D1563772

Developing Discourse Practices in Adolescence and Adulthood

Editors

Richard Beach

Susan Hynds

Volume XXXIX in the Series
ADVANCES IN DISCOURSE PROCESSES
Roy O. Freedle, Editor

ABLEX PUBLISHING CORPORATION
NORWOOD, NEW JERSEY

Printed in the United States of America.

Library of Congress Cataloging-in-Publication Data

Developing Discourse Practices in Adolescence and Adulthood /
    editors, Richard Beach, Susan Hynds.
        p.   cm. — (Advances in discourse processes ; v. 39)
    Includes bibliographical references.
    ISBN 0-89391-602-1. — ISBN 0-89391-662-5 (pbk.)
    1. Language arts.   2. English language—Discourse analysis.
3. Discourse analysis, Literary.   I. Beach, Richard.   II. Hynds,
Susan.   III. Series.
LB1631.B38   1990
302.2′244—dc20   90-428
                                                        CIP

Ablex Publishing Corporation
355 Chestnut St.
Norwood, NJ 07648

Table of Contents

iii

Preface to the Series

Roy O. Freedle

Series Editor

This series of volumes provides a forum for the cross-fertilization of ideas from a diverse number of disciplines, all of which share a common interest in discourse—be it prose comprehension and recall, dialogue analysis, text grammar construction, computer simulation of natural language, cross-cultural comparisons of communicative competence or other related topics. The problems posed by multisentence contexts and the methods required to investigate them, while not always unique to discourse, are still sufficiently distinct as to benefit from the organized model of scientific interaction made possible by this series.

Scholars working in the discourse area from the perspective of sociolinguistics, psycholinguistics, ethnomethodology and the sociology of language, educational psychology (e.g., teacher-student interaction), the philosophy of language, computational linguistics, and related sub-areas are invited to submit manuscripts of monograph or book length to the series editor. Edited collections of original papers resulting from conferences will also be considered.

Volumes in the Series

The Authors

Deborah Appleman, Department of Education, Carleton College, Northfield, MN

Carolyn Ball, English Department, University of Pittsburgh, Pittsburgh, PA

Dorothy Barnes, School of Education, The University of Leeds, Leeds, Britain

Douglas Barnes, School of Education, The University of Leeds, Leeds, Britain

David Bartholomae, English Department, University of Pittsburgh, Pittsburgh, PA

Richard Beach, Department of Curriculum and Instruction, College of Education, University of Minnesota, Minneapolis, MN

Marilyn Cooper, Department of Humanities, Michigan Technological University, Houghton, MI

Marion Crowhurst, Department of Language Education, University of British Columbia, Vancouver, Canada

Marc Davison, Department of Educational Psychology, University of Minnesota, Minneapolis, MN

Laura Dice, English Department, University of Pittsburgh, Pittsburgh, PA

Sharon Dorsey, Columbus Public Schools, Columbus, OH

Cheryl Geisler, Department of Language, Literature, and Communication, Rensselaer Polytechnic Institute, Troy, NY

Gail Hawisher, Department of English, University of Illinois, Urbana, IL

Russell Hunt, Department of Psychology, St. Thomas University, Fredericton, New Brunswick, Canada

Susan Hynds, School of Education, Syracuse University, Syracuse NY

James Jewett, Department of Psychology, St. Thomas University, Fredericton, New Brunswick, Canada

Peter Johnston, Department of Reading, State University of New York at Albany, Albany, NY

C. H. Knoblauch, Department of English, State University of New York at Albany, Albany, NY

Barry Kroll, Department of English, University of Indiana, Bloomington, IN

Susan Lytle, Graduate School of Education, University of Pennsylvania, Philadelphia, PA

James Marshall, Linguist Center, University of Iowa, Iowa City, IA

Louise Phelps, Department of English, Syracuse University, Syracuse, NY

Alan Purves, Center for Writing and Literacy, State University of New York at Albany, Albany, NY

James A. Reither, Department of Psychology, St. Thomas University, Fredericton, New Brunswick, Canada

Katherine Schultz, Graduate School of Education, University of Pennsylvania, Philadelphia, PA

Cai Svennson, Department of Communication Studies, University of Linkoping, Linkoping, Sweden

Robert Tierney, Department of Educational Theory and Practice, Language, Literature, and Reading, The Ohio State University, Columbus, OH

Douglas Vipond, Department of Psychology, St. Thomas University, Fredericton, New Brunswick, Canada

I

1
Introduction: A Model of Discourse Development

Richard Beach
Susan Hynds

While it is generally assumed that much of the world's population is more literate than in the past, there is some question as to how competent people are in using their acquired abilities. While the majority of people may be able to read and write, they may not be able to use their reading and writing to develop beliefs and ideas, communicate clearly to others, formulate a sense of individual self, think critically, function as informed citizens to affect social and political change, establish personal relationships, or participate in cultural communities. Definitions of "functional literacy" fail to take into account these varied uses of reading and writing within a society.

This collection of theory and research addresses the question of how adolescents and adults develop as readers and writers and what promotes or impedes such development. We believe that one major impediment to fostering such growth is the limited conception of literacy currently shaping educational policy.

LIMITATIONS OF CURRENT THEORETICAL PERSPECTIVES ON LITERACY DEVELOPMENT

At present, curricula and competency examinations are driven by one of three theoretical perspectives: "cognitivist," "expressionist," or "social contextualist" (Berlin, 1988). While each perspective offers a valuable contribution to an understanding of literacy development in adolescence and adulthood, each is somewhat incomplete in isolation. As this introductory chapter will demonstrate, and as the essays in this volume collectively argue, an integrated perspective moves beyond a view of literacy as isolated skills or techniques and conceives of discourse as constituted by social strategies and discourse practices. Before presenting such a model, we will briefly review the limitations of current theoretical perspectives.

Limitations of Cognitivist Models

From a cognitivist perspective (Flower & Hayes, 1981; Scardamalia, Bereiter, & Goelman, 1982) growth is defined in terms of distinct cognitive behaviors. For example, in "cognitivist" approaches to writing research, composing aloud protocols are typically analyzed to detect those cognitive moves employed by more versus less experienced writers. From this perspective, the difficulties associated with reading and writing are often attributed to developmental deficiencies in attaining particular cognitive stages. For example, largely based on Piagetian notions of egocentrism, difficulties in understanding or producing discourse are defined in terms of difficulties in recognizing a narrator, character, or audience's perspective (Applebee, 1978; Moffett, 1968).

However, attempts to generalize about behaviors characteristic of a certain stage, and instructional approaches designed to move "novices" to the level of "experts" often ignore the influences of social or rhetorical contexts on determining and communicating meaning (Applebee, 1985; Cooper, 1984, 1986). Within unfamiliar contexts, even experienced readers and writers are, by definition, novices. Kroll (1986) has suggested that the complexity of particular writing tasks may interfere with social-cognitive processes. Correspondingly, within certain familiar discourse contexts, writers may never need to infer particular audience characteristics. Thus, it is problematic to define "expertness" apart from a knowledge of the contexts within which literate persons must function. Even if such definitions can be made, simply teaching novices to behave like experts will not necessarily make them so.

Furthermore, cognitive stage models are not "air tight," in that they often fail to account for variation within age levels or across individual persons' behavior. For example, labeling women according to Kohlberg's stages of moral development fails to consider their culturally-driven propensity to consider the consequences of actions or decisions on human relationships (Gilligan, 1983).

Finally, the ways in which "developmental tasks" are posed often influence resulting conclusions about development. For example, contrary to the assumption that "egocentric" early adolescents are less able to conceive of audience, Donaldson (1978) found that they can, given authentic, purposeful rhetorical contexts, define audience characteristics, although these definitions may not be as elaborate as those of adults. Rubin (1984) also argues that many less developed writers differ from more developed writers, not in their inability to recognize differences in perspectives, but in their inability to utilize strategies for adapting writing to those differences.

Thus, definitions of "expert" readers and writers are difficult to formulate in terms of discrete cognitive stages because the meaning derived from reading and writing varies according to distinct social or cultural contexts.

Limitations of Expressionist Models

Berlin (1988) notes that, from an "expressionist" perspective, writing serves to foster honest, authentic expression of the "self" or personal "voice" (Elbow, 1975; MacCrorie, 1980, 1984; Murray, 1986). Instructional approaches based on this notion have promoted reading and writing as a way of discovering and understanding personal experience. Students are encouraged to explore their own topics for writing (Calkins, 1983, 1986; Graves, 1983), to develop their own authentic voice (MacCrorie, 1980, 1984; Murray, 1986), and to bring inchoate thoughts to consciousness through free writing and other expressive writing techniques (Elbow, 1975). Readers are encouraged to find personal meaning in literary texts through writing in journal or logs, or to explore self by creating autobiographical narratives or short stories or their own classroom literature (Atwell, 1987; Butler & Turbill, 1984).

However, assumptions that the "self" is an autonomous entity, and advice such as "think for yourself" or "express yourself" may mislead students in assuming that their ideas are "within" themselves as opposed to being socially constructed through relationships with others. While it is hoped that students develop an increasing sense of their own self-concept through reading and writing (Salvatori, 1983), the "self" as "reader" or "writer" ultimately rests on social or cultural conceptions of roles, purposes, and motives.

Limitations of Current Social Contextualist Perspectives

From a "contextualist" perspective, meaning is socially constructed (Faigley, 1986; Brandt, 1986). Thus, readers and writers learn to construct meaning through engaging in discourse practices driven by social motives and goals in different contexts. They may conceive of the same text as a "descriptive," "persuasive," "polemic," or "a plea for humanity," each conception reflecting a different view of the social relationship between text, author, or audience.

As Tompkins (1988) argues in her discussion of poststructuralist criticism, however, readers and writers do not simply apply knowledge of the methods of poststructuralist criticism. They are constituted by their discourse. Similarly, Marilyn Cooper (Chapter 3) proposes that various discourse practices shape readers' and writers' very identities and personalities as language users.

While this "contextualist" perspective is currently fashionable (Bartholomae, 1985; Cooper, 1986; Faigley, 1986; Perelman, 1986) there are certain limitations to some versions of that perspective. As Paul Hernadi (1988) argues, arbitrary distinctions between selves as socially defined roles and as subjective identities "fragment the total makeup of human life" (p. 754). That is, just as readers and writers develop social identities through discourse practices, they also develop subjective identities. Reading and writing foster "lasting—periodically reexperienceable—expression to otherwise fleeting thoughts and sayings." As Hernadi notes:

> Besides reconnecting my public person with the private, a reflective reading of my own writing enables me to experience existential continuity between different phases of an evolving self—I am in any moment who I have just become—in the deeply historical sense of ever identical, yet ever changing, selfhood. (p. 745)
>
> Thus, teaching readers and writers to imitate social conventions or to fit within the "norms" of particular discourse communities can ignore the role of literacy in forming each reader's and writer's individual subjectively experienced "self."

In addition to excluding a consideration of the development of subjective identity, some versions of a contextualist perspective define growth as merely acquiring a *knowledge* of speech act, social, and literary conventions constituted by and constituting social contexts (Beach, 1985; Mailloux, 1982; Rabinowitz, 1987). However, in a critique of her own earlier espousal of such a position, Cooper (Chapter 3) argues that it is not enough to simply know conventions; readers and writers need to be able to employ "discourse practices" which enable them to read and create texts.

Discourse conventions, Cooper proposes, are arbitrary verbal rules, as opposed to discourse practices, which involve "what people do," as motivated by social purposes and values. Thus, teaching discourse conventions involves presenting verbal maxims, whereas teaching discourse practices involves putting readers and writers into situations where they must use language for socially motivated purposes.

A third limitation of a contextualist perspective, as illustrated by Knoblach and Johnston's deconstructivist critique of various conceptions of literacy development (Chapter 14), is that one's conception of contexts is itself a subjective phenomenon. That is, what educators, curriculum planners, and test makers believe about a society "is readily transmuted to a myth about human growth that ratifies educational practices designed to replicate those beliefs and instill those traits or capacities" (p. 319, this volume). Because the "context of literacy" is often influenced by the hidden agendas of educational policy makers, literate persons need not develop a blind conformity to the "conventions" of discourse, but a critical consciousness about the implicit power relationships and political dimensions of language learning in schools.

Thus, while cognitivist, expressivist, and contextualist perspectives offer valuable information about how people grow as readers and writers, when taken in isolation, each fragments and limits our understanding of literacy development during adolescence and adulthood. Further, as the following section will show, approaches to teaching and testing based on only one perspective are similarly limited.

Limitations of Current Approaches to Curriculum and Assessment

In the past, attempts to teach or measure cognitive skills or processes apart from social and cultural contexts rested on the assumption that certain standard curricular approaches could apply to all students. "Teacher-proof" textbook activities geared to "everystudent" presupposed an attitude towards literacy that neutralized "personal, social, and political sanctions; indeed, its independence from any substantive context and therefore content" (De Castell, Luke, & Egan, 1986, p. 106).

Often, in contrast to authentic and thoughtful "transactions," students experience reading and writing as momentary "snapshot performances" stripped of actual, "real-world" purposes and audiences. Rather than literacy skills, students often acquire "test-taking skills" or "language tricks" (Edelsky & Harmon, 1988) associated with success on standardized tests—skills that bear little relationship with the competencies employed in real-world reading and writing situations (Chapter 2). Thus, a decontextualized, skills-based approach to teaching and testing is severely limited.

Similarly, curricular approaches based solely on the expressivist position have been criticized for their unrealistic attitude toward the value of personal expression and their failure to recognize "real-world" issues of status and power within the larger society in which literate persons must function.

Social contextualist models can also be criticized in that they may promote the idea that students need to imitate "recognized discourse conventions" (Culler, 1975; Mailloux, 1982), sometimes at the expense of understanding the power and status issues underlying these conventions or developing unique individual perspectives through discourse practices. Thus, one might ask "whose cultural norms should students adopt: the teacher's, authorities in the field, or their own?"

Further, as Cooper (Chapter 3) argues, while readers and writers may acquire knowledge of conventions (i.e., that titles function symbolically), or while they may memorize the "facts" of language use, they may not be able to put their knowledge to use in actual discourse practices. As a result, many traditional instructional methods are based on imparting knowledge about language rather than engaging students in activities designed to foster learning to use language in purposeful ways.

What is needed is a model of development that simultaneously recognizes the cognitive underpinnings of discourse, the individual identities of readers and writers, and the social nature of language. Furthermore, as opposed to defining discourse in terms of discrete skills or techniques, such a model should explain the multiple orientations that readers and writers must appropriate in their discourse practices. The model presented in the following section will provide a framework for understanding the theories and issues addressed in this collection.

A MODEL OF DISCOURSE DEVELOPMENT: FROM SKILLS AND CONVENTIONS TO DISCOURSE PRACTICES

The chapters in this volume support the notion that, rather than acquiring discrete cognitive skills, or discourse conventions, readers and writers learn to engage in "discourse practices," (Chapter 3) directed toward particular social or pragmatic ends (Harste, 1985). Through engaging in such practices, literate persons develop self-definitions as readers and writers.

For example, readers of literature not only acquire genre strategies necessary for reading, they define themselves as readers through the acquisition of those strategies (i.e., being a "mystery buff") (Rabinowitz, 1987). Similarly, women readers of romance novels seek to verify their own cultural roles as nurturers in the home by identifying with the heroines' own nurturing roles (Radway, 1984).

The ways in which individuals define themselves as readers and writers greatly influence their motivation to learn. For example, so-called "remedial readers" often lack a sense of their own efficacy as "readers" in deliberately and strategically employing comprehension strategies (Johnston & Winograd, 1985). In a series of case studies, Hynds (1989) found that readers' views of themselves as readers were influenced by their experiences in and outside of the literature classroom. Often students with incomplete or limited views of reading failed to employ necessary social cognitive processes in their interpretations of literature.

In addition to developing the subjective identities of readers and writers, such discourse practices also serve to establish and define social relationships. For example, for many adolescents, knowledge of sports serves as a "bond" to create and sustain social relationships. The incentive to learn how to participate in "sports talk" is therefore driven by and perpetuates a social need for community.

Acquiring Attitudes Toward Knowledge

In a strategic and socially-situated view of discourse, readers and writers must learn that certain linguistic or rhetorical practices are particularly appropriate for certain audiences, purposes, and situations (Brown & Herndl, 1986; Odell & Goswami, 1982; Flower & Hayes, 1986). Beyond this, however, they must also be aware of the potential relativity and arbitrariness of language rules, realizing that discourse conventions are often implicit and ill-defined agreements.

Thus, growth is not just a process of socialization or "accommodation" (Bartholomae, 1985), involving imitation of others, but a conscious awareness of options, which include either adapting to or opposing accepted conventions and norms. Reflective judgement, or the understanding that knowledge is relative (Chapter 12) contributes to element of what it means to be literate in adolescence and adulthood.

Developing Multiple Stances

Readers and writers develop alternative ways of conceiving of the same context, alternatives reflecting competing attitudes and values—what Cazden (1988) defines as "mixed systems." They learn that meaning is constituted by institutional or disciplinary perspectives—that government officials will differ from Marxist economists in their conceptions of an economic report. They consequently learn to vary their stances or orientations (Hunt & Vipond, 1986; Vipond & Hunt, 1984) according to the social context.

This collection is based on the premise that four basic stances underlie the discourse practices of adolescents and adults: *social, textual, institutional,* and *field* (see Figure 1.1). These four stances will form an organizing rubric for the chapters in this volume.

Adopting a social stance entails the practices of exchanging or negotiating ideas in a collaborative manner. Adopting a textual stance entails at-

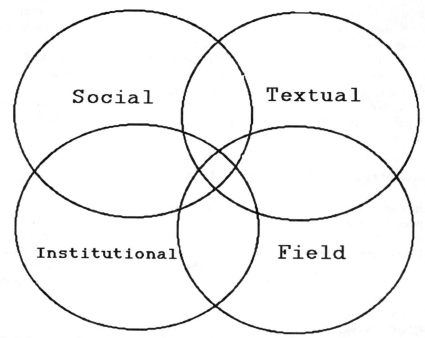

Figure 1.1. Stances Constituting Discourse Development.

tending to certain text features and conventions. Adopting an institutional stance entails understanding ideas or assuming roles/language consistent with certain institutional norms of the academy, classroom, government, corporation, or community. And, adopting a field stance entails understanding ideas in terms of the practices endorsed by particular academic disciplines (i.e., chemistry, psychology, literary criticism, philosophy, etc.), or a body of knowledge or expertise (i.e., music criticism, automobile mechanics, French cooking, etc.).

In adolescence and adulthood, readers and writers learn to appropriate all four stances. For instance, in writing a biology lab report, a student may discuss the report with an instructor (social), organize the information according to a "report format" (textual), test out the findings according to "the scientific method" (institutional), and relate the results to other research in biology (field). As they engage in discourse practices, students also learn to effectively mesh these stances. Biology students may learn to "talk like biologists," combining social and field stances. Or, they may recognize that the lab report needs to be written in a manner consistent with the practices of a particular school, combining text and institutional stances. Often, failure to succeed in a particular discourse practice can be explained by failure to be conscious of and appropriate all four stances simultaneously. For example, a student who is unaware that academic journal writing involves all four stances may ignore the informal social dimensions of the assignment, inappropriately writing entries as mini expository entries. Or perhaps a student may keep a diarylike account of the school day, ignoring the institutional expectation that students will focus on the academic subject matter of the course.

Further, these different stances may conflict, so that by focusing on one stance, a reader or writer may ignore another. A music critic who knows a lot about jazz (field) may write a music review for a school newspaper that does not follow the text practices (textual) endorsed by that school (institutional). The following section will redefine growth in reading and writing among adolescents and adults in terms of their ability to learn and adopt these four stances in their discourse practices.

Social stance. In adopting a social stance, readers and writers conceive of texts in terms of social or conversational practices. Based on his extensive research on the development of social knowledge, Elliot Turiel (1983) notes that "development entails an expanding social knowledge and an increasing complexity of social interactions" (p.7). As developmental research in speech communication and written language suggests (Crockett, 1965; O'Keefe & Delia, 1982; Piche, Rubin, & Turner, 1980; Rubin, 1984; Kroll, 1978, 1986), growth in knowledge of social/conversational practices is reflected in an increasing awareness of the unique nature of particular social/rhetorical contexts. Readers and writers also learn to recognize the competing rhetorical perspectives and attitudes of participants and audiences within that mutually constructed context. Based on their perception of a context, persons learn to vary their own roles, orientations, rhetorical strategies, register, or speech acts according to their conceptions of the beliefs, knowledge, needs, goals, plans, and attitudes constituting that context.

For example, writers learn, as in any conversation, to assess their text in terms of being relevant to the topic, of saying no more than necessary, being sincere, or being truthful—Grice's maxims of conversation (Cooper, 1986). And, as in conversation, they learn to assess the appropriateness of speech within certain types of social contexts—ceremonies, social meetings, business transactions, family gatherings, and so on.

Readers apply these learned social practices in making inferences about literary texts (Beach, 1985; Beach & Brown, 1987; Pratt, 1976). For example, in *A Speech Act Theory of Literary Discourse*, Pratt demonstrates how readers may use the Grician maxims of sufficiency and relevancy to make inferences about a narrator's attributes. Beach's developmental research (1985; Beach & Brown, 1987; Beach & Wendler, 1987) indicates that readers who are more knowledgeable of certain social practices are better able to infer the symbolic meanings of literary texts than less knowledgeable readers. Hynds (1985, 1989) has demonstrated that readers must view the social dimensions of literary texts similarly to the way they view the events of their own lives, learning, among other things, to make inferences about the actions and motivations of literary characters.

Writers acquire the ability to use rhetorical strategies to define and foster social relationships. Analysis of memos written by adults and secondary students in role-play sessions indicated that adults were more likely to initially refer to writer/audience relationships than the secondary students (Beach & Anson, 1988).

Moreover, the degree to which teachers perceive texts in terms of a social transaction influences their response to those texts. As research on "dialogue-journal writing" indicates (Staton, Shuy, Kreeft, & Reed, 1988), teachers responding in a dialogic, collaborative manner may encourage students to adopt an exploratory, social stance. Thus, if reading and writing is a social transaction, then teachers' and students' conceptions of text practices shape the learning occurring in that transaction.

However, despite the growing support for the value of collaborative writing (Daiute, 1986); much of the writing done in schools rarely includes collaborative writing, limiting the use of social, oral interaction with others as a means of generating text (Brown & Herndl, 1986). This emphasis on solitary writing conflicts with the fact that, according to research on the Myers Briggs Personality Inventory, 70 percent of adolescents are extroverts, who prefer to generate ideas through talking out their ideas with others (Myers & McCaulley, 1985). Similarly, very little attention is devoted to the usefulness of collaborative learning approaches to literary response and interpretation (Straw, 1989). Thus, while social/conversational discourse is central to development, reading and writing instruction often fails to exploit its full potential.

Textual stance. In contrast to formulistic approaches to text understanding and production, the "textual stance" necessary for competent discourse practices in adolescence and adulthood involves the recognition that text conventions and genres are socially situated. It is problematic to define text "genres" or "forms" apart from their social, interpretive, and rhetorical contexts. "Reading like a political analyst," or "writing like a scientist" involves far more than simply understanding the form of a suspense novel or a scientific report. It involves a complex understanding of what makes editorials and novels work the way they do on particular readers—how form and function, as well as readers' and writers' subjective perceptions, transact and interrelate to create particular meanings.

Adopting a textual stance involves employing several discourse strategies. For instance, readers must learn to filter out extraneous information and attend to those aspects most significant for understanding a text (Rabinowitz, 1987). In reading a narrative, for example, they learn to recognize what Labov defines as "evaluations"—asides, comments, or syntactic deviations ("I was really, really nervous") that signal "unusualness" or violations of social practices and help them to understand the point of a story (Vipond & Hunt, 1984).

Similarly, in responding to their own and others' texts, writers must learn to recognize rhetorical goals and strategies appropriate for particular texts. For example, in responding to a peer's essay, a writer may note that "as a reader," he or she is accustomed to finding evidence to support an opinion in a persuasive essay. In this manner, writers learn to base their perceptions of "good writing" not on the degree to which they prescriptively followed the model of a "good essay," but on the degree to which they strategically adapted their writing to a variety of social and rhetorical purposes.

Readers and writers learn to employ particular textual stances through sharing and discussing texts with others. For example, young males training to become Jewish rabbis learn a set of practices for interpreting religious texts, practices distinct from those employed by readers of no particular religious background. As Gee (1988) notes, "One always and only learns to interpret texts of a certain type in certain ways through having access to … social settings where texts of that type are read in those ways" (p. 209). Thus, a purely formalistic definition of textual stance is useless, because, regardless of surface form or genre, acceptable discourse practices in reading and writing change from one interpretive and social context to another.

Bruner (1986) illustrates the idea of a textual stance by arguing that narrative serves as a way of knowing about experience. Readers and writers learn certain narrative practices—dramatizing the unusual, building suspense, accentuating conflict—as ways of altering their own and others' perceptions of experience. Thus, when readers and writers appropriate a variety of textual stances, they attend to a host of implicit social and rhetorical purposes, often changing their attitudes toward experience in the process.

Part of adopting a textual stance involves recognizing that textual conventions in one medium may be inappropriate for another. In contrast to sustained, extended political speeches of the past, contemporary discourse as employed on television often tends to fragment exploration of ideas or insights in superficial manner (Postman, 1985) and is inappropriate for academic discourse. Without knowledge of academic or disciplinary practices, students may mimic the talk show's guests or television commercial's speaker to advance claims with no evidence or no consideration of alternative perspectives or underlying value assumptions.

Unfortunately, rather than approaching reading and writing as a way of knowing and shaping experience, English instructors often approach these discourse practices as a process of adhering to prescriptively defined formalistic conceptions of texts and genres as models to be mimicked. Since a knowledge of textual forms alone provides little understanding of the complex interaction of social and rhetorical strategies underlying particular text practices, many students have difficulty understanding and producing texts.

Institutional stance. In conceiving of texts from an institutional stance, readers and writers are concerned with the roles, styles, functions, attitudes, or modes of thinking as appropriate within institutions such as the academy, governmental agency, workplace, peer group, family, and so forth.

In applying particular institutional stances, readers can infer different meanings for the same texts. For example, one reader may interpret a newspaper editorial favoring reduction in defense spending from the perspective of "academic" logical analysis (perceiving the editorial "as lacking sufficient evidence"). Another reader may interpret the same editorial from the perspective of concerned community citizen (as "providing needed funds for the social problems of our community"). Another person reading from the stance of a corporate executive could interpret the article as "jeopardizing our business." Still another, operating from the stance of a newspaper/mass media consumer could interpret the editorial as "reflecting the 'liberal' press."

Writers and readers learn to employ "institutional discourse," or, in the academy, what Knoblach and Johnston (Chapter 14) define as the "prose of the schools," by varying the degree of formality or assertiveness according to differences in their own and their audience's status, power, needs, knowledge, or abilities (Beach, 1983; Cooper, 1986). Such discourse practices eventually shape not only the language context, but the ideas and attitudes of the language users themselves.

As Kenneth Burke (1969) demonstrates in his "dramatistic" analysis, people engage in discourse practices that are institutionally sanctioned and designed to further the roles, purposes, and attitudes of particular agencies. For example, business managers learn to employ nominalizations in memos to employees (i.e., "the desired-corporate approach implies the essentiality of your position") in order to shift the focus from employees as individual agents to the corporation as agent and employees as "agency" (Brown & Herndl, 1986).

Some institutions may value certain discourse practices more than others. The government/community, by conceiving of reading and writing primarily as skills necessary for economic success, may argue for the need for grammar instruction in a district's schools under the assumption that "correct grammar" is a necessary prerequisite for economic success. Thus, instruction in part-to-whole language skills becomes a curricular staple for all citizens. However, as Odell and Goswami (1984) have demonstrated, such generic instruction fails to address the contextually specific literacy needs of people in the workplace, where roles and status issues are sharply defined.

While students in the academy are encouraged to "assert your own ideas," those that enter the corporation must initially learn to muffle their assertiveness. In their study, *Corporate Cultures*, Deal and Kennedy (1982) found that newly hired employees often violated assumed practices by conversing with others in an overly confident, assertive, serious manner, rather than learning to adopt more of a "back-slapping, small-talk," deferential role appropriate for beginning employees.

Similarly, writing in corporate or business settings, employees must shift their styles or registers according to differences in status (Odell & Goswami, 1984) and revise the "extended text" practices associated with expository essays in order to write memos, prepare reports, or lists of items for presentations using overheads. Further, the "reflective judgment" acquired in the academy may conflict with the "practical thinking" employed in community or business institutions. Thus, the practices employed in one institution may not transfer to other institutions.

Practices may also vary within institutions. A comparison of preferred literary response styles across different countries indicated that students in different countries are socialized to employ certain response strategies. For example, American secondary students are socialized to focus primarily on critical interpretation of literary texts, a response style that differs from those of secondary students in other countries (Purves, 1981).

Similarly, writing survey studies (Anderson, 1985; Anson, 1989) reveal that the nature and amount of writing varies considerably across different schools or colleges, often due to differences in teachers' attitudes or familiarity with using writing. In some cases, the institutional "ethos" discourages free flow of ideas, creating writing anxiety (Bloom, 1985). Peer groups or families may differ considerably in their uses of reading and writing, resulting, as Svennson found (1985), in differences in level of interpretation.

Thus, in adopting an institutional stance, adolescents and adults must learn that conventions and expectations for discourse vary, both between and within particular institutions.

Field stance. Adopting a field stance entails conceiving of texts in terms of those practices associated with specific fields or academic disciplines: the natural and social sciences, literature, humanities, business, fine arts, medicine, law, and so on, or with certain bodies of knowledge or acquired expertise. Field knowledge is not necessarily synonymous with the knowledge gained in academic disciplines. For example, a stock market analyst acquires certain strategies for analyzing financial reports based on knowledge of the stock market and attitudes of investors—knowledge that is typically gained after the years of formal schooling.

Rather than considering fields as distinct bodies of knowledge, we are conceiving of fields as prototypical ways of thinking based on certain models or metaphors endemic to a discipline (Schwartz & Ogilvy, 1979). For example, in terms of what constitutes a valid explanation or "good reason," social scientists value careful inquiry regarding information and values. In contrast, natural scientists value objective, empirical research, while mathematicians value relationships between concepts (Orton, Avery, & Lawrenz, 1989).

However, it is difficult, if not impossible to clearly demarcate different fields or disciplines, or "academic" and "nonacademic" contexts of a discipline. For example, Anson (1989) notes that:

> A field of study such as microbiology, firmly seated in the school of medicine, will often share the discourse practices of the field of medicine as a whole, including its lexicon and its structural, stylistic, and rhetorical features. In turn, the medical research conducted (and reported on) in the academic institution adds to and influences the field's professional discourse. Microbiologists reporting on research under the auspices of profit-making private laboratories will share with academic microbiologists some assumptions about and knowledge of the practices of writing within the field. (p. 7)

Within different fields, individuals will adopt different stances. For example, within literary criticism, persons may learn to employ the strategies of a Marxist, feminist, structuralist, Freudian, deconstructivist, or semiotic critic. Similarly, the same literature professor may present a paper at the Modern Language Association conference employing one stance or style, while employing quite a different style in presenting to the National Council of Teachers of English.

As adolescents and adults develop knowledge of discourse practices in particular fields, they may develop a clearer sense of their own self-concept. Correspondingly, as they learn to value their own perspectives, they develop the ability and the motivation to understand particular fields or disciplines. As Paulo Freire (1973) argues, Brazilian peasants acquire "critical consciousness" by learning to "demythologize reality" in everyday social situations in order to recognize the value and legitimacy of their own ideas.

In an analysis of changes in women's self-concept, Belenky, Clinchy, Goldberger, and Tarule (1986) analyzed the growth in women's ways of knowing, drawing on Perry's developmental stages. In contrast to Perry's male undergraduates, Belenky et al.'s women represented a continuum from "silence" and "received knowledge" (paralleling Perry's absolutist thinking) to "subjective voice" (in which they learn to express their own opinions and ideas, particularly about their own experiences). The study found that growth at this stage often resulted not from academic experiences but from personal or work experiences—a divorce, a new job, or travel. Once the women in the study learned to trust the validity of their own opinions and ideas—to listen to their own "subjective voice," they further developed "procedural knowledge" based on academic and professional experiences, leading to the final stage of "constructed knowledge," building their self-concept around their own beliefs. These developmental findings point to the importance of recognizing the value of one's own ideas as a precursor to acquiring academic practices or "procedural knowledge."

Students are therefore, as Bartholomae (1985) argues, being "accommodated" into certain practices constituting thinking within a field. Rather than simply acquiring knowledge of these field practices as a set of inert, theoretical principles, students best learn these practices within the context of real-world applications (Bransford, Sherwood, Rieser, & Vye, 1986). In learning these practices, students must often unlearn or abandon certain ways of thinking, often totally restructuring their conceptual frameworks (Marzano et al., 1988).

For example, in learning to apply logical analyses, students must revise their common sensical assumptions about truth. As Marzano et al. argue, in order to help students learn to revise or restructure their approaches, teachers need to employ "imaginative teaching that relies heavily on oral discourse (especially Socratic dialogue) and analogies, metaphors, and physical models ..." (p. 128), interaction that creates disequilibrium between familiar practices and new, unfamiliar practices.

Thus, adolescents and adults engage in discourse practices that enable them to distinguish institutional requisites and discourse conventions from those of larger fields and disciplines. As they develop field knowledge, they experience heightened confidence and self-efficacy as readers and writers by abandoning old ways of thinking and adapting to new philosophical and theoretical viewpoints (Powell, 1985).

HOW DO ADOLESCENTS AND ADULTS DEVELOP AS READERS AND WRITERS?

The chapters in this volume put forth several alternative conceptions of growth in reading and writing—conceptions that recognize the limitations of current cognitivist, expressivist, and contextualist perspectives. We will briefly survey these conceptions before discussing their implications.

The two introductory essays of this collection by Barnes and Barnes and by Cooper posit that reading and writing are social activities and that readers and writers grow by acquiring social strategies or discourse practices within certain contexts. This conception of development or growth, as derived from Vygotsky, Burke, Halliday, and Bahktin recognizes development as motivated by the social or cultural need to define self in relationship to others and to derive cultural meanings from everyday experience.

Both introductory chapters support the idea that "reading" and "writing" refer to "a range of practices which are not all necessarily similar to those found in lessons" (Barnes & Barnes p. 34, this volume). Barnes and Barnes argue that different "versions of English" (i.e., "engaged" or "detached") are taught in different schools. Not surprisingly, the version of English supported by a particular school is directly connected to the mode of examination typical of that school, and subtly reinforces students' cultural identity and status.

In distinguishing "discourse conventions" from "discourse practices," Marilyn Cooper's chapter differentiates instruction based on arbitrary rules of language from instruction that places students into realistic contexts where they must engage in language practices motivated by real social purposes and values. Using language in social interaction influences and shapes not only the language, but the ideas, attitudes, and identity of the language user. Thus, students become "participants in the process of development rather than as passive recipients of a static body of knowledge (see p. 80, this volume).

The next four chapters explicate the development of a "social" stance toward discourse. Cheryl Geisler begins by combining a view of literacy as "natural conversation" with a view of literacy as the artful construction of autonomous text. Her concept of "artful conversation" attempts to integrate individuals' everyday understandings with the often unfamiliar world of texts. Through open-ended, dialogic, "transactional" (Rosenblatt, 1984) exchange with a text or peer, readers' and writers' perceptions are challenged, resulting in new meanings and ideas. In contrast, simply using reading and writing to extract, restate, or duplicate existing meanings reifies status quo perceptions. Geisler argues that adopting a social stance toward discourse involves a knowledge of the turn-taking practices constituting ways by which conversants share and extend their conversation. Her comparison of novice and experienced philosophers' discourse demonstrates that within the field of philosophy, students learn to acquire ways of conversing unique to that field.

The emerging field of "dialogics" (Bialostosky, 1986; Bakhtin, 1981; Rorty, 1979) focuses on how meaning of ideas emerges from social interaction. In their view of the social dimensions of reading, Vipond, Hunt,

Jewett, and Reither define the ability to adopt a "point-driven" orientation not in terms of inferring a main idea, gist, or moral, but as a process of understanding the literary text as an intentional act of communication by an author. Drawing on Labov's (1972) notion of "tellability" of oral anecdotes as constituted by social interaction, they define "dialogic" reading as a process whereby readers "imagine themselves to be in conversation with authors and texts" (see p. 113). They distinguish such reading from "information-driven" and "story-driven" reading, where the reader's attention is directed to information to be derived, or immersion in the story. "A full reading capacity," the authors argue, involves the flexibility to use the stance most appropriate to the "specific conjunction of text, purpose, and situation" (see p. 131).

In the next chapter, Cai Svensson argues that reading ability and literary interpretive skill are culturally determined, particularly by students' exposure to reading in the home. Readers' "cultural socialization" within and outside the classroom contributes to their knowledge and use of interpretive strategies and conventions in poetry understanding. Developing a "cultivated disposition" toward reading means more than simply *learning about* literature; it means understanding and employing a knowledge of interpretive strategies and norms essential for reading.

James Marshall finds that the ways in which students are socialized to write about literature in school influences their literary interpretations. In schools, Marshall argues, writing assignments typically proceed from personal narrative in the lower grades to public argument in the higher grades, on the assumption that the latter is more cognitively advanced than the former. Contrary to that assumption, Marshall concludes that personal, informal writing is no less valuable or cognitively complex than formal analytic writing. Both types of writing are valuable in eliciting different ways of thinking about literature. Marshall calls for a "dialogic" approach to literature teaching that allows students to respond from a variety of perspectives and to examine those perspectives at the same time.

Thus, in developing a "social" stance, readers and writers must participate in language practices that allow them to understand and adapt their orientations to the conversational dimensions of discourse, to become aware of the various interpretive norms and strategies operating in their social context, and to use language dialogically—in ways that engage them in various types of thinking about reading and writing.

The subsequent four chapters focus in part on the development of "textual stances" toward discourse. Marion Crowhurst examines the patterns of persuasive writing produced by 10–12-year-olds, and concludes that, rather than a exhibiting a total "failure" to produce successful argumentative discourse, many younger students develop arguments through playing with language in a variety of forms, including narrative and dialogue. Thus, the "dismal" performance of younger children on such tasks in national competency examinations might stem from a failure to employ formal written language forms and to generate interesting information within unfamiliar formal writing tasks.

Crowhurst argues that the a-rhetorical and a-contextual nature of most large scale assessment tasks often prohibits students from experimenting with language in ways more appropriate for their current abilities. Similar to Marshall in this volume, Crowhurst criticizes the assumption that "development" in writing must proceed in a lock-step fashion from narrative to argument. Such an approach, Crowhurst argues, keeps younger children from experiencing a variety of language forms and functions until late in the primary grades.

Just as writers and readers adopt stances which allow them to understand the different forms and functions of texts, individuals who judge texts (teachers, evaluators, literary critics) operate out of particular textual stances as well. In their analysis of the criteria employed in rating expository essays, Purves and Hawisher found that texts are rated according to culturally-bound models of writing. These "models in the head" exert a powerful influence on writing instruction and performance. As Gee (1988) points out, one of the unfortunate aspects of much school-based literacy instruction is that the underlying criteria for rating texts are often implicit rather than explicit. Keeping the assumptions implicit perpetuates the "two-tier" social structure by "empowering those mainstream children who already have them and disempowering those children who do not and for whom they are never rendered visible" (p. 209). Given the arbitrary nature of the criteria, Purves and Hawisher argue for the need to make those criteria explicit—to know that they are "conventional and human and not divine" (see p. 197, this volume).

Developing a textual stance also involves the ability to compare and connect current and past texts. Developing the idea of literary socialization, Beach, Appleman, and Dorsey examine secondary students' ability to define intertextual links between prior and current texts through free writing and mapping. The authors contrast a "text-based" conception of literature (which treats texts as autonomous entities) and an "intertextual" conception (which conceives of texts as representative of generic ways of knowing literature). By examining the level of abstraction and degree of elaboration at different phases of the process, they found that less able students made intertextual links involving character traits or plot, as opposed to more able students, who tended to define such links in terms of literary themes. The authors suggest teaching methods focused on intertextual connections (i.e., thematic, topical, archetypal connections among texts), as opposed to methods focused on historical periods or literary classifications.

In his chapter, Robert Tierney traces the limitations of current reading instruction, assessment, and research to prevailing simplistic conceptions of text understanding. He argues that these conceptions emphasize text comprehension at the expense of more complex processes of meaning making: affective experiences, image making, perspective taking, and relating the text to readers' purposes, needs, and lives.

Thus, developing a textual stance involves understanding the complex relationship between the forms and functions of texts (i.e., experimenting with the "persuasive" elements of narrative or dialogue). Further, developing such a stance involves recognizing and responding to the culturally-bound and often hidden criteria of evaluators and teachers, as well as comparing the themes, topics, content, and context of current and past texts.

The next three essays in this collection focus on the institutional stances necessary for functioning within schools. Within the academy, it is hoped that students will ultimately learn to formulate, test out, and reflect on the validity of their own ideas and those of authorities. Thus, as Patricia Bizzell (1986) posits, and as William Perry's developmental research indicates, college students move from a rigid, "dualist" orientation involving absolutist thinking to an ability to entertain optional perspectives to a "relativist" perspective—the ability to test out and determine the validity of a range of different perspectives to a "commitment in relativism"—a propensity to act according to one's own well-formulated beliefs.

Davison, Kitchener, and King review theory and research on the development of "reflective judgment" as related to the ability to cope with "ill-structured problems," problems for which learned practices are momentarily inadequate. The fact that they find that levels of development of "reflective judgment" increase with levels of schooling suggests that involvement in "academic" discourse practices fosters such thinking. The authors strongly urge approaches to the teaching of writing that provide ill-structured problems, as opposed to "puzzles" (problems with simplistic, unidimensional solutions).

While the need to provide supporting evidence is an essential aspect of academic thinking, students must learn to adopt a skeptical attitude towards that evidence. In his chapter, Barry Kroll discusses one instance of teaching reflective judgement through encounters with ill-structured problems. He analyzes changes in freshmen composition students' thinking over the period of a semester in a course involving reading and writing about different, and often discrepant, accounts of the Vietnam War. In the beginning of the course, many students assumed that texts were believable and accountable to the truth. However, after studying texts presenting conflicting evidence about particular battles in the war and by reflecting on their perceptions using exploratory journal writing, the students became less dogmatic and more intuitive and analytical in their thinking, acquiring, what Rexford Brown defines as a "literacy of thoughtfulness." Such thoughtfulness was characterized by a curiosity about the intrinsic worth of ideas, a willingness to withhold judgment and adopt a tentative stance, an understanding of the need to provide supporting evidence, a sense of persistence, and a commitment to humane values and truthfulness (Orton, Avery, & Lawrenz, 1989). In keeping with the view of discourse development supported by others in this volume, rather than presenting arbitrary rules and conventions for "evaluating evidence," Kroll immersed his students in a variety of discourse practices that forced them to engage in and develop reflective thinking.

Just as students need to be skeptical in their acceptance of authorities and knowledge, they need to recognize the limitations of "the prose of the schools." Applying a deconstructivist critique to various conceptions of literacy reflecting different institutional stances, Knoblauch and Johnston argue for the need to be "free from . . . other people's dominating uses of language" (p. 327). They suggest involving students in discourse practices that, in the conceptions of Barthes and Derrida, involve "reading playfully." They advocate that readers and writers reading and continually recognize power of language as a subversive form of institutional control.

Thus, adopting an institutional stance means becoming aware of the variety of institutional perspectives within which literate people work and live (i.e., the workplace, the government, the academy, etc.). As this awareness develops, adolescents and adults must become conscious and critical of what constitutes "knowledge" and "authority" within and outside of particular institutions. Specifically, within the context of the academy, readers and writers must become aware of the sociopolitical nature of language.

The final three chapters in this volume focus on the development of particular field stances within and outside of the traditional classroom. In their chapter, Ball, Dice, and Bartholmae discuss the ways in which students learn to employ certain essay-writing practices within certain academic disciplines. In some cases, students' essays receive positive evaluations from instructors even if those essays have little substance. Because the instructors are pleased that students are employing appropriate practices, they reward their students for accommodating to their particular field.

Moving outside the academy to the field of adult literacy, Lytle and Schultz criticize the limitations of traditional assessment techniques as failing to provide valid measures of adults' own discourse strategies developed in the context of urban life. According to the authors, such standardized tests tend to label adults as "deficient" learners and contribute to a view of low skilled adults as "part of an 'epidemic' and . . . illiteracy as a disease or pathology" (see p. 360, this volume). They contrast the "autonomous" model of literacy (which assumes that literacy is a set of skills to be mastered) with an "ideological" model (which recognizes the social nature of literacy practices). Part of competent assessment, they argue is determining adults' perceptions of "what counts as literacy" through qualitative inquiry methods such as open-ended interview techniques. In their program of "learner-centered" assessment, adults are active participants in understanding and assessing their own literate practices. Thus, they develop literate behaviors in the context of assessing their own progress.

In the final chapter, Phelps, drawing on her experience in designing a "literacy program" for Syracuse University, develops a heuristic for thinking about curriculum development. The resulting model attempts to integrate what we know about discourse development with what we are beginning to understand about how language operates within particular social, institutional, and field contexts. She emphasizes the need for students to experience "developmental tensions" that challenge their familiar modes of thinking.

Thus, within and outside of the academy, adolescents and adults must develop particular field stances which enable them to understand prototypical ways of thinking associated with particular disciplines or fields of study. Students in classrooms learn that in order to succeed in school, they must infer the perspectives and ways of thinking valued by teachers. Outside of the traditional classroom, adults learn to become literate by becoming more aware of their own attitudes and presumptions about what it means to be or become literate. In assessing and understanding their own growth, they develop not a single "literacy," but "multiple literacies" (Chapter 16) that enable them to function within a variety of fields and institutions.

STANCES AND THE DEVELOPMENT OF DISCOURSE PRACTICES

These then are four stances shaping growth in discourse practices. While we have described them as distinct, the essays in this collection suggest that readers and writers learn to combine and integrate these stances.

For example, the students in Geisler's research are learning to converse socially within the field of philosophy, learning to "talk like a philosopher." And the readers in Vipond, Hunt, Jewett, and Reither's study learned to vary their orientations according to differences in practices associated with different types of texts. In writing persuasive essays within an academic context, as Crowhurst suggests, students learn to mesh knowledge of text practices with "academic" or "field" practices constituting certain roles, orientations, or interpretative/rhetorical strategies ("being a student," "being a literary critic;" "analyzing the imagery patterns," "being a feminist reader," etc.).

Developmentally, this is a crucial, but difficult step for students because it requires them, in Bartholomae's (1985) words, to "invent the university." They must redefine their roles and strategies in terms of often new and unfamiliar social contexts. For example, while they may be familiar with the textbook organizational model of the "five paragraph theme," in a freshman literature class taught by a feminist, they are asked to critique the sex-role portrayals of characters in a Hemingway story. Within that social and political context, a purely formalistic stance does not enable them to function successfully.

Engaging in certain practices enhances critical awareness of the limitations of other practices. For example, in the academy, students learn to critically examine the content or language of what is being said as opposed to simply how it is being said. Acquiring such an attitude towards language provides them with a critical orientation towards a mass-media, consumer culture obsessed with "style" (Ewen, 1988) and "performance" of language rather than meaning.

However, rather than reinforcing each other, discourse practices often conflict with each other, creating ambiguous directions for socialization. As Barnes and Barnes suggest, the formalist ways of reading and writing acquired in by less-advantaged "basic skills" English courses conflict with those practices employed in certain "real-world" institutions or fields, making it more difficult for these students to acquire these institutional or field practices. Similarly, the practices associated with certain fields— the ability to openly express or critically analyze ideas, may be deemed as inappropriate within certain institutions such as the workplace.

Unfortunately, language "skills" are often taught as separate phenomena, so that students never learn to adopt and integrate a variety of stances in their discourse practices. In an analysis of writing in an organic chemistry course, Powell (1985) found that students employed a wide range of different field practices: chemistry, biology, medicine, mathematics, and chemical engineering. In order to write effective lab reports, he needed to model ways of integrating discourse stances and practices typical of these different fields.

Moreover, individual teachers may operate under quite different ideological orientations (Herrington, 1985; Mosenthall, 1984). Even within one field such as English, a student may encounter teachers who employ or evaluate writing or reading in radically different ways. Further, different schools operate according to different ideological orientations, as Barnes and Barnes have demonstrated.

Finally, schools often fail to provide an environment rich in "ill-structured problems." Many students engage in rote learning of accepted conventions and facts about language, rather than purposeful and socially motivated discourse practices. Language learning in schools becomes a "puzzle" to be solved rather than an active, involved experience.

GROWTH IN READING AND WRITING: TOWARDS WHAT END

These conflicts between practices raises the question as to what is the ultimate goal of literacy education. Recent criticisms of lack of "cultural literacy" reflect certain assumptions about what is or should be learned in reading and writing about literature. Critics such as Hirsch (1987) and Bloom (1987) argue that because students lack knowledge of familiar authors and texts, they are unable to understand current texts as drawing on past literary traditions and themes. They prescriptively assume that knowledge about authors and texts constitutes what it means to be "literate" within a culture.

At the other end of the spectrum, Gee (1988) and Graff (1987) argue that the "literacy crisis" is a myth in that the presumed goals of literacy—increasing economic power, higher levels of education, and greater degree of political participation and tolerance are not necessarily found in relatively "literate" societies. They are therefore skeptical about justifications of literacy development based on improved social and economic growth. For example, Gee (1988) points to Sweden, a country which, through the church, instituted a literacy campaign in the 18th century. Despite the success of this campaign, Sweden has not necessarily benefited economically.

As these critics charge, rather than enhancing economic opportunity, much literacy instruction simply perpetuates economic inequality, reflecting rather than transforming the social order. For example, Goodlad's (1984) analysis of English instruction in American secondary schools echoes Barnes and Barnes findings documenting the existence of a "two-tier" economic system with two different institutional stances constituted by different social, text, and field practices.

In the upper tier—in schools and/or classes populated by students from the upper socioeconomic strata, instruction is more than likely to foster open-ended expression of ideas, reading of literature, extended writing, and relatively effective teaching. In contrast, students in classes populated by students in the lower strata are more likely to experience focus on language mechanics and usage, reading of nonliterary texts, "correct answer" worksheets, and less effective teaching. This pattern begins in the first several years of schooling; students from homes with opportunity for literacy activities begin with a "head start," while students from homes without literacy activities never "catch up."

As a result, "deviant" students in schools, often from blue-collar backgrounds, demonstrate "resistance" to the academic expectations in schools as a political statement against these practices (Erickson, 1984). Or students may parody the "student" role in order to define or portray a sense of individuality—a manifestation of what Robert Brooke (1987) calls an expression of the "underlife." Or, as do many poor urban students, they drop out of school, often foreclosing further literacy development.

Some chapters in this volume have demonstrated that discourse practices also vary across different cultures. As demonstrated by the recent controversy over bilingual education, all of this poses distinct problems for students' socialization in a multicultural society. In addition to learning the discourse practices of their home culture, students must also acquire the often unfamiliar discourse practices of the majority culture. While the essays in this collection suggest that disequilibrium may enhance development, the disequilibrium generated by cross-cultural differences may be so overwhelming as to paralyze potential for growth.

The opportunities for individuals to participate in various discourse practices, for instance, in the amount and kinds of reading and writing varies considerably across different cultures. As Svennson has demonstrated, some readers lack the cultural socialization at home that contributes to knowledge of literary interpretive strategies. Schools can also fail to provide adequate opportunities for students to engage in purposeful discourse practices. While one would assume that most instructional time is devoted to reading and writing, analyses of classrooms indicate that students actually spend little time reading and writing (Applebee, 1985; Goodlad, 1984). What little writing that does occur is typically confined to a paragraph or less (Applebee, 1985).

In addition, readers and writers vary in their participation in different discourse practices due to differences in social development, such as their motivation or volition to learn (Johnston & Winograd, 1985). In her case study research on adolescents' responses to literature, Hynds (1989) demonstrated that beyond competence for interpreting literature, students also needed to develop the pragmatic skill to "succeed" in the literature classroom, as well as the volition to read for personal purposes, beyond the minimal requirements of passing a test. The degree to which readers and writers perceive discourse practices as socially purposeful may enhance their motivation. In his study of students' perceptions of school writing, Applebee (1985) found that although teachers were employing a "process approach," students often perceived little or no purpose in their writing.

As Barnes and Barnes, Crowhurst, and Lytle and Schultz argue, in "real world" social contexts, people are reading and writing in order to fulfill their own purposes or needs. Lytle and Schultz's assessment techniques attempt to help adults articulate their own uses of literacy as related to their perceived purposes or needs. All of this suggests that growth in reading and writing requires and ideally fosters an increased sense of personal and social efficacy (Coles & Wall, 1987; Salvatori, 1983).

Thus, literacy instruction must reach far beyond the teaching and testing of cognitive skills in order to provide opportunities to employ those practices necessary for a meaningful life. Current skills-based instruction and assessment programs have disenfranchised less able students and those from nonmainstream cultures. Further, teaching only cognitive skills or formal conventions of language is no guarantee that adolescents and adults will be able to successfully engage in purposeful discourse practices. Finally, the decontextualized and depersonalized approaches to reading and writing "competency" that students experience in the classroom often diminish or destroy their motivation to engage in discourse practices beyond the context of formal schooling.

IMPLICATIONS FOR EDUCATIONAL POLICY

The chapters in this book, taken as a composite, suggest the several implications for educational policy and curriculum development. Rather than organizing the English curriculum according to topics or "bodies of knowledge" to be "covered" (i.e., "the paragraph," "elements of the short story," etc.) educators should provide students with a variety of opportunities to engage in language practices designed to develop particular stances toward discourse. For example, activities such as free writing, think-alouds, role playing, and so on can be built around the response strategies of engaging, conceiving, connecting, explaining, interpreting, and judging (Beach, 1987).

These stances are not acquired in one lesson. Students develop more elaborate discourse strategies by extensive language practices in different contexts. For example, they learn to mutually define intertextual links from repeated experiences of sharing texts with other students. This suggests that the curriculum needs to be based on the principles of consistency, reiteration, and elaboration of practices over time.

Further, as Knoblach and Johnston suggest, both teachers and students needs to be constantly turning the curriculum inside out, reexamining its underlying assumptions. Students often detect that "hidden agenda" practices of a specific classroom conflict with explicitly stated goals and evaluative criteria. Both Purves and Hawisher, and Ball, Dice, and Bartholomae recommend that instructors and students make explicit their underlying purposes and value assumptions, a process which itself is a valuable learning activity.

Learning can also be approached as a social (rather than a solitary) activity. Many essays in this collection suggest that informal, social activities, collaborative learning groups, "reciprocal teaching," or dialogue-journal writing help students acquire a social stance toward discourse. In social activities such as these, teachers can create disequilibrium or what Phelps defines as "developmental tensions" by asking students to grapple with "ill-structured problems."

Students should also be encouraged to adopt multiple stances toward discourse. For example, students could consider their own essay in terms of its potential social impact, its use of rhetorical strategies, its conformity to an institutional role, or its reliance on the knowledge of a certain field. As Terry Eagleton (1983) suggests, and Cooper demonstrates in this volume, students are therefore examining the effects of their own and others' texts on themselves and wider audiences. Thus, they learn how their texts reflect and influence their respective economic or cultural contexts, and ultimately their own attitudes and values.

In order to provide helpful, descriptive, "reader-based" evaluation of students' writing, teachers need to be able to describe students' discourse practices—what it is that students are doing in their reading and writing and how those practices influenced their social response. For example, rather than judge a paper according to deficiencies relative to a text model, teachers can describe their own responses as readers to these practices, conveying to students the ways in which the writing affects them. This helps students define the connection between what they are doing with their writing and how those practices influenced their audience.

Rather than basing assessment on isolated, a-rhetorical, "snapshot" performances, these essays suggest that assessment be based on the uses of discourse or composing strategies within particular social contexts (Faigley, Cherry, Jolliffe, & Skinner, 1985). Furthermore, any valid determination of growth needs to examine reading and writing over a period of time. By examining writing produced in actual rhetorical/social contexts and collected in a "portfolio," judges can ascertain the ways in which writers operated within and responded to a particular social context as opposed to the degree to which the writing conformed to a predetermined set of criteria standardized across different contexts.

Thus, these essays argue that readers and writers grow by acquiring social, textual, institutional, and field discourse practices. They learn to integrate these different practices, and to recognize the conflicts between them. In the process, they learn that reading and writing, rather than simply ends in themselves, are social activities that illuminate and enrich the lives of literate people.

REFERENCES

Anderson, P. (1985). What survey research tells us about writing at work. In L. Odell & D. Goswami (Eds.), *Writing in nonacademic settings* (pp. 3–83). New York: Guilford.

Anson, C. (1989). Toward a multidimensional model of writing in the academic disciplines. In D. Jolliffe (Ed.), *Advances in writing research. Volume Two: Writing in academic disciplines* (pp. 1–33). Norwood, NJ: Ablex.

Applebee, A. (1978). *The child's concept of story.* Chicago: University of Chicago Press.

Applebee, A. (1985). *Contexts for learning to write.* Norwood, NJ: Ablex.

Atwell, N. (1987). *In the middle.* Upper Montclair, NJ: Boynton/Cook.

Bakhtin, M. M. (1981). *The dialogic imagination: Four essays by M. M. Bakhtin.* (M. Holquist, Ed.). Austin: University of Texas Press.

Bartholomae, D. (1985). Inventing the university. In M. Rose (Ed.), *When a writer can't write* (pp. 134–165). New York: Guilford.

Beach, R. (1982). The pragmatics of self-assessing. In R. Sudol (Ed.), *Revising: New essays for the teaching of writing* (pp. 71–83). Urbana, IL: National Council of Teachers of English.

Beach, R. (1985). Discourse conventions and researching response to literary dialogue. In C. Cooper (Ed.), *Researching response to literature and the teaching of literature* (pp. 103–127). Norwood, NJ: Ablex.

Beach, R. (1987). Strategic teaching in literature. In B. Jones, A. Palincsar, D. Ogle, & E. Carr (Eds.), *Cognitive strategies for instruction* (pp. 139–159). Alexandria, VA: Association for Supervision and Curriculum Development.

Beach, R., & Brown, R. (1987). Discourse conventions and literary inference: Toward a theoretical model. In R. Tierney, P. Anders, & J. Mitchell (Eds.), *Understanding readers' understanding* (pp. 147–173). Hillsdale, NJ: Erlbaum.

Beach, R., & Wendler, W. (1987). Developmental differences in response to a story. *Research in the Teaching of English, 21,* 286–297.

Beach, R., & Anson, C. (1988). The pragmatics of memo-writing: Developmental differences in the use of rhetorical strategies. *Written Communication, 5,* 157–183.

Belenky, M., Clinchy, B., Goldberger, N., & Tarule, J. (1986). *Women's ways of knowing.* New York: Basic Books.

Berlin, J. (1988). Rhetoric and ideology in the writing class. *College English, 50,* 477–494.

Bialostosky, D. (1986). Dialogics as an art of discourse in literary criticism. *PMLA, 10,* 788–798.

Bizzell, P. (1986). What happens when basic writers come to college? *College Composition and Communication, 37*, 294–301.

Bloom, A. (1987). *The closing of the American mind.* New York: Simon & Schuster.

Bloom, L. (1985). Anxious writers in context: Graduate school and beyond. In M. Rose (Ed.), *When a writer can't write* (pp. 119–133). New York: Guilford.

Brandt, D. (1986). Toward an understanding of context in composition. *Written Communication, 3*, 139–157.

Bransford, J., Sherwood, R., Reiser, J., & Vye, N. (1986). Teaching thinking and problem-solving: Research foundations. *American Psychologist, 41*, 1087–1089

Brooke, R. (1987). Studies in the underlife. *College Composition and Communication, 38*, 154–182.

Brown, R., & Herndl, C. (1986). An ethnographic study of corporate writing: Job status as reflected in written text. In B. Couture (Ed.), *Functional approaches to writing: Research implications* (pp. 11–28). Norwood, NJ: Ablex.

Brown, R., & Herndl, C. (1986). An ethnographic study of corporate writing: Job status as reflected in written text. In B. Couture (Ed.), *Functional approaches to writing: Research implications.* Norwood, NJ: Ablex.

Bruner, J. (1986). *Actual minds, possible worlds.* Cambridge: Harvard University Press.

Burke, K. (1969). *A grammar of motives.* Berkeley, CA: University of California Press.

Butler, A., & Turbill, J. (1984). *Towards a reading-writing classroom.* Portsmouth, NH: Heinemann Educational Books.

Calkins, L. M. (1983). *Lessons from a child: On the teaching and learning of writing.* Exeter, NH: Heinemann Educational Books.

Calkins, L. M. (1986). *The art of teaching writing.* Portsmouth, NH: Heinemann Educational Books.

Cazden, C. (1988). *Classroom discourse: The language of teaching and learning.* Portsmouth, NH: Heinemann.

Coles, N., & Wall, S. (1987). Conflict and power in the reader-responses of adult basic writers. *College English, 49*, 298–314.

Cooper, M. (1984). The pragmatics of form: How do writers discover what they do. In R. Beach & L. Bridwell (Eds.), *New directions in composition research* (pp. 109–126). New York: Guilford.

Cooper, M. (1986). The ecology of writing. *College English, 48*, 364–75.

Crockett, W. (1965). Cognitive complexity and impression formation. In B. Maher (Ed.), *Progress in experimental personality research* (Vol. 2). New York: Academic Press.

Culler, J. (1975). *Structuralist poetics.* Ithaca, NY: Cornell University Press.

Daiute, C. (1986). Do 1 and 1 make 2? Patterns of influence by collaborative authors. *Written Communication, 3*, 382–408.

de Castell, S., Luke, A., & Egan, K. (1986). On defining literary. In S. de Castell, A. Luke, & K. Egan (Eds.), *Literacy, society, and schooling.* Cambridge: Cambridge University Press.

Deal, T., & Kennedy, A. (1982). *Corporate cultures*. Reading, MA: Addison-Wesley.

Donaldson, M. (1978). *Children's minds*. Glasglow: Collins Press.

Eagleton, T. (1983). *Literary theory*. Minneapolis: University of Minnesota Press.

Edelsky, C., & Harman, S. (1988). One more critique of reading tests—with two differences. *English Education, 20*, 157–171.

Elbow, P. (1975). *Writing without teachers*. New York: Oxford UP.

Erickson, R. (1984). School literacy, reasoning, and civility: An anthropologist's perspective. *Review of Educational Research, 54*, 525–546.

Ewen, S. (1988). *All-consuming images*. New York: Basic Books.

Faigley, L. (1986). Competing theories of process: A critique and a proposal. *College English, 48*, 527–542.

Faigley, L., Cherry, R., Jolliffe, D., & Skinner, A (1985). *Assessing writers' knowledge and processes of composing*. Norwood, NJ: Ablex.

Flower, L., & Hayes, J. (1981). A cognitive process theory of writing. *College Composition and Communication, 35*, 365–387.

Flower, L., & Hayes, J. (1986). Detection, diagnosis, and the strategies of revision. *College Composition and Communication, 37*, 16–55.

Freire, P. (1973). *Education for critical consciousness*. New York: Continuum.

Gee, J. P. (1988). The legacies of literacy: From Plato to Freire through Harvey Graff. *Harvard Educational Review, 58*, 200–212.

Gilligan, C. (1983). *In a different voice*. Cambridge: Harvard UP.

Graff, H. J. (1987). *The legacies of literacy*. Bloomington, IN: Indiana University Press.

Goodlad, J. (1984). *A place called school*. New York: McGraw-Hill.

Graves, D. (1983). *Writing: Teachers and children at work*. Portsmouth, NH: Heinemann.

Harste, J. (1985). Portrait of a new paradigm: Reading comprehension research. In A. Crismore (Ed.), *Landscapes* (Chap. 12, pp. 1–24). Bloomington, IN: Center for Reading and Language studies, College of Education, University of Indiana.

Hernadi, P. (1988). Doing, making, meaning: Toward a theory of verbal practice. *PMLA, 103*, 749–758.

Herrington, A. (1985). Writing in academic settings: A study of the contexts for writing in two college chemical engineering courses. *Research in the Teaching of English, 19*, 331–359.

Hirsch, E. D. (1987). *Cultural literacy: What every American needs to know*.

Hunt, R., & Vipond, D. (1986). Evaluations in literary reading. *Text, 6*, 53–71.

Hynds, S. (1985). Interpersonal cognitive complexity and the literary response processes of adolescent readers. *Research in the Teaching of English, 19*, 386–402.

Hynds, S. (1989). Bringing life to literature and literature to life: Social constructs and contexts of four adolescent readers. *Research in the teaching of English, 23*, 30–61.

Johnston, P., & Winograd, P. (1985). Passive failure in reading. *Journal of Reading Behavior, 27*, 279–302.

Kroll, B. (1978). Cognitive egocentrism and the problem of audience awareness in written discourse. *Research in the Teaching of English, 12*, 269–281.

Kroll, B. (1986). Explaining how to play a game: The development of informative writing skills. *Written Communication, 3,* 195–218.

Labov, W. (1972). *The Language of the inner city.* Philadephia: University of Pennsylvania Press.

MacCrorie, K. (1980). *Telling writing* (3rd ed.). Upper Montclair, NJ: Boynton/COOK.

MacCrorie, K. (1984). *Writing to be read* (3rd ed.). Upper Montclair, NJ: Boynton/Cook.

Mailloux, S. (1982). *Interpretive conventions.* Ithaca, NY: Cornell. University Press.

Marzano, R., et al. (1988). *Dimensions of thinking.* Alexandria, VA: Association for Supervision and Curriculum Development.

Moffett, J. (1968). *Teaching the universe of discourse.* Boston: Houghton Mifflin.

Mosenthall, P. (1984). The effect of classroom ideology on children's production of narrative text. *American Educational Research Journal, 21,* 679–689.

Murray, D. (1986). *A writer teaches writing.* Boston: Houghton Mifflin.

Myers, I., & McCaulley, M. (1985). *A guide to the development and use of the Myers-Briggs type indicator.* Palo Alto, CA: Consulting Psychologists Press.

O'Keefe B. J., & Delia, J.G. (1982). Impression formation and message production. In M. E. Roloff & C. R. Berger. (Eds.), *Social cognition and communication* (pp. 33–72). Beverly Hills, CA: Sage.

Odell, L., & Goswami, D. (1982). Writing in a nonacademic setting. *Research in the Teaching of English, 42,* 35–43.

Orton, R., Avery, P., & Lawrenz, F. (1989). Values education: Cutting across the disciplines. *The High School Journal, 72,* 124–129.

Pereleman, L. (1986). The context of classroom writing. *College English, 48,* 471–483.

Piché, G. Rubin, D., & Turner, L. (1980). Training for referential communication in writing. *Research in the Teaching of English, 14,* 309–318.

Postman, N. (1985). *Amusing ourselves to death.* New York: Viking.

Powell, A. (1985). A chemist's view of writing, reading, and thinking across the curriculum. *College Composition and Communication, 36,* 414–418.

Purves, A. (1981). *Reading and literature: American achievement in perspective.* Urbana, IL: National Council of Teachers of English.

Pratt, L. (1976). *A speech act theory of literary discourse.* Bloomington, IN: Indiana University Press.

Rabinowitz, P. (1987). *Before reading.* Ithaca, NY: Cornell UP.

Radway, J. (1984). *Reading the romance: Women, patriarchy, and popular literature.* Chapel Hill, NC: University of North Carolina Press

Rorty, R. (1979). *Philosophy and the mirror of nature.* Princeton, NJ: Princeton University Press.

Rosenblatt, L. (1978). *The reader, the text, the poem: The transactional theory of the literary work.* Carbondals, IL: Southern Illinois University Press.

Rubin, D. (1984). Social cognition and written communication. *Written Communication, 1,* 211–246.

Salvatori, M. (1983). Reading and writing a text. *College English, 45,* 657–666.

Scardamalia, M., Bereiter, C., & Goelman, H. (1982). The role of production factors in writing ability. In M. Nystrand (Ed.), *What writers know* (pp. 173–210). New York: Academic Press.

Schwartz, P., & Ogilvy, J. (1979). *The emergent paradigm: Changing patterns of and belief.* Menlo Park, CA: Values and Lifestyles Program.

Staton, J., Shuy, R. W., Peyton, J. K., & Read, L. (Eds). (1988). *Interactive writing in dialogue journals: Linguistic, social, and cognitive views.* Norwood, NJ: Ablex.

Straw, S. (1989). Collaborative learning and reading for theme in poetry. *Reading-Canada-Lecture, 7,* 42–51.

Svennson, C. (1985). *The construction of poetic meaning.* Linkoping, Sweden: Liber.

Tompkins, J. (1988). A short course in post-structuralism. *College English, 50,* 733–747.

Turiel, E. (1983). *The development of social knowledge: Mortality and convention.* Cambridge, England: Cambridge University Press.

Vipond, D., & Hunt, R. (1984). Point-driven understanding: Pragmatic and cognitive dimensions of literacy reading. *Poetics 13,* 261–277.

2
Reading and Writing as Social Action

Douglas Barnes
Dorothy Barnes

LITERACY AS SOCIAL PRACTICES RATHER THAN SKILLS

It is not easy to penetrate the taken-for-granted assumptions about writing and reading which we share with other researchers and teachers, and indeed with the general public, since we were all socialized into them in elementary school. We learned to think of reading and writing as sets of generic skills, irrespective of their content and purpose, and to take it for granted that the reading and writing which we learned in school would be universally applicable. Nevertheless, it is worth asking how the kinds of reading and writing which are required of students in lessons relate to those which they are already engaged in outside the curriculum, including graffiti, signs on bedroom doors, and notes passed surreptitiously during the class. The terms "reading" and "writing" refer to a range of practices which are not all necessarily similar to those found in lessons. This chapter considers some of the ways in which literate activities in schools vary according to the contexts, uses, and purposes of the communication. Literacy is a sociocultural phenomenon, and we must not allow the familiarity of reading and writing as school activities to blind us to differences which may have important implications both for the goals and methods of teaching.

In this chapter we use some of our own research materials to illustrate differences in the teaching of reading and writing in schools and colleges in the U.K., and then more briefly in other countries, and to explore the contextual differences which accompany them. These are not merely differences in pedagogy but qualitative differences in what is to be learned. We are particularly interested into exploring differences between school conceptions of literacy and those enacted in adult life.

Literacy in Our Lives

If we see literacy not as a set of general skills, but as clusters of practices embedded in the lives and purposes of those who read and write, we can expect differences in the nature of the reading and writing to appear in social groupings of all kinds. These may be whole nations, insofar as each displays a discrete cultural milieu, or sections of the community in whose lives writing or reading play different roles and therefore carry different meanings. Or it may be different institutions, including schools, in which particular kinds of reading and writing may be linked with particular functions and values which they have in that context.

Reading and writing, like speaking and listening, are not just a matter of arranging words in sentences: they involve acting upon others, so that competence in them involves sensitivity to interpersonal relationships as well as understanding of those aspects of the world which form the subject matter. It is for this reason that we have called this chapter "Reading and writing as social action." Heath (1983) has shown something of what this means in practice by her analysis of the functions of reading and writing in particular communities. For example, in one community reading might be instrumental, news-related, recreational, critical/educational, or confirmational, and writing might be memory aids, reinforcement for oral messages, social-interactional, financial, or expository. Even more valuable are the brief indications that she gives of the ways in which each of these practices relates to particular social actions: the definition of expository writing, for example, includes, "Writer envisions or 'knows' audience and attempts to include only those definitions and facts believed not to be known to the addressee." The analysis illustrates very persuasively how intimately the practices that constitute literacy are embedded in a repertoire of contextualized cultural performances. Literacy can thus be seen as the result of socialization into culturally embedded practices, such as keeping records in commerce, or fullfilling the requirements of a religion, as well as meeting the needs of schooling.

Literacy in Schools

The teaching of reading and writing is likely to be profoundly impaired if it ignores the ways in which literacy is embedded in social contexts: This chapter will explore the implications of the embedded nature of literacy for teaching. It must be understood that school literacy is not excluded from the general rubric: Schools also display their own versions of reading and writing in response to the specific functions that these play in educational milieux, especially in the assessment of students. As Street (1984) shows, in everyday life outside schools and colleges it is unusual for people to read and write essays and compositions; far more common forms of writing are lists, labels, signs, checks, records of business transactions, tables, charters, warning labels, instructions, and forms to be completed. Continuous texts occur mainly in the form of fiction or of newspaper and magazine articles, which have their own rationale. In pointing out this difference between texts in and out of schools, we are not of course implying that schools should devote themselves mainly to texts that perform a transactional function: Education has wider concerns than merely reflecting the ways of life beyond its boundaries.

VERSIONS OF ENGLISH

In 1979–82 we carried out a qualitative study of the teaching of English in the upper forms of a sample of U.K. high schools and of colleges of Further Education (F.E.)[1] (Barnes, Barnes, & Clarke, 1984). We called our study of these courses "Versions of English" because our central purpose was to penetrate behind the rhetoric of English teaching. We wanted to test the hypotheses that the English curriculum offered to one set of students differed radically from the version of the English curriculum experienced by other students, and that these differences could be related both to the identities of the students and to the institutional contexts in which the courses were taught.

The versions of writing required of students in different institutional contexts differed profoundly within schools, between different schools, and between schools and F.E. colleges. We had set up the study so as to sample schools in different contexts, inner city, suburban, and in a small town with many prosperous commuters. Within each school we sampled high, middle and low "streams" ("tracks" in North American terminology), and we also saw to it that different forms of leaving examination were

---

[1] *Versions of English* is a quasiethnographic study of how language arts curricula were being put into practice in a sample of schools and colleges in England. It focused upon the curricula offered to students in their last year of compulsory education in schools (equivalent to Grade 10) and in their first year of postcompulsory education in schools and colleges of further education (that is, students aged 15–16 and 16–17 years). Most U.K. students leave their schools at 16 years of age, some of them proceeding to F.E. Colleges, where most follow vocational courses which normally include compulsory elements of study in Communications. A minority of students (those preparing for secretarial work) follow courses in English. The various versions of English were characterized on the basis of extensive classroom observation, inspection of documentary evidence, interviews with teachers and with a sample (one-third) of the students, as well as analysis of writing done by the students interviewed.

represented.[2] In all of the schools we studied, parents' socioeconomic status was a strong predictor of the "stream" to which their son or daughter had been assigned. Thus, when we are discussing curricular differences according to streams we are indirectly also examining the ways in which differences in the kind of schooling vary according to different social backgrounds.

We identified four contrasting models for writing which occurred in the practices and justifications of teachers of English in U.K. high schools. First we distinguish "engaged" from "detached" approaches, and then subdivide each of them; the four resulting paradigms can then be related to the contexts in which we found them, although the actual practices of the teachers were more complex.

	APPROACH	PARADIGM
1.	engaged	"cultural tradition"
2.	engaged	"personal growth"
3.	detached	"belles lettres"
4.	detached	"basic skills"

Engaged Approaches to Writing

Teachers whose preference is for the students to aim for "engaged" writing usually set out to involve their first-hand interest and experience. In spite of this concern for the learner the array of preferred topics and styles in such writing is not infinite; those assigned topics included Loneliness, Jobs Around the House, Family Holidays, Bringing One's Boy/Girl Friend Home, and Family Arguments. This list would be misleading if it suggested to the reader a discussion of such topics at a distance and in general terms, for the essence of the "engaged" approaches is the exploration of the writer's attitudes and experiences through story or anecdote. Students focus upon describing the uniqueness and emotional quality of first-hand experience. When general issues appear they are dealt with through the particular experience of a participant. For examples, attitudes towards war are often represented through imaginary letters written by a soldier. The values by which such writings is measured are literary; the models are drawn from the novels and autobiographical writings of the earlier part of this

---

[2] The pattern of sampling which we designed amounted to posing a set of hypotheses about how the English curriculum varied; some of these hypotheses were supported by what we observed, but not all of them. In describing the differences that we found in literacy practices it has been necessary to use a certain ruthlessness in outlining ideal types which partly disguises the variations within each of them. Nevertheless, the differences in overall tendency are marked enough to justify this.

century, all characterized by an introspective concern with their protago-
nists' subjectivity. "Truth to experience" is highly valued, but it is truth
filtered through the novelist's eyes. The experience explored in such writing is individualistic and concerned primarily with close relationships, particularly in the family, yet what the students are learning can equally be
described as the tacit requirements of a literary genre.

Although teachers who recommend the "engaged" approaches frequently characterize them as enabling students to engage in reflective rec-
reation of first-hand experience, they usually find their apotheosis in fictional writing. Here are its achievements at their most impressive at the
beginning of a story written by an able student:

> Billy sat on his father's knee, his back bent, picking thoughtfully at his shirt
> buttons; Aunt Pol was talking to his father while she did the washing. They
> seemed to like talking to each other, thought Billy; after all, they were sister
> and brother. He thought back two Saturdays to the first time his father had
> come—the first time Billy had met his father. It seemed terribly long ago,
> yet very vivid in his mind. Ever since his aunt had mentioned his father, two
> years since, he had very much looked forward to seeing him.... He felt it
> would cause a change, and at seven years of age he felt the time was ripe
> for a change ...

From the point of view of an "engaged" account of writing, this would be
described as the exploration through fiction of virtual experience rather
than of first-hand events and perceptions. However, it is equally, and possibly more significantly, the remarkably skillful exploitation of a genre, a
particular kind of "realistic" short story. What this student has "learned"
is as much about the requirements and stylistic expectations of this genre
as about "experience," though the two are clearly not mutually exclusive
(Medway, 1986). In the schools we visited, the engaged approaches appeared in two forms which we call "cultural tradition" and "personal
growth," two sides of the same coin. The "cultural tradition" paradigm
showed itself most clearly in the study of literature, and very often had the
marked ethical coloring associated with the Cambridge school of criticism
(allied to "the New Criticism" in North America). The literary works were
held to give the students access to more sensitive readings of human experience. This often coexisted with a "personal growth" perspective on writing, though the writing of more able students of this age was dominated
by the requirements of the literature examination. Writing about first-hand
experience was claimed to give the students the opportunity to understand and reevaluate that experience. Fiction was thought to perform a
similar function, though more obliquely. One consequence of this view
was that it almost entirely omitted any writing that was designed to engage

directly in action: to use James Britton's terms it was "poetic" not "transactional" (Britton, Burgess, Martin, McLeod, & Rosen, 1975). With less able students for whom reading adult literature presented difficulties, the "personal growth" paradigm turned strongly towards the students' own writing, usually with a marked preponderence of fiction, which the students themselves preferred. It was as if the students' own writing was being ascribed part of the function that adult literature was to play for their more able contemporaries, the provision of a range of virtual experiences which might extend the students' sensibilities.

Many students are unable or unwilling to utilize school writing to carry out a reflective enquiry into their own lives, and fall back upon a flat unexpressive style that gives nothing away. Here a less able girl imagines herself in a year's time:

> Its Monday and I get up at eight o'clock. I dress and have breakfast. Then I go out to get the morning paper. Then my Dad got up at eight thirty and when he was dressed we both went into the shop through the door . . .

The rest of the piece is in similar vein. She may be writing about something that matters to her, but she is not exploring the texture of experience in the way that the rhetoric would require. Such writing is not infrequent, even from more able students, particularly boys.

In spite of this, there is much to be said for the assumptions that underlie the engaged approach. Pupils do indeed write better when they are grappling with a topic that matters to them, since their concern in ordering and representing that interest becomes the dynamic that drives their ordering of text. However, the engaged approach is limited to a central focus upon quasiliterary forms of writing, which turns students' attention away from writing addressed to particular audiences and situations. Moreover, the "personal growth" alternative can threaten areas of experience which students prefer to keep private. In any case, students of high school age are not usually writing for themselves (though they may if they are fortunate be addressing a teacher who has a personal interest in them), but really for an assessor; the personal growth paradigm then becomes an academic fiction.

Detached Approaches to Writing

In our schools we found "detached" accounts which presented writing as a set of skills to be mastered with little or no reference to the purposes or experiences of the writer. These approaches appeared in two forms, "belles lettres" and "basic skills," which appeared to correspond with the teachers' view of what their students were capable of. In the "belles let-tres" paradigm, the more able students were expected to write with skill and liveliness without necessarily committing themselves deeply to what they wrote. When they wrote about literature their concern was to demon-strate knowledge of the text, rather than to respond to it for themselves. What was valued in this paradigm was the ability to produce acceptable performances on topics of no particular interest to the writer. In charac-terizing this approach to writing as "belles lettres," we do not intend to imply that young people cannot learn from play with words, from pastiche, or from writing which is not close to their concerns. Here is a successful practitioner writing about "Holidays Abroad":

> Let me begin by stating the obvious—we English are streets ahead when it comes to holidaying abroad. We're the ones who really make the holiday go. It's not Germans you'll find dancing on the tables in the beer kellers, but we English—throwing ourselves into the holiday spirit with gusto. . . .

This is skillful light entertainment, which represents a considerable achievement for a 16-year-old. Such skills are undoubtedly to be valued; our task here is to note how different the underlying values and precon-ceptions of such writing are from those illustrated above as characteristic of an "engaged" paradigm.

Not many young people achieved such control of tone in their writing. A typical "belles lettres" topic is "Fire," and for one student this led to the following:

> The flames looked like people running after you, shouting death, dressed in falmboyant [sic] clothing. The tips of flames looked like daggers, cutting in to everything. The tree which had been captured by the flames looked like mourners all in black . . .

This illustrates some limitations of the "belles lettres" approach to writing. The girl who wrote this has considerable control over language, but has been betrayed into mimicking "fine writing," which in this piece has led to a mechanical search for similes. Writing has become not a struggle to represent her perceptions of experience but an attempt to provide a verbal display of a kind which her teacher will value. The writers of both "Holi-days Abroad" and "Fire" had their attention firmly upon their audiences; their subjective purposes played a lesser role.

In a number of schools a second "detached" paradigm appeared, usu-ally in classes for less able students. The "basic skills" paradigm treated writing as a set of skills that could be practiced through exercises and short tasks quite independently of the purposes and interests of the writer.

Often the students did little continuous writing of the kind that requires the writer him or herself to organize the material. One teacher observed made a practice of providing her class of not-very-able 16-year-olds with a structure for each piece of writing made up of leading sentences and indicators of content for each paragraph, a procedure likely to rob them of the experience of having to order their ideas. As Langer (1984) has pointed out, it is often the least able students who are given so much "scaffolding" in structuring continuous writing that they seldom have the demand made on them to structure a piece for themselves. All teachers emphasized the importance of conforming to orthographic conventions, but the practice of these became a major concern in the "basic skills" paradigm, as if the content were of secondary importance.

The skills celebrated in the belles lettres paradigm were those of a certain kind of journalism, in contrast with engaged approaches which looked rather towards novel writing or autobiography. Writing was thus treated as a set of skills that might be learned in general for later application in various situations. It is our experience that though some students thrive on this, many find it impossible to commit themselves seriously to lengthy writing tasks that appear to have no purpose beyond the teacher's or examiner's whim.

The "basic skills" paradigm seems to us to be entirely unacceptable. Practicing conventions and completing written exercises out of context is a quite ineffective way of preparing to engage with real issues for real audiences: The "whole" of literacy is quite different in kind from the sum of its parts.

We have indicated some undoubted differences between the writing that is encouraged by "engaged" and "detached" approaches, yet they have much in common as they are interpreted in U.K. schools. For example, the writing tasks set by teachers whose approach we characterize as "detached" are likely to be just as much bound to quasiliterary models—light journalism, for example, as in the "Holidays Abroad" passage—as those from teachers we would call "engaged." In contrast, we were more likely to find writing tasks intended to match adult writing in the world outside education in colleges of further education.

Writing, Examination Modes, and Social Class

It was no great surprise to us to find the four paradigms—cultural tradition, personal growth, belles lettres, and basic skills—but what was unexpected was to find that they were systematically related to modes of examination. Most of the secondary students were being prepared for one or other of the leaving examinations that are available to U.K. students at 16 years of age. Some students were to be assessed through formal examination papers, some solely through coursework selected and evaluated by their teachers, and some through a combination of both these methods. A clear connection appeared between the predominant paradigm of writing in each class and the form of examination used. Classes being prepared for assessment through coursework tended to display one or other of the "engaged" paradigms; those being prepared for assessment through an examination paper commonly displayed the "detached"; and those prepared for mixed examinations displayed aspects of both. It was not clear whether the mode of examination determined the kind of writing favored or vice versa; in many cases the choice of examination had been made by a school administrator and not by the teacher. What is important for our purposes is to note that although all of these students were being taught writing within the framework of a course called "English," what they were experiencing as "writing" differed radically from one class to another, as did the qualities and priorities being advanced both explicitly and tacitly by their teachers. Which of the paradigms was experienced by a particular student depended partly upon the form of examination chosen in the school and partly upon whether he or she had been assigned to a higher or lower "stream." Thus the working-class students who predominated in the lower streams were more likely to experience the teaching of writing either through a personal growth approach or a basic skills approach, or a combination of the two.

Though social class was thus related to the curriculum through the streaming system, we did not find that social background of the schools as a whole had a similar effect. Although some theorists (Bowles, 1971; Anyon, 1981, for example) predict a correspondence between the social class context of the school and the modes of cultural transmission experienced by students, we did not find such a correspondence shaping the teaching of writing. One city center school took a predominantly engaged approach and the other a mixed one that appeared to depend upon each teacher's priorities. One suburban school was markedly "detached" with a great emphasis upon decontextualized language exercises; the other showed a variety of approaches. In the small town schools, where the proportion of middle class parents was much higher than elsewhere, writing was taught predominantly through "engaged" approaches, but these teachers did differ from the other schools by being markedly more willing to engage with controversial and critical issues relevant to the lives of the students. For some students in these classes, writing became *inter alia* a tool for disentangling controversial issues, whereas elsewhere the reproduction of acceptable stereotypes was more highly valued.

It seemed probable that schools were transmitting to different groups of students different versions of the cultural meaning of both reading and writing. For some students in lower streams, reading and writing were solely a means of taking and reproducing meanings controlled by other persons; the mode of teaching literacy was encouraging them to become passive and uncritical in their approaches to written text. In contrast, for other students reading and writing were presented as means of taking part in the dialogues—written and spoken—that constitute the conversation of mankind. In this way, children from families of a low socioeconomic status may be further disabled from taking a full part in their future adult lives.

VERSIONS OF READING IN SCHOOLS

Just as a range of models can be identified in writing, we found similar models shaping reading instruction. Adult readers can contrast what they have read attentively in the last few days with the kinds of reading typical of the classroom. They have probably spent as much time, if not more, in reading notices, instructions, recipes, timetables, reports of meetings, newspaper articles, and academic papers as they have reading what they think of as "books." Yet if we casually ask people whether they read much they will generally presume we are talking about leisure time reading and will reply in terms of magazines or novels; for many ordinary folk out of school, just as for English teachers in schools, the term "reading" has become synonomous with reading fiction. Indeed, most of the teachers we interviewed told us that their primary goal was that their students should read habitually for pleasure, though this often did not correspond well with their classroom practices.

As a result of this, high school students experience two contrasting kinds of reading; in English classes, reading is generally identified with the reading of fiction, the property of the English department, while in the remainder of the curriculum it performs a very narrow function in relation to textbooks. The content in the lessons which teachers designate "reading" becomes specialized in the kind of texts which demand of the reader commitment and involvement—what we describe as "literature." Teachers of subjects other than English expect students to read, of course, but usually regard their ability to do so as unproblematic. Students in science or geography or history are faced with tasks quite unlike reading for pleasure. Textbooks are usually compressed, with little of the repetition and supporting detail that characterizes adult books on similar topics, and often without much recognition of the disputes, value issues, and human implications that make the topics potentially exciting. Such texts face the reader with unique problems, though the teachers who use them are usually entirely unaware of this. In this chapter however we are concerned with the teaching of literacy, and not its uses elsewhere in the curriculum.

The Content of Literature Lessons

We have been using the term "literature" as though we all attach the same meaning to it, but we found that there is considerable variation in what the term is understood to refer to according to its context. It may well be that wider comparisons could be made between practices in different countries, but although we have observed some differences in the books that are read in literature classes in the U.K., Canada, and Australia, there does not appear to be systematic patterning in the variations.

In the *Versions of English* study, however, we were able to observe systematic variation in the books which were used with the students of different ability and of different social background. In U.K. schools the selection of texts is not entirely at the whim of individual teachers and departments even though there is some freedom of choice. We found that three characteristics distinguished the texts studied by high status classes: They came from the established canon of English literature, they were likely to be set in a period or milieu far removed from the present day-to-day life of their readers, and they tended to be substantial enough to demand considerable perseverance. Examples include novels by Dickens, Charlotte Brontë, Hardy, Wilkie Collins, and H.G. Wells. The study of drama for these "top" classes usually implied Shakespeare, but two of the teachers had chosen Arthur Miller's *The Crucible* instead. All these classes were studying poetry by concentrating on two or three poets and, although some teachers had chosen Goldsmith, the Romantic poets, or Hardy, by far the most popular poets were those who came into prominence in England in the 1960s: R. S. Thomas, Philip Larkin, and Ted Hughes.

In contrast the prose texts being used in the courses preparing students for a literature paper in the lower status C.S.E. examination did not come from the same corpus of literature. They were typically works with predominantly urban and realistic settings and written by well-known writers within the last 20 or 30 years; short stories were more frequently chosen than novels. No one in these classes was reading a Shakespeare play; drama, for them, was represented by modern three act plays with a serious purpose which had been theatrical successes in their day. When poetry was read, it was only as an occasional not a regular lesson. No one poet or poetry book was being studied; classes were reading isolated poems ranging from traditional ballads to twentieth century writers.

For the third group of students who were members of classes not taking a separate examination in literature, the "bottom" sets, no outside authority nominated texts so the choice lay entirely with the school and individual teacher. We found that some of the more accessible books read by the other classes were being used, but here we became aware of a new corpus of books emerging, produced in the last 10 or so years specifically for the teen-age market. Their brightly colored covers were designed to catch the eye and, though their message was different, they often looked like those displayed on railway bookstalls. These were the titles that some of our teachers were least happy with. As one teacher said, "I can teach *Animal Farm* 25 times and find it worthwhile. . . . would say the same of some Barstow and Sillitoe [fiction writers of the 1960s], but not *Us Boys of Westcroft.*"

Some of the differences in the texts chosen for different classes could be explained by referring to their difficulty; for example, the language of Shakespeare is not readily accessible to any student of this age and its difficulty would alienate the less able readers. But this explanation would be too simplistic: ease of understanding did not seem to be the major criterion governing choice, but rather a much more complex cultural divide. Some books conferred on their readers a cachet apart from their intrinsic worth: they signified that students who read them belonged to a cultural elite. The very fact that a student was in a class reading *Romeo and Juliet* and *The Woman in White* accorded that student a different cultural status from those who read *Billy Liar* and *To Sir with Love*.

Thus, the literature courses, like those in other subjects, were ascribing a cultural identity and status to each student. None of the teachers in our U.K. study explicitly referred to this cultural divide, although one young teacher spoke of his unease at the temptation to limit the less able to a diet of stories set in the context of urban working-class family life. In Australia, however, this cultural divide was thrown into sharp relief by one teacher's deliberate attempt to subvert it. In a Melbourne technical (low-status) school a class of predominantly non-native English speakers was struggling cheerfully with *Macbeth*. Their teacher had convinced them of the social advantage—the cultural capital—which they would gain from being able to claim they had studied a Shakespeare play; they were saving money so that they could visit a theater to see it performed, dining out in appropriate style beforehand.

Thus "teaching reading" in high school is far from being value-free. According to the "stream" to which they have been assigned, students are offered differing models of what constitutes literature, models which imply tacit social identities. At the same time they participate in different experiences of what constitutes taking meaning from a text, which may be even more significant than the texts chosen.

Versions of Reading as Classroom Practices

If we turn from choice of texts to their treatment in lessons, we find that the themes and topics which teachers directed attention to were much less diverse than the variation in titles studied would suggest. The teacher we quoted earlier referred to Orwell's *Animal Farm* but we came across very few other texts which were concerned with social or other large-scale issues. Teachers almost always focused on character and personal relationships within a domestic setting, especially when they were asking students to write. In a lesson when students and teacher were discussing *A Taste of Honey* in preparation for a literary essay, students touched on a wide range of issues about prejudice and inner-city life, yet when they were asked to write, it was about the relationship between two characters in the play. When we observed a class talking about *The Crucible* it was Elizabeth's character they were concerned with; we came across no discussion of, nor even reference to, the Salem witch trials as a parallel to the Communist witch hunt led by McCarthy, which was Miller's overt purpose in writing the play. Many of the teachers whom we interviewed would have endorsed Inglis' view (1981) that "literature is the readiest vehicle for talking about moral seriousness," but in the classroom most of them restricted their concern to personal and private morality. Class discussion of literature may have provided the first steps towards literary criticism; in most classes it was far from providing students with a general model for critical discussion.

Even more significant was the different interpretation that was attached to the activity "reading" as it was experienced by the different groups. If we ask ourselves what constituted "learning to read" for these literature courses, the answer must be complex. For the two classes being prepared for literature examinations, the primary task was to become familiar with the text. In another context Rosen and Rosen (1973) wrote, "There is a deep lack of confidence in the power of literature to do its work and a profound conviction that unless literature can be converted into the hard currency of familiar school learning it has not earned its keep" (p. 195). A parallel concern was that students should learn to interpret works of literature in conventionally acceptable ways: teaching literature includes inducting the young into particular ways of perceiving and evaluating people and events (Eagleton, 1983).

For the top and middle groups of students, much of the time given to literature was taken up by close reading of the text. Most of the English teachers in the "Versions of English" study expressed in interviews and in written policy statements how deeply they were committed to literature teaching. If they succeeded in making their students "hooked on books," they believed that they were not only providing them with a source of pleasure, but also "enlarging their emotional lives." Yet the activities they set up for their students and the kinds of reading which they encouraged often seemed to make this outcome unlikely. Some teachers were pre-occupied with local details: they took the class through the text para-graph by paragraph, pausing to check every few lines on the students' understanding of ideas and of individual words. For some teachers this seemed to be the only conceivable method of teaching for an examina-tion. We believe such laborious control of students' reading to be unpro-ductive: there are other ways of aiding those who require help with diffi-cult passages. There were many occasions when students seemed to be expected to take over the teacher's interpretation without internalizing it: the authority was external, and the student's own response was not asked for.

Thus the pressure of examinations provoked some teachers to a dis-trust of their students' ability, so that they spent most of the lessons in providing them with ready-made commentaries on the literary works be-ing read, instead of helping them to construct readings for themselves. Some went further and placed their emphasis upon the memorizing of details of the texts as if a novel was a textbook in geography, except that it was "ficts" not facts that were to be learned. Though no teachers were entirely free of such influence, many resisted it. For example, in one class that was reading *The Woman in White* in preparation for a particularly rigorous examination, students read some sections individually at home, but in class the presentation of the text was a shared activity, a semidra-matic reading, with students as characters and the teacher as narrator. There were few breaks for explanation, and to an observer the reading was remarkably effective. When the students had finished the book, they worked in groups through a list of questions which the teacher had pre-pared, and then presented the results of their discussions to the whole class. In their reporting back, the teacher accepted their views and their ways of expressing them, including one student's formulation: "Anything exciting tends to be spaced out ... not clumped all in one place." Ar-guments about the "wetness" of the character Laura were encouraged; opinions were not at this stage expected to be couched in orthodox lit-erary critical terminology. This teacher had so successfully initiated his students into his expectations about how a text should be read that he was able to hand over much of the actual reading to them. He was allow-ing them to move towards understanding at their own pace, and not im-posing an interpretation or expecting them to focus on minutiae before they had responded to the book as a whole. He had made available to students the implicit or explicit principles that inform the activity so that they could operate them for themselves. For this class, the reading of liter-ature involved their own perceptions of how the world is; the struggle to recreate the text and the struggle to understand experience became one.

For students of the lowest status, however, the emphasis fell upon enjoyment and fostering the habit of reading fiction, though it is not clear how successful the courses were in this. For them reading seemed not unlike the elementary school model of reading—the story at the end of the day. Individual reading was used as a reward for conscientious work or to fill in the gaps when the slower members of the class were finishing written tasks. For this group of students, the class reading of a novel was an undemanding activity unpunctuated by cross-questioning about meaning or reflective talk about the characters or action. In some schools and for some teachers it seemed that the less able the student the less time had to be spent on explanation, rather than the reverse, as one might expect.

Teaching methods varied according to the teacher and to the ethos of the English department. Teachers who repeatedly enacted for their students that reading literature seriously entailed accepting an authoritative explanation were manifestly transmitting a message about their future relationship with literature, a message that we believe to be disabling. Some classroom practices however were more calculated to encourage students to develop their own interpretations. For example, one teacher followed the suggestion of a student and joined in with the class as they prepared a dramatized reading of Keats' *Eve of St Agnes.* As in writing, so in reading; built into classroom activities are roles for the students. We must hope that they do not learn the more passive roles too effectively.

Literature teaching as we know it always contains elements of induction into current ways of interpreting texts: we might ask ourselves whether learning to read literature is of necessity an introduction to a particular ideology. The essence of reading is reconstructing text on the basis of the reader's cultural resources; there is no reason to treat adolescent students as if they had no experience or cultural resources upon which to base an interpretation. To deprive students of the opportunity of making the work their own—that is, of bringing their own experience to bear upon it—is to fail to teach them to read. The task of the teacher of language arts is neither to transmit information about literature nor to teach decontextualized reading skills; it is to help students become readers, to find that books can play an important part in their lives. This cannot be achieved without helping each reader to experience that progressive interpenetration of text and experience that is the sole justification of any reading that goes beyond simple messages of fact. This necessitates reading that either answers some of the reader's practical concerns or presents fictional images that strongly engage him or her.

Comprehension Exercises: Another Model of Reading

These methods of literature instruction reflect models of what constitutes reading. Models also come from two other sources: from the uses made of textbooks elsewhere in the curriculum, and from an activity called "comprehension." In Great Britain and Australia, "comprehension" or "clear thinking" is considered important in English lessons for 16-year-olds. The practice seems to imply that the reading of literature is unlikely to advance the ability to study texts closely, for example in the way we had to study the manual when learning to use the word processor on which this paper is being written. In England, in common with a test of writing abilities, "comprehension" is given a special status by being a compulsory element in all English examinations taken at 16 years of age, so that it is included in all courses. The word "comprehension" seems to imply that the activities practiced and tested can be taken unambiguously to represent the process of taking meaning from a text, but of course the matter is more problematic than that. The exercises and tests that are used amount to a stipulative definition of what reading is, so it behooves us to notice what they include and what they omit.

Students practice this activity by working through so-called "comprehension exercises," passages usually of prose followed by lists of questions to be answered. The passages chosen are not taken from the texts students are studying, but are looked at in isolation, although they may sometimes be linked by a common theme. Context did not here seem to define subject matter; we could not say this or that topic was suitable for the high- or low-status classes. Passages appeared to be randomly chosen, some from newspapers of 20 years ago, some from works of local history, other from travel writing, from autobiography, and so on.

Most significant were the questions set, since these directed the students' reading, what they attended to, where they placed the emphasis and the level of interpretation required. Questions requiring the paraphrase of sentences and the interpretation of individual words and phrases dominated the lists, as if to tell the students to pay most attention to minutiae. Questions requiring students to interpret the text played a less important role; the demand to relate the contents of the passages to the world outside was almost entirely missing.

Comprehension tests thus imply that reading is a matter of attending in detail to words and phrases, sometimes looking at paragraphs, but never expecting to relate what is read to the reader's life and concerns. No doubt no-one had designed the comprehension tests with the intention of communicating this version of reading, yet the message projected by them is unmistakable.

Reading Inside and Outside Schools

The particular requirements of secondary schooling have generated their own versions of reading, some appearing only in English lessons, others elsewhere in the curriculum. Though the latter must be at least as important in forming students' expectations, our purpose here is to characterize the former. As we have already shown, the choice of texts for different groups of students signals to them a social identity, which is often reinforced by the learning activities that are planned for them. In high school English lessons in the U.K., the teaching of reading frequently involves the transmission by teachers of authoritative accounts of the meaning and significance of texts, thus depriving the students of the opportunity of reconstructing the meaning for themselves. This is not only a misleading model of reading, but implies a passive picture of the reader, inappropriate for a democratic society in which the critical acumen of citizens is a matter of prime importance. At worst, the influence of examinations leads to reducing the reading of literature to the memorizing of "facts." For the least academically successful students, the teacher's efforts may be directed primarily towards encouraging them to enjoy reading fiction, with the result that they are given minimal help in the process of constructing meaning. Fortunately, many teachers resist the pressures towards teaching of this kind and endeavor to involve the students in the construction of interpretations, since they realize that the students' developing understanding and experience of the world outside schools is a crucial element in their expanding abilities as readers.

These characteristics of reading in English lessons derive from various sources, among them the demands for accreditation and the fact that most English teachers look to university departments of English literature for their values and model of reading. In other curriculum subjects, such as science, quite different models of what constitutes reading (and writing) define teachers' strategies. That is, what constitutes reading in schools is defined by the functions that reading performs in that context.

Outside schools, reading is similarly not just a matter of decoding text: as with writing, our reading arises from our current projects and relationships with people. We read carefully and attentively what we want to understand because there are actions needing to be accomplished or because we want to master the subject matter for our own personal interest. It is these intentions that organize and focus the strategies by which we understand and reconstruct the texts we read. That is, we read a text not in the abstract but in the context of our own precise concerns. When we pick up a practical handbook or another work of information; we read it seeking details or ideas that confirm or challenge our expectations. Both relevance and interpretation are partly created by our own priorities and concerns. It is equally true that we read fiction from the perspective of our current needs, for we have no other basis on which to construct a meaning. Competence in reading is not in the least a matter of mastering a hierarchy of skills: to understand a text the reader must have knowledge of the matters dealt with as well as the ability to reconstruct the social assumptions being made by the writer. Thus learning to read includes the whole of the reader's understanding of the world: it includes the ability to marshal what we know in order to make appropriate predictions of what the writer intends. To teach reading as a set of decontextualized skills is ineffective because it radically misrepresents the abilities on which the understanding of text is based. This is why we have criticized teachers who exclude their students from the reconstruction of meaning, as if their experience and cultural resources were irrelevant. On the contrary, they are of central importance, since for the student they are the sole source of understanding.

COLLEGES OF FURTHER EDUCATION

Marked differences appeared when we compared school paradigms for reading and writing with those to be found in the colleges of further education. At 16 years of age school students can end their education, or stay in schools to take advanced courses, or attend an F.E. college usually to follow a vocationally oriented curriculum. In all the schools we visited, the underlying assumptions about writing were literary: the unspoken model was a continuous text intended to be read as a whole, and addressed to an unknown audience who would read it in an unpredictable context. In U.K. high schools a writing lesson frequently begins with the reading of several short poems and prose extracts on the topic at hand, and these are discussed in terms of the experiences dealt with. Autobiographical passages presenting experiences of social isolation may be used, for example, to introduce a discussion and a writing task on the subject of "loneliness." We surmise that this reading of verse and prose passages not only indicates the boundaries of the topic but provides models for the kinds of writing that will be acceptable. Even in classes exemplifying the basic skills model, the unspoken ideal appeared to be a literary one.

Most students in F.E. colleges study the subject Communications as a compulsory part of a unified vocational course. A minority of students, mainly preparing for secretarial work, study English in a form not unlike what we have called "detached" when describing school curricula. Literature has very little place in any of the courses, and even the decontextualized prose extracts which some classes may study will be unlikely to come from a literary source. Unlike English teachers in schools, lecturers made no claims for the civilizing effects of literary study.[3] Their priorities were elsewhere: one lecturer, although he held a higher degree in English literature, insisted that he had no right to presume that his student apprentices needed the personal satisfactions he gained from exploring his deeper feelings through literary reading and writing. We met only one lecturer who advocated literary study and included it in his (English) course, perhaps with the intention of gentrifying the future typists. (The reader may share our fleeting vision of a secretary quoting Keats' *Ode to a Nightingale* to her astounded employer.)

Communications Courses in F.E.

All students were experiencing some form of tuition in writing as part of a Communications course, but written tasks in F.E. colleges were based on entirely different preconceptions from those in schools. Whereas school English often turned inwards towards the experience of individuals, Communications courses in F.E. were explicitly directed towards the outer world, particularly to the worlds of business and industrial production. Much writing which is done in people's everyday lives relates to ongoing activities and projects in a particular social and institutional context. We write a note for a colleague, leave a notice pinned to a door, fill in a form, scribble some jottings in a meeting, produce a short paper for a superior, compose a letter of complaint, or write minutes. The writing in each case is intended for a specific audience, and often relates to a particular occasion. Much of it can be read selectively, and does not rely for its effect on perusal of the whole. It often arises not as an activity in its own right but as part of the continuing projects of our daily lives. In all these ways it contrasts with the kinds of writing found in schools, where the predominant literary model implies that the text will be read as a whole and that the intended audience is general and unknown. (Of course, most students realize that they are in fact writing for their teacher's eye alone: the general audience is an educational fiction.)

Writing in colleges, however, purported to be concerned with action in the real world. F.E. lecturers believed that their values were drawn from

[3] Students attend colleges of further education voluntarily, and choose the courses that they follow. The colleges' attitude to students is different from that of the schools: whereas the schools take a paternalistic responsibility for the personal and moral development of students, the colleges accept a quasicontractual relationship with the students, who are treated more as autonomous adults. This description overstates the contrast between the two: for example, colleges take a more paternalistic attitude to certain lower ability students who attend government-sponsored courses. Nevertheless, the contrast does point to some underlying cultural differences between colleges and schools that affect the courses that are taught, including the versions of reading and writing.

appropriate and effective action in practical contexts, in contrast with the concern shown by some school teachers with sensibility and the authentic exploration of experience. While schools are still concerning themselves with improving the "comprehension tests" which we have described, courses in further education have been developing another format for reading and writing which might be called "the situated assignment." Starting from the assumption that in "real life" most of our reading and writing is situated within a context which includes an audience and purpose, F. E. lecturers have invented situations in which the student needs to read carefully in order to undertake further tasks, written and spoken. One college was using an assignment which set up an imaginary situation in which a legal company wished to obtain insurance against loss by burglary: a map of the premises, an application form for insurance cover, and some other information was provided. The students' tasks included making written notes in preparation for a telephone call, completing the form of application, and writing two letters to the insurance firm and a memorandum to the writer's imaginary superior. In another course which we observed, the students were given an assignment based upon a detailed street map of houses which were to be rewired for electrical power. Students were to decide what facilities would be required for the work force and where they should be placed. Tasks included listing the facilities, explaining the criteria used in choosing sites on the map, drafting a letter to a local official to explain the services required, and completing a formal report to the employer. Since such tasks are deeply embedded in the particular needs of the situation, in the latter case the work of electrical contractors, the criteria by which the writing was judged necessarily included knowledge of technical matters and relevance and accuracy in dealing with them. Another assignment widely used with less able students in F.E. colleges required them to carry out in simulation some of the planning needed to prepare for a motoring holiday in Europe. The tasks included recording a telephone message to a shop that sold camping equipment, filling in a form of application for a passport, and writing a letter to a firm that arranged the booking of places in campsites.

It must be clear from these three examples how distant the goals, expectations, and models that lie behind this kind of writing are from those that lie behind any of the four paradigms found in schools. The students are not merely learning to write; they are also learning to take up a role, usually a work role.[4]

---

[4] In drawing this contrast between school and college writing we are both oversimplifying the differences within each of them and relying heavily upon the self-report of teachers and lecturers, which did not always represent accurately all aspects of the teaching we observed. However, this enables us to draw attention to underlying tendencies and processes that some participants were only partially aware of.

The colleges of further education are concerned to maintain their status by attracting and holding students, and this is achieved by persuading young people—and often their employers too—that the courses are relevant to the demands to be met at work. Writing, like other aspects of the curriculum, must therefore be deeply embedded in a version of social reality, which proved to be largely a special construct of the F.E. college subculture. Writing had to answer to a view of the needs of industrial and commercial concerns and their employees. It was to this view of industry that many F.E. lecturers turned to legitimate their conceptions of writing. School teachers of English, however, somewhat protected from immediate economic pressures, turned for their ultimate legitimation to the academic world of English literature in which they had been trained. In all cases, however, the goals drawn from these sources were somewhat modified by the more immediate demands of the examinations for which they were preparing their students. In the case of F.E., Communications can be seen as an invention of certain official bodies in the U.K. which provide vocational examinations and thereby shape the goals of F.E. colleges.

Gender Differences in Further Education

In the area of business studies, female and male students experienced different kinds of writing. Vocational courses for secretarial work, filled almost entirely by young women, usually included an "English" element, while the more general courses in business studies, with a slight preponderance of males, required students to study Communications. The English courses, which focused upon essay writing and comprehension tests, were strongly "detached" in approach, with considerable emphasis upon accuracy and conformity to expectations. In class, there was little or no discussion of the content of writing: examination essays were to display control of the surface features of language, while the expected content was conventional.

The difference between the English and the Communications courses was striking, even when both were taught in the same department of business studies. In Communications there was considerable emphasis upon taking responsibility and making choices. The writing and reading tasks were not bounded by typical examination composition tasks but by the quasirealistic assignments already described. The tacit learning for the two groups of students was quite different. The two groups were defined by their job aspirations, which appeared to be influenced (but not determined) by gender stereotypes.

We have pointed out that the "situated assignments" typical of Communications courses act as a preliminary socialization into both the knowledge and the attitudes of industry and commerce. The work role the young people are learning includes not only the ability to produce particular modes of text, but also any knowledge relevant to the job itself which is needed in order to produce those texts. Turning to English courses in further education, it might similarly be argued that in ignoring content in favor of conventional accuracy, future keyboard workers were being prepared for their repetitive tasks. Moreover—and this is of particular interest—the students following both kinds of course were being presented with values which might make them as future employees more sympathetic to their employers' perspectives, intentions, and attitudes. Learning to write therefore involved acquiring a set of social attitudes.

DIFFERENCES BETWEEN COUNTRIES

If we turn from differences between institutions in one country to differences between countries, some equally striking divergencies appear, as for example when U.K. practices in the teaching of writing in high school are compared to those in Canada and the United States. English teachers in the U.K. act upon a "learning by doing" rhetoric, attempting to find topics which will interest their students in the belief that the struggle to express thoughts and feelings on a matter of personal importance will lead them to develop greater control over their language resources. The underlying rationale is that when writers compose, they attend to the emerging meanings rather than to language structures. "Teaching writing" under such circumstances becomes a matter of discussing possible topics with students in such a way as to catch their interest, and giving written and spoken advice and response after the event. Such teaching tends to be atheoretical, and closely linked to the subject matter being discussed and written about. Bereiter and Scardamalia (1982), who can be taken to represent one North American tradition, dismiss "expressive" writing which "draws on highly salient memory content that the child has some urge to express" (p. 8) as irrelevant to their search for ways of teaching general schemata that will guide children's writing on topics that are less important to them. This dismissal is itself an interesting cultural phenomenon, since one would judge a priori that successful writing under some conditions would throw useful light on writing under other conditions. To eliminate purposeful writing from the attempt to model all writing tells us much about the assumptions of the researchers.

A generation of U.K. writers on this topic (Britton et al., 1975; Holbrook, 1964; Dixon, 1975) saw the desire to share meanings as the dynamic that enables the skilled writer to select, develop strategies and substrategies, organize, generate text, and criticize—all this in the service of the wish to communicate something of importance. North American writers are less homogeneous in their views: one tradition (Smith, 1982; Graves, 1983, for example) would support a similar account of the teaching of writing, acknowledging the importance of the writer's purposes, and of helping the student to become aware of the tacit expectations of the teacher and other readers. An alternative tradition firmly established in the teaching methods of many North American teachers assumes that there are general principles that can guide the skilled writer on any topic, even in the absence of personal interest in the subject matter. The model of a writer on which this latter is based appears to be the journalist, or—perhaps more significantly—the examination candidate who has to perform with or without any interest in the matter in hand.

It is worth considering how this latter approach is likely to affect students' practices in writing. In the perception of the students the abstract prescriptions become somewhat simplified, of course. A group of eleventh grade students in a Canadian high school offered us this prescription for constructing an essay:

> You start off and have your thesis; you have your main body with several paragraphs, discussing and referring back to your thesis; then you have your conclusion. . . .

It was less clear, however, how far they shaped their writings at the bidding of this recipe. In discussing such general schemes, Langer and Applebee (1984) argues on the basis of case studies of school students that such a framework may prove irrelevant to the main tasks of composition. One young writer found that "the framework required her to know where she was going before she had explored" her understanding of the matter in hand. An essential part of composition is the gradual construction of a system of purposes and subpurposes which will provide a structure for the eventual document. To expect the writer to work within an a priori abstract framework "ignores the discovery element in writing." As Langer and Applebee put it "Language events are driven by their purposes not simply by their forms" (p. 172). If the second North American approach outlined above expects the student writer to conform to an abstract structure without going through some of the essential processes of composition, the dominant U.K. approach also gives students little help with those processes. Initial discussion of the topic, often based on the reading of literary passages, may support the students by helping them to find some personal relevance in the matter, and perhaps gives them some evidence of an interested audience, but U.K. teachers of English seldom offer general instruction in shaping a piece of writing; the shape is expected to emerge from the writer's struggle with a topic of some urgency to him or her.

If it is fair to say that the underlying model for writing in the North American mainstream is the journalistic article, then that for the U.K. is the semiautobiographical short story. The espoused values of the two are quite distinct. (This is not to ignore the presence in North America of alternative perspectives.) The outcome of such cultural differences is that students on either side of the Atlantic may both be "learning to write," but what they are learning is different.

It is not our intention to establish a preference between these two perspectives. The one supports students in using writing to create quasiliterary artifacts which at best constitute ways of exploring actual or possible experiences; it is highly individualistic, and tends to isolate the individual student with the struggle to find something in his or her personal experience that seems important enough to write about in an engaged manner, and fails to offer help in the structuring of writing. The other perspective prepares young people for writing at others' bidding, and proposes a framework for doing so that is intended to offer help but may not do so. Both perspectives encapsulate models of writing very unlike those enacted in the world outside schools and colleges, and this throws doubts upon the adequacy of either for the teaching of writing.

SCHOOLING AND THE WORLD OUTSIDE

There is always a gap between school activities and the activities of people outside school, for state education systems are set up partly to withdraw young people from direct response to the adult world, including market forces that might exploit them. For all the benefits of this withdrawal, the result for schooling is a pervasive unreality, since students engage in activities which have no direct effect upon their own or other people's lives except through the mediation of certification. When we adults write it is in order to influence someone, as a basis for teaching, to maintain contact with a friend, to record some ideas, or to join in an academic debate. When a student writes it is to obtain a grade from a teacher who often gives no response to the content of the message, but only assesses aspects of the medium which may be invisible to the student. It is thus important to realize that school and college writing, most of which is done in response to another person's bidding and solely for evaluation, is qualitatively different from most writing in adult life. Education creates modes of writing which are unique and distant from those we engage in during our lives: this is not, of course, to imply that they perform no useful function.

Examinations play a central role in the maintenance of these special models of what constitutes writing, since for teachers and for older students the qualifications sought provide a very persuasive argument about those aspects of writing which should be attended to. This may affect educational research into writing also: the model of writing which underlies the research carried out by Bereiter, Scardamalia and their associates has been powerfully influenced by the writing recognised and rewarded in the course of educational assessment. Writing at the bidding of someone else, though common in schools, is an activity *sui generis*. Bereiter and Scardamalia (1982) justify this noting that "skilled writers can demonstrate on demand, whether a given task has intrinsic worth to them or not" (p. 47), which is indeed true for those whose living depends on writing to order. Embedded in tasks of this kind is a model of the writer as employee: it might be argued that what is being learned is not only the so-called generic skills of writing but the practices appropriate to writing directed by others. At work, however, writing is intended to be read for its content and not merely to be assessed.

The teachers in schools gave an oblique account of the relevance of reading and writing to their students' future lives. One English department saw their central task as "to expose [students] to facts, information, and ideas" so as "to widen their often narrow boundaries and reveal to them how rich life can be." Since these teachers were teaching in one of the small town schools where the students were far from economically deprived, this perspective can be taken to reflect a generation later the effects of the Cambridge views of the 1940s and 1950s. English teachers in this school and some others perceived themselves to be standing out against a pervasive decline in the quality of life that affected both the prosperous and the poor. Literary study was seen as a bulwark against this socioethical decline, and this affected profoundly how both reading and writing was represented in the curriculum. In departments that took this view of their responsibilities it was not possible to regard literacy either as a set of skills ("Basic skills") nor as a tool to be used at work in adult life, as in the F. E. colleges. Literacy was about the development of moral sensibility, a campaign against capitulation to corrupt and corrupting economic forces.

In contrast, F. E. lecturers sometimes appeared to believe that the writing and reading that they taught would have a direct relevance to their students' future lives, though other lecturers expressed doubts about this. We have described above three writing tasks which we found in colleges, one concerned with positioning facilities on a work site, another with the insurance of legal premises, and the third with arranging a holiday in Europe. At first glance all three appear to be practically relevant. Yet the lecturer who was supervising the rewiring simulation told us that when he was a technical worker he had not been given responsibility for tasks of the kind simulated until he moved up into junior management. Similarly, it seems unlikely that a clerk would be expected to arrange for insurance cover. Moreover, the students whom we talked to seemed much more likely to buy a "package" holiday in Europe than to plan one for themselves. The tasks did not merely provide practice in writing but operated as anticipatory socialization for those students who aspired to management and to middle-class patterns of leisure. Their relevance to action in the real world appeared to be more cosmetic than real. In effect, the writing was creating competitive goals for young people who might otherwise have accepted passively a lowly economic and social status. It is thus impossible to consider students' achievement in such writing simply in terms of developing language skills, for success depended equally upon internalizing the values and practices of management, or at least of a social group to which most of them did not belong.

SOME IMPLICATIONS FOR THE TEACHING OF LITERACY

Our purpose has been to propose an alternative way of looking at literacy practices in schools. Reading and writing have traditionally been thought of as sets of generic skills which can be learned in one context and conveniently applied for different purposes elsewhere. But learning to read and write is very far from being merely a matter of learning to decode or encode text. We have sought to substitute for this the idea that since reading and writing are inseparable from the uses to which they are put they can equally by seen as sets of sociocultural practices specific to the characteristics of a situation. This change of emphasis implies that in learning to read and write the student must not only learn skills but also undergo an induction into taken-for-granted views of how the world is, including suitable content for texts, ways of going about writing and reading, preferred interpretations, and priorities for the forms of literacy which should be valued.

In using the phrase "social action" in the title of this chapter we indicate that reading and writing are social activities which arise from a commitment to persons and to projects. This central idea can be further developed in several ways. First, in developing successful written communication, interaction or dialogue with others is crucial. As writers we need feedback from our readers, and as readers we need to share with others the complexities of understanding, testing our first responses on one another. It is through interaction with others that we purposefully participate in, and even sometimes help to create, discourse modes which are then open to individual or group exploration, exploitation, and development. As young children we take part in relationships first in the family, then with peers and wider groups because our participation matters to us: We want to join in, to be recognized and responded to, to influence the course of events. We learn to talk because we want to influence the world, or at least the groups we belong to, and it has been a misconception to see learning to communicate in writing as entirely different in kind from learning to talk. Teaching reading and writing in ways that fail to capture the learners' purposes is very likely to be ineffective; it not infrequently produces those who can read but do not.

The second implication of literacy as social action is that our competence as readers and writers is far from being content-free: our development as readers and writers is part of the development of our understanding of the world. From this point of view, literacy development depends upon the expansion of the areas of interest and understanding into which we can project ourselves as readers and as writers. Thus the "discourse modes" mentioned in the previous paragraph are not just composed of linguistic resources but include more central understanding of the world. We can therefore call them "areas of interest and understanding" as appropriately as "discourse modes."

A third implication is that learning to communicate is not only content-specific but also context-specific. Our ability to participate with others, to take on appropriate roles in writing to them, and to foresee what they need to know is a social competence that we learn for specific groups of people, and not in general. Our ability to reconstruct the probable meaning and tone of what others have written is similarly social and specific. Both depend on our awareness of the tacit meanings available in a group, and our ability to respond to the demands of a specific audience and situation. That is, both depend upon a participant's experience of a social milieu.

We are suggesting that the development of reading and writing takes place for adolescents and adults through the gradual extension of the range of milieux—both as ways of knowing and understanding the world and as ways of communicating and sharing with other people. (We believe that a similar conception is implicit in the formulation "ways of taking meaning" [S. B. Heath, 1983].) An education in language arts that does not take account of these characteristics is likely to be ineffective for at least some students, and perhaps for a large number.

School writing is itself socially located in practices that are inseparable from the functions it performs there, such as providing a convenient basis for assessment, or engaging the students in rehearsing content while freeing the teacher for other activities. In schools and colleges much writing exists only to satisfy the teacher that work has been done. In some schools we visited teachers tried to make the work more realistic by encouraging students to read and write mainly about interpersonal experiences. In other schools there was a repertoire of pseudotopics (Town and Country, Corporal Punishment, and so on) which provided a content without requiring more than everyday knowledge. In both cases this led to a lack of engagement with public issues and unreality in both reading and writing.

If literacy develops through the students gradually expanding their ability to participate in a range of communicative milieux, then ideally teachers should collaborate with them to find writing tasks that influence events, and reading that throws light on their concerns and helps them to see the world differently. For example, we know of a class of students in a mining area that set out to investigate a proposal to mine coal in an area of rich farmers. They interviewed all the groups that were involved, read newspapers and books about the issues, discussed and reordered the material they were collecting, eventually producing a pamphlet that amounted to a critical contribution to the debate. Such activities would hardly constitute the whole of a well-balanced course in English, but they would fill some of the gaps that we have identified in the language arts curriculum.

The social contexts of reading too are important, implying a dialogic response. We can see reading as a series of alternative models of how to take meaning from a text and how to adopt implied roles, some throwing more responsibility on the reader than others. Reading can assign or confirm cultural status, imply that an authoritative interpretation is available from expert sources elsewhere, and encourage or discourage critical engagement with the author's intentions. What happens in a lesson in which a poem or short story is being studied may signal clearly who "owns" the meaning of the text, whether it belongs to the students or whether they have to take it from an authoritative source.

What kind of teaching of reading and writing to older students would correspond to the view of literacy as social action? Certainly authoritative explanations of works of literature are inimical to it, as is the practice of stressing the conventions in writing at the expense of communication. Language exercises of all kinds are inappropriate. The ideal would be to help learners to become involved in a range of authentic communicative exchanges in various situations in which they can play an active part, and at the same time to devise opportunities for them to reflect upon the new abilities and understandings that they are acquiring.

We have pointed out that literacy practices in schools differ from those outside, and have thereby implied that some changes in teaching methods would be appropriate. To reduce the complexities of classroom management to a few brief principles is not always helpful to practicing teachers, yet it does seem necessary to make explicit what has been implicit in the earlier parts of this chapter.[5] We have attempted to represent our priorities

---

[5] Our criticisms of the practices of many of the teachers whom we observed in the *Versions of English* study makes it proper that we should make explicit our own preferred approach. We hesitate to do so, since we know well that teachers operate in constraining contexts provided by the expectations of senior colleagues, of students, and of parents, and beneath the shadow of various systems of accreditation, and so are far from being free agents. It is the success of a minority of teachers whom we observed to break free of these constraints that makes us feel that it is proper to propose an approach.

as five principles. The teaching of reading and writing to older students should:

1. Involve the learners' concerns.
2. Be based upon interactive exploration of topics and texts.
3. (Writing) should be addressed to real audiences that respond.
4. (Reading) should either be pleasurable or seek information relevant to some issue owned by the reader.
5. Both should be linked whenever possible with action in the real world.

Writing and reading in schools should involve the concerns of learners because it is on this basis that a writer selects and orders material, and a reader interprets and reconstructs the meaning of a text. But it is not enough for a teacher to select topics thought to be relevant to students: the students should be brought into the negotiation of topics, and into the planning of projects that they themselves have had a hand in formulating. Students often become habituated to accepting any topic from a teacher, however inappropriate; the active construction of a topic which they feel they own is a far more likely basis for committed writing.

This leads logically to the second principle, that reading and writing should arise from and be part of social interaction. The isolated writer addressing himself to an imaginary audience is largely a romantic myth; communication, even the most original, arises from a background of shared meanings and experiences. Our ideal English classroom is a place of ongoing talk between teacher and student, and student and student; projects to inquire into issues of importance, and the consequent reading and writing, arise out of this matrix of talk with the help of the teacher but by agreement with the students. Nor does this context mean that works of literature cannot be read for their own sake; sharing in the process of constructing meaning greatly strengthens young people in their struggle with difficult works and deepens their enjoyment of others. In contrast, the teacher who presents him or herself as a source of authoritative interpretations is disabling them from becoming readers in their own right.

Much of what goes on in a classroom must necessarily be at a distance from ordinary life. However, as often as possible the reading and writing, like the talking, should be linked to action in the world beyond the school walls. There is no justification for treating reading and writing in high schools as no more than the learning of skills for use elsewhere. We should avoid what James Britton calls "dummy runs" and see to it that all reading and writing is "for real."

Writing is not likely to challenge the writer to reorganize thought at some depth if it is merely addressed to a teacher who will give it no more than a cursory reading and a grade. Of far more value to the writer is writing that is addressed to a real audience who will read and respond. For example, in recent years we have heard of teachers who have taken a high school class on a series of visits to an elementary class: typically each older student interviews a younger about his or her preferences in stories, composes a story to be read to the child on the next visit, and then later revises it in the light of the child's responses, finally presenting a fair copy. But this is only of many possibilities for finding real audiences in spite of the constraints of the classroom. The example also illustrates the role that can be played by interaction in encouraging older students to approach their writing in a more reflective manner, taking the needs of audience into account, and provides occasion for discussing such matters in class.

It is perhaps not enough merely to say that reading should either be for pleasure or to find information related to a purpose recognized as worthwhile by the reader. Even in reading for pleasure we can gain from sharing our experiences with others, finding in our exchanges with them confirmation of some responses and provocation to reconsider others. As teachers we can support pupils' reading in many ways; what is destructive of reading is to treat the text as a source of facts to be learned. Nor is it helpful for the teacher to take over the task of interpretation, as if we adults had access to an eternally prescribed correct meaning. Each student needs the experience of making sense of texts by relating them to his or her own experience, concerns, and mythologies.

To summarize the principles of language teaching so briefly is to risk caricature. Our two major points are: first, that students' ability to read and write develops through the extension of their experience into new discourse areas, which include the substantive understanding of topics as well as sensitivity to social contexts and the communicative behavior appropriate to them. (We have not had the space in this account to do justice to students' reflection upon the processes of reading and writing: it is this that will increase their access to the tacit ground rules that underlie successful communication in various contexts.) Second, students are more likely to move into new discourse modes if they engage with issues that are real to them in their everyday or their fantasy lives.

REFERENCES

Anyon, J. (1981). Social class and school knowledge. *Curriculum inquiry, 11*(1), 3–42.

Barnes, D., Barnes, & Clarke, S. R. (1984). *Versions of English.* London: Heinemann.

Bereiter, C., & Scardamalia, M. (1982). From conversation to composition. In R.

Glaser (Ed.), *Advances in instructional psychology No. 2* (pp. 1–64). Hillsdale, NJ: Erlbaum.

Britton, J., Burgess, T., Martin, N., McLeod, A., & Rosen, H. (1975). *The development of writing abilities 11–18.* London: Macmillan.

Bowles, S. (1971). Unequal education and the reproduction of the social division of labor. In J. Karabel & A. H. Halsey (Eds.), *Power and ideology in education.* New York: Oxford University Press.

Dixon, J. (1975). *Growth through English* (3rd ed.). Huddersfield: NATE/Oxford University Press.

Eagleton, T. (1983). *Literary theory.* Oxford: Blackwell.

Graves, D. (1983). *Writing: Teachers and children at work.* Exeter, NH: Heinemann.

Heath, S. B. (1983). *Ways with words.* Cambridge: Cambridge University Press.

Holbrook, D. (1964). *The secret places.* London: Methuen.

Inglis, F. (1981). *The promise of happiness: Value and meaning in children's fiction.* Cambridge: Cambridge University Press.

Langer, J. A., & Applebee, A. N. (1984). Language, learning and interaction: A framework for the teaching of writing. In A. N. Applebee (Ed.), *Contexts for learning to write* (pp. 169–181). Norwood, NJ: Ablex.

Medway, P. (1986). What gets written about. In A. Wilkinson (Ed.), *The writing of writing* (pp. 22–39). Milton Keynes: Open University Press.

Rosen, C., & Rosen, H. (1973). *The language of primary school children.* Harmondsworth, Middlesex.: Penguin Books.

Smith, F. (1982). *Writing and the writer.* London: Heinemann.

Street, B. V. (1984). *Literacy in theory and practice.* Cambridge: Cambridge University Press.

3

The Answers Are Not in the Back of the Book: Developing Discourse Practices in First-Year English

Marilyn M. Cooper

Two weeks into the term, one of my students in the first quarter of First-Year English included in his assigned weekly written responses to the book we were reading the following complaint:

> This false need subject we're discussing now in class is such a debatable topic. We've written a paper and weekly writings and even compared ideas on the computer disk. I don't know if I'm getting more or less confussed [sic] with the subject.
> The answers to this class are not in the back of the book. Or for that matter within the text either. This makes it very hard to get a firm concept to write about. Marcuse has written his book, his theory. Sure he may be much further educated than all of us, especially us students, but who is to say his theory is more correct than the next guys?
> All we can do is read his theory and analyze it and discuss it. This is sort of frustrating because he writes in such a manner that it's not ever "black and white." So we can speculate on what he exactly means but in the end of this we can't say, "OK this is what he meant when he wrote . . ." Theory is turning out to be a very abstract study.[1]

The book was Herbert Marcuse's *One-Dimensional Man,* a critique of the technological society that we felt would surely engage our students, the majority of whom are planning to be engineers. We had told them that in this book Marcuse presents a theory, and that the use of theories in science and in other fields of inquiry was to help us think about phenomena

---

[1] I have made no corrections in the students' writing cited in this chapter.

in new ways. Thus, we said, when you encounter a theory, the most useful response is not to ask whether it is true or correct but rather to ask questions like, "How does this work?" and "If this is true, what does it tell me about _____?" And we said that these were the kind of questions we would expect them to ask as they read and the kind of questions we would expect them to answer in their writing in the course.

This student—and many others like him—told us quite directly that this was not the kind of reading and writing they were used to doing and not the kind they were comfortable with either. They were used to questions that have unambiguous, "black and white" answers, answers that could be and were printed in the back of the book or to which explicit answers could be found in particular passages in the book. They were used to writing about "firm concepts," the correctness of which both writer and reader could be expected to agree on. They found the kind of reading and writing we were asking them to do confusing, frustrating, abstract—at least at first.[2]

Their reactions were not unusual nor were they necessarily bad. Trying new things is often difficult and frustrating but also often worthwhile; and, besides, in the process of explaining to us what they found difficult about these practices, they began to understand them better and to understand why we were asking them to engage in them. In this chapter I will argue that development in reading and writing involves developing new discourse practices, and that people are motivated to develop new practices in situations in which they find such practices valuable.

Development of reading and writing is often conceived in terms of acquiring the varied sets of rules or conventions that enable these activities. The influence of linguistic theories of language development cannot be overrated here: Clearly it is Noam Chomsky and his disciples who have led us to think of reading and writing as first and foremost cognitive skills that draw on knowledge of the appropriate conventions. But both language development and the development of reading and writing can be conceived differently, in ways that do not contradict the cognitive view but that focus instead on the social context and consequences of reading and writing. M. A. K. Halliday has long argued that social and psychophysiological approaches to language development are complementary, not contradictory, and that, in fact, one can be seen in terms of the other:

> just as the view of language as knowledge, which is essentially an individual orientation, can be used to direct attention outwards, through such concepts

---

[2] The difference between what students were used to doing and what we were expecting them to do is well characterized by William Perry as the difference between the dualist position of intellectual development and the relativist position, though as Patricia Bizzell points out (1984), the difference is probably better characterized as a matter of socialization rather than cognitive development: The relativist position simply encodes the discursive practices of the academic establishment.

as the speech act, towards language in society, so the essentially social interpretation of language as behavior can be used to direct attention onto the
individual, placing him in the human environment . . . and explaining his linguistic potential, as speaker-hearer and writer-reader, in these terms. (Halliday, 1978, p. 15)

Even within the psychological sphere, one can emphasize the importance
of social factors and see language and its development not in terms of
rules of syntax, but rather in terms of a *"resource*—resource for meaning,
with meaning defined in terms of function" (Halliday, 1978, p. 17). And, as
Halliday argues, it is the social view of language that is most relevant in
an educational context:

> From this point of view, language is the medium through which a human
> being becomes a personality, in consequence of his membership of society
> and his occupancy of social roles. . . . the formation of the personality is itself
> a social process, or a complex of social processes, and language—by virtue
> of its social functions—plays the key part in it. (p. 15)

The social view of language development encourages us to see education
as a process in which people become actors in society by developing language practices that serve functions that are valued by the society.

With regard to the development of reading and writing in particular,
Brian Street similarly argues that what he calls the ideological model of
literacy does not neglect the technical aspects that the autonomous model
focuses on independently of social context. Instead, scholars who assume
the ideological model attempt to understand "the technical skill or the
cognitive aspects of the reading and writing . . . as they are encapsulated
within cultural wholes and within structures of power" (Street, 1986, p. 2).
The model of writing I proposed in "The Ecology of Writing" (Cooper,
1986) is intended to be an inclusive model in this sense. I suggested that
students learn to write not simply by learning to think differently but by
"developing the habits and skills"—practices—that engage them in the
systems that constitute the activity of writing within a society.

Some scholars have characterized this ecological model as a description of an ideal discourse community, but I am uncomfortable with this
characterization for a number of reasons.[3] For one thing, the notion of
discourse community is often elucidated in terms of sets of conventions,
rules that readers and writers must learn and use in order to be a member
of that community. To me discourse conventions, at least in this sense,
are useful in explaining what people who are within a discourse community know. But they are not useful in explaining why members of a dis-

---

[3] See Freed and Broadhead, 1987. For further discussion of my attitude toward the notion
of discourse communities, see Cooper and Holzman, 1989.

course community do what they do when they read and write, nor are they useful in explaining how these people got to be members of a particular discourse community.

In other words, in focusing on discourse conventions, one is led to view reading and writing solely from a cognitive perspective. What I have been arguing for since 1986 is that the inclusion of the social perspective on reading and writing will help us understand more completely what we are trying to do in the writing classroom. In order to extend this argument here to the question of how people develop as readers and writers, I will begin by considering in some detail a distinction between things about reading and writing one learns as arbitrary rules and things one learns to do by reading and writing in particular situations. I will call the first sort of thing discourse conventions and the second, discourse practices. Even though "convention" has been used in a general sense to refer to both of these sorts of things, I believe that the narrower sense I propose here is in accord with the way it is intended in many recent discussions of writing theory and with the way it has been used by other theorists of language.

Conventions and practices are alike in some ways: once learned, both direct behavior unconsciously, and both vary from situation to situation. Because of these similarities, both are useful notions in explaining why people who are reading and writing in new situations often seem incompetent to their teachers or their supervisors—and to themselves. But in thinking about how people develop as readers and writers, two differences between conventions and practices are important, and it is these differences that I will focus on in the first two-thirds of this chapter. The first difference is that conventions are arbitrary, while practices are motivated by purposes or values. To elucidate this difference, I will contrast Saussure's theory of language as an acontextual system with Grice's theory of meaning as purposeful behavior. The second difference is that conventions are explained with reference to verbally explicit rules, while practices are explained with reference to what people do. And to elucidate this difference, I will turn to Wittgenstein's theory of language-games, which contains the hypothesis that action is prior to cognition.

Both differences reflect the opposed yet complementary cognitive and social perspectives on reading and writing: The cognitive approach sees language behavior in terms of arbitrary conventions and rules which can be made explicit, while the social approach sees language behavior in terms of purposeful action motivated by social contexts. And, thus, these differences imply different pedagogical practices. If we think of learning to read and write as a matter of learning arbitrary conventions, we will encourage students to focus on the nature of the conventions themselves and how they differ in different discourse communities. In contrast, if we think of learning to read and write as a matter of learning to behave differently in different contexts, we will encourage students to focus on elements of social context that motivate the practices of reading and writing. In the last third of this essay, I will discuss how students in a first-year writing class can be trained to develop discourse practices by putting them in situations where such practices are appropriate and useful.

PRACTICES AS MOTIVATED BEHAVIOR

Conventions arise in order to coordinate behavior when there are equally effective ways to achieve the same thing: The choice among these ways is arbitrary, and the only thing that matters is that all people choose the same way (Lewis, 1969). "Dog" and "chien" are equally effective ways to refer to this domestic mammal; it doesn't matter what we call it as long as the people we're conversing with call it the same thing. It was Saussure, of course, who most memorably insisted that language is conventional in this way, pointing out that the link between signifier and signified is unmotivated, not dependent on any natural connection. For Saussure, this fundamental arbitrariness of language, which explains both why languages can change and why they are resistant to change, makes language different from other human institutions: "Unlike language, other human institutions—customs, laws, etc.—are all based in varying degrees on the natural relations of things; all have of necessity adapted the means employed to the ends pursued" (Saussure, 1966, p. 75).

But when we start to look at language not as Saussure did, as "a system that has a potential existence in each brain" (p. 14), but rather as a kind of communicative behavior, it begins to look more like other human institutions in that the means employed do have a connection with the ends pursued. Saussure himself notes that the language system is not solely determined by the principle of arbitrariness but also by the principle of rationality: Order and regularity are introduced into language because it is a system to be used by people, who rely on such things as order and regularity to make sense of their world. Thus, some signs are "relatively motivated" in that we connect them with other signs in order to understand them: "farmer" is relatively motivated by "farm"; "twenty-one" is relatively motivated by "twenty" and "one." The regularities of syntax are similarly motivated; people would find an utterly chaotic syntax unlearnable. When we go beyond the level of signifier-signified correlations (which were the focus of Saussure's linguistics) and beyond the level of syntax (which is the focus of Chomsky's linguistics) to the level of the structure of discourses, we find that motivation plays an even greater role. To take a simple example, turn taking in conversation can be seen to be motivated by the physical fact that it is difficult to distinguish language when lots of people are talking at once and by a cultural belief in the right of individuals to exclusive attention.

Practices, in contrast with conventions, are motivated by values and beliefs; for complex sets of reasons, they are seen to be the most effective way to achieve something. Practices are as they are because the people who engage in them are as they are and because the contexts in which they take place are as they are. Kenneth Burke (1984) has offered one explanation of the social context that motivated the language of "firm" concepts my student argued for in his response quoted above. Hypothesizing a flock of birds who had developed different ways of feeding and escaping, and who had developed the capacity for speech, Burke argues that a language that relied on fixed concepts would be more adaptive than one that relied on suggestion; to resolve the "muddle" created by their now heterogeneous society, "the most intelligent birds would insist upon the perfection of a strict and unambiguous nomenclature" (p. 56). The situation, he implies, is analogous to the situation in the Middle Ages, when learned Latin was introduced to connect the heterogeneous cultures of Western Europe, and "to the situation now, when we find the attempt to erect a communicative medium that will lie across many diverse disciplines, distinct ways of living, different psychoses" (p. 56). If my student's desire for firm concepts is a discourse practice motivated, at least in part, by the muddle of the highly pluralistic American society, the discourse practices of academia are similarly motivated by the perceived needs of academia. For example, the requirements for backing up claims with evidence, for linking one's claims to contemporary research, and for considering the models on which observations and claims depend are motivated by the academic community's interest in consensus and coherence, which in turn is motivated by such things as the anti-intellectualism and fragmentation of contemporary American society.

When people share values, there is no need to set up arbitrary conventions to coordinate behavior; when a group of people is not interested in cooperating to achieve shared goals, it is impossible to control behavior through conventions. The speech-act theorist Paul Grice has long protested the grounding of meaning in the notion of conventions, insisting instead that communication is based on the rational behavior of people who need to cooperate to achieve social goals. In the first of his lectures delivered at Harvard in 1967, he argued:

> while remarking is no doubt a conventional act in *some* sense (since it involves the use of linguistic devices, which are in *some* sense conventional), I doubt whether so unpretentious an act as remarking is a conventional act in the . . . fairly strong sense [of conforming to constitutive rules]. . . . It seems to me more than likely that the nature of a remark could be explained with-

out reference to such matters; the inappropriateness of remarks that failed
to satisfy such putative rules might be consequential upon other features
which remarks characteristically have, together perhaps with some more
general principles governing communication or even rational behaviour as
such. (Grice, 1967)

When he goes on in his second lecture to formulate some general principles, or maxims, governing communication, he again emphasizes that they
are at base not "quasi-contractual":

> The conversational maxims ... are specifically connected (I hope) with the
> particular purposes that talk (and so, talk exchange) is adapted to serve and
> is primarily employed to serve.... I would like to be able to think of the
> standard type of conversational practice not merely as something that all or
> most do *in fact* follow but as something that it is *reasonable* for us to follow,
> that we *should not* abandon. (Grice, 1975, pp. 47–48)

Striving, at least at times, to say what one believes to be true, for example,
is not a rule that we *do* follow, nor is it a convention that we follow only
because most everyone else follows it. It is, rather, a practice connected
with a purpose we have for conversation—the exchange of information.
If no one ever told the truth, we could not rationally use conversation to
fulfill this purpose.

Revisiting the subject of meaning in 1982, Grice reiterated his doubts
about the utility of the notion of convention, suggesting that what had
been left out of accounts of meaning to date was "the notion of value
[which] is absolutely critical to the idea of rationality, or of a rational being" (Grice, 1982, p. 238). In a preliminary consideration of language,
thought, and reality, Grice demonstrates that value in the sense of advantage or benefit is also deeply implicated in the nature of meaning, which
he defines as the soul-to-soul transference of psychological states in a way
that benefits the "creatures" involved.[4] He observes that

> the operation of such creatures as I have been talking about is at least in
> certain circumstances going to be helped and furthered if there is what one
> might think of as shared experience. In particular, if psychological states
> which initially attach to one creature can be transmitted or transferred or
> reproduced in another creature ..., that would be advantageous. (p. 227)

A further general condition on meaning is that the psychological states be
connected to reality, again because such a connection would be advanta-

---

[4] Nevertheless, Grice's interest in the transfer of psychological states means that his theory of meaning is more cognitively oriented than socially oriented.

geous: Only if true beliefs and experiences were transmitted (at least sometimes) could communication be considered useful. Thus he suggests that "to say what a word means in a language is to say what it is in general optimal for speakers of that language to do with that word, or what use they are to make of it; what particular intentions on particular occasions it is proper for them to have, or optimal for them to have" (p. 239).

Grice develops the role of evaluation in determining meaning in part to counter the argument by Stephen Schiffer and others that his earlier account of meaning in terms of the recognition of speaker's intention was fatally flawed by an infinite regress such that the speakers and hearers could never live up to the requisite conditions. This objection carries weight only if one equates meaning with strict adherence to ideals. If, in contrast, one considers meaning in terms of optimal use, one can explain why such "logically impossible and also desirable" intentions are often *deemed* to be satisfied. What Grice suggests is that in "the sublunary world" speakers and hearers operate in terms of what they evaluate as advantageous in the particular situation, and, therefore, the conditions on meaning must include a "licence to apply the word non-strictly to things which in some way approach or approximate to the ideal cases" (p. 241). His example of this licence emphasizes the importance of such things as power and expediency in the determination of how words are beneficially applied to situations:

> in Oxford on one occasion, there was a difficulty between an incoming provost and a college rule that dogs were not allowed in college: the governing body passed a resolution deeming the new provost's dog to be a cat. I suspect that crucially, we do a lot of deeming, though perhaps not always in such an entertaining fashion. (p. 242)

Grice has never excluded conventionality as a part of what characterizes meaning, but in this discussion he makes particularly clear his contention that meaning does not rely on convention but rather on such acts of evaluation.

Still, despite his emphasis on social value in this 1982 article, Grice's theories cannot be characterized as social in orientation. He says he is engaged here in "philosophical psychology" (p. 223), and his remarks about value rarely stray beyond what is advantageous for speakers and hearers considered as ahistorical, isolated, rational individuals. Nevertheless, the very fact that he frames his predominantly psychological account of meaning in terms of value casts doubt on the essentiality of the notion of convention in explaining communication and complements a broader perspective in which discourse practices are seen to be motivated by social values. If word meanings are dependent on speaker's meanings which are in turn dependent on evaluations of what it is optimal for an expression to mean in a particular situation, it is even more probable that discourse practices (which are the product of multiple evaluations of what is beneficial in multiple complex situations) depend not on arbitrary conventions but on socially mediated beliefs and purposes.

PRACTICES AS SOCIAL ACTION

The second difference between conventions and practices is more clearly connected to the difference between the cognitive and social perspectives on language. Conventions encode what people know about what it is best to do or proper to do in situations, while practices are what people do in response to the demands of social interaction. Though one need not be able to verbalize conventions in order to follow them, it is always possible to capture them in words, and they are explained to those not in the know in verbal form. Language conventions, for example, may be explained to native speakers on the basis of their knowledge of the language (not "runned," "ran") or to second-language speakers on the basis of their knowledge of language rules ("run" takes an irregular past tense "ran"). If learners do not pick up conventions by deduction from observing the behavior of others, the conventions must be explained, for they are arbitrary and thus there is no rational reason for them to be as they are.

Conventions are, moreover, subsequent to and dependent on human action. Though they may guide action once they are established, they arise in social behavior and beneficially guide behavior only as long as the consensus out of which they arose lasts. The verbal formulation of conventions often arises when a powerful elite resists the fading of consensus, and in this situation even practices may be transformed into arbitrary rules. Burke analyzes this process in terms of law and custom:

> At first, law is hardly more than the codification of custom. But its formulation probably occurs because the customs are ceasing to possess unquestioned authority among the group as a whole, whereas a fraction of the group would greatly profit by the continuance of the old habits. Law is thus an educative, or manipulative device. (Burke, 1984, p. 186n)

Burke's linking of education with manipulation in this context emphasizes the repressive effect of teaching discourse practices as conventions and suggests that when we do so it may be in order to preserve our own privileges or the privileges of the elite group on which we depend. Later he points out the dangers of attempting "to reverse the process and mold custom by legislative fiat" more explicitly, explaining that "not only does it tend to 'liquidate' customary sanctions, but it attempts to establish new sanctions inimical to the demands of the group as a whole" (Burke, 1984, p. 270n).

Practices, in contrast, are not dependent on nor subsequent to rules or laws; they are not codifications of behavior but rather are in themselves forms of social behavior. Since practices are what we habitually do, descriptions of them sound odd, superfluous. Greeting practices in our society include smiling and nodding, shaking hands, hugging and kissing. Practices such as these are developed and learned concurrently by people acting in complex social situations, motivated by complex evaluations of such things as how formal the situation is, how well the people know each other, what relation they have to one another, what sex and age they are. Practices are thus inherently less stable than conventions, for they are governed not by verbal formulae nor by traditional knowledge but rather by the exigencies of the immediate situation. Two people may change their greeting practices in response to increasing intimacy, or to their current mood, or to the length of time since they last met.

Bakhtin (1981) offered an early correction to Saussure's definition of language, noting that the conservative, centripetal force of the "unitary language" (which leads to the notion of language as a matter of convention) is opposed by the revolutionary, centrifugal force of heteroglossia, the tendency of language to diversify in response to social situations (p. 272). But because of the delay in the transmission of Bakhtin's writings to the West, it was Wittgenstein who argued most influentially that language is not just a unitary system but more fundamentally a way of behaving: As he said, it is not thinking but *"acting,* which lies at the bottom of the language-game" (1969, sec. 204). Language-games are practices developed to cope with certain situations; when we encounter a similar situation, we draw on these practices automatically and perhaps adapt them to fit new features of the situation. Wittgenstein, of course, is the source of Grice's belief that language practices are motivated: Even though we may not be conscious of their usefulness every time we engage in them, they compel us on the basis of this evaluation. But while Grice locates the motivation in principles of rationality, Wittgenstein looks instead to the social functions of language. Thus, while both find the notion of value central to language, Wittgenstein's equation of meaning and action is more useful to us in developing a social theory of the development of discourse practices than is Grice's equation of meaning and intention.

Wittgenstein's social perspective is especially notable in his discussions of how one learns language-games and how language-games develop and change, for in all these discussions he rejects the notion that language depends on private mental states in favor of the idea that language is a product of public, shared social practices. His argument rests on a reversal of the relationship between mental states and language use we normally assume, as David Bloor (1983) makes clear in his recent study of Wittgenstein's social theory of knowledge:

> What, though, are we going to say about all the subjective feelings, images and states of consciousness that attend the meaningful use of words and gestures (or what Wittgenstein sometimes called 'signs')? According to the theories that have just been rejected, these inner events were the causes of the outward performances. If they are to be denied this role, then what status do they have? Wittgenstein's answer was that they are mere by-products. They are not the causes of our ability to use words or signs, they are the effects of that ability. Wittgenstein therefore reversed the direction of causality assumed in psychological theories of meaning and said: 'the mental experiences which accompany the use of a sign undoubtedly are caused by our usage of the sign in a particular system of language' (1965, p. 78). (Bloor, 1983, p. 19)

For Wittgenstein, cognitive knowledge of the conventions of language is dependent on and a consequence of training in social practices, or language-games. If, as he argues, the mental states that accompany language use are not the causes but the effects of language use, then the inculcation of these mental states cannot be expected to bring about the understanding necessary to engage in language-games. For example, we learn such things as how to read a novel not by learning to think in the proper ways— to imagine the world described in a novel, for example, rather than trying to connect it with reality—but rather by interacting with others through language—by talking about what we read in novels differently than we talk about what we read in newspapers. It is not our intention to treat the world of the novel as imaginary that allows us to say such things as "unicorns can be tamed only by virgins" and not be thought of as crazy; it is instead our participation in the language-game of novels, where such statements are motivated by the evaluation of inventiveness as beneficial, that causes us to think of imaginary worlds.[5]

Wittgenstein deploys several arguments against the essentiality of mental states in learning language-games, all of which add up to the argument that the theory of meaning as a social practice provides simpler and more consistent explanations of such things as what it means to obey a rule or how one comes to understand an ostensive definition. Wittgenstein argues that obeying a rule or understanding what "red" refers to is a matter of grasping the function of the rule or the sign in a particular language-game, and one grasps this by participating in the language-game. If, instead, we

---

[5] Of course, reading novels is only one of the language-games that values inventiveness and that enables us to think about imaginary worlds.

conceive of obeying a rule as a matter of grasping the intentions of the rule-giver, we run into the same problem I noted earlier in connection with Grice's intentionally based theory of meaning:

> So when you gave the order $+2$ you meant that he was to write 10002 after 1000—and did you also mean that he should write 1868 after 1866, and 100036 after 100034, and so on—an infinite number of such propositions? (Wittgenstein, 1968, sec. 186)

People do not, for very good reasons, normally have such infinite intentions, nor is it necessary or possible for us to grasp intentions of this sort and use them as a guide to action. In order to understand how to follow the order $+2$ one must understand not only what sort of operation $+2$ suggests but also the purpose of following an order of this kind. In other words, to follow the order $+2$ you must be trained in the language-game in which this order is embedded: You must be trained to write down sequences of numbers when you are given orders of this form and you must have some notion of why you are doing this (and, of course, you must understand how the order $+2$ differs from the order $+1$, say, or $+3$). Wittgenstein explains that it is our belief that intentions determine such complicated operations that makes our ability to obey a rule seem to be a mysterious phenomenon (1968, sec. 188). When, instead, we think of obeying a rule as the result of being trained in the operations involved, the process seems straightforward and, more importantly, something that can be directly taught.

This belief that obeying a rule depends on grasping intentions is a common cause of failures in the writing class. For example, instructors who give an assignment to "write an essay in which you describe your home town" often assume that the purpose of descriptive essays and the strategies—the use of focus, detail, evaluation—necessary to write a successful descriptive essay are somehow determined by the command. And even if instructors try to make their intentions clearer by explaining that description is a way of making a point and listing the necessary strategies, students often cannot figure out what point their description might make or what details are necessary. Such assignments, like the command $+2$, rely on the students' grasping the purpose of the language-game in which they are embedded, not on grasping the intentions of the instructor. And this understanding comes through the activity of engaging in the language-game.

That it is the context of language-games and not intentions that determines meaning is even clearer in Wittgenstein's discussion of ostensive definition. Ostensive definition is one of those everyday processes that can seem mysterious if we think about it very long; it is, for example, one of the ways we instruct children in concepts such as "red" or "round." A parent points to a ball and says "round," and points to a plate and says "round," and points to the moon and says "round," and the child understands what round is. But how, Wittgenstein asks, *does* the child understand this? Not, he answers, by learning how to look at these objects in a particular way, but rather by understanding that the purpose of the game is the definition of characteristics important to communication.

> You attend to the shape, sometimes by tracing it, sometimes by screwing up your eyes so as not to see the colour clearly, and in many other ways. I want to say: This is the sort of thing that happens *while* one 'directs one's attention to this or that'. But it isn't these things by themselves that make us say someone is attending to the shape, the colour, and so on. Just as a move in chess doesn't consist simply in moving a piece in such-and-such a way on the board—nor yet in one's thoughts and feelings as one makes the move; but in the circumstances that we call "playing a game of chess", "solving a chess problem", and so on. (Wittgenstein, 1968, sec. 33)

The circumstances of language-games—their purposes, the way they are related to other language-games—are what makes possible such things as ostensive definitions and moves in chess. What we overlook in the ostensive teaching of the concept "round" to a child is the interaction that gives the process of attending to objects in a certain way its purpose: the child listening as a story is read to her, for example, and interrupting to ask, "what's 'round?' " Wittgenstein concludes:

> neither the expression "to intend the definition in such-and-such a way" nor the expression "to interpret the definition in such-and-such a way" stands for a process which accompanies the giving and hearing of the definition. (Wittgenstein, 1968, sec. 34)

Instead, such actions are moves in language-games; they are social actions, not cognitive processes nor physical processes.

Bloor explains why it is so difficult to grasp the nature of such actions as these:

> The significance of a piece of pointing behaviour taken in isolation is indeed difficult to discern, but that is not because it is hidden in the mind, but because it depends on the surrounding activity. Its meaning is perfectly open to view, it is on the surface, but it is spread out over time and shared with others. (Bloor, 1983, p. 13)

It is our insistence on looking at these actions in isolation, our insistence that their meaning is determined by the mental states that accompany them and not by the context in which they are imbedded, that makes them seem mysterious. As Bloor says, "The strange properties of mental states derive from the fact that they are really properties of groups of people which have been imputed to individuals or individual actions" (Bloor, 1983, p. 20). The complicated intentions imputed to Grice's speakers or to rulegivers are also often seen to characterize the thinking of writers and readers, whose knowledge of their plans and goals and purposes seem impossibly detailed and explicit. Wittgenstein suggests that if we seek the source of these complexities in social structure rather than in mental states we are more likely to be successful in explaining how people learn to use language.

Like Grice, when Wittgenstein turns to an analysis of the origin of language-games, he finds that evaluation plays an essential role. In *The Blue Book*, he discusses why language changes:

> Our ordinary language, which of all possible notations is the one which pervades all our life, holds our mind rigidly in one position, as it were, and in this position sometimes it feels cramped, having a desire for other positions as well. Thus we sometimes wish for a notation which stresses a difference more strongly, makes it more obvious, than ordinary language does, or one which in a particular case uses more closely similar forms of expression than our ordinary language. Our mental cramp is loosened when we are shown the notations which fulfill these needs. These needs can be of the greatest variety. (Wittgenstein, 1965, p. 59)

Language responds to the needs of its users, not, as Saussure also points out, to the needs of individual users, but rather to the needs of the group. Language-games develop within the context of social interactions, as Bloor explains:

> What Wittenstein was referring to by 'needs' were the very things that sociologists refer to under the heading of social interests. Needs are not individual appetites, but are best construed as collective phenomena. When we detect a change in a language-game we must look for a shift in the goals and purposes of its players which is sufficiently wide-spread and sufficiently uniform to yield that change.... What institutions are best served ... which can be most easily justified.... Who gains advantage? These are the kind of questions that will lead us to the interests that structure language-games. (Bloor, 1983, p. 49)

Bloor points to Lewis' (1912) definition of inference in the language-game of formal logic as an example of a practice which is supposed to rely on the validity of the formal proofs Lewis offers. Bloor argues that the formal rigor of Lewis' proofs could be challenged, just as Lewis challenged

Russell, but they are not challenged because they rely on traditional assumptions of formal logic. Thus, "despite their rigorous formal character they rest on a taken-for-granted basis" (Bloor, 1983, p. 131). And why are these traditional, taken-for-granted assumptions allowed to stand? Wittgenstein "would say that if the Lewis proofs are deemed valid it is because they represent a stable language-game. If they are deemed invalid it is because we are wanting to replace one language-game by another" (Bloor, 1983, p. 131). The significance of this is that the structure of language-games can be explicated with reference to rules, conventions, rigorous procedures—but only to a point. Eventually we reach a point where the reason things are as they are must be explained with reference to what is advantageous or of benefit to those engaging in the language-game. People do not operate in the ideal world of logical necessity or purely arbitrary convention. The validity of Lewis' proofs and Oxford's rule against dogs as well as the willing suspension of disbelief and use of detail in descriptive writing ultimately depends on our evaluation of the usefulness of these practices in the situations we find ourselves in, not on the rigor or clarity of the systems we use to define them. As Wittgenstein and Grice have taught us, in the sublunary world of language-games, we do a lot of deeming.

The importance of social value is also obvious in Wittgenstein's discussion of how language-games are learned. Such learning, he argues, is characterized not by explanation of conventions but by training in practices. In the hypothetical primitive language of builders, the apprentice is trained to bring a block, pillar, slab, or beam when the master builder calls out one of these words, and the ostensive teaching of these words is a secondary part of this activity:

> Don't you understand the call "Slab!" if you act upon it in such-and-such a way?—Doubtless the ostensive teaching helped to bring this about; but only together with a particular training. With different training the same ostensive teaching of these words would have effected a quite different understanding. (1968, sec. 6)

The understanding of such commands as "Slab!" depends on the apprentice's involvement in the building task. He understands that his fetching of slabs, blocks, and so forth in the order in which they are called for fulfills a certain function within the process, that it leads to the successful completion of a task in which he has a role to play and sees as valuable in some way. The lesson here for those of us who wish to help our students develop new discourse practices is that teaching them the conventions of the formal essay, for example, will not by itself lead to their understanding what a formal essay is meant to do. Instead, we must teach them the purposes and values of these practices, for only then will they understand what they are being trained for and what our directions to "add detail" or "state your main point" mean.

Finally, it is important to realize that when we think of the development of reading and writing in terms of practices rather than conventions, we also must see students as participants in the process of development rather than as passive recipients of a static body of knowledge. Wittgenstein's apprentice builder has a role to play at the same time he is learning. As I explained in "The Ecology of Writing," the systems that connect writers are made and remade in the act of writing. Thus, when we ask students to write in new situations and formats, what is changed is not only the students but also the systems of ideas, purposes, interactions, norms, and forms that make up the writing activity (Cooper, 1986, pp. 368–369). From this perspective, development of reading and writing appears to involve most essentially the development of new discursive practices within a society rather than the acquisition of cognitive skills by individuals. In developing new discursive practices readers and writers will begin to think differently or think about different things, but the difference in their thinking is a result, not the cause, of the new practices. And, similarly, new conventions simply encode new practices; they do not cause the changes in practices. As Bloor says, "Humans don't solve the problem because they can formulate the rule; they can formulate the rule because they can solve the problem" (Bloor, 1983, p. 173).

DISCOURSE PRACTICES IN FIRST-YEAR ENGLISH

In order to clarify how students can become involved in the process of developing new discursive practices I want to consider again that First-Year English class that was struggling to understand Marcuse. The course was designed as part of a two-quarter sequence that focused on students learning to write from sources. As writing from sources is not a purpose in itself, we were looking for ways to immerse students in some kind of inquiry that they would find valuable. Since a large majority of our students are preparing for technological careers (as engineers, technical writers, computer system designers, for example), we thought that they might find valuable an understanding of how technology affects society. Marcuse's argument that technology, rather than enhancing life, perverts social values and denies to individuals the freedom to choose their own goals challenges our students' socially constructed vision of themselves as the society's problem-solvers (those Dow Chemical advertisements spring to mind). We thought this challenge might inspire them to search for information and arguments to use in refutation. And for the most part they did live up to our expectations, taking on the project of understanding and applying Marcuse's theories as their own.

One of the methods we developed to help them accomplish this project was an asynchronous computer conference which they were required to contribute to weekly.[6] The directions on how they should participate in this discussion were simple:

> Your purpose here is to discuss the ideas Marcuse presents in *One-Dimensional Man*, especially how they relate to the research you are doing. You can respond to my questions, bring up questions and points of your own and ask for response from your classmates and from me, and you can—and should—respond to your classmates' questions, points, problems.

I did not tell them exactly how they were to respond or how to bring up points and questions for I knew I could rely on some skills they already had: Both in in-class discussions and in out-of-class "bull sessions," they get a lot of experience of talking with one another about things that are important to them, trying to figure out what they believe, connecting what they read and what they are taught with their lives. And I knew they would develop new practices as necessary to serve their purposes in this course, which we had carefully and repeatedly defined: to understand and apply Marcuse's theories.

The discussions were wide-ranging and, particularly in this class, quite prolix, with some students contributing a whole single-spaced page of writing at a time. As I began to analyze what my students did in these written discussions, I began to see how being placed in this situation encouraged them to both learn and create discourse practices that serve the goals of scholarly inquiry. In this essay I want to examine just three practices that engaging in this discussion trained them in: using different perspectives to come up with new ideas, developing ideas through discussion, and using information to support a point. These practices are significant ones, for they enable a writer to develop the complexity that is valued—and required—in scholarly argument, the kind of complexity that the student I quoted at the beginning of this article found frustrating at first.

USING DIFFERENT PERSPECTIVES TO COME UP WITH NEW IDEAS

To help my students understand Marcuse's arguments, I occasionally directed their attention to particular passages in the book, as a means of

---

[6] The conference was stored on a disk kept in the department's Center for Computer-Assisted Language Instruction: Students went to the center at their convenience, picked up the disk, read all entries written since they last wrote, and added their new entry.

training them to pay close attention to Marcuse's precise meanings. Their first impulse was to explain the meaning of these passages by relating them to their own beliefs and experiences. But as the discussion progressed, they also became aware that this practice was not sufficient to make sense of Marcuse's divergent ideas. It was at this point that they picked up on the suggestion I offered in class that trying to see things from someone else's perspective could be a useful practice.

Early in the second quarter I asked them to discuss a pair of passages in which Marcuse argues that "a transition to a higher stage of civilization" could be achieved if the goal of technical progress were established as "the pacification of the struggle for existence" (1964, p. 227), or, in other words, if technology devoted itself to freeing people from the oppressive demands of getting enough food to eat and so forth. Phil's[7] discussion of these passages demonstrates not only how he uses his own beliefs in his interpretation but also his awareness that one's perspective guides what one says about particular problems:

> In the line "the pacification of the struggle for existence" Marcuse is trying to relay the idea of destroying competition in society. Destroying competition would be accomplished through the use of harnessing technology and controlling it so as to provide society [with] all of its mandatory needs. Thus, by destroying competition there would be no "struggle for existence." With all of society's true needs supplied to it, society would then divert its energies away from existence and to a yet unknown direction or area. This direction or area, Marcuse believes, would be the factor that would raise society to a new level, a new order.... Marcuse is a Marxist, period. He can't but help think the way he does.... With the elimination of competition, Marcuse believes that society will form a new order, and that it will. But, with the elimination of competition, will not society become lazy and lose its driving force? Society will become a bunch of vegetables that don't think or do anything; it will just exist. I must disagree with Marcuse because of the capitalistic philosophies that are instilled in me and which I agree with.
>
> Phil

Phil recognizes that it is because he believes in capitalism that he disagrees with Marcuse. But he does not recognize that it is in part because he has translated Marcuse's ideas into capitalistic terms that Marcuse's goal for society makes no sense to him. As another student, Dan, notes, Marcuse never mentions competition in the passages under discussion: "I cannot see where the idea of competition comes into play anywhere, please correct me if I am wrong." The connection between competition and the struggle for existence is made via Phil's and the other students'

---

[7] I have used pseudonyms for all students. I have not altered their sex; there were initially only two women in the class, and both dropped the course by the end of the third week.

tacit belief in social Darwinism, in which social life is explained in terms of what Herbert Spencer called the survival of the fittest, a notion which makes unrestricted competition for goods and services seem not only legitimate but also inevitable. Thus, Phil sees Marcuse's "pacification of the struggle for existence" as a call for the elimination of competition.

Chuck, pointing out that his practice differs from that of other students, arrives at a more accurate definition of what Marcuse means in the passage:

> My ideas on "the pacification of the struggle for existence" stand in a different light than the rest. I look at what Marcuse wants in order to explain the quote. I look at the quote in this light. Marcuse wants us to be peaceful in our development. He wants us to use the circle of technology building politics which builds society which builds technology to increase society and ease the struggle for existence. But, to not struggle for existence might destroy society and there will be no need for "the pacification of the struggle for existence."

Chuck explicitly tries to understand Marcuse's perspective, to define what Marcuse means in this passage by relating it to his understanding of Marcuse's overall point in the discussion. Marcuse's "circle of technology"—the idea that technology simply inspires society to want more technology for its own sake—had been discussed in class and in the computer conference at length, and Chuck explains how the "new direction of technical progress" that Marcuse calls for will change this circle. It's a pretty good explanation—but it doesn't help Chuck understand why Marcuse thinks society could be transformed in this way; he says, "to not struggle for existence might destroy society." Thus, Chuck, though he defines Marcuse's ideas better than Phil does, in the end simply rejects them too.

Doug's discussion of the passage is more productive: Like Chuck, he tries to understand Marcuse's perspective, but in doing so he realizes that what Marcuse is calling for requires a radical turnaround in thinking. Doug's success in recognizing the value of a different perspective is largely due to his careful reading of other entries in the conference, especially Phil's, to which he responds:

> In response to [Phil's] entry. You may think that everyone would turn into vegetables but the problem is Marcuse's ideas can't really be tried. Everything would have to turn completely around. If it were possible to try, I still think no one would veg out. Marcuse's ideas do not only deal with society's external aspects, but society's mental aspects. That is why no one, I think, would veg out. Marcuse was trying to rationalize a society that not only provided for everyone, but when it came to doing something, it would be for the well being of everyone. His society would have absolutely no one think-

ing for themselves. That is why your capitalistic train of thought seems not to be able to rationalize this. The main question now is, if we could change would we? (If we were able to change to Marcuse's ideal society, in thought and action).

Doug points out two ways in which Marcuse's ideas conflict with the "capitalistic train of thought." First, he says, Marcuse believes that people can be motivated by mental as well as external "aspects," that people won't "veg out" because they strive for "mental" goals such as the betterment of society as much as they strive for "external" things like material goods. Second, he says, in Marcuse's society people think more about "the well being of everyone" than about their own individual wants and needs. Doug's identification of the differences between Marcuse's perspective and Phil's perspective allows him to explain why our society doesn't change and inspires him to ask the question that preoccupied many students later in the conference—whether we want to change our society in this way.

As the quarter went on, more students found that Marcuse's perpective on the technological society helped them explain things they noticed and that bothered them about our society. Dan said:

> As we get farther into this course, I find myself agreeing with some of the points that Marcuse makes. That doesn't mean I agree with his philosophy, I am just saying that he makes many good points that we could use to better our society. . . . Like Marcuse says in the quote we [sic] wrote on p 242, if industry would produce less of this "profitable waste" society would be better off. The money spent on these waste items could be spent on bettering society. I agree it would be very difficult to do this because technology already has a very strong hold over us. Now this doesn't mean that I am against technology, technology is very useful and I wouldn't want to live without it. It is just that I think it is time for us to get a hold of what technology is doing to us.

As Dan's careful abjuration of Marcuse's "philosophy" and his protestation that he is not against technology demonstrates, Marcuse's perspective was one most students did not wish to be associated with and found hard to accept in general. But through discussing his ideas in class and in the computer conference they discovered that looking at things from a different perspective, even a perspective one doesn't entirely agree with, can be a valuable practice. In these discussions, they encountered problems like profitable waste that they saw as important but that they couldn't understand from their current perspective. When they discovered that looking at such problems from another perspective allowed them to understand the problems better and come up with ways to resolve them, the purpose of using different perspectives became obvious and the practice of shifting perspectives became valuable to them. At the end of the second quarter, Bruce wrote, "Even though I would say I am an anti-Marcuse, this course has opened my mind up to some of the problems with our society today."

DEVELOPING IDEAS THROUGH DISCUSSION

As the exchanges between students in the computer conference demonstrate, peer discussion was an important part of the course. I told my students that most writers developed their ideas by discussing them with their colleagues and friends, and, thus, in this writing course they would get lots of practice in using discussion to help them in their writing. When we met in the classroom, they met in groups to discuss *One-Dimensional Man* and their research projects; when we met in the computer center, they wrote comments on each other's papers or contributed to the computer conference. I did not lecture, nor did I often explain Marcuse's ideas. One student described my "teaching style" as sometimes "frustrating" (a word that seems to turn up frequently in my students' comments): "she would not always give you an answer to your Qusetions. She would more often than not answer your question with another question." But by the end of the course he also understood the value of peer discussion:

> NOw as i think back i am very glad she did that becuase i had to figure things out on my own and therefor formed my own opinions and ideas. This was a new teaching style for me because aost [most] teacher will tell you in what way you are expected to think, "Doc" let you form your own ideas, and i see they are waorking by reading other peoples writtings and listening to coversations, there are a multitude of opinions on marcuse's ideas and i think that the teaching of our marcuse english instructors is the reason.[8]

I quote "Pete" at length here partly to assure you that my students are not always frustrated even though I demand a lot of them, but also to emphasize that peer discussions are significantly different from class discussions led by a teacher. In peer discussions, students are more likely to see themselves as responsible for the ideas that are discussed and the way in which the discussion proceeds. This is true even when a teacher participates in these discussions as long as the teacher's participation is minimal and the students' attention remains focused for the most part on each other. When students see themselves as responsible for understanding and developing

---

[8] As is especially evident here, contributions to computer conferences are frequently as casual in style and as full of mistakes as oral conversations are.

ideas, they begin to see more clearly how other people's opinions can help them.

At the beginning of the written discussion in the computer conference, students indicated their awareness of the value of other people's opinions mostly by asking for correction or for comments on what they had said. Doug concluded one early entry by saying, "This is what I think Marcuse is trying to say, please tell me if you agree or am I so wrong it's pathetic." Chuck, as usual, commented on why he was doing what he was doing: "I like to comment on other peoples' work. So, later they will have a reason to comment on mine. . . . Please, I welcome comments, then I can learn."[9] Later, they acknowledged that reading what others had to say about difficult parts of *One-Dimensional Man* helped them figure it out themselves: Bruce started an entry by saying, "I found it a little hard to understand the passage, but, from what everybody else wrote about it, I have a better idea." These students are not simply paying lip service to the academic commonplace that listening to other people's opinions can clarify your own ideas; they are aware that the activity of writing in the computer conference is useful to them in fulfilling the requirements of the course to understand and apply Marcuse's theories.

But once the discussion proceeded beyond explications of passages and staking out of positions to a more complex discussion of ideas, students began to realize the full value of discussion in developing ideas. Throughout the computer conference, Jim seemed more accepting than most students of Marcuse's ideas. Though he stoutly proclaimed his allegiance to capitalism and his satisfaction with the status quo, he also repeatedly pointed out the way in which the profit motive distorted our values. Late in the course, he wrote in this vein again:

> The material base for domination, as Marcuse speaks of, I feel is the profit motive we are so graciously aware of. This repression of thought, creation of false needs, and the glorifying of these products through mass communication, all deal with the ever present technology. Cutting production costs, marketing a variety of products, and selling goods actually needed or not needed, all seem to play into the hands of making money. . . . I feel it is this capitalistic, profit-based, society that determines what the media will communicate, and the stores will stock on their shelves. What can we do though? What I am afraid of is how generations to come will be like. I have two nephews, who watch these technobots, or whatever on T.V.. They buy transformers, and seemingly want to blow everything up. Even kids are getting more technologically oriented.

---

[9] Students develop their own forms for asking for help in these conferences: Both Dan, whom I quoted earlier, and Chuck picked up the "please" form from Doug. In another first-year writing conference students developed an "any other ideas?" form.

For reasons I cannot entirely fathom, Jim's comments in this entry sparked a revelation in Phil. Phil had been so adamant in his opposition to Marcuse's ideas that at one point he exploded at the other students, writing at the beginning of an entry, "You people are a bunch of Marxists!!!!!!" As a result he was jokingly labeled "the DEFENDER OF CAPITALISTIC WAYS, the TRUE RED BLOODED AMERICAN" by Doug. But now Phil wrote:

> I like what [Jim] wrote alot. I've been trying to defend everything that you have been cutting down. But now I guess I see whats wrong. [Jim] said that the profit motive is the driving motive behind all technological advancements and thats pretty much true. American society always wants more, and more and more. Where's the cut off line, I mean does it ever end. I can't understand how people can just continue to want to make money. After you have so much I would think it would get boring after a while. I think thats the major problem with our society, it does'nt know when to say enough.

I should say that such sudden breakthroughs in understanding are not overwhelmingly common, nor did Phil understand a great deal of Marcuse's perspective. Nevertheless, by the end of the course most students learned the value of discussing ideas with one another. Confronted with difficult ideas that their instructor would not explain, they learned to ask questions and hazard answers and to make and criticize hypotheses because these practices helped them achieve their purposes in the course.

Doug, who was outgoing and popular with his classmates, proved to be especially proficient in developing ideas through discussion. The ideas in his entry I quoted earlier were developed not only through his participation in the computer conference but also in talking with his group in class. Later in the conference he made an especially acute observation:

> Another thing I would like to point out to everyone is our attitude. While reading through the files I noticed how everyone was disagreeing with society, (except [Phil]) and saying different things were bad. Then all of a sudden everyone starts saying stuff like it's bad but I like it. Aren't there passages in the book that talk about people saying things are bad and then say oh what the heck. Like the guy with the new car, the man on the subway, and the other one, I don't remember what it is. If you don't see what I'm saying, reread some of the previous stuff and watch for a change in attitude.

Doug is referring to Marcuse's idea of the harmonizing realization, the method by which the technological society aborts criticism of itself: Negative observations like the fact that one's new automobile soon "will deteriorate and need repair; that its beauty and surface are cheap, its power unnecessary, its size idiotic; and that [one] will not find a parking place" (Marcuse, 1964, p. 226) are "harmonized"—obliterated—by realizations like "the other guy has to live, too" and "we have it much better than before" (p. 226). Doug cleverly notices and brings to his classmates' attention the prevalence of such "realizations" in their own comments, increasing both his own and the others' understanding of the import of Marcuse's argument. In the succeeding entry, Mark applauded Doug's observation and drew a lesson from it: "Good point, [Doug].... If we are happy with what we have and what is available, then we might never have a chance to obtain something better."

USING INFORMATION TO SUPPORT A POINT

The third practice students learn better by engaging in academic discourse than by listening to a teacher's instructions is the use of evidence to back up points. In commenting on drafts of each others' essays, they copy my demands for "more quotes from the book" and "evidence to back up your claims," but as they argue with one another in the computer conference, they supply such evidence with no prompting from me. And, often, the evidence they supply is decidedly not something I could have suggested.

In the discussion of the role of competition in society I referred to earlier, students used a diverse array of evidence to back up their points. Mark drew on the research he was doing on genetic engineering to argue that competition was not always good:

> As our society is set up now, competition makes transplants and other highly technical operations only available to those who can afford them. Also with the shortage of organs compared to the number of people needing them, the price is even higher. Competition for these rare organs and for the highly trained doctors makes it extremly difficult, expensive, and requires a substantial length of time to wait for an organ. People in our society NOW have been selling body parts on the black market so thay can get out of finacial problems. In a classless society, there would not be any competition for these organs and doctors. They would be served on a first come first serve basis or on their need or urgency.

Chuck replied using evidence drawn from popular culture: "[Mark], there will always be competition for items that have a limited supply, such as organs and fossil feuls. In the movie "Road Warriors" All of society was destroyed and yet, the competition for scarce items was greater than ever." Although from our point of view the way Chuck uses the movie is rather naive, he demonstrates in his comment his understanding of what kinds of evidence his classmates will find convincing. In their arguments, other students used as evidence such things as the arms race, social security, John Lennon's songs, their experience in ROTC, a televised interview of Timothy Leary, a teacher's story about an electronics company where he was once employed, a state proposal to tax illegal drugs, the information they were gathering for their essays, and, occasionally, a quotation from *One-Dimensional Man.*

I drew my students' attention to all three of these practices (and others) in my comments in class, in the computer conference, and on their writing. Many of these practices are very well known if not often described, practices that are automated behavior in most academic writers. They are also practices that are related to practices in other discourses with which students are more familiar. It is difficult to discern exactly what each of these—my explicit knowledge and teaching, their implicit knowledge, and the activities the students were engaged in—contributed to their learning of these practices. Still, observing my students' use and adaptations of the practices of academic discourse, especially in the computer conference, I cannot help but believe that their judgments of what behavior is valuable in achieving their purposes are the most significant factor in their learning and adopting these practices as their own.

Designing courses that stimulate students to develop discourse practices that they—and other academics—find valuable requires us to focus on different concerns than those we might otherwise consider. If we want to train them in the practices of academic inquiry, to learn to use reading and writing as a means of discovering and developing knowledge in a field, we need to begin by defining for ourselves the language-game of academic inquiry in its entirety—its purposes, its history, its institutions, the norms and forms of interaction. Then we can plan assignments and activities that engage students in this language-game, that enable them, like Wittgenstein's apprentice builder, to learn through doing. As they make the purposes of this game their own, they will begin to develop and discover practices that are valuable to them because the practices achieve these purposes. What practices are most valuable and what order in which they should be discovered cannot be determined in advance or dictated by the instructor. Training is a matter of guiding individual behavior, not of transmitting an ideal system of thinking.

What Wittgenstein observed of philosophy is also true of much current thought about how people become readers and .vriters: "There is a kind of general disease of thinking which always looks for (and finds) what would be called a mental state from which all our acts spring as from a reservoir" (Wittgenstein, 1965, p. 143). I am not suggesting in contrast that all our acts spring from the reservoir of social interaction, for to do so would be to ignore the dialectical interaction between thought and action and between individual and society that is at the heart of all discourse. What I am suggesting is that we think of our students as not merely individual minds in need of development but rather as people who have social as well as intellectual needs and desires and who are capable of evaluating and participating in their own learning. In any case, such a perspective, if not conclusively more efficacious, is certainly more interesting for both students and teachers.

REFERENCES

Bakhtin, M. M. (1981). *The dialogic imagination* (M. Holquist, Ed.; C. Emerson & M. Holquist, Trans.). Austin: University of Texas Press.

Bizzell, P. (1984). William Perry and liberal education. *College English, 46*, 447–54.

Bloor, D. (1983). *Wittgenstein: A social theory of knowledge.* New York: Columbia University Press.

Burke, K. (1984). *Permanence and change: An anatomy of purpose* (3rd ed.). Berkeley: University of California Press.

Cooper, M. M. (1986). The ecology of writing. *College English, 48*, 364–75.

Cooper, M. M., & Holzman, M. (1989). *Writing as social action.* Portsmouth, NH: Boynton-Cook.

Freed, R. C., & Broadhead, G. J. (1987). Discourse communities, sacred texts, and institutional norms. *College Composition and Communication, 38*, 154–65.

Grice, H. P. (1967). *Logic and conversation.* William James Lectures, Mimeo. Cambridge, MA: Harvard University Press.

Grice, H. P. (1975). Logic and conversation. In P. Cole & J. L. Morgan (Eds.), *Syntax and semantics, Vol. 3: Speech acts* (pp. 41–58). New York: Academic Press.

Grice, H. P. (1982). Meaning revisited. In N. V. Smith (Ed.), *Mutual knowledge* (pp. 223–243). New York: Academic Press.

Halliday, M. A. K. (1978). *Language as social semiotic: The social interpretation of language and meaning.* London: Edward Arnold.

Lewis, C. (1912). Implication and the algebra of logic. *Mind, 21*, 522–531.

Lewis, D. K. (1969). *Convention: A philosophical analysis.* Cambridge: Harvard University Press.

Marcuse, H. (1964). *One-dimensional man.* Boston: Beacon Press.

Saussure, F. de. (1966). *Course in general linguistics* (C. Bally & A. Sechehaye in collaboration with A. Riedlinger, Eds.; W. Baskin, Trans.). New York: McGraw-Hill.

Schiffer, S. R. (1972). *Meaning.* Oxford: Clarendon Press.

Street, B. V. (1986). Literacy practices and literacy myths. Mimeo.

Wittgenstein, L. (1965). *The blue and brown books* (2nd ed.). New York: Harper & Row.

Wittgenstein, L. (1968). *Philosophical investigations* (G. E. M. Anscombe, Trans.; 3rd ed.). New York: Macmillan.

Wittgenstein, L. (1969). *On certainty* (G. E. M. Anscombe & G. H. von Wright, Eds.; D. Paul & G. E. M. Anscombe, Trans.). New York: Harper & Row.

II
The Social Stance

4

The Artful Conversation: Characterizing the Development of Advanced Literacy*

Cheryl Geisler

Reformers in literacy education have become increasingly critical of a model of decontextualized reading and writing that divorces reader from writer and affect from intellect. Critiques have arisen on two complementary fronts. Many researchers in child language acquisition have argued that the acquisition of literacy skills is a natural process in which students adapt oral strategies to written contexts (Graves & Hansen, 1983; Heath & Branscombe, 1985; Knoblauch & Brannon, 1984; Pearson & Tierney, 1984; Schafer, 1981; Smith, 1985). In a similar vein, researchers in adult literacy have shown that texts usually perceived as autonomous contributions to knowledge are, in fact, part of an ongoing dialogue within specialized communities (Bartholomae, 1985; Bazerman, 1985; Bizzell, 1982; Bruffee, 1984; Gilbert & Mulkay, 1984; Latour & Woolgar, 1979; LeFevre, 1987; McCloskey, 1985; Myers, 1985).

In making these arguments, researchers have relied upon a model of literacy as natural conversation. In this model, a writer is seen as taking a turn in a conversation that both responds to previous writers and invites response from future writers. As I will discuss below, this model makes certain important corrections to a more traditional model of literacy as the conscious or artful construction of autonomous texts. Nevertheless, it may lead educators to underestimate both the work that students must do to acquire advanced literacy practices and the help they need to do so. In

*Research presented here was supported by a grant from the Fund for the Improvement of Post-Secondary Education to the author and David S. Kaufer, Christine M. Neuwirth, and Preston Covey at Carnegie Mellon University.

this paper, I will begin by reviewing a growing body of empirical evidence that suggests that neither decontextualized art nor natural conversation is an adequate description of advanced literacy practices. Then, drawing on advances made by cognitive researchers on the nature of expertise, I will suggest an alternative model of literacy as "artful conversation."

LITERACY AS DECONTEXTUALIZED ART

The model of literacy as natural conversation has usually been promoted as an alternative to a model held by an older research tradition in which literacy was seen as a fundamental break with rather than extension of conversational skills. According to this model, practices of written interpretation depart from oral conversation by being:

- *Depersonalized,* independent of affect
- *Decontextualized,* possible without knowledge of time and place of authorship
- *Universal,* oriented toward the construction of knowledge independent of any single individual's life or work.

In a line of argument first articulated by Goody and Watt (1963), literacy was seen to create a representation for thought that could be more systematically manipulated than oral conversation. In the permanent and spatial organization of written texts, logical and historical inconsistencies easily overlooked in an oral system would become more noticeable. This recognition, according to Goody and Watt, was essential for the development of modern Western culture.

Many theoreticians, especially literary critics, have also emphasized the artful manipulation present in writing but absent in conversation. In an essay entitled "The Writer's Audience is Always a Fiction," Walter Ong (1975) described the process by which an author fictionalizes an audience. First, the writer builds an image of the audience through acquaintance "not from daily life but from earlier writers who were fictionalizing in their imagination" (p. 60). Second, the writer, if skillful, creates a new fiction to which readers must then learn to conform. In a symmetrical line of argument, Foucault (1977) has claimed that the author is also a fiction, one created by society to give coherence and locate responsibility for texts. In reality, according to Foucault, the author has characteristics independent of the person who actually penned the text.

Empirical support for these theoretical descriptions of literacy as decontextualized art was first developed by a student of Vygotsky's, A. R. Luria. At a time when Western psychology was firmly in the grip of behaviorism, Vygotsky (1962) had emphasized that language, especially the schooled language of literacy, was a tool by which humans could manipulate their own thinking processes, moving beyond simple reflex actions to analytic thinking. Encouraged by Vygotsky, Luria (1976) studied the impact of literacy and schooling on peasants in the early stages of collectivization in the U.S.S.R.. He found significant differences between those who were preliterate and those with even just a few weeks of schooling. These recently literate people had developed the ability to reason in a decontextualized manner, focusing on the logic of statements presented to them, a form of reasoning not employed by the preliterates.

Since Luria, empirical investigations have suggested that decontextualization and artful construction may be characteristics of a special kind of literacy entrenched in Western-style schooling. Scribner and Cole (1981), for example, found that members of a West African tribe who acquired literacy in Western-style schools showed the cognitive effects documented by Luria. Those who had acquired literacy through religious study of the Koran or through one-to-one tutoring among friends and family, however, did not show these changes. In a cross-cultural study of Athabascan attitudes toward literacy, Scollon and Scollon (1981) found that Native Americans distinguished between Western "book-like" language and their own conversational strategies. According to the Scollons, even Western conversational strategies have been influenced by "essayist" literacy. In confirmation, they documented differences between their own daughter's tendency to decontextualize and fictionalize herself in oral narratives and the narrative strategies naturally used by Athabascan children.

Several studies of children's language acquisition processes have also suggested that literacy involves a kind of artful manipulation not required of oral conversation. In a now classic article, David Olson (1977) described the child learning to read and write as moving away from interpretive processes dependent on the contexts of production to interpretive processes that relied solely on the meaning explicitly and autonomously represented in the text. Following up on this claim, Olson and Torrance (1981) reported a series of developmental studies which suggest that children must learn to treat the meaning of a text as independent of pragmatics in order to draw logically correct conclusions. Similarly, Bereiter and Scardamalia (1982) have argued that students learning to write must decouple their oral conversational system from the external turn-taking rhythm of an interlocutor. To further this end, they recommend that teachers replace standard classroom interventions which perpetuate students' dependencies on external input with procedural facilitations designed to help them to function autonomously.

A longitudinal study by Wells (1986) offers the most recent evidence that mastery of written language calls for skills not required by oral conversation. Tracking 128 children from shortly after their first birthdays until the last year of elementary school, Wells found that overall school achievement after the age of five was unrelated to oral language skill. Even though these children varied in their control of speaking and listening, these competencies appeared to be peripheral to the school curriculum. Control of written language, however, was a strong predictor of school success.

Supported, then, by arguments and evidence from historians, anthropologists, psychologists, linguists, and some educators, a rich tradition exists for considering literacy a decontextualized art different from conversational practice. As discussed below, however, these arguments have come under increasing attack by sociologists, cognitive psychologists, and educational reformers who characterize the notion of autonomous text making as a myth that only serves to disenfranchise large segments of our society.

LITERACY AS NATURAL CONVERSATION

In contrast to viewing literacy as decontextualized art, conceiving of literacy as natural conversation usually means describing the interpretive processes relied upon by readers and writers as:

- *Interpersonal*, part of an ongoing relationship between two or more persons
- *Contextual*, constructed with consideration of the context in which the text was produced and published
- *Local*, affected by the past experience of the reader and affecting the future of that reader.

Attacks on the model of literacy as decontextualized art began with sociologists studying the professional practices of specialized communities, especially those characterized as scientific. In a landmark study of scientific discourse, Gilbert and Mulkay (1984) found that scientists can account for their research findings in two radically different ways. When they use an empiricist repertoire, they give accounts focused on depersonalized facts from the physical world. When they use a more contingent repertoire, however, they emphasize intuition, personality, and the local conditions of specific laboratories. According to Gilbert and Mulkay, scientists systematically suppress the contingent repertoire in favor of the empiricist repertoire when they publish. As a result, their published accounts can lead those outside of their community to take their descriptions of decontextualized objectivity at face value. In a similar vein,

McCloskey (1985) has shown that the claims for a take-it-or-leave-it objectivity made by publishing economists mask a practice that, in fact, is quite interpersonal and conversational.

Studies of writing in nonacademic settings have further documented the ways in which texts that seem to be autonomous artifacts are, in fact, deeply embedded in a social context. Reviewing published accounts of inventive processes in numerous fields, for example, LeFevre (1987) has argued that the rhetorical invention of ideas in writing involves a social, collective collaboration. According to LeFevre, the more favored Platonic view of writing as the product of the solitary individual has little descriptive value. In a case study following in the same line of research, Myers (1985) has shown how grant proposals evolve as a result of a dialogue between a granting agency and research scientists. Revisions made by the researchers he studied were driven less by the need to characterize their research findings and more by the need to answer objections that might be raised by the program officer and reviewers.

The argument for the conversational nature of advanced literacy practices has also been confirmed by a growing body of cognitive research in reading and writing. Lundeberg (1987), for example, found differences in the reading strategies of more and less experienced practioners of law. Lawyers and law professors asked to read complicated legal briefs made use of contextual information about the parties involved, the type of court, the date of the decisions, and the name of the judge in making sense of the text. Novices, on the other hand, ignored this information. In a similar vein, Haas and Flower (1988) found that more experienced readers use a class of rhetorical reading strategies not drawn upon by less experienced readers. These strategies were aimed at constructing a rhetorical situation for the text by accounting for the author's purpose, context, and effect on the audience. Using slightly different methods, Bazerman (1985) found that physicists focused on the names of individuals and research groups in deciding what to read to keep up with the literature.

Educators too have begun to emphasize the conversational nature of literacy. Bizzell (1982) and Bartholomae (1985), for example, have argued that college students often write poorly not because they are deficient in basic skills but because they are outsiders to the conversation of the university. Learning to write, then, becomes a matter of taking on a voice of authority, locating oneself in a discourse, and assuming the right to participate. In Chapter 5, Vipond, Hunt, Jewett, and Reither use a similar line of argument to account for the fact that the university faculty in their study generally used point-driven reading while college students did not. According to these authors, the college students were reading in an experimental situation which may not have authorized them to engage the text conversationally. The university faculty, on the other hand, may have felt more free to reflect on the authorial intention behind the text and thus to construct its "point."

Evidence is accumulating, then, that in both production and interpretation, more advanced literacy practices are characterized by greater attention to the conversation in which the text is embedded. In fact, these studies suggest that the only readers and writers who employ a model of literacy as decontextualized art are the outsiders—the nonscientists looking at scientific publications, the inexperienced law student reading legal briefs, the inexperienced or unauthorized reader of literary texts. Picking up on this finding, many educational reformers have concluded that schooling that perpetuates the myth of the autonomous text serves only to limit advanced literacy to those few who, by virtue of a privileged background, come to school already possessing an insider's understanding of literate conversations. Those without this advantage, however, are only mislead by the decontextualized practices fostered in school settings (Cazden, in press; Cook-Gumperz, 1986).

A STUDY OF ACADEMIC DISCOURSE

While evidence concerning the contextualized or rhetorical nature of literacy is now substantial enough to dismiss any simple model of the autonomous text, other evidence continues to support the notion that, at least as far as Western essayist literacy is concerned, substantial art is involved. Rather than seeing natural conversation and decontextualized art as competing alternatives, I would like to suggest that advanced literacy practices may require a little of both. In particular, a study with which I have been involved for the past few years illustrates the ways that both art and conversation may be complexly intermingled.

The purpose of this study (Geisler, in press) was to describe the goals, activities, and knowledge representations used by experienced and inexperienced readers/writers when asked to write an essay in response to the previous literature in an area. This kind of essay in which one reviews the range of opinion in an area and argues for one's own position is typical of academic discourse and often becomes an assignment in the typical college writing course (Kaufer, Geisler, & Neuwirth, 1989).

Since we were interested in the case-based reasoning typical of ethical philosophy, we choose to ask participants to work on the issue of paternalism. Paternalistic interference is an issue in ethics because it appears to violate widespread assumptions about individual rights and yet occasionally to appear to be justified. John Stuart Mill claimed that the individual had exclusive rights to make decisions regarding his or her own welfare. This "harm principle" has become the basis for many ethicists' discussions on the nature of individual rights. Paternalism is a problem in these discussions because it involves interference by one person in the affairs of another for that person's "own good" and thus appears to violate the harm principle. Nevertheless, few would argue that this kind of interference cannot be justified in some cases: Parents' paternalism toward their children; teachers' toward their students; government's toward the mentally incompetent. In an effort to determine the boundaries between justified and unjustified action, ethical philosophers have offered conflicting definitions of paternalistic interference and conflicting specification of the conditions under which it can be justified.

Four individuals were asked to read and write about this issue. Two were "insiders"—Ph.D. level philosophers familiar with ethical issues, but unfamiliar with the topic and readings used in the project. Two were "outsiders"—second-semester college freshmen unfamiliar with the technical issues of ethics, but both experienced with paternalism in their own lives. These four individuals were asked to read the same set of eight articles on paternalism and write an original essay defining paternalistic interference and describing the conditions, if any, under which it could be justified.

All four participants worked on this reading/writing task at their own rate for between 30 and 60 hours over 10 to 15 weeks. They were asked to think aloud into a tape recorder whenever they worked, to meet with a member of the research team for an interview between each working session, and to keep all of the writing they produced. The think-aloud protocols, interview transcripts, and texts formed the data on which the following discussion is based.

RESULTS

Many critics of current educational practices have pointed out that much schooled literacy does not give students an opportunity to engage in reading and writing for purposes other than reporting on what they have learned (Applebee, 1984; Britton, Burgess, Martin, Mcleod, & Rosen, 1975). Given the opportunity to use literacy for more conversational purposes, the argument goes, students could make use of their natural conversational skills. Thus, the first thing to note about the results of this case study is that both the freshmen and the philosophers adopted the same goal of putting forward their own position on paternalism. The students' thinking-aloud protocols leave little doubt that they realized that the task involved more than simple reportage on a specialized literature. They knew they had to make decisions about where they stood.

In addition to adopting the same overall goal for the task, both the stu-

	Conversational Practice	Literacy Practice
Turn 1:	Speaker 1 proposes context by speaking	Writer proposes context by writing
Turn 2:		Reader reads
		Reader reflects
		Reader organizes
	Speaker 2 responds	Reader drafts/revises
Turn 3:	Speaker 1 repairs misunderstandings	

Figure 4.1.   A Comparison of the Structure of Activities of Conversational and Literate Practices.

dents and the philosophers employed the same basic structure of activities to complete the task. All began by reading, followed with a period of reflecting, moved to organizing, and then finally to drafting interspersed with revising. As an activities structure, this pattern departs from the standard pattern of oral conversation in several significant respects. As described most clearly by Heritage (1984), participants in an oral conversation use some variant of a three-turn sequence in an oral conversation. As shown in the first column of Figure 4.1, in the first turn, a speaker proposes a given context by using the first part of an adjacency pair such as a greeting, question, or invitation. In the next turn, the second speaker responds with (a) the preferred or expected response, (b) the dispreferred response plus some account for it, or (c) a completely unexpected response. Finally, in an optional third turn, the first speaker may repair any misunderstandings indicated in the second speaker's turn.

Unaccounted for in this oral structure are the periods of reflection and organizing used by all four participants to complete the advanced literacy task in this study. As illustrated in the second column of Figure 4.1, all four participants gave themselves what amounts to a "time out" from the normal oral imperative to make an immediate response to the previous speaker's turn.

Despite the fact that the structure of activities used by the four participants departed in significant ways from that of natural conversation, several analyses did confirm earlier suggestions that insiders use more conversational strategies. In this study, the distinguishing concept was that of authorship. A global analysis of the kinds of knowledge representations being developed by the philosophers and students during their working time showed large differences in their attention to who authored the readings. The students attended to authorship an average of 3.5 times in each 1,000 words of think-aloud protocol while the philosophers attended at least twice as often in the case of Philosopher 1 and almost four times as often in the case of Philosopher 2. This result confirms previously reviewed research (Bazerman, 1985; Haas & Flower, 1988; Lundeberg, 1987) which showed attention to authorship to be a distinguishing trait of insider behavior. Since attention to authorship is a prerequisite for a literacy practice that is conversational, this evidence further supports a conversational model.

An analysis of the texts produced as a result of this differential attention, however, again suggests that this conversation was far from natural. Consistent with the protocol analysis, the final texts written by the philosophers referred to other authors more often than did those of the freshmen (0 and 12 times for the students; 44 and 74 times for the philosophers). These references to authors, however, did not simply reflect the philosophers' unordered conversational responses to the authors they had read. An excerpt from one of the philosopher's texts illustrates:

(52) The prominence of such examples as these in the discussion of the moral status of paternalism suggests to Dworkin (source one above) the following "rough" definition of paternalism (pg. 7):

(53) D1: "Paternalism is the interference with a person's liberty of action justified by reasons referring exclusively to the welfare, good, happiness, needs, interests, or values of the person being coerced."

(54) The definition D1 is faulty in several respects, and is not made any better by Dworkin's admission that it is "rough." (55) First, as it stands, if the definition is right, there can be no unjustified (i.e. wrong) paternalistic action for D1 says paternalism is justified. (56) Doubtless this is part of the "roughness". (57) Perhaps what Dworkin intends is something like the following:

(58) D1': "Paternalism is interference with a person's liberty of action of such a sort that if justified at all it is justified exclusively by its positive bearing on the welfare, good, happiness, needs, interests or values of the person being coerced."

(59) But this will not work, as can be seen from Example 3 above. (60) In the case of the drug laws, potential buyers who can't buy because the product is not on the market are not coerced at all though they are the ones whose benefit is intended.

This excerpt by Philosopher 2 follows what we have come to call the "faulty path/main path" structure used in much academic discourse including philosophy. An author using this structure attempts to convince readers to take his position or "main path" on an issue by characterizing and dismissing previous approaches as "faulty paths." The order in which each approach is discussed is determined by its distance from the author's

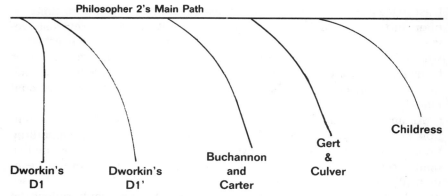

Figure 4.2.   The Main Path / Faulty Path Structure Used by Philosopher 2.

main path. More faulty approaches are characterized and dismissed early; less easy-to-dismiss approaches are discussed later.

In the excerpt above, Philosopher 2 invokes the faulty path/main path structure with Dworkin's extremely faulty approach. Next he rewords Dworkin's definition to produce a more plausible position—"perhaps what Dworkin intends"—but then goes on to critique this position on additional grounds. Following this excerpt, Philosopher 2 characterizes and critiques, in turn, the positions taken by Buchannon and Carter, by Gert and Culver, and finally by Childress with whom he most closely agrees (see Figure 4.2).

This faulty path/main path structure deviates from a standard pattern of conversational response in several ways. First, the order in which the authors are responded to has been manipulated according to a metric of "faultiness" along which Philosopher 2 wants his readers to measure the definitions. He finds Dworkin's definition with which he started the most faulty and Childress' definition with which he ended the most plausible. The others lie somewhere in between. The effect of this manipulation is gradually to move readers from a position at some distance from the "main path" he wants them to take closer to that path until they are finally willing to go along with his own line of argument. Thus, instead of simply responding to the "conversation" of previous texts, he is artfully manipulating it in order to bring readers around to his own point of view.

Second, the authors themselves are not treated as actual human beings with normal conversational rights, but are taken as representatives of more abstract approaches to the issue. This abstraction is demonstrated in Philosopher 2's text in three ways. To begin with, Philosopher 2 actually characterizes Dworkin as responding to examples such as he himself has created ("The prominence of such examples as these . . . suggests to Dworkin"). As a history of the conversation, this presentation is implausible, suggesting as it does that Dworkin is responding to Philosopher 2 rather than the other way around. Second, Philosopher 2 takes the liberty of manipulating Dworkin's definition, feeling free to create a more plausible position than his interlocutor presents if it helps to further his point. The result is, in effect, a conversational turn with a constructed interlocutor. Finally, Philosopher 2 combines the positions taken by two different authors, Buchannon and Carter, into a single approach to highlight a fault which his own position will avoid.

None of these characteristics deviate from the conventions of academic writing, but all indicate the kind of additional "art" required beyond that expected in daily conversation. One additional convention suggested but not directly manifested in the philosophers' behavior also supports this distinction. When Philosopher 2 rewords Dworkin's definition of paternalism, he justifies his action as helping Dworkin to say what he might have meant to say. In doing so, he is exercising a kind of conversational "right of repair." In oral conversation, this right normally belongs to the person who made the original statement—in this case, to Dworkin. While it is not inconceivable that a helpful conversationalist might suggest a repair to keep the conversation going, this seems more likely in written than in oral contexts.

In addition, the right of repair allowed the original "speaker" in written discourse is generally more restricted than that allowed in oral contexts. As Heritage describes it, the first speaker in an oral conversation has almost unlimited right of repair—not just to misunderstandings attributable to the listener, but also to misspeakings that are his or her own fault. Thus, if a first speaker sees that a statement is having unwanted or unanticipated consequences, she or he can attempt a repair to avoid an embarrassing or conflicted situation. When the conversation is written, however, a first speaker/writer loses much of this right of repair. In some kinds of literary criticism, in fact, the author's clarifications of intention are considered irrelevant to proper interpretation.

In summary, the practices of these philosophers can be characterized in some respects as both "conversational" and "artful." They are conversational in so far as the philosophers are responsive to the authors of previous texts. They are artful insofar as these authors are characterized as representatives of abstract approaches to an issue, characterizations that are constructed solely for the purpose of providing a contrast with the philosophers' own positions. The student practices, showing much less attention to authorships, exhibit neither these conversational nor artful characteristics.

"ARTFUL CONVERSATION": A MODEL OF ADVANCED LITERACY

Why then do both these writers borrow some conventions from an everyday practice like conversation while, at the same time, deviating from these conventions in significant ways? An answer to this question has been systematically pursued in research by cognitive scientists studying the nature of expertise in complex knowledge-rich domains. In domains like chess (Chase & Simon, 1973), physics (Larkin, McDermott, Simon, & Simon, 1981), radiology (Lesgold, Feltovich, Glaser, & Wang, 1981), and the social sciences (Voss, Greene, Post, & Penner, 1983), experts appear to conceive of the entities with which they work in a highly abstract way whereas novices work with representations at the literal or everyday level (see Glaser, 1984, for a review). In dealing with a problem in social sciences, for example, experts consider the impact of abstractions like bureaucracy and infrastructure whereas novices work with more concrete entities like fertilizer and tractors (Voss, Greene, Post, & Penner, 1983).

Applied to the phenomenon of advanced literacy practices, this characterization of expertise suggests that students who learn more sophisticated literacy practices may have more abstract and artful representations of written conversations. Even though the entities involved—authors, audience, discussion—appear to have real-world referents and perfectly literal meanings, a more careful description such as that given here suggests they cannot be mapped directly onto particular people and particular chronologies. Thus, an author is not simply an interlocutor; an audience does not simply have characteristics that can be determined by a readership survey; a discussion does not have a chronology that can be unambiguously determined by reference to the records. In each case, participants in advanced literacy craft abstract representations of these entities, probably in the reflective time out that seems to distinguish the activities structure of oral and written practice.

How is the development of such abstractions accomplished? While few studies of the development of advanced literacy have been done, longitudinal studies of knowledge restructuring in other domains have been conducted. In particular, educational researchers have begun to investigate the process by which the transformation of knowledge from literal to abstract entities takes place in science and mathematics. In a recent review, Vosniadou and Brewer (1987) characterize this transformation as a "radical restructuring" in which students are confronted with the facts for which their naive view cannot account and, as a consequence, replace their model with a more expert representation.

This model of radical restructuring would have several advantages when applied to the development of advanced literacy. First, it would allow us to attribute the similarities between advanced literacy practices and natural conversation to the fact that one is the transformation of the other. Second, it would allow us to explain the differences between them as the effects of the restructuring. Thus, the explanation would be that expertise in advanced literacy, like many other types of expertise, involves the replacement of a more literal everyday representation of conversation with a more sophisticated and abstract representation of artful conversation.

Such an extension of the current theory of expertise will, unfortunately, be insufficient to describe advanced literacy practices. A functional model of literacy expertise must, I believe, allow the writer to live both in the intertextual abstract world of advanced literacy and in the literal, everyday, interpersonal world. That is, writers must see other authors not only as constructs that they can create and manipulate on the page, but also as people whom they may meet professionally or socially, with whom they may eventually coauthor or argue. The everyday, literal world where affairs may more often be conducted through the oral medium must be integrated with the more abstract world of published interchange, not replaced by it. Thus functioning in advanced literacy cannot mean simply giving up an everyday conversational model for a more decontextualized model, but finding ways to sustain the transition between the two, maintaining facility to operate in both.

What I am suggesting is a multiple representation hypothesis. That is, instead of describing expertise as the replacement of one representation with another, we can describe it as the ability to maintain more than one. A variation of this hypothesis was first put forward by Bereiter and Scardamalia (1987) who suggested that writers have to work in two "problem spaces"—a rhetorical problem space and a content problem space. In the rhetorical problem space, according to these authors, a writer works out answers to the question, "What do I say?" In the content problem space, he or she works out answers to "What do I mean?" Reflection in writing is fostered, then, by an intimate interaction between these two spaces.

While Bereiter and Scardamalia do not explicitly deal within the interaction of literal and abstract entities, they do suggest that advanced literacy may be one of the most complicated types of expertise yet studied. A study by Dyson (1988) bears this out. Using participant-observation with a set of children over a two-year period beginning with kindergarten, Dyson found that the acquisition of writing skills involved,

> not simply learning to create a unified text world but to move among multiple worlds, carrying out multiple roles and coordinating multiple space/time structures. That is, to grow as writers of imaginary worlds—and, by inference, other sorts of text worlds as well—children must differentiate, and

work to resolve the tensions among, the varied symbolic and social worlds within which they write, worlds with differing dimensions of time and space.

Dyson further argues that these multiple worlds, while operating along distinct space/time dimensions, must nevertheless be "permeable" or linked to each other.

Dyson's description of the multiple worlds of the writer was developed to show the intersections between children's fictional narratives and their lives at home and in the classroom. As her review of the literature suggests, narrative theory has long recognized that storytellers negotiate transitions between the here-and-now and the then-and-done both for themselves and their readers. The evidence reviewed above suggests, however, that this multiple representation hypothesis can be extended from narrative discourse to discourse that is highly argumentative and perhaps to all types of advanced literacy practices.

IMPLICATIONS FOR TEACHING

Many have argued that the educational system and even Western civilization needs to seriously reconsider the model of decontextualized literacy promoted for several centuries. Recommendations from these reformers tend to emphasize the child as a natural writer and the students' authority over the text. While concurring with these recommendations, I believe that as they become more commonly implemented they will be found to be an inadequate preparation for advanced literacy. In my own experience, simply inviting students to treat themselves and other authors as conversational partners leads to several kinds of systematic mistakes on their part.

First, students often assume they may use the same interpersonal grounds for rejecting other authors' positions as they use for disagreeing in oral conversation. Ad hominum attacks, however, are not considered acceptable in much of written argument. Second, students often expect to have a more global right of repair than the community allows. Thus, when readers misunderstand their intentions, they may expect to be able to simply restate their meaning rather than revise the original text. Finally, students may be unable to treat other author's positions hypothetically. Unless they feel free to "play with" the positions they have discovered in the literature, they will be unable to move beyond what other authors have said to construct an original position of their own.

On the other hand, educating students to a decontextualized practice, as is more common now, leads to systematic errors as well. Students see little connection between texts and their personal experience. They read for information without considering authorial intention. And their reading is uncritical, allowing them only to accept or reject other authors' positions. Most insidiously, they see little reason to participate in-authoring texts themselves.

A more adequate approach to advanced literacy practices may require our students to operate, like Alice-through-the-Looking-Glass, in two adjacent worlds. At every point in her journey, Alice can make local meaning and coherence of her circumstances, whether she be standing in her normal world, walking through the mirror, or wandering in the topsy-turvy world on the other side. But taken together these worlds do not add up to a coherent whole and she does not try to make them do so. By forcing our students into the mold of either natural conversation or decontextualized art, however, we may be falling into the trap that Alice avoids.

A more fruitful avenue, one I have tried to suggest with the concept of artful conversation, would be to examine reading and writing as practices that, like the looking glass, give us ways to go between the everyday world and the world of texts without ever finally resolving the difference between them. Students must realize that texts are the results of the experiences, struggles, values, and intentions of human beings like themselves. This understanding will empower them to draw on their everyday experiences and assume the authority to interpret and to author. At the same time, they must understand that once they enter into the world of texts, their conversation will run according to conventions different from everyday interchanges. They must, therefore, make an effort to learn the ways of conversing in these intertextual worlds. Asking our students to build these multiple representations will enable them negotiate the duality of context inherent in reading and writing and give them a way to link their experience in the here-and-now with the domain of timeless truths they find in books.

REFERENCES

Applebee, A. N. (Ed.). (1984). *Contexts for learning to write: Studies of secondary school instruction*. Norwood, NJ: Ablex.

Bartholomae, D. (1985). Inventing the university. In M. Rose (Ed.), *When a writer can't write: Studies in writer's block and other composing process problems* (pp. 134–165). New York: Guilford Press.

Bazerman, C. (1985). Physicists reading physics: Schema-laden purposes and purpose-laden schema. *Written Communication, 2,* 3–23.

Bereiter, C., & Scardamalia, M. (1982). From conversation to composition: The role of instruction in a developmental processes. In R. Glaser (Ed.), *Advances in instructional psychology, Vol. 2* (pp. 1–64). Hillsdale, NJ: Erlbaum.

Bereiter, C., & Scardamalia, M. (1987). Fostering reflective processes. In *The psychology of written composition* (pp. 299–317). Hillsdale, NJ: Erlbaum.

Bizzell, P. (1982). College composition: Initiation into the academic discourse community. *Curriculum Inquiry, 12,* 191–207.

Britton, J., Burgess, T., Martin, N., McLeod, A., & Rosen, H. (1975). *The development of writing abilities (11–18).* Schools Research Council Studies. London: Macmillan Education.

Bruffee, K. A. (1984). Collaborative learning and the "conversation of mankind." *College English, 46,* 635–652.

Cazden, C. B. (in press). The myth of the autonomous text. To appear in D. M. Topping (Ed.), *Third International Conference on Thinking.* Hillsdale, NJ: Erlbaum.

Chase, W. G., & Simon, H. A. (1973). Perception in chess. *Cognitive Psychology, 4,* 55–81.

Cook-Gumperz, J. (1986). Literacy and schooling: An unchanging equation? In J. Cook-Gumperz (Ed.), *The social construction of literacy* (pp. 16–44). Cambridge: Cambridge University Press.

Dyson, A. H. (1988). Negotiating multiple worlds: The space/time dimensions of young children's composing. *Research in the Teaching of English, 22,* 355–390.

Foucault, M. (1977). What is an author? In M. Foucault (Ed.), *Language, countermemory and practice.* Ithaca: Cornell University Press.

Geisler, C. (in press). Toward a sociocognitive model of literacy: Constructing mental models in a philosophical conversation. To appear in C. Bazerman & J. Paradis (Eds.), *Textual dynamics of the professions.* Madison, WI: University of Wisconsin Press.

Gilbert, G. N., & Mulkay, M. (1984). *Opening Pandora's box: A sociological analysis of scientific discourse.* Cambridge: Cambridge University Press.

Glaser, R. (1984). Education and thinking: The role of knowledge. *American Psychologist, 39,* 93–104.

Goody, J., & Watt, I. (1963). The consequences of literacy. *Comparative Studies in Society and History, 5,* 304–326, 332–345.

Graves, D., & Hansen, J. (1983). The author's chair. *Language Arts, 60,* 176–183.

Haas, C., & Flower, L. (1988). Rhetorical reading strategies and the construction of meaning. *College Composition and Communication, 39,* 167–183.

Heritage, J. (1984). *Garfinkel and ethnomethodology.* Cambridge: Polity Press.

Heath, S. B., & Branscombe, A. (1985). "Intelligent writing" in an audience community: Teacher, students, and researcher. In S. W. Freedman (Ed.), *The acquisition of written language: Response and revision* (pp. 3–32). Norwood, NJ: Ablex.

Kaufer, D., Geisler, C., & Neuwirth, C. (1989). *Arguing from sources: Exploring issues through reading and writing.* San Diego: Harcourt Brace Jovanovich.

Knoblauch, C. H., & Brannon, L. (1984). *Rhetorical traditions and the teaching of writing.* Upper Montclair, NJ: Boynton/Cook.

Larkin, J. A., McDermott, J., Simon, D. P., & Simon, H. A. (1981). Models of competence. *Cognitive Science, 4,* 317–345.

Latour, B., & Woolgar, S. (1979). *Laboratory life: The social construction of scientific facts.* London: Sage.

LeFevre, K. B. (1987). *Invention as a social act.* Carbondale: Southern Illinois University Press.

Lesgold, A. M., Feltovich, P. J., Glaser, R., & Wang, Y. (1981). *The acquisition of perceptual diagnostic skill in radiology* (Tech. Rep. No. PDS-1). Pittsburgh, PA: University of Pittsburgh, Learning Research & Development Center.

Lundeberg, M. A. (1987). Metacognitive aspects of reading comprehension: Studying understanding in legal case analysis. *Reading Research Quarterly, 22,* 407–432.

Luria, A. R. (1976). *Cognitive development: Its cultural and social foundations.* Cambridge, MA: Harvard University Press.

McCloskey, D. N. (1985). *The rhetoric of economics.* Madison, WI: The University of Wisconsin Press.

Myers, G. (1985). The social construction of two biologists' proposals. *Written Communication, 2,* 219–245.

Olson, D. R. (1977). From utterance to text: The bias of language in speech and writing. *Harvard Educational Review, 47,* 257–281.

Olson, D. R., & Torrance, N. (1981). Learning to meet the requirements of written text: Language development in the school years. In C. H. Frederiksen & J. F. Dominic (Eds.), *Writing: The nature, development, and teaching of written communication* (pp. 235–255). Hillsdale, NJ: Erlbaum.

Ong, W. (1975). The writer's audience is always a fiction. *PMLA, 90,* 9–21.

Pearson, D. R., & Tierney, R. J. (1984). On becoming a thoughtful reader: Learning to read like a writer. In A. C. Purves & O. Niles (Eds.), *Becoming readers in a complex society* (pp. 144–173). Chicago: University of Chicago Press.

Schafer, J. (1981). The linguistic analysis of spoken and written texts. In B. Kroll & R. Vann (Eds.), *Exploring speaking-writing connections and contrasts* (pp. 1–31). Urbana, IL: National Council of Teachers of English.

Scollon, R., & Scollon, S. B. K. (1981). *Narrative, literacy and face in interethnic communication.* Norwood, NJ: Ablex.

Scribner, S., & Cole, M. (1981). *The psychology of literacy.* Cambridge, MA: Harvard University Press.

Smith, F. (1985). A metaphor for literacy: Creating worlds or shunting information? In D. Olson, N. Torrance, & A. Hildyard (Eds.), *Literacy, language, and learning: The nature and consequences of reading and writing* (pp. 195–216). Cambridge: Cambridge University Press.

Vosniadou, S., & Brewer, W. (1987). Theories of knowledge restructuring in development. *Review of Educational Research, 57,* 51–67.

Voss, J. F., Greene, T. R., Post, T. A., & Penner, B. C. (1983). Problem solving skill in the social sciences. In G. H. Bower (Ed.), *The psychology of learning and motivation: Advances in research and theory* (Vol. 17, pp. 165–213). New York: Academic Press.

Vygotsky, L. S. (1962). *Thought and language.* Cambridge, MA: MIT Press.

Wells, G. (1986). *The meaning makers: Children learning language and using language to learn.* Portsmouth, NH: Heinemann.

5
Making Sense of Reading*

Douglas Vipond
Russell A. Hunt
James Jewett
James A. Reither

Reading researchers and literary theorists alike tend to assume that they know how the general reader will respond to a particular text, but humans are a contrary lot. We were forcefully reminded of this in a recent investigation, when we asked people to read John McPhee's "In Virgin Forest" (1987). Here is a sample of the responses when the interviewer, Jim, asked the readers what they made of the piece (the readers' names are fictitious):

Julie: Oh, I don't know, it was boring.
Jim: Boring?
Julie: Yeah, basically.

Jim: What did you make of "In Virgin Forest"?
Carole: I'm not going to say it was interesting, but it's nice that there is a place like that.

Jim: What did you make of "In Virgin Forest"?
Rita: What *can* you make of it?
Jim: I don't know. Did you want it to go on?
Rita: No. No. I wanted it to end. It was confusing.

Carl: I liked it. It was informative. It's interesting because you catch a touch of—well, [it] presents an image of an untouched virgin forest in the middle of a very developed region. That's kind of an interesting contradiction in some sense.

Jim: What did you make of "In Virgin Forest"?
Don: I loved it.

---

*This work was supported by grant 410-87-0647 from the Social Sciences and Humanities Research Council of Canada. We thank the 15 readers who participated in the study, and Sharon Ayer and Joyce Belliveau, who transcribed the tapes.

110

How can we account for the range of response to "In Virgin Forest" or, for that matter, to any text? What does the diversity of response imply about "reading"? One might dismiss the question by saying that the different responses are simply due to differences among readers—we all know that people differ—and drop the matter there. The problem with such an approach, of course, is that it leaves texts themselves out of consideration. Differences among texts (which are about as large as differences among people) must play some role in the diversity of response. If readers did no more than "read themselves," we would have no way of accounting for the fact that the same person responds differently to different texts.

The prevailing view, therefore—it has become almost a truism, both in reading research and in literary theory—is that reading must be understood as an *interaction* between reader and text. That view is an improvement on reader-based or text-based accounts, but even it is too simple. The interactive approach ignores or underestimates the degree to which a person can respond to the same text differently on different occasions, in different situations. Louise Rosenblatt (1985) therefore insists that the most appropriate way to understand the reading event is not as interaction but as *trans*action, "a unique coming-together of a particular personality and a particular text *at a particular time and place under particular circumstances*" (p. 104, emphasis added). For example, it makes a difference whether you are reading a short story for enjoyment, in the comfort of your own living room, or if you're reading it in a classroom or laboratory, expecting to be tested on its details.

Readers, texts, and situations—in ways that seem to be so fluid and dynamic as to defy explanation—somehow mesh, and result in the activities we call "reading" and "responding." Is it possible to make sense out of all this? Can a "transactional" approach help us account for the diversity of response to texts? And, perhaps most important, what are the implications of such a view of reading for educators who are concerned to help people grow and develop as readers?

We don't pretend to have definitive answers to these difficult questions. Over the past several years, though, we have developed a conceptual approach to reading that may at least allow them to be asked within a specific framework (Hunt & Vipond, 1985, 1986, 1987; Vipond & Hunt, 1984, 1987, 1989). In brief, we claim that there are identifiable types or "modes" of reading and response, and that which mode is dominant depends on the complex transaction between reader and text, shaped by the situation in which the reading occurs. In this chapter we outline the model and then use it to account for responses—such as those of Julie, Carole, and so on, above—obtained in a recent investigation of reading and response. Finally, we discuss some educational implications of this work.

Modes of Reading

We claim that reading is not a unitary activity. Instead, there are different types, stances, or "modes." For any given reading event one of three modes will be dominant: information-driven, story-driven, or point-driven. *Information-driven* reading dominates when the reader's central goal is to learn from the text, to acquire information from it. We read in an information-driven mode when we are, for example, studying for an exam, following a recipe, checking a fact in a dictionary or encyclopedia, or reading the label on a medicine bottle. The second mode, *story-driven* reading, dominates when the reader is concerned with the "lived-through experience" of the reading. Story-driven reading operates as though the text were a plain glass window on a storyworld; readers try to immerse themselves in a world of events, characters, and settings. We expect to read in a story-driven way when we read for enjoyment, when we go to the bookstore looking for a "good read," a "page-turner."

In a rough-and-ready way, information- and story-driven modes of reading correspond to Rosenblatt's (1938/1976, 1978) classic distinction between the "efferent" stance (which is concerned with carrying information away from reading) and the "aesthetic" stance (concerned with lived-through experience). We differ from Rosenblatt, however, because we posit a third mode, one which we believe is especially appropriate for texts often deemed "literary." We call this *point-driven* reading (Vipond & Hunt, 1984) or, equivalently, *dialogic* reading (see below). That is, we divide Rosenblatt's aesthetic stance into two modes: story-driven and point-driven.

The term *point* comes from sociolinguistic analyses of conversational storytelling. William Labov (1972) and Livia Polanyi (1979, 1985) have shown that participants in a conversation expect narrators to be "getting at" something. Listeners expect a story to be point-ed, to have some purpose that makes it tellable in the situational or thematic context. Labov and Polanyi have also shown that points are constructed on the basis of what they call the evaluation structure of text. Anything that is incongruous with respect to social, cultural, or textual norms is potentially evaluative; incongruities (figures of speech, for example) serve as *invitations* to share the narrator's beliefs, ideas, attitudes, perceptions, or values (Hunt & Vipond, 1986). Points, therefore, are not "in" the story but have to be constructed on the basis of evaluations that are recognized and accepted. In some cases they are literally "negotiated" by listener and narrator (Polanyi, 1979). If follows that there is no such thing as *the* point.

By analogy, point-driven reading entails the effort to understand the text as a purposeful act of communication. This is not to say point-driven reading is a more advanced type developmentally; nor is it to say that what the author intended is what the text "really" means (to say that would be to adopt the intentional fallacy; Wimsatt & Beardsley, 1949). Rather, readers in point-driven mode are trying to construct for themselves plausible meanings, a process invoked and shaped by their expectation that the author has created the text out of what Linda Flower (1988) calls a "web of purpose." Thus, as Flower notes in connection with a related concept, the rhetorical reading strategy, "readers use their inferences about the author's plans, goals, and context to help construct a meaningful text" (p. 540). It may be worth underlining that point-driven reading does not entail the intentional fallacy: Readers may impute intentionality to the text and have a sense of authorial purpose without knowing anything at all, even the name, of the actual historical author.

Particularly important for point-driven reading is that when readers see incongruities as *intentional* (i.e., they see them as potential evaluations rather than as inexplicable anomalies), they may consider themselves invited to construct and reconstruct possible points.

It is crucial to keep in mind in this context that "point" should not be reductively equated with "gist," "theme," "message," or "moral." In the sociolinguistic literature, and as we are using it here, point is what renders a specific story tellable by a particular narrator to a particular audience in a particular situation. As Labov has noted, when stories lack point it is obvious: The listener responds "So what?" Dialogue is interrupted. Using the analogy of Anne Freadman (1987), a story is like a shot in a tennis match—it acquires its meaning, its point, from its position and role in the game between the players. To catch the tennis ball and throw it back, to tell a pointless story, ends the game, abrogates the dialogue.

Thus, an alternative and in some ways more useful term than point-driven reading is "dialogic" reading. The term *dialogic* emphasizes that in this type of transaction, readers imagine themselves to be in conversation with authors and texts. Meaning-making is a collaborative process (Phelps, 1985)—a dialogue—between authors and readers, even though, again, there is no requirement that what the actual, historical author intended and what the reader constructs must be congruent. The term *dialogic* is helpful, then, because it foregrounds the analogy between reading and conversational story listening.

The collaborative/communicative features we have attributed to point-driven or dialogic reading are true to some degree of *all* reading. To read—to understand language at all—is to use a symbol system that one shares with other people and whose very origin lies in social interaction (Vygotsky, 1934/1986). Furthermore, any type of reading would probably be impossible if one did not make the fundamental assumption that the text was the product of an intentional being. Even so, we believe it is still useful to make a distinction between reading events in which the text is treated primarily as an opportunity to "make contact" with an intentional author (as in dialogic reading), and events in which readers' attention is focused elsewhere—on what they can learn from the text (information-driven reading) or on their experiential immersion in a storyworld (story-driven reading).

The Reader, the Text, the Situation

Which of the three modes will predominate in any given reading event depends on the configuration of reader, text, and situation. A reading event is a transaction between reader and text, conditioned by the physical, social, and cultural situation in which it occurs. *Readers* differ in personality, intelligence, and motivation; they bring characteristic preferences, styles, needs, and histories of success and failure with different modes to the transaction. *Texts* differ because they invite, reward, repay, or—in James J. Gibson's (1979) useful term—"afford" being read in certain modes, but constrain or "block" being read in other ways. One text (a romance, for example) might afford story-driven reading, a second (a traditional novel) might afford both story-driven and dialogic reading, whereas a third (a medicine bottle label) might afford information-driven reading. Other combinations, of course, are possible: The point is that although it may be *possible* to read any text in any way—one can read *Hamlet* for information regarding Elizabethan assumptions about Denmark, or a telephone book as an expression of the purposes and character of the phone company—certain modes tend to work better (and, by convention, tend to be used) with certain texts.

We use the term *situation* to represent task demands, the physical and social setting, and the historical, cultural, and ideological contexts that shape reading events in silent but profound ways (Eagleton, 1983). Like texts, situations can be seen as affording certain modes and constraining others. Task demands, for example, promote different types of reading and response (see Chapter 7): Readers who expect to be asked "What happens in this story?" are likely to engage in story-driven reading, whereas readers who expect to be tested on details are likely to read in an information-driven way.

Sociocultural context can also influence reading mode. Consider two different groups of people, students and faculty members, who participate in the same research project. The students, participating in the social role of "subjects," may be more likely for that reason to read in an information-driven way, whereas faculty members, participating as "collaborators," may be more likely to read dialogically (see Danziger, 1985; and Wood &

Kroger, 1985, for more on the distinction between subjects and collaborators).

Now we can begin to see why it is so difficult to account for a given reader's response to a certain text in a particular situation. Even if one makes the simplifying assumption, as we do, that mode of response directly reflects mode of reading, it is difficult to know which mode of reading will predominate on any given occasion: It depends on the interplay between what the text affords and what the reader is prepared and motivated to do, a transaction shaped by task demands and other aspects of the situational matrix in which the reading is embedded.

Another problem is that even though the modes are distinct conceptually, in practice it is difficult to identify a single reading as belonging to a specific mode. One reason for the difficulty is that a reader may engage in different modes during reading. For example, someone who begins reading a work of literary fiction in story-driven mode may, perhaps because of accumulating incongruities (evaluations), shift to a more dialogic stance. A second reason for difficulty is that, in practice, the modes seldom exist in pure form. More likely, they overlap, each instance of reading incorporating some elements of all three. It is highly unlikely that a reading that was primarily story-driven, for example, could avoid entirely some attempt to construct authorial purpose; at the same time, there would almost certainly be some attempt to learn or remember specific textual information. And who can read *Othello*, no matter how "dialogically," without wanting to know what happens next? It is a question of precedence.

Previous Experiments on Reading and Response

Support for this model comes from a number of experiments we have conducted. In one (Hunt & Vipond, 1985, Experiment 3), 70 first-year undergraduates read three short stories. After every page of reading the students received one of three tasks: a plot task (designed to encourage story-driven reading), a detail task (to encourage information-driven reading), or a frame task (to encourage dialogic reading). Reading speeds, which were presumed to reflect the influence of mode, differed as a function of task, with the detail task resulting in the slowest reading times overall and the plot task the fastest. The most interesting result, however, concerned the frame task. Unlike the students who were reading for plot or for details, the students reading for "point" tended to slow down over the last few pages of each story. We suspect that this slowing occurred because they were trying to construct a meaning for the text that was consistent with a framing letter they had seen just before reading, a task that became more urgent as the end of the story drew closer.

In another experiment (Vipond & Hunt, 1989), people read "The Day We Got Our Own Back," a literary short story by Maeve Brennan. This experiment was designed as a $2 \times 2 \times 2$ factorial, in which text (evaluated vs. nonevaluated versions of the story), task (plot vs. frame task), and modality (silent vs. oral reading) were manipulated. Ninety-six first-year undergraduates and, for comparison purposes, twelve faculty members, took part. During and after their reading of "The Day We Got Our Own Back," the participants were given a variety of tasks, all of which were quantified and subjected to statistical tests. Results indicated, among other things, that readers were sensitive to the evaluative structure of the story; that the faculty members tended to be more "dialogic" than the undergraduates; and that, among undergraduates, the frame task was associated with more dialogic responses than the plot task.

In broad outline, these two experiments support the three modes/reader-text-situation model outlined above. First, they suggest that task demands can drive readers to use specific modes, as indicated by in-process and post-reading measures. Second, they suggest that the different modes tend to be used differentially by different groups of readers. Third, they suggest that variations in the evaluation structure of text affect some aspects of reading and response.

Useful as they are in establishing the plausibility of the model, however, experiments such as these do not (nor are they intended to) allow us to understand the complexities of the reading-response process. The controlled, experimental approach of these studies gives us the broad outlines; what is required now is a more descriptive, qualitative approach to fill in some of the details. That is the purpose of the present study.

A different way of saying this is to say that in the present investigation we are willing to trade "control" for "regularity" (Rubin, 1989). The data of this study consist of what readers say; our purpose is to identify and account for regularities in these verbal responses. More specifically, we will try to classify the protocols (or parts of them) as predominantly information-driven, story-driven, or dialogic, giving examples of each. Next, we will attempt to make sense of the different types of response by considering how modes of reading are either afforded or constrained by different configurations of reader-text-situation.

METHOD

Readers

Readers were recruited from St. Thomas University, a small, liberal arts, undergraduate institution. Because we wanted to study a broad range of readers we selected five people from each of three groups: (a) first-year university students; (b) fourth-year university students; and (c) faculty members. The first-year students, who were approximately 18 years old, were fulfilling a participation requirement for their introductory psychology course. The first five students to sign up (Carole, Joan, Karen, Larry, Martha) were included in the study; that is, we had no control over who participated from this group. That was not the case for the other two groups, however. We invited five fourth-year students whom we considered to be "good" students. Three were honors students in psychology (Becky, Julie, Rita), one was an honors student in English (Eric), and the other was majoring in history (Kevin). The fourth-year students were each approximately 21 years old with the exception of Eric, a 32-year-old. Similarly, we invited five faculty members whom we thought would be interested, and willing to participate, in a lengthy study. With one exception (Don), the faculty members could be considered "junior," having less than four years' teaching experience. They were in their early- to mid-30s. It is worth noting that the faculty participants were members of various university departments: social sciences (Ben), humanities (Will), education (Don), and social work (Carl, Ellen).

Members of the English department were specifically excluded, however, because we found in earlier work (Vipond & Hunt, 1989) that the detached, analytic kind of reading often practiced by "professional" readers, although clearly of interest, poses a set of problems different from the ones we wished to study here. (But see below, p. 129.)

In summary, the 15 readers in this study represent about as wide a range of interests and abilities as was possible within this university community.

Texts

The participants read and talked about four texts. We chose texts that represented a range of difficulty, genre, and authorial visibility. All, for practical reasons, were fairly short. All, in our view, afforded "literary" reading, although not all were fictional. Two of the texts ("Metaphors" and "The Sun on Mount Royal") were very short "postcard" stories by the New Brunswick author Kent Thompson, published in the collection *Leaping Up Sliding Away* (1986). Despite their brevity (one page or less), postcard stories are readily identifiable as conventional short stories, featuring plots, settings, and characters.

"In Virgin Forest," published anonymously in "The Talk of the Town" section of *The New Yorker* (July 6, 1987), was written by John McPhee (personal communication, February 1988). "In Virgin Forest" is an evocative description of the Hutcheson Memorial Forest near New Brunswick, New Jersey, written in McPhee's "aesthetic nonfictional prose" style (Schuster, 1985).

"Some Approaches to the Problem of the Shortage of Time" (henceforth, "Time"), by Ursula K. Le Guin, could be described as a satirical postmodern fiction; it was published in the collection *The Compass Rose* (1982). Although fictional, "Time" is anything but a conventional story. Le Guin delivers a pseudoscientific, parodic treatise on how the problem of the shortage of time might be solved; she presents cosmological, chemical, and political solutions. Although we did not try to ascertain the "reading level" of the texts, intuitively it seems that the two Thompson stories would be fairly accessible for most readers, the McPhee piece difficult, and the Le Guin text very difficult.

The study proper was preceded by a discussion of two fragmentary warmup texts. The first was a paragraph from the St. Thomas University calendar. The second was a paragraph from Maeve Brennan's short story, "The Day We Got Our Own Back."

Procedure

Each reader was interviewed by one of the authors (JJ) for two sessions, each lasting up to two hours, and separated by an interval ranging from two to seven days. The sessions were semistructured interviews: While the interviewer had a list of questions and topics, he also tried to create a "client-centered" atmosphere, following up interesting leads and allowing the reader to establish closure. In short, topics were explored exhaustively. Considerable effort was made to ensure that readers were comfortable, and in general they reported that they experienced little tension or constraint.

To establish rapport, and to learn something about the reader's background, the first session began with a leisurely discussion of the reader's like and dislikes. The readers were asked to name specific titles and authors they enjoyed or had read recently. The two warmup texts were then read and discussed, followed by the four texts described above. The order of texts was varied unsystematically across readers, except that the two Thompson stories, being in the same book, were always read consecutively. The instructions emphasized that the participants should try to read as "normally" as possible, take as much time as desired, and that no tests of memory would be given.

What happened next is unusual in reading research: In an attempt to change the way readers saw the texts as "framed" (Reid, 1988)—and thus to make the situation one that less strongly invited information-driven reading—the readers were handed an actual published copy of the text they were to read. For "In Virgin Forest," they were handed a July 6, 1987 copy of *The New Yorker*. For the two Thompson pieces, they were handed *Leaping Up Sliding Away*. For the Le Guin story, they were handed *The Compass Rose*. While the reader was reading, the interviewer busied himself with other work in a far corner of the room.

Immediately following reading the readers were asked what they made of the piece, which usually turned into a freewheeling discussion of what they liked and disliked about it. This was followed by a "discourse-based interview" (see below), and then a discussion of "probes" about each text (see below). After all four texts had been discussed in this manner, there was a final wrapup in which the readers were invited to reconsider each text in turn, making any final comments they wished.

Discourse-based interview. Lee Odell and Dixie Goswami (1982; Odell, Goswami, & Herrington, 1983) devised the discourse-based interview as a means of studying the tacit knowledge of writers in nonacademic settings. For example, the writer of a letter was shown his original expression, "Dear Ron," along with one or more alternatives prepared by the researchers: for example, "Dear Mr. Bunch." The writer was asked whether he would be willing to substitute the alternative for the original, and if not, why not. Often, in discussing reasons for their preference, writers reveal a knowledge of purpose and context that might otherwise go unnoticed (Paré, 1988).

For the present study we adapted the discourse-based interview in order to study the tacit knowledge of *readers*. For each text, we prepared several sets of alternatives or "branches." The first branch was the original sentence, exactly as it appeared in the text. The other two branches were either paraphrases of the original or semantically-altered versions (see p. 125 for an example).

The reader was shown these branches only after reading the entire text and discussing the "what do you make of it?" question. To get the reader talking about the different branches, the interviewer would say something like this: "Suppose alternative B were in the text instead of A. Would that make a difference to your reading?" (Note that the reader was *not* asked, Which one is best? Pilot work indicated that that question tends to stifle discussion.) If the reader agreed it would make a difference, the interviewer then asked, "What sort of difference would it make?" Readers who thought it would not make a difference were asked if they saw any difference at all between the branches. After discussion (often extensive), the procedure was repeated for alternative C.

The reason for using this task is that we wanted to see whether readers have a tacit concept of "authorial purpose." (We have found that it is something that many of them do not mention spontaneously.) Because the task focuses attention on the differences between the original sentence and our alternatives, it invites—although it does not require—the reader to consider and to comment on authorial or textual purpose. This task, in other words, helps create a situation in which dialogic responses are afforded.

Two sets of branches were prepared for each of the Thompson stories, four for "In Virgin Forest," and three for "Time." To help the participants get used to the procedure, the warmup texts each had one set of branches.

Probes. Following the discourse-based interview, the readers were asked whether they agreed or disagreed with a number of statements about the text that "other people" had allegedly made. Most of the probes had a rather critical, negative tone. For instance, one probe for "In Virgin Forest" was, "There are too many facts, all mixed up, which makes it very hard to remember things." In the present study, as in previous research, we found that such statements elicit a range of response from "strongly agree" to "strongly disagree." More to the point—and as we will see in the next section—probes are effective in stimulating discussion concerning the readers' own responses, the text, the writer's purposes and abilities, and so on. In this discussion readers often reveal frustration or even hostility towards a text, which would be unacceptable in more traditional "English class" modes of response. Possibly readers are willing to reveal these feelings because the probe format lessens their responsibility: They are merely agreeing with what someone else has already said.

In any case, the probes must be understood as tasks that afford (but do not determine) different modes of response. For example, "There are too many facts, all mixed up, which makes it very hard to remember things," invites an information-driven response, whereas "The story doesn't feel complete—you want to know what happens next" (said about a postcard story), affords a story-driven response.

To summarize: Fifteen readers (five each of first-year students, fourth-year students, and faculty members) read and discussed four texts presented in their original formats—two very short stories, a *New Yorker* article, and a satirical postmodern fiction. Each reader participated in up to four hours of reading and talking. The sessions were tape-recorded and later transcribed in their entirety, yielding 40–50 pages of transcript for each reader.

Now, how to make sense of all this talk?

FINDINGS AND ACCOUNTINGS

In this section we present excerpts from the transcripts to illustrate different modes of reading and response. For each text, we will try to make sense of "all this talk" by considering differences in the reader-text-situation configuration.

"Metaphors" and "The Sun on Mount Royal"

The two fictional postcard stories by Kent Thompson strongly afford story-driven reading. Organized as narratives, they allow readers to immerse themselves in an accessible and familiar (to our readers) story-world of settings, characters, and events. They also afford dialogic reading, however, because a reader who asked, "What is this about? What is Thompson getting at here?" would be able to construct a satisfactory response. In particular, the title of "Metaphors," and the unresolved plot structure of "The Sun on Mount Royal," invite consideration of authorial purpose. The stories do not invite information-driven reading (although of course they could be so read under appropriate circumstances).

Probably because they can be read just for the story line, these two texts evoked many clearly story-driven responses. For example, immediately after reading "Metaphors," Carole gives a plot summary—a classic story-driven response.

Jim: What did you make of that piece?

Carole: That there is a problem in the family and that Gary, the father, was not being fair to his son and his wife could not accept that and she wanted things to change. He said that he would try and then practically turned it around and said that he couldn't in a matter of seconds, and she decided she was going to do something about it and leave for a short period of time.

In general, people reading in story-driven mode expect the plot to be resolved and therefore they tend to be disappointed with "modern" unresolved stories such as "The Sun on Mount Royal." (Thompson actually alludes to this convention when he ends the story with a question: "Was this to be the end of her story?") Here Rita is agreeing with the statement, "The story doesn't feel complete—you want to know that happens next":

Rita: It's like she doesn't want to love somebody right away after her marriage is broken up so you're sort of wondering, Is she going to or is she not?—just going to walk on by—so you don't feel it's complete. Like I said, you do want to know what happens next—what's going to happen. Will she marry this guy or will he move in or—? Anything's possible, so I would strongly agree with that one.

Carole's objection, also reflecting a story-driven response, has to do with incompleteness of character rather than plot. This is in response to the probe, "You certainly do come to understand a lot about this woman in five paragraphs, don't you?"

Carole: I don't know if it's a lot. (...) I consider to be a lot knowing exactly what the problem was with her marriage and why it was such a problem, whatever this problem was and how many kids she had, how long did she have to wait, what her career is and what kind of relationship is she actually having with this new man. I think there's more. I would like to know more.

     Although Rita and Carole objected to the story, it was precisely because of the story that Martha liked "The Sun on Mount Royal."

Jim: What did you make of that little piece?
Martha: Interesting.
Jim: Did you like it?
Martha: Yeah. I did.
Jim: O.K. Maybe if you talked about what you liked about it. Maybe what you thought interesting would come through.
Martha: Oh, just the story line—nice story line, that she left her husband and thought she met someone else that would fulfill the fantasy she had or the image—her next lover—and to discover that he probably had just as many faults as her husband and that she'd probably fall into the same situation she did with him.

     Earlier we mentioned that it is difficult, in practice, to identify a single reading as belonging to a specific mode. For example, despite her comments above, it would be inaccurate to classify Martha as a "story-driven reader," because later in the interview she invokes authorial intention to support her disagreement with the statement, "The story doesn't feel complete—you want to know what happens next." (This supports, incidentally, the view that different post-reading tasks invite different modes of response.)

Jim: Is that a strong disagreement again or just a disagreement? Just going to try to get a degree of your disagreement.
Martha: O.K. I don't know if I'd say it's strong or not, because that's the end of the story and so I think it's the way the author wanted to leave it end and let you decide. (...) It would be nice to know what happens next but I think it would take a few more pages, you know, it could go on and on—tell about her husband and the kids. It's just—the story—its purpose is to present that little scenario and end with that question.
Jim: And what?
Martha: You know, leaving you to wonder what will she do—to let you investigate the situation further and maybe place yourself in her situation.

We might say that readers who want to "investigate the situation further" are taking a dialogic stance: They seem to consider reading to be an ongoing conversation or dialogue between themselves and the text (or the author responsible for it). That is, whereas the story-driven reader expects to become immersed in an interesting story-world for as long as the actual, physical reading lasts, the dialogic reader expects to be able to think about and "converse" with the text after the physical reading is finished. (Perhaps for this reason, people in our investigation who read dialogically sometimes wanted to take a copy of the text home with them.) The clearest example of this dialogic type of response in our corpus was Don's comment, during the wrapup, about "Metaphors":

Jim: Is there anything about "Metaphors"? (. . .)
Don: Well, I think the idea of thinking of down the line of the metaphors that people use to—to think about their own development is interesting—I haven't tended to use that way of thinking and so that's an idea that I will explore and probably see it both in my own thought and other people's thought.
Jim: When people use metaphors?
Don: Specifically using metaphors to think about their own development and problem-solving. (. . .) I'll think on that for quite awhile now and see how far I can extend that idea and see what use it has to me and then, somewhere down the line, I make a judgment on it.

In summary, "Metaphors" affords both story-driven and dialogic reading, and it was so read by our readers. In one respect (its open-endedness), "The Sun on Mount Royal" resists conventional story-driven reading; some readers disliked it for that reason. The extreme brevity of the stories may also have constrained story-driven reading to some extent. In general, however, what the texts afforded, what the readers were prepared to do, and what the situation required, were in reasonable harmony for these two stories.

"In Virgin Forest"

In contrast to the postcard stories, "In Virgin Forest" does not readily afford story-driven reading because it is not organized as a narrative. It does, however, invite a dialogic stance: There are many places where McPhee may be taken as inviting his readers to share a perception, a belief, or an attitude; typically, these are conveyed by metaphors, similes, and other "discourse evaluations" (Hunt & Vipond, 1986). To some extent, the text also affords information-driven reading. There is, indeed, a great deal of factual information about forests (one in particular) in this piece; a person can learn a great deal from it. However, the text is not particularly conducive to "pure" information-driven reading: the facts are there, but they are not arranged in conventional "textbook" fashion, and there are no information-acquisition aids such as headings or diagrams. In brief, "In Virgin Forest" can be said to invite a mixture of dialogic and information-driven reading. Someone reading "In Virgin Forest" in a pure information-driven mode, at least in this setting, would likely feel frustrated by its abundant detail and lack of textbook structure.

We found instances of both information-driven and dialogic types of response. Becky is an example of a reader who—perhaps somewhat reluctantly—takes an information-driven stance:

Jim: What did you make of that piece? (...)
Becky: Well, it's about forests. I don't know, it was very descriptive, a lot of information in it and history, some geography because it talks about different places. I'm sure if you were interested in botany you'd find it very interesting. (...) I didn't like it but that's just my opinion because I'm not into plants and trees and that stuff, I guess. It was kind of—it was a very instructional reading. I wouldn't read it for enjoyment, I don't think. That's it.

An information-driven approach was not invariably associated with disliking the text. Although his reading was largely dialogic, Don reported enjoying the piece in part because of what he learned from it:

Don: Well, I come from [a place] where there aren't very many trees and so I love any kind of forested area because it's something that intrigues me. (...) There's a lot of tidbits of information in there that are kind of intriguing as well. The whole idea of the developmental process of the forest is something I know very little about. I enjoyed that opportunity to get a few more insights in that whole area.

Probably because they were trying to read the text factually, as straight information, some readers agreed that "There are too many facts, all mixed up, which makes it very hard to remember things."

Rita: It jumps around and goes—it's mumbo-jumbo, actually. It talks about one thing and then talks about another and then it might go back to that, and then you just get confused of what's going on, and yeah, it would be hard to remember things.

Note that Rita does not question the presupposition that one ought to be able to remember things from "In Virgin Forest."

If people reading in an information-driven way are primarily interested in getting the facts from the text, people reading dialogically are concerned with constructing points or engaging in conversation. The different stances became apparent during the discourse-based interview, when readers were asked if it would make a difference to them if the original sentence (A) were replaced by either of our alternatives (B or C); for example:

(A)   In 1981, gypsy moths tore off the canopy, and sunlight sprayed the floor.
(B)   In 1981, an invasion of gypsy moths ate much of the leaf cover and allowed sunlight to spray the floor.
(C)   An infestation of gypsy moths tore off the canopy in 1981, allowing sunlight onto the forest floor.

Becky: No, B wouldn't make a difference because they're saying the same thing—the gypsy moths ate the top and so the sunlight just came through (. . .). So it's the same thing. A and B are the same. I think C would mean the same as well.

If one is concerned only with getting the information, Becky is right; there is no difference between A, B, and C. If anything, a case could be made for preferring the more explicit, less "literary" alternatives, B and C. On the other hand, if one is reading dialogically, attempting to see what the author might be getting at, "tore off" and "sprayed" stand out as evaluations that afford the opportunity to share a perception with McPhee, as Ellen does:

Ellen: There's no difference in terms of the actual factual information, you know, [A and B are] both basically saying the same thing, but the image that comes to me when I read "gypsy moths tore off the canopy"—I get a sense of the voraciousness with which they would eat the leaves, you know. Where "ate much of the leaf cover" just doesn't capture that, how fast that can happen.

In other parts of the interview, too, some readers made responses indicative of a dialogic mode. This is Martha, disagreeing with the probe, "The language is too fancy. All of that playing around with description makes it harder to understand."

Martha: The language—it's a little bit fancy but it lets you know that the author—sees—the forest as worthy of description and wants to have you that same impression of the forest when you read, you know. It's not ugly or sterile. He describes it so you'll have a better understanding of how he feels about it.

Thus, people who read "In Virgin Forest" dialogically tended to attribute to McPhee or the text some purpose beyond that of conveying a lot of facts about forests. In response to the statement, "It's a description of a forest—you'd only be interested in it if you were interested in forests," Ben said:

Ben: Well, I would disagree with that. There is no point in writing something and
         distributing it to such a wide audience if it is simply about some very spe-
         cific aspect of the world. But I think they're making a comment about the
         relationship between man and his environment and using another example
         of an area of virgin forest which is on the verge of extinction. (...) So I
         don't think that it is just about trees—it's about our relationship to the envi-
         ronment.

In summary, we infer that people like Becky, Rita, and Julie read the text in a more or less "pure" information-driven fashion and therefore saw no important difference between McPhee's literary language and our more prosaic alternatives. However—and despite its wealth of factual information—"In Virgin Forest" does not readily afford a pure information-driven approach in the way that a textbook, for instance, does. People who tried to read it in an information-driven way were therefore understandably frustrated. In contrast, people reading dialogically assumed that the purpose of the article was something other than teaching the reader about forests. Ellen, Ben, and Martha, among others, were not distressed that they couldn't remember all the facts. They believed they had a sense of what the article was getting at, and this was more important than being able to remember it.

But where do these assumptions—the stances that people adopt towards texts—come from? Different configurations of reader-text-situation go part way toward accounting for why the people in our investigation read "In Virgin Forest" differently. Consider first the reader. One possibility is that some readers have learned that factual texts afford only information-driven reading: It is as if the presence of facts and details, in the absence of narrative structure, "drive" such readers towards this stance (Mitchell, 1982). Related to this is the question of familiarity with the conventions of a particular genre. For instance, readers who know *The New Yorker* (Don, Ben, Eric were familiar with the magazine, and Ellen is a regular reader) have experienced "aesthetic nonfictional prose" before, whereas people unfamiliar with the magazine (Becky, Rita, Larry) tended to find McPhee's style alien and alienating. This is not a simple matter of reading ability, either. Becky, Julie, and Rita are highly capable students and they have no problem with articles in the *Journal of Experimental Psychology*—yet they were flummoxed by McPhee.

Granted that readers bring different knowledge and expectations to their reading, it would be a mistake to attribute all the important effects to differences in "cultural literacy" (Hirsch, 1987). It is also important, for instance, to consider how the situation was different for different readers, and may thereby have predisposed them to different modes. Recall that for the first-year students, the investigation was an "experiment" carried out in an academic setting, sponsored by the "Psychology Department," for which they received course credit. For first- and fourth-year students (except Eric), the interviewer, Jim, was a person older and with higher academic status than themselves, and this person, moreover, was representing two even older, higher-ranking "professors." All of these factors may have conspired to create a situation in which information-driven reading was the appropriate, "academic" mode to use. The social situation was different for the faculty members, however. Obviously they were not receiving course credit; presumably they were participating as a way of collaborating with two of their colleagues. And, from the faculty members' perspective, the interviewer was a person younger and with lower academic status than themselves. In short, the students in this investigation may have played the role of "subjects," whereas the professors took the role of "collaborators."

Whatever social roles they adopted in this study, we cannot overlook the primary sociocultural roles of our participants—"students" and "professors"—which may also have influenced the modes of reading and response that we encountered. In fact, as a very rough and only partly accurate summary of the responses to "In Virgin Forest," we might say that the students "studied" and the professors "professed."

"Some Approaches to the Problem of the Shortage of Time"

Le Guin's "Time" is the most difficult text we used. Although part of the difficulty is due to its vocabulary, which features such interesting neologisms as *chronocrystallization* and *petropsychotoxin*, it is mainly due to the fact that "Time" doesn't just afford but virtually requires the reader to adopt a dialogic stance—to ask: What in the world is she getting at? In this respect it differs from "In Virgin Forest." Both texts resist story-driven reading; however, whereas "In Virgin Forest" can be successfully read, at least in part, as a factual account, to read "Time" as a factual account is surely to misinterpret Le Guin's satirical intent. (It would be like taking Swift's "A Modest Proposal" as a reasonable plan for population control.) In fact, it could be argued that one of the purposes of "Time" is to satirize those who would read it as nonfiction!

Nevertheless, our readers were divided. Some found it a "spoof," "put-on," or "joke," whereas others considered it "incomprehensible" or "boring." This division corresponds, roughly, to a division between those who read "Time" dialogically and those who did not. Readers who classified the piece as a satire tended to have ideas about what its point or purpose might be.

Ellen: I liked the way whoever's writing this pokes fun at this whole notion of trying to save time and have more time to do things and all that. (. . .) One of the things I liked or something that I enjoyed is the spoof on our whole preoccupation with time and the use of time and making it such a lofty sort of topic to be studied by these international groups and this sort of thing.

Readers who considered the text to be satirical were not put off by the vocabulary. Reading dialogically, they considered the neologisms to be part of the joke Le Guin is playing, part of her point. Ben is asked whether he agrees with the statement, "All that technical vocabulary makes it impossible to remember things."

Ben: But it is not "technical," it is technical gobbledegook. If you take it seriously I am sure that it would be hard to understand. It's not intended to be expressed in that way.

Other readers were distressed by the "technical" language, however. They did not connect the difficult terminology with the text's possible rhetorical aims, but instead tried to make sense of it, literally. However, *chronocrystallization* and the like are not easily interpreted, and therefore it is understandable that these readers found "Time" "over my head" (Rita) or "above my reading level" (Martha). This suggests that one's stance towards texts may well be more important for reading than knowledge per se. Presumably none of our readers knew what *petropsychotoxin* means; the difference is that only some of them assumed they *should* know.

Similarly, some believed they were acquiring legitimate scientific information from the piece. For instance, asked whether he agreed with the statement, "I think it's funny," Larry said:

Larry: No. I totally disagree. (. . .) I felt the approach of it was serious—to me, anyway—because it is all scientific.

Jim: I guess I should start off by saying, "What did you make of the whole piece?"

Carole: That everyone is trying to find a way to stop time from decreasing. It seems to me that something is going to shorten time.

But much later in the interview, during the wrapup, Carole finds out that "Time" is fiction.

Carole: I don't like it any more.
Jim: You don't like it any more. O.K., you want to tell me why you don't like it any more?
Carole: Because I thought it was real. I just thought that this was a problem that I didn't know about and that's why I'm interested. I thought, "God, I didn't know that we're losing time! How do you lose time?" and stuff. Now I realize that it's not true so now I don't like it anymore.
Jim: O.K., kind of neat.
Carole: It just seems fake now.

In summary, "Time" appears to be almost incomprehensible unless one assumes that it is intended to be read as satire. It affords dialogic reading but only *appears* to afford an information-driven stance. Its language is, as Ben said, "technical gobbledegook," but it is just scientific-sounding enough that a reader could be fooled by it. Why were some of the readers fooled? We assume some people read "Time" in an information-driven mode for the same reasons that "In Virgin Forest" was sometimes read that way (see that discussion): Either these readers do not have the dialogic mode available, or else they have it available but for a variety of situational reasons, they considered the information-driven mode to be the appropriate one to use.

Professional and Associative Responses: More Modes?

Most of our readers' responses can be accounted for by positing three reading modes, but there were some comments that seem to fall outside this scheme. The first of these is the detached, analytical type of response that critics and English professors tend to make (and which we tried to exclude by not inviting English professors to participate). Eric is particularly adept at this kind of "professional reading." Here, for instance, he wonders whether Thompson doesn't attempt too much in "Metaphors" in too short a space:

Eric: In the end it works, but in the body of it (. . .) it jumps back and forth a little too much, from Gary, to her, to the kid: bing, bing, bing, bing. I mean, it's clear what he's trying to do—he's trying to give you a little bit of everybody—but I don't know that you can give that much of everybody and still have any continuity. The story line follows through, but it's just too choppy.

At present the status of professional reading is unclear to us. Perhaps it is a mixed mode (dialogic, information-driven) that has been learned and conventionalized. What is clear is that professional reading is a relatively "noncooperative" type: It is not a matter of engaging in a conversation but of stepping back to observe (and, often, to pass judgment on) how authors accomplish what they do.

At the opposite extreme, readers sometimes stay within themselves, attending to their own images, memories, and associations. It is important to distinguish this "reader-based" type of response (MacLean, 1986) from the other modes. No matter which mode they are using, people could never make sense of text if they did not use their knowledge and experience (Kintsch, 1988); similarly, the act of reading would be nonsensical if it did not affect their knowledge and experience. In dialogic reading, this back-and-forth interplay between text and experience is, of course, especially important; it is in focal attention. When the text is used not as a conversational partner, however, but as a pretext for exploring one's own memories and images, one has drifted into what may be called an "associative" mode; the dialogue has become a monologue. Both dialogic and associative reading, then, feature what Steen Larsen and Uffe Seilman (1987) call *personal remindings;* the difference is that in dialogic reading the remindings illuminate and are relevant to the text (they contribute to the ongoing conversation), whereas in associative mode remindings tend to be an end in themselves.

For example, Ellen, whose reading of "In Virgin Forest" was mainly dialogic, seems to have read the text at least partly in associative mode:

Jim: What did you make of "In Virgin Forest"?
Ellen: Well, it's kind of a nice story about a virgin forest. I was having images of when I was—I lived in Manitoba for a year and I went to Riding Mountain National Park and there are some areas in the park that are, I guess, virgin prairie and they have never been done unto by people, and it's fascinating to see what—I have images of what that area, that ground was like, you know, with these very fragile-looking, sort of reedy kind of grass and feathery sort of stuff that looks like wheat but was very short.

At least momentarily, it seems that Ellen has dropped out of her dialogue with the text in order to explore her own associations. An even more extreme example comes from Larry. "In Virgin Forest" contains a reference to a group of Germans who once visited Hutcheson Forest, and Larry said that reminded him of Nazis and what they did to the Jews: "I don't know why I was thinking that but I was," he said. "I was like in another imaginary world."

As in the case of professional reading, it is not clear whether associative reading is best considered a separate mode or whether it represents some combination of the others. For now, though, these problems will have to be left unresolved.

EDUCATIONAL IMPLICATIONS

We have argued that much of the variability in what people say about texts can be understood by assuming that there are three main modes of reading and response—information-driven, story-driven, and dialogic (point-driven)—and that which mode is predominant on a given occasion depends on the configuration of reader, text, and situation. Most (although not all) of the responses made by the 15 readers in this investigation could be accounted for by this scheme.

Note that we do not claim that any one of the three modes is "the best" or the most advanced developmentally. "Best" begs too many questions: Best for whom? For which texts? Under what circumstances?

Asking these questions helps us come to grips with some otherwise puzzling findings. For example, although all the texts used afforded dialogic reading, not all our readers responded to them dialogically. It is not irrelevant, however, that the texts were still *our* texts and the participants were reading for *our* purposes, not their own. In this situation, story- and information-driven reading may indeed have been the most appropriate modes to use. It is at least possible that in other circumstances—specifically, when reading their chosen texts for their own purposes—these readers read dialogically.

No one mode is best, but we do suggest that full reading capacity requires that the reader be able to use, flexibly, whichever mode or modes is most appropriate to the specific conjunction of text, purpose, and situation. Given that texts and situations vary, readers who are able to move freely in and out of any of the modes, or any combination of them, would be more likely to be satisfied with their engagement in the reading process, would be likely to read a greater variety of texts, and would, by most external criteria, be judged more "successful" than those readers restricted to one or two modes. Conversely, readers who are comfortable with, say, just one mode would be frustrated by texts or situations that didn't afford that stance.

These concerns lead directly to a discussion of how educational systems and teachers can support development of full reading capacity. If our goal is to enable students to read in all of the modes identified here, there are, according to this model, two obvious places where leverage may be exerted.

The first is the *text*. To help readers develop proficiency with particular modes, teachers should select texts that afford those modes. As Robert Calfee (1982) has argued in a slightly different context, schools sometimes defeat their own purposes by neglecting to consider the text-task configuration. Calfee points out that in many reading series, information (e.g., about different cultures) is presented by means of a story, a practice that may lead to difficulties in retrieval. His reasoning is that a narratively-organized memory representation may make it more difficult for the student to remember factual information. From our vantage point, there may also be an acquisition problem: Information-driven reading may be constrained by the use of texts that strongly afford story-driven reading.

Similarly, dialogic reading is unlikely to occur if texts are used that afford only story- or information-driven stances. For instance, basal readers—which are carefully monitored for "readability"—are not, we think, monitored for the degree to which they invite young readers to construct the narrative as a purposeful, pointed communicative act (Bruce, 1981). Therefore, it is unlikely that such texts will be read dialogically, or, consequently, that children will learn to use this mode.

The *situation* is the second place leverage may be applied to help students develop a range of reading modes. A reader's stance towards text depends in part on the task he or she expects to perform. For instance, a student who anticipates questions of the type, "What color was the heroine's coat?" is likely to read in an information-driven way. Questions about texts that imply there is one right answer or that require students to identify "the" theme, also invite information-driven reading—not to mention the more disturbing fact that they tend to alienate students from reading itself (Hynds, 1989). Simplistic, *ex cathedra* statements about "what the author meant" often function in classrooms to end discussion rather to promote dialogue, and are therefore effectively information-driven. On the other hand, many of the questions found in literature anthologies that are far less efferent in their assumptions (especially questions regarding the motivations of characters and the plausibility of plot) invite students to stay within the story-world of characters and events—that is, to engage predominantly in story-driven reading.

Of course there are many occasions when it is appropriate to read texts to acquire information or to experience the story. However, if texts are treated *only* as repositories of facts (or alternatively as enjoyable stories), a student will not be encouraged to see reading as dialogue, and will thus fail to develop full reading capacity. The prevalence of the authoritative textbook (Luke, de Castell, & Luke, 1983), the compulsive testing for comprehension and obsession with accountability (Smith, 1986), the widespread adoption of the "banking" system of education (Freire, 1970)—all suggest that in our schools today it is the information-driven mode that prevails.

How can the situation be altered to encourage a more balanced picture; specifically, to give greater attention to dialogic reading? Although a full discussion of this issue is beyond the scope of this chapter, some helpful models are provided by Language Experience and Whole Language approaches (e.g., Harste, Woodward, & Burke, 1984; Newman, 1985). Reading and writing in such classrooms are relatively dialogic because the texts tend not to be anthologies, textbooks, or basal readers but occasioned pieces, written, often collaboratively, by classmates you know and work and play with. Similarly, at the postsecondary level there are pedagogical approaches in which dialogic reading is made the situationally appropriate mode. A number of us at St. Thomas University, for instance, design our courses as "collaborative investigations" (Hunt, Parkhill, Reither, & Vipond, 1988; Reither & Vipond, 1989). In brief, the instructor sets a research question for the class, casting the students as members of an investigative team or "task force"; the critical point here is that reading and writing in these classrooms become the chief means by which the collective project is defined and advanced.

We believe that which mode of reading is dominant on a given occasion depends on the interplay among the reader's purposes and abilities, the text's affordances, and the situation's constraints. Our intention is that this model will afford a way of thinking that helps account for what happens— and what doesn't happen—in classrooms and living rooms as well as in reading laboratories.

REFERENCES

Bruce, B. C. (1981). *A new point of view on children's stories* (Reading Education Report No. 25). Champaign, IL: Center for the Study of Reading.

Calfee, R. (1982). Some theoretical and practical ramifications of story grammars. *Journal of Pragmatics, 6,* 441–450.

Danziger, K. (1985). The origins of the psychological experiment as a social institution. *American Psychologist, 40,* 133–140.

Eagleton, T. (1983). *Literary theory: An introduction.* Oxford: Basil Blackwell.

Flower, L. (1988). The construction of purpose in writing and reading. *College English, 50,* 528–550.

Freadman, A. (1987). Anyone for tennis? In I. Reid (Ed.), *The place of genre in learning: Current debates* (pp. 91–124). Geelong, Australia: Deakin University Centre for Studies in Literary Education.

Freire, P. (1970). *Pedagogy of the oppressed* (M. B. Ramos, Trans.). New York: Continuum.

Gibson, J. J. (1979). *The ecological approach to visual perception.* Boston: Houghton Mifflin.

Harste, J. C., Woodward, V. A., & Burke, C. M. (1984). *Language stories and literacy lessons.* Portsmouth, NH: Heinemann.

Hirsch, E. D., Jr. (1987). *Cultural literacy: What every American needs to know.* Boston: Houghton Mifflin.

Hunt, R. A., Parkhill, T., Reither, J. A., & Vipond, D. (1988, March). *Writing under the curriculum: Learning to write by using writing to teach.* Panel presentation at the Conference on College Composition and Communication, St. Louis, Missouri.

Hunt, R. A., & Vipond, D. (1985). Crash-testing a transactional model of literary reading. *Reader: Essays in Reader-Oriented Theory, Criticism, and Pedagogy,* No. 14, 23–39.

Hunt, R. A., & Vipond, D. (1986). Evaluations in literary reading. *TEXT, 6,* 53–71.

Hunt, R. A., & Vipond, D. (1987). Aesthetic reading: Some strategies for research. *English Quarterly, 20,* 178–183.

Hynds, S. (1989). Bringing life to literature and literature to life: Social constructs and contexts of four adolescent readers. *Research in the Teaching of English, 23,* 30–61.

Kintsch, W. (1988). The role of knowledge in discourse comprehension: A construction-integration model. *Psychological Review, 95,* 163–182.

Labov, W. (1972). *Language in the inner city: Studies in the Black English Vernacular.* Philadelphia: University of Pennsylvania Press.

Larsen, S. F., & Seilman, U. (1988). Personal remindings while reading literature. TEXT, 8, 411–429.

Le Guin, U. K. (1982). *The compass rose.* Toronto: Bantam Books.

Luke, C., de Castell, S., & Luke, A. (1983). Beyond criticism: The authority of the school text. *Curriculum Inquiry, 13*(2), 111–127.

MacLean, M. (1986). A framework for analyzing reader-text interactions. *Journal of Research and Development in Education, 19*(2), 16–21.

McPhee, J. (1987, July 6). In virgin forest. *The New Yorker,* pp. 21–23.

Mitchell, C. A. (1982). Exploring the aesthetic response: "I just read novels and that sort of thing." *English Quarterly, 15,* 67–77.

Newman, J. M. (1985). *Whole language: Theory in use.* Portsmouth, NH: Heinemann.

Odell, L., & Goswami, D. (1982). Writing in a non-academic setting. *Research in the Teaching of English, 16,* 201–223.

Odell, L., Goswami, D., & Herrington, A. (1983). The discourse-based interview: A procedure for exploring the tacit knowledge of writers in nonacademic settings. In P. Mosenthal, L. Tamor, & S. A. Walmsley (Eds.), *Research on writing: Principles and methods* (pp. 221–236). New York and London: Longman.

Paré, A. (1988, August). *What can we learn from real world writing?* Paper presented at the meetings of the Canadian Council of Teachers of English, St. John's, Newfoundland.

Phelps, L. W. (1985). Dialectics of coherence: Toward an integrative theory. *College English, 47,* 12–29.

Polanyi, L. (1979). So what's the point? *Semiotica, 25* (3/4), 207–241.

Polanyi, L. (1985). *Telling the American story: A structural and cultural analysis of conversational storytelling.* Norwood, NJ: Ablex.

Reid, I. (1988). Genre and framing: The case of epitaphs. *Poetics, 17,* 25–35.

Reither, J. A., & Vipond, D. (1989). Writing as collaboration. *College English, 51,* 855–867.

Rosenblatt, L. M. (1976). *Literature as exploration* (3rd ed.). New York: Barnes and Noble. (Original work published 1938)

Rosenblatt, L. M. (1978). *The reader, the text, the poem: The transactional theory of the literary work.* Carbondale: Southern Illinois University Press.

Rosenblatt, L. M. (1985). Transaction versus interaction: A terminological rescue operation. *Research in the Teaching of English, 19,* 96–107.

Rubin, D. C. (in press). Issues of regularity and control: Confessions of a regularity freak. In L. W. Poon, D. C. Rubin, & B. A. Wilson (Eds.), *Everyday cognition in adulthood and later life* (pp. 84–103). New York: Cambridge University Press.

Schuster, C. I. (1985). Mikhail Bakhtin as rhetorical theorist. *College English, 47,* 594–607.

Smith, F. (1986). *Insult to intelligence: The bureaucratic invasion of our classrooms.* New York: Arbor House.

Thompson, K. (1986). *Leaping up sliding away.* Fredericton, NB: Fiddlehead Poetry Books & Goose Lane Editions.

Vipond, D., & Hunt, R. A. (1984). Point-driven understanding: Pragmatic and cognitive dimensions of literary reading. *Poetics, 13,* 261–277.

Vipond, D., & Hunt, R. A. (1987). Shunting information or making contact? Assumptions for research on aesthetic reading. *English Quarterly, 20,* 131–136.

Vipond, D., & Hunt, R. A. (1989). Literary processing and response as transaction: Evidence for the contribution of readers, texts, and situations. In D. Meutsch & R. Viehoff (Eds.), *Comprehension of literary discourse: Interdisciplinary approaches* (pp. 155–174). Berlin: de Gruyter.

Vygotsky, L. S. (1986). *Thought and language* (A. Kozulin, Rev. and Ed.). Cambridge, MA: MIT Press. (Original work published 1934)

Wimsatt, W. K., & Beardsley, M. C. (1949). The intentional fallacy. *Sewanee Review, 57,* 31–55.

Wood, L. A., & Kroger, R. O. (1985). Can we revive the classical experiment for social psychology? *Canadian Psychology, 26,* 282–291.

6

The Development of Poetic Understanding During Adolescence

Cai Svensson

In recent years researchers in the fields of language and reading development have become increasingly concerned about reading ability as an aspect of the more general process of cultural socialization. From this perspective, reading ability is conceived of as shaped by an individual's or a group's sociocultural and sociohistorical conditions (e.g. Heath, 1983; Cochran-Smith, 1984; Svensson, 1985). These conditions or cultural determinants of literacy, reading ability, and literary interpretive skill include the preschool home environment and exposure to literature instruction.

Literature instruction, as well as other kinds of literacy-related activities, have several functions, for example, the promotion of cultural communication, the promotion of a cultural loyalty, and the development of individuality (Purves, 1988, pp. 25–26). The first of these functions enables the student—on the basis of acquired interests, norms, strategies, and so on—to communicate with a circle wider than his or her home, peers, or local community. This promotion of *cultural communication* requires the student to learn the cultural norms of semantics, morphology, syntax, text structures, literary and tropological allusions, and pragmatics. The students acquire the second function, a *cultural loyalty*, by accepting and valuing those norms, strategies, and so on. A culturally loyal student would have certain expectations about what texts are and how they should be read. And he or she would expect others in the culture to follow those same norms. Not until the literate student has profited from the first two functions is he or she able to become independent of the culture and develop his or her *individuality*. Before one has learned to communicate within the culture, deviation from those norms, strategies, and so on is seen as "naive, illiterate, or childish."

The literary-poetic aspect of literacy is a highly specialized "competence" that is generally acquired slowly and incompletely, from literature instruction during adolescence. The general aim of this study has been to investigate children's and adolescents' gradual growth towards mastery of a number of basic norms and strategies constituting literary interpretation. The study was designed to assess children's and adolescents' spontaneous interpretations of potentially symbolic poetry as a function of factors like tale-telling habits of the home, reading of fiction, reading of nonfiction, length of reading time, and depth of intention in reading.

First I discuss the strategic or socialization approach to literary study. According to this view literary interpretive skill is to a large extent dependent on conventions and procedures that are socially based and distributed. I then argue that students acquire literary interpretive skill by accomodating norms and strategies specific to the literary community, by cultural socialization facilitated by so-called "significant others," who act in accordance with culturally defined conduct. Finally, presenting the study, I briefly review a number of contributions to the empirical study of symbol interpretation.

THEORETICAL BACKGROUND

The Strategic Approach to Literary Study

In his essay *How to recognize a poem when you see one*, Fish (1980) has elaborated upon the "strategic" approach to the reading process. The interpretation of poetry, to Fish, is a matter of having acquired certain assumptions concerning what poems are and look like. Governed by these assumptions (or norms), the reader starts to perform corresponding operations, that is, interpretive strategies (or procedures). As soon as the text is identified as a poem (*inter alia* on the basis of assumptions actualized by the situation or the context, for example, of being a literary student in a classroom), students apply a set of norms bearing upon poetry: the assumption that poems are more complex than other texts, that they express a central insight, that they are wholes unified by the central insight, and that everything about a poem is significant (pp. 326–327).

Unfortunately, Fish is neither very careful nor systematic in keeping norms apart from the corresponding interpretive strategies. However, some of his norms shape particular literary strategies. For example, if a reader is guided by an expectation of a dense and intricate composition, he or she will, for instance, look for latent ambiguities, alliterative and consonantal patterns, or meanings that "deconstrue" the meaning that first arises. A reader who assumes that the text is unified by the expression of a central insight will try to find such an essential whole.

To give our concepts more stringent and systematic definitions, let us draw slightly on van Dijk and Kintsch (1983). For the purpose of this study, "interpretive norm" refers to a basic assumption ("representation") concerning what literature, novels, poems, and so on are, how they should be dealt with, and what results this dealing with them will yield. In what follows "interpretive strategy" refers to a global assumption ("representation") of the means of reaching this goal. As such, an interpretive strategy is understood as a general instruction for the carrying out of each necessary step in the sense-making activity based on the interpretive norms. An interpretive strategy presupposes a number of subordinate and more detailed procedures. It seems reasonable to assume the existence of hierarchies of strategies, so that, for example, a number of substrategies may be understood as making up a strategy. The interpretation of literature, hence, is a rule-governed activity in the sense of being determined by interpretive norms. However, readers may differ in their ability to employ interpretive strategies.

Jonathan Culler in his *Structuralist Poetics* (1975) agrees with Fish's position that both the text and the reader play roles subordinate to an internalized system of reading conventions, which make up literary competence. Literary meaning, hence, is a communal affair, the outcome of rules publically agreed upon, not a matter of individual response to authorial cues in the text. These conventions are (Culler, 1975, pp. 113–115):

1. The "rule of significance," which states that the poem is to be read "as expressing a significant attitude to some problem concerning man and/or his relation to the universe."
2. "The conventions of metaphorical coherence," which state that "one should attempt through semantic transformations to produce coherence on the levels of both tenor and vehicle," that is, on both the literal and the figurative levels.
3. The "convention of thematic unity," which states that the different elements of a poem are to be integrated into a unified whole.

In addition, Culler suggests a fourth role: "The convention which allows one to inscribe the poem in a poetic tradition" (pp. 113–115; see also Rabinowitz (1987) for further discussion of interpretive conventions).

The norms and strategies mentioned above may be said to constitute conditions for the interpretation of literary symbols. A poetry reader is predisposed to be active and cooperative, that is, to take up an interpretive or "subjective" attitude (not a descriptive or "objective" attitude). Further, the poetry reader is looking for and creating enigmas and gaps to solve and fill out.

By assuming that poems deal with essentials and express central insights, a reader infers the larger significance of elements (objects, images, actions). This conferment of wider significances turns the elements in question into either types or symbols, depending on which meaning is generalized—that of the normal or that of the symbol-creating contexts. Approaching a poem which seems to be platitudinous or dealing with banalities, the reader's expectations of larger significance are violated. The reader expects that the text must refer over and beyond itself, that is, represent symbolic objects. The kind of symbolism that results from this mechanism of Panofsky (1953) is called *disguised*, that is, the text or the painting can be interpreted both realistically and symbolically (i.e., readers can attribute a coherent meaning also on a literal level; cf. Culler's conventions of metaphoric coherence). The other class of symbols, the so-called *open* symbols, is the product of quite a different norm or assumption, which states that poems are coherent and consistent, logical and meaningful (i.e., it is possible to give them that kind of interpretation; cf. Culler's "convention of thematic unity").

Cultural Determinants of Literary Interpretive Skill

It is possible to discriminate fairly roughly between *cognitive-developmental* and *cultural-developmental* studies in the field of developmental aesthetics. The former orientation ranges from studies that directly apply the Piagetian apparatus (particularly the stage-theory) to the aesthetic realm (e.g. Machotka, 1961, 1966; Pflederer-Zimmermann, 1967; Hardy-Brown, 1979), to works that employ this developmental framework modified as to two of its main principles, namely, those of universality and spontaneousness (e.g., Gardner, Winner, & Kircher, 1975; Madeja, 1978). Some efforts aim at a construction of an autonomous cognitive-developmental theory of aesthetic experience parallel to but more or less independent of the works of Piaget on scientific development and Kohlberg on moral development (e.g., Parsons, 1976; Parsons, Johnston, & Durham, 1978).

The cultural-developmental orientation still seems to be in its initial stage. As a more downright socialization approach it is less amenable to assumptions like those of universality and spontaneousness, and rather emphasizes sociocultural factors like education and cultural exposure (e.g., Rosario, 1977, 1978; Rosario & Collazo, 1981; Heath, 1983; Cochran-Smith, 1984; Svensson, 1985).

The acquisition of aesthetic skills is conceived of as a special case of socialization and cultural transmission. The child and adolescent are seen as gradually, by means of internalization, "taking over" the "sub-world," the aesthetic (literary) community, with its set of relevancies, norms, and strategies. Development is to a great extent looked upon as equal to learning.

Very few researchers in the field of the empirical study of art and literature have accomplished research within the confines of such a reference model. Purves and Beach (1972, p. 20) in their comprehensive review of the research in response to literature, reading interests, and the teaching of literature, conclude that we still know little about the relationship "between the environment of the student and response." Most of the studies in the field obviously fail to recognize that literary reception is founded on relevancies, norms, and strategies that are socioculturally derived and distributed.

A few investigations employ broad variables like "social class," "socioeconomic status," and "ethnicity." Furthermore, they seem to be inconclusive; some can report a significant correlation between sociocultural status and some aspect of literary response (e.g., Monson, 1966; Barchas, 1971; Purves, 1981), whereas others cannot (e.g., Burgdorff, 1966; McCloskey, 1966).

Two studies, however, briefly consider "home literary environment" as a functional predisposition for literary competence and reading interest. This variable is reported to be a powerful determinant, a more powerful one than socioeconomic status and intelligence (Wollner, 1949; Hansen, 1967). Research efforts of this kind deserve amplification. The accomplishment of such an enterprise, however, presupposes a set of relevant, well-defined, and more closely specified cultural determinants. A suggestion concerning factors matching these criteria may very well be derived from the positions advocated by particularly Olson (1970) and Bourdieu (1968).

Tajfel (1969, pp. 359–360) may help us briefly summarize the *types* of factors influencing development:

1. *Functional salience* means that "because of certain ecological properties of the environment in which an individual lives, some discriminations become to him more important than others."
2. *Familiarity* refers to "the fact that individuals living in a culture *may* be exposed to types of human artifacts unfamiliar to those living in another culture. These artifacts may be characterized by some general properties which are common to a very large variety of objects."
3. *Systems of communication* employed in a culture refers to the fact that language, visual and auditory symbols, "accepted modes of expression in art," and so on "all share some common characteristics:

they often mediate between the individual and his surroundings, they may focus his attention on some aspects of his environment and deflect it from others, or they may impose idiosyncratic cultural classifications on the world in which he lives."

Thus, inspired by Olson, we may presume that the development towards mastery of literary interpretive skills is promoted by means of early exposure to, or rather, *the carrying out of performatory activities* in relation to various forms of literary works of art (and the like). The child may, for example, listen to, tell, write, or draw fairy tales and stories. Each performatory activity is carried out in a specific medium which requires that new information about this medium and the literary genre in general is acquired. The carrying out of many different acts in various media, hence, increases the child's knowledge of the literary genre. The effect of this early *familiarity* with the literary medium, by virtue of its culture-dependent functional salience, is a *cultivated disposition*. This disposition is motivational as well as cognitive in nature and constitutes the more or less necessary condition for further systematic literary schooling, both formal and informal. Without the tendency to ascribe value to the performatory activities mentioned above, and without the cognitive tools (norms and strategies) needed to carry them out the child may have difficulty with literature instruction in school.

Bourdieu (1968) argues thoroughly that the mechanism of *familiarization* is operative in aesthetic development. Aesthetic competence is acquired through familiarization by repeated perceptions of works of art. By way of these exposures, the individual comes to master the "code," the rules, or the aesthetic categories which govern the production and reception (including appreciation) of these works. The repeated perception of works of art "encourages the unconscious interiorization of the rules," which constitute "the instruments of appropriation," the necessary fundamental conditions for the deciphering and appreciation of works of art (p. 601). Thus, by means of this mechanism, the norms and conventions discussed by Culler and Fish can be "transmitted" to children and adolescents. This, however, does not necessarily imply a view of the child as passive. The approach is fully compatible with notions of the child as an active agent who plays an important role in his or her own development by transacting with the environment (see below and Svensson, 1985, p. 46).

From a sociocultural macro point of view *the story-telling interaction* may be conceived of as an instance of "the socially structured ways in which society organizes the kinds of tasks that the growing child faces and the kind of tools (both mental and physical) that the young child is provided to master those tasks" (Cole & Griffin, 1980, p. 346). It is likely that by means of the "tool" par preference, language, "little lessons" take place in the tale-telling situation. Researchers in the field of language and second language acquisition have observed the occurrence of such lessons, which consist of, for instance, adult confirmations, corrections, and elaborations (sometimes to structurally higher levels) of the child's earliest reactions to his everyday world "here and now" (see Clark & Clark, 1977, pp. 320–331 for a review). This aspect of the significant other's role in the process of socialization is certainly more or less operative in the acquisition of literary competence, too (cf. Bleich, 1978, pp. 135–137; Cochran-Smith, 1984). In the story telling interaction the child is encouraged to take up an interpretive attitude, to be attentive to unifying themes and conventionalized motifs, to consider the story's relevance to his/her own life, and so on. Thus, this pleasurable encounter is well suited to implant in the child the basic norms and strategies for the interpretation of literature, including symbolic poetry, the main concern of this study.

In addition to the amount and quality of previous literary competence *the length of schooling, the presence of a propitious cultural athmosphere* (Bourdieu, 1968, p. 606), and a supportive and culturally wealthy home environment may also influence the level of interpretation.

Instruction per se, of course, does not guarantee an increased ability to interpret and appreciate literary texts, though in-school experiences might to a certain extent be expected, somewhat unavoidably, to promote this ability. Literature instruction, however, usually presupposes a cultivated disposition and a propitious cultural atmosphere in the home environment. Teachers' problems in the classroom are to a great extent due to the fact that many pupils lack the presupposed prerequisites, due to factors outside school. Rigid cognitive developmental approaches to instruction are perhaps especially unfortunate in this respect, since they seem to conceptualize literary interpretive ability as a "competence" based on more or less universal "structures" underlying thinking and experience, "structures" unrelated to background sociocultural factors. Almost every instructional problem, even the most obviously value-related ones, therefore tends to be understood as a "competence problem." Pupils from sociocultural groups other than those favored by the school system consequently run the risk of being regarded as incompetent or untalented. It is not possible (and not always justifiable) to "administer" changes in forms of life.

The cultural developmental approach to literary study and instruction, on the other hand, is more sensitive to influences on a sociocultural level. And it is less inclined to construct models of the reading process or stages in literary understanding. Instead, it is focused on the factors influencing the acquisition of various interpretive norms and strategies. Because those rules and procedures are socially based and acquired, they cannot be codified in terms of models or stage theories. When age-bound regularities are determined, they are better understood as the result of society's ways of structuring children's activities. These ways are more uniform in culturally homogenous societies, like Sweden, than in other societies.

Even though we accept the assumption that children develop certain increasingly complex cognitive structures, these structures are by no means independent of culture-specific ecological properties of the environment. Different aspects of the arts to most children (at least in Western cultures) are more or less inescapable elements of their socially constructed reality. Performatory acts with regard to aesthetic media may be expected to promote children's cognitive growth. Therefore, "underlying structures" might just as well be conceived of as the results of literary activities rather than the prerequisites for such activities. From a cultural developmental point of view many cognitive developmental models of the reading process and aesthetic development engage in circular reasoning, in presupposing what should be proved. However, their descriptive categories can be reinterpreted within a cultural developmental frame of reference. At least in this respect the cognitive developmental and the cultural developmental approaches are not mutually exclusive. Otherwise they represent different *perspectives* (see, for example, Giorgi, 1970) as well as different theories and methods.

Research on the Interpretation of Aesthetic Symbols

Very few studies have explicitly set out to examine empirically the interpretive processes involved in the interpretation of aesthetic symbols. The only one dealing specifically with the subject, Hardy-Brown (1979), is an attempt at demonstrating the general applicability of the notion of formal operations to the analysis of poetry.

Hardy-Brown compared the performance of 30 college students on a Piagetian formal operations test (including the chemical task, the flexibility of rods task, a ratio problem, and a proportional reasoning task) with their interpretation of two symbolic poems. It was hypothesized that the subjects would respond to the poems, especially as to the dimension literal-symbolic, in accordance with their level of formal thought. (The conception of symbolism employed by Hardy-Brown is in line with that argued for in the present study. See below.) The results of the study showed that there was a significant correlation between response category regarding one of the poems and level of logical operational thought on the other.

Here the crucial issue is whether a Piagetian framework is applicable to literary response. One plausible objection that may be raised is that the Piagetian perspective employed tends to bias the notion of aesthetic perception towards mere logical problem solving, leaving little room for the creative and exploratory dimension of that activity. Hardy-Brown's operationalization of poetry interpretation required a high degree of plainness, consistency, and integration in the readers' reasoning about the poems.

But even if one accepts Hardy-Brown's somewhat strained conception of aesthetic perception, her results may nevertheless be disputed. The association between operational level and literary interpretive skills might of course be due to other factors at a sociocultural level, for example of the kind discussed above. The only additional variables considered by Hardy-Brown are "academic major" and "self-reported number of books read," neither of which turned out to be significantly related to the operational level. Needless to say, several other and more relevant variables should be taken into account before it is possible to draw any safe conclusions

Another cognitive-psychological approach to poetic communication is furnished by Shimron (1980) in a process-oriented study which focuses certain predispositions and interpretive strategies characteristic of poetry readers. It was predicted that a reader of poetic discourse exhibits a liability to "process a maximum of information from memory schemes that are evoked during reading," and a "readiness to process information expressed similarly to metaphors." The latter predisposition implies the processing of "pieces of information whose meanings would not be considered consistent if taken literally" (p. 43). This phenomenon is called "open symbolism." Shimron assumes that the basic processes of comprehending a regular text (e.g., recall of memory schemes, developing hypotheses, and test of relevance) apply just as much to poetry (p. 47). But in addition he suggests that there are two other kinds of processes involved in the reading of poetic discourse, to wit, those of discovering and comparing analogies, and drawing conclusions from these comparisons (p. 43).

Drawing on Miller's (1976) model of reading, Shimron tested his hypotheses in a minor "experiment" in which six university students were given one line at a time of a contemporary poem and asked to express what they understood of the text so far. Their comments were recorded, analyzed, and found to confirm the hypotheses. Shimron's findings reflect a social-constructivist approach. However, the reliance on, for example, the notion of memory schemes makes his model experimentally unwieldy, especially when applied to more extensive and complex discourses.

Parsons, Johnston, and Durham (1978), in attempting to establish developmental trends in the perception of paintings, found that interpretations at a nonliteral level appear rather late in the course of development, somewhere around the 10th to 12th grades: "There is a much greater awareness of the variety of attitudes possible toward any subject matter. In addition, what is referred to is often formulated as something more abstract than before, 'winning and losing', 'sadness at war' (p. 91). One of the 12th-graders cited, for example, provides the following interpretation of Marc Chagall's "Circus": "I think that a circus has overtones on life. In a sense it represents life and is also a chance to get away from life" (p. 91). This boy no doubt is in possession of norms and strategies that enable him to create meanings at a symbolic level.

THE STUDY

Question and Hypotheses

The purpose of this study is to chart the development of children's and adolescents' gradual growth towards aesthetic understanding. This development is conceived of in terms of acquiring socially based norms and strategies that govern, in this case, the interpretation of contemporary potentially symbolic poetry.

An additional general aim is to determine the relationships between readers' sociocultural background and their level of interpretation. The background variables examined include: tale-telling habits of the home, reading of fiction, reading of nonfiction, length of reading time, and depth of intention.

"Tale-telling habits of the home" is an indicator of the opportunities for *early repeated exposure to the literary medium* in the home. The variable "reading of fiction," together with "reading of nonfiction" reveals the possible effects of the amount of reading in general. In addition, "reading of fiction" is essential as a possible indicator of a *sustained cultivated disposition.* A third factor of importance is *degree of commitment to the aesthetic enclave of meaning* and its media specific activities. It is, in addition to "reading of fiction," operationalized as depth of intention in reading, that is, the ability or tendency to report and specify significant literary experiences. "Length of reading-time" is related to the variable of reading in general and is defined as the length of the time used on each reading occasion. Thus, the general question of this study may be stated as follows:

What interpretive strategies are practiced by readers at various age-levels and levels of cultivated disposition in order to make sense of poetry.

In accordance with the theoretical assumptions in previous sections it may be hypothesized that the number of interpretive responses, including symbolic interpretations, increase with age. The interpretation of poetry presupposes a cooperative attitude based on certain norms and strategies that are slowly and gradually acquired through informal and formal schooling.

Inasmuch as the effectiveness of this more or less systematic instruction is dependent on the amount and quality of predisposing experiences, it may also be expected that readers characterized by a pronounced cultivated disposition will exhibit more such interpretive and symbolic interpretations, than will readers with a less marked inclination of that kind.

Method

Subjects. Seventy-two subjects, equally divided between females and males at each of three age-levels (modal and median ages 11, 14, and 18) participated in the study. Subjects were selected at random from their classes, although, by prearrangement, a few children with known learning disabilities were eliminated from the selection procedure. The sample was drawn from six similar schools located in socially heterogenous but predominantly middle-class school districts in Sweden. The three grade-levels were as far as possible matched with respect to the social character of the school districts. The 24 eighteen-year-olds were pupils attending vocational or academic courses of two- or three-year duration.

Material. From a large number of contemporary poetic works reviewed for the study 23 poems were selected in accordance with the following criteria: They should be relatively short, of approximately the same length, unrhymed and written by well-established Swedish authors. By means of a number of pilot studies four poems were ultimately selected (see Figure 6.1). They all emerged as written in a style comprehensible to children and adolescents, as containing at least one motif implying symbolic meanings, and as being open to symbolic as well as nonsymbolic interpretation (defined for the purpose of this study as diguised symbolism). The four poems were recorded on tape by the experimenter, and books were produced which presented the texts, one on every other page. The order of the works presented was counterbalanced across age, sex, schools, and courses.

Procedure. Each subject was brought into a quiet room where he or she was seen individually by the experimenter for approximately 40 minutes. After the usual precautions had been taken to make the subject feel at ease, he or she was told that the study was about children's and adolescents' conceptions of poems, and that he or she would hear four short poems on a tape. The poems were presented one at a time, and the subjects were asked after each presentation, having had time to consider the poem: "What do you think this poem is about?" After this first session the subject was asked a number of follow-up questions (see Svensson, 1985), and finally he or she was asked to fill out a questionnaire. The questionnaire comprised questions intended to measure the degree of cultivated

Autumn walk	*It is this persistent wind*

Autumn walk

A man walks through the woods on
a day of changing light.
Meets few people, stops, gazes at
the autumn sky.
He heads for the churchyard and
none follows him.

It is this persistent wind

It is this persistent wind.
It just gets stronger.

One after the other the old trees fall
here in the garden.

before the fruit has had time to
ripen.

The light and the beetle

Light
– on everything and everyone.
Even the smallest beetle has a
shadow which he cannot run away
from.

Deep, deep in my heart

Deep, deep in my heart I know
everything about the sea.
With closed eyes I see it before me.
Far, far from the sea I listen evening
after evening to the voice of the sea.

Figure 6.1.   The Poems Used as Material in the Study. (Here as Verbatim Translations from the Swedish Originals.)

disposition operationalized as tale-telling habits of the home environment, opportunities for establishing early reading habits (the reading of fiction and nonfiction), length of reading time, and depth of intention in reading. The questionnaire was answered in writing by each of the subjects in about ten minutes.

Scoring. Each recorded interview session was transcribed in its entirety and a protocol was established for each of the subjects. The responses on the first question were coded into one of six categories. Examples of each type of response and the criteria used to define the categories are presented below (Table 6.1). It should be noted that the coding manual does not necessarily imply any grading of the categories involved. Although the figurative responses can be expected to occur later in the course of socialization, it does not seem reasonable in each specific case to classify them as a category at a higher level than literal responses. The type of symbolism involved, disguised symbolism, is possible to interpret symbolically as well as nonsymbolically. There might be cases in which a literal response to a certain poem of this kind is regarded as a higher form of response, from the perspective of a specific interpretive community.

Reliability was established by two independent judges on a 30% subset

Table 6.1. Interpretations of Sample Poems.

Category	Definition and guidelines for scoring	Examples*
Literal descriptive	An interpretation is offered that consists of nothing but what is explicitly expressed in the poem. No point is noted; no enigma is indicated and/or responded to.	The wind blows and trees fall. It's about a beetle that can't run away from his shadow.
Literal interpretive	An interpretation is presented that—on a literal level—at least partly goes beyond what is explicitly expressed in the poem. A point or an enigma is created and occasionally expounded.	It's a gardener who is sad because his fruit falls off before it has had time to ripen. Even though the beetle is small it has a shadow like people have.
Mixed literal —thematic	A thematic statement is made, but other parts of the interpretation offered still indicate a literal reading.	The smallest beetle is important. Like people it has a shadow which it can't run away from. Old things have the least staying power. The wind blows the trees over.
Thematic	The response consists of a generalized inference concerning a surface point or enigma. An abstracted overall meaning or organizing principle is proposed, sometimes in the form of a saying or a saying-like wording. The point of departure and subject of the summarizing statement is an element (image, object, situation, etc.) understood as type.	Nothing can stop the natural forces You should pay regard to animals even though they are small.
Mixed literal-symbolic	Either there is an individual element in a whole given a symbolic meaning, while the rest is approached literally, or there is a vacillation between a literal and a symbolic approach to the whole work or parts of it.	Some sort of a storm. A power that has made a mess of it. Everyone and everything are created out of one cause, and there is no getting away from that fact. The sun is the cause of all life. Then you have a shadow.
Symbolic	Some sort of abstracted summarizing statement is made which entails an implicit or explicit analogical (one-to-one) transference of the symbolic element(s) to some other specific object(s), image(s), etc., which it is (they are) supposed to represent. The meaning of the symbolic element(s) is attached as accompanying (part of a) story, tradition or myth. The point of departure and subject of the summarizing statement is an element (image, object, situation, etc.) understood as symbol.	It's about an evil power that you can't counteract. The light is God, the beetle people and shadow their sins.

*The examples refer to the poems *It is this persistent wind* by Urban Andersson and *The light and the beetle* by Bo Setterlind.

Table 6.2.   Percentage of Response Types at Each Age-Level on the Symbol Interpretation Task.

Age (in years)	No answer/ I don't know	Literal- descr.	Literal- Interpr.	Mixed literal- thematic	Thematic	Mixed literal- symbolic	Symbolic
11	4	23	59	2	4	4	4
14	2	19	57	0	4	1	17
18	6	12	33	4	2	8	35

of the protocols (92% agreement was obtained). The remaining protocols were coded by one judge. For the purpose of hypotheses testing by means of chi-square analyses the categories were collapsed into two overall categories, a symbolic and a nonsymbolic variable. Items on the questionnaire were scored by the assignment of values ranging from one to four. In accordance with the median a group of high scorers and a group of low scorers were established on the two variables (symbolic and non symbolic). High and low groups on each variable were compared with respect to their performance on the interpretation task. The association was examined by means of chi-square analysis. The accepted significance level was 5%.

Results

The percentage of response types at each age-level on the symbol interpretation task is presented in Table 6.2. A preliminary analysis of sex effect revealed no significant effects, and for this reason the sex variable was eliminated from further considerations of the results of this task.

Forty-nine percent of the 18-year-olds', 22% of the 14-year-olds', and 14% of the 11-year-olds' interpretations are figurative (responses classified as mixed literal-thematic, thematic, mixed literal-symbolic, or symbolic). The greater part of these responses were symbolic. For the literal interpretations the differences are to be found particularly between the 11- and 14-year-olds, on the one hand, and the 18-year-olds on the other. Literal interpretations are approximately twice as common in the two younger groups as in the oldest group. The same holds for the descriptive responses. There were no differences between the poems with regard to response types elicited in the age groups.

In order to examine the effects of age for symbolic and non-symbolic responses, chi-square analyses were computed. The response categories were collapsed into two main categories: symbolic and nonsymbolic interpretations. The symbolic category included symbolic and mixed literal-symbolic interpretations, while the nonsymbolic category included the

Table 6.3. Number of Subjects at Each Age-Level Who Responded Non-Symbolically and Symbolically on the Symbol Interpretation Task.[a]

| Category | Age-levels | | | |
	11	14	18	Total
No symbolic interpretation	19	15	7	41
At least one symbolic interpretation	5	9	17	31
Total	24	24	24	72

[a]$\chi^2 = 12.69 > 5.99$; $p < 0.05$.

Table 6.4. The Association Between Predisposing Experiences and Performance on the Symbol Interpretation Task.

| Predisposing experience | High scorer | Low scorer | Chi-square test | | |
| Name | Number of symbolic interpretations | | | | |
	>0 0	>0 0	χ^2	p	s
Tale-telling habits of the home	20 14	11 27	6.53>3.84,	p<0.05	s
Reading of fiction	23 19	8 22	5.63>3.84,	p<0.05	s
Depth of intention in reading	23 19	8 22	5.63>3.84,	p<0.05	s
Reading of non-fiction	19 14	12 27	5.24>3.84,	p<0.05	s
Length of reading-time	12 8	19 33	3.24<3.84,	p>0.05	ns

remaining responses. In accordance with the median the subjects were divided into two groups: those yielding at least one symbolic response, and those yielding no symbolic response at all (Table 6.3).

Table 6.3 shows a significant effect of age for symbolic and nonsymbolic types of response. The effect is significant in the theoretically predicted direction and seems to be due mainly to the difference between the two younger groups on the one hand and the oldest group on the other.

According to one of the hypotheses there would also be an effect of predisposing experiences on the readers' performance on the symbol interpretation task. In order to test this hypothesis the proportion of subjects who yielded at least one symbolic interpretation and those who yielded no symbolic interpretation at all were compared among the high scorers and low scorers on each variable of predisposing experiences (Table 6.4).

A chi-square analysis comparing the number of high scorers and low scorers on each variable across age revealed no significant effects except for the reading of nonfiction: $= 16.45 > 3.84, p < 0.05$. A similar computation across sex obtained significant effects for tale-telling habits ($= 10.92 > 3.84, p < 0.05$) and the reading of fiction ($= 4.59 > 3.84, p > 0.05$).

The high scorers and low scorers on each variable were compared with respect to their tendency to respond symbolically. As shown, the number of subjects who responded with at least one symbolic interpretation is greater among the high scorers on the variables of "tale-telling habits of the home," "depth of intention in reading," "reading of fiction," and "reading of non fiction." There were no significant effects of sex.

To sum up, the results indicate that the number of interpretive and figurative responses increases with age and amount of certain predisposing experiences. Symbolic strategies occur even in the group of 11-year-olds, which contains insignificantly fewer symbol interpreters than does the group of 14-year-olds. The oldest group contains by far the greatest number of symbol interpreters. More than two-third of the 18-year-olds provided at least one symbolic response. (For extensive qualitative analyses of the responses obtained on the symbol interpretation task, see Svensson, 1987.)

DISCUSSION

Interpretive Norms and Strategies

The results of the study show that there are features of ordinary readers' sense-making activities constituted by socialization into the literary community. These invariant features, which here have been conceptualized as interpretive strategies governed by certain norms and relevancies, are possible to characterize as indicative of the readers' gradual growth into the literary community.

This socialization involves learning to infer significant meanings or central insights that integrate each part of the text into a unified and consistent whole. Such a happy outcome of the reader's encounter with the sequence of squiggles presupposes an active and cooperative posture on the part of the reader through the creation of gaps or enigmas, and the generalization of elements into types or symbols.

The data obtained on the symbol interpretation task were possible to classify into categories along the dimensions of interpretive-descriptive, or subjective-objective. The descriptive responses revealed no traces of an intensive sense-making activity such as the solving of enigmas or the filling in of gaps.

The interpretive responses ranged from literal via thematic to symbolic interpretations. The literal-interpretive responses are the results of various strategies of going beyond the information given. Gaps are noticed and filled in, points are suggested, extrapolations are carried out, and so on. Sometimes even the principle of significance is obeyed. Otherwise, generalization seems to be the major means of meeting the demands of this principle.

In providing a thematic response, readers draw on some kind of supplemented meaning (e.g., point or enigma) which is generalized and ascribed a broader significance. The generalized element is a person, an action, a situation, and so on, representative of a type. This means that the supplemented meaning still refers to the literal level, or to the meaning of the normal contexts (see the coding manual above for some illustrative examples). Yet, the generalized statement in most cases expresses a "significant attitude to some problem concerning man and/or his relation to the universe" (see above) and, thus, the principle of central insight has been respected. This interpretive type qualifies as a figurative interpretation inasmuch as the reader who creates it transcends the purely representational meaning. Moreover, the thematic interpretation expresses an organizing principle or a theme of the work.

In symbolic reading, not only the principles of significance and thematic unity are operative but also the principle of metaphoric coherence. The latter norm states that one should attempt through semantic transformations to produce coherence on both the literal and figurative levels by integrating each element of the work into a unified whole. Not all symbol interpreters were successful in this respect. Their responses have been classified as mixed literal-symbolic. In a symbolic interpretation the generalized element is not apprehended as type but as symbol, that is, as transcending the meaning of the normal contexts, as referring to an enclave of meaning other than the world of everyday knowledge (see the coding manual above for some illustrative examples).

Some of the norms or principles, underlying the various interpretive strategies and types were explicitly articulated by some of the subjects in their dealing with the tasks of the follow-up questions. They preferred to justify their symbolic interpretations by referring to the principle of significance, and the general principle of cooperation was clearly expressed when they discussed the concept of interpretation. And when asked if there were in the poems any odd or unusual elements, the principle of thematic unity was consciously actualized by some of the readers. The following example from the interview material indicates that the reader has an awareness of the principles of cooperation and significance:

Interviewer: You said about this poem "The light and the beetle" that it is about everybody having some imperfection they want to disguise, or maybe about Destiny, which you cannot escape. What makes you think it is about that and not about light and a beetle?

Carl-Peter (aged 18): Well, why, well, I always look for a hidden meaning when

I read stuff like this. I can't ... An author like that doesn't
sit down and write about a beetle. He's got to have something to describe, otherwise you wouldn't ... they wouldn't
get well-known.

A Cultural-Developmental Perspective

In the present study, differences in age are assumed to represent differences in the length of the time of exposure to aesthetic and other media,
or stages in the process of familiarization within the aesthetic universe of
meaning. Older readers have in general had the opportunity to practice
various interpretive strategies in the literary medium for a longer time
than have younger readers. Moreover, systematic formal instruction
within the aesthetic realm occurs late in the course of schooling and becomes increasingly specialized. Norms, strategies, vocabulary, and so on
bearing on poetry reading are generally not taught systematically until the
10th or 11th grades, as suggested by the current textbooks and curricula
employed in Sweden (for research of the effects of instruction on aesthetic growth, see, e.g., Silverman, Winner, & Gardner, 1976).

The hypotheses of the study were supported. The number of interpretive responses, including figurative interpretations like symbolic responses, increased with age and amount of predisposing experiences. The
results confirm the assumption that the interpretation of poetry presupposes a specific posture based on certain norms and strategies that are
slowly and gradually acquired. The significant association between the
performance on the interpretation task and four of the variables of predisposing experiences indicates the importance of a propitious home environment, familiarity with the medium of fiction (including poetry), and a
deep engagement in the response to literature. Early and regular exposure
to the literary medium in the form of fairy tales, stories, songs, and so on
promotes a tendency to attach value to works of literature and in an ability
to appropriate them by means of basic rules, procedures, and generic categories. The results show that such a cultivated disposition is related to a
regular and keen reading of fiction later in childhood and adolescence.
This reading in turn, and together with the early acquaintance with fairy
tales and so on, functions as a prerequisite for the appropriation of more
advanced works of literature, like the poems in this study, and for formal,
systematic schooling as regards the interpretation of literature.

In addition, the results indicate that a substantial amount of general
reading, including the reading of newspapers, journals, and so on, is a predictor of the use of figurative and symbolic strategies in the interpretation
of poetry. Irrespective of the relatedness of this variable to the other variables, it seems reasonable to assume an effect of a close acquaintance

with written language per se on the readers' performance on the symbol interpretation task.

Although no one group of readers favored literal-descriptive responses, these occurred particularly among the younger and poorly predisposed subjects. Those subjects who approached the poems descriptively lacked the appropriate posture of intensive reading and action and gave no proof of specific interpretive strategies, such as the construction of enigmas or points. However, only a very few of the readers responded consistently in this descriptive manner. Hence, the vast majority of the subjects provided at least one stated response indicative of a more active construction of meaning. In so doing they suggested an interpretation partially based on a filled-in gap, a solved enigma, or an apprehended point. This literal-interpretive response type was by far the most frequent one in the two youngest groups.

The strategies of generalizing elements of the poems into types or symbols were practiced at all age levels. The resulting interpretive types, thematic and symbolic, can be conceived of as a means of satisfying the principle of significance, in that they express a central insight or a significant attitude to some problem concerning the individual and/or her/his relation to the universe (see the coding manual above for some illustrative examples). This principle was operative particularly among the 18-year-olds, who, accordingly, offered by far the greatest number of figurative interpretations, especially symbolic ones. The symbolic response type was in fact the most frequent one among the oldest subjects.

The principle of cooperation, of intensive processing of literary works of art, is acquired early in the family or school context. Children are encouraged to carry out (in speech and in writing) more productive performatory activities in relation to, for example, fairy tales and stories. By modifying the tales and the stories, or creating their own tales and stories, children not only extend their knowledge of the literary medium but also come to take up an appropriate posture vis-á-vis literary works of art. Hence, 11-year-olds are, in general, able to apply to the reading of poetry the strategy of creating enigmas or points.

Hence, children acquire some of the most basic conventions concerning literary interpretation by means of interacting with adults. In these encounters children learn the rule of cooperative negotiation and an interpretive attitude towards literature. Also more specific conventions, such as applying literature to reality and reality to literature, are acquired in these interactive events (Cochran-Smith, 1984). Later on in the course of literary socialization a similar mechanism is operative in literary instruction, which further contributes to the elaboration of students' literary knowledge, including conventionalized motifs and genre-related expectations.

These interactive encounters entail "guidance in a medium," an instructional means through which the child and adolescent is oriented towards essential features of the medium, for example points and themes. The performing of various activities in relation to a medium, for example, promotes the development of distinctions in that medium and in the perceptual world in general (Olson, 1970). These activities provide the occasion for gaining new information from the perceptual world, including the literary medium. By means of the various forms of instruction mentioned in this article the child's and the adolescent's picking up of further information in this respect can be facilitated.

The principle of intensive reading is not only a norm tied to the genre of fiction in general but also a more or less unavoidable element of the socialization process, for example in the form of tale-telling interactions. The strategy of thematic reading presupposes the ability to identify/produce enigmas and points. Since it is also associated with a more genre-specific norm, namely the principle of significance, thematic interpretations can be expected to occur later than can the literal-interpretive ones. From data it is evident, first, that thematic interpretations were given only in exceptional cases by subjects who favored purely descriptive responses, and, second, that the percentage of thematic interpretations increased with age and degree of cultivated disposition.

Both the symbolic and the thematic strategies involve generalization, and both are related to the principle of significance. This would imply that they are appropriated approximately simultaneously in the course of socialization. On the other hand, the thematic interpretations are based on generalizations of enigmas or points, which refer to the literal level of meaning. In that respect they are closer to the literal-interpretive responses. However, the results are inconclusive. Further research is needed to elucidate the developmental relationship between thematic and symbolic response types.

With the symbolic interpretations, however, the developmental pattern is more distinct. Their number increases with age. On the whole, the results suggest that before the age of 15 symbolic strategies are not in general use and are employed predominantly in relation to uncomplicated texts and by highly predisposed readers. At the age of 18 such strategies are common.

That a frequent use of symbolic strategies in the interpretation of poetry occurs relatively late indicates the long-term character of the acquisition of literary sense-making strategies. Even granted a high degree of cultivated disposition in its various aspects, the mastering of symbolic strategies seems to presuppose long-term exposure to the literary medium, including poetry. Through this exposure the significant themes and motifs, including possible symbolic meanings characteristic of the aesthetic realm, are slowly and gradually assimilated. Some of these themes or meanings overlap with or are possible to substitute for popular notions or cultural notions in general. Hence, cultural exposure in general is a factor of some importance. Beach and Wendler's (1987) analysis of differences between high school and college students' inferences about story characters also suggests that readers' knowledge of literary conventions are derived not only from reading but also from social experiences.

Moreover, even though a symbolic awareness is at least nascently present in a good number of the younger readers, a skilled employment of symbolic strategies requires a long period of applying these strategies through the systematic and specialized literary instruction in upper secondary school.

Again, however, the importance of cultivated disposition should be emphasized. It is an interesting fact that even some 11-year-olds, due to their culturally propitious home environment, obviously exhibit some of the most advanced interpretive behaviors characteristic of the literary community. And it is equally noteworthy that some of the 18-year-olds, due to their low degree of cultivated disposition, still seem after 12 years of schooling, entirely unaware of the symbolic dimension of literature.

The developmental trends obtained in this study, along the dimensions descriptive-interpretive and literal-figurative, corroborate the earlier reported findings of Silverman et al. (1976), Applebee (1978), Parsons et al. (1978), Rosenstiel, Morison, Silverman, and Gardner (1978), and Hardy-Brown (1979).

Implications for the Teaching of Literature

A strategy-oriented approach to literature instruction undoubtedly implies a number of considerable advantages in comparison with more traditional models of teaching. The cultural-developmental view is, of course, educationally more rewarding than are theories that neglect or underestimate the sociocultural basis of learning and thinking. And even though the long-term character of the acquisition of various aesthetic skills and their unequal social distribution might seem distressing, aesthetic development from a cultural-developmental point of view is to a large extent open to instructional influences.

The "strategic" approach makes possible a systematic and developmentally adapted sequencing of literature instruction. To a certain extent literature instruction will then be comparable to models employed by disciplines like language and second-language instruction. It would exceed the scope of this article to dwell more concretely on the presentation of this approach. Suffice it here to refer to Steinley's (1982) and Probst's (1984) excellent applications of similar ideas to literature instruction.

The "strategic" approach, moreover, stresses learning underlying norms and procedures involved in interpreting texts. This means increased possibilities to utilize and build upon the students' already existing proficiencies. In fact, most students already master a number of basic norms and strategies for making sense of literary discourse, though these skills are not always recognized as such by traditionally educated teachers, who often take their own content-oriented, academic knowledge as their point of departure. New interpretive strategies should be practiced in content-domains which are already appreciated and mastered (e.g., children's literature, advertisments, lyrics of popular songs, proverbs and sayings).

Among the more specific teaching techniques to be recommended are class discussions. In these discussions the students are encouraged to identify gaps to fill out, enigmas to solve, and to generalize these supplemented meanings into an overall meaning of the literary work. Sometimes in relation to certain texts it might be advisable for the teacher to point out and suggest gaps and enigmas for the students. Also more structured techniques consisting of preformulated questionnaires may serve the same purpose. The principle of thematic unity and the strategy of thematic reading may very well be practiced on fables and stories with a plain moral. (For further teaching techniques in accordance with the assumptions of this chapter, see Probst, 1984.)

To be able to assimilate further concepts and experiences with already existing ones children and adolescents also need help in making their conceptions explicit. The major tool for the accomplishment of this task is language. An essential aspect of literature instruction is to furnish an appropriate vocabulary by means of interpretive exercises and metacognitive talk. Through the latter activity our students also may gain insights into the basic norms and strategies underlying the interpretation of literary texts and be provided with opportunities to reflect upon and try out their conceptions of the interpretive process and the value and purpose of the reading of fiction.

When increased literary awareness is our instructional goal, the strategy-oriented approach is even more appropriate, if not self-evident. If "literary awareness" is defined as *the ability to make the sense-making norms, strategies, and so on, opaque, to pay attention to them in their own right,* then it is an essential task to help our literature student make explicit the various elements of their sense-making activities per se. It is a reasonable assumption that increased awareness of the interpretive process improves literary interpretive skill (see Svensson, 1985, for a discussion of and some empirical support for this assumption).

It seems important to provide young readers with opportunities not only for regular and broad reading but also for pleasurable experiences in that respect. The affective-motivational aspect of predisposing experiences must not be underestimated.

Broad reading here also implies opportunities for the carrying out of various performatory activities in relation to different media. The teaching of literature must not be confined to only "literary" literature. Neither should it be restricted to reading activity but include also reasoning and production.

REFERENCES

Applebee, A. N. (1978). *The child's concept of story.* Chicago: University of Chicago Press.

Barchas, S. E. (1971). *Expressed reading interests of children of differing ethnic groups.* Unpublished doctoral dissertation, University of Arizona, Tuscon, AZ.

Beach, R., & Wendler, L. (1987, October). Developmental differences in response to a story. *Research in the Teaching of English, 21*(3), 286–297

Bleich, D. (1978). *Subjective criticism.* Baltimore: The Johns Hopkins University Press.

Bourdieu, P. (1968). Outline of a sociological theory of art perception. *International Social Science Journal, 20,* 589–612.

Burgdorff, A. B. (1966). *A study of the ability of intermediate-grade children to draw inferences from selections of children's literature.* Unpublished doctoral dissertation, Ball State University, Muncie, IN.

Clark, H. H., & Clark, E. V. (1977). *Psychology of language. An introduction to psycholinguistics.* New York: Harcourt Brace Jovanivich, Inc.

Cochran-Smith, M. (1984). *The making of a reader.* Norwood, NJ: Ablex.

Cole, M., & Griffin, P. (1980). Cultural amplifiers reconsidered. In D. R. Olson (Ed.), *The social foundations of language and thought: Essays in honor of Jerome S. Bruner* (pp. 343–364). New York & London: W. W. Norton & Company.

Culler, J. (1975). *Structuralist poetics. Structuralism, linguistics and the study of literature.* London and Henley: Routledge & Kegan Paul.

van Dijk, T. A., & Kintsch, W. (1983). *Strategies of discourse comprehension.* New York: Academic Press.

Fish, S. (1980). *Is there a text in this class? The authority of interpretive communities.* Cambridge MA and London: Harvard University Press.

Gardner, H., Winner, E., & Kircher, M. (1975). Children's conceptions of the arts. *Journal of Aesthetic Education, 9,* 60–77.

Giorgi, A. (1970). *Psychology as a human science.* New York: Harper and Row.

Hansen, H. S. (1967). *The relationship between the home literary environment and selfcommitment to independent reading.* Unpublished doctoral dissertation, University of Wisconsin, Green Bay, WI.

Hardy-Brown, K. (1979). Formal operations and the issue of generalizability: The analysis of poetry by college students. *Human Development, 22*, 127–136.

Heath, S. B. (1983). *Ways with words.* Cambridge: Cambridge University Press.

Machotka, P. (1961). *The development of aesthetic criteria in childhood.* Unpublished doctoral dissertation, Harvard University, Cambridge, MA.

Machotka, P. (1966). Aesthetic criteria in childhood. *Child Development, 37*, 877–885.

Madéja, S. S. (1978). Introduction. In S. S. Madéja (Ed.), *The arts, cognition, and basic skills.* St. Louis, MO: Cemrel, Inc.

McCloskey, E. F. (1966). *A study of the free reading habits of sixth grade negroe boys living in disadvantage areas in the city of New York.* Unpublished doctoral dissertation, Columbia University, New York.

Miller, G. A. (1976). Text comprehension skills and process models of text comprehension. In H. Singer & R. B. Rudell (Eds.), *Theoretical models and processes of reading* (2nd ed., pp. 709–729). Newark, NJ: International Reading Association.

Monson, D. L. (1966). *Children's responses to humorous situations in literature.* Unpublished doctoral dissertation, University of Minnesota, Minneapolis, MN.

Olson, D. R. (1970). *Cognitive development. The child's acquisition of diagonality.* New York and London: Academic Press.

Panofsky, E. (1953). *Early Netherlandish painting.* Cambridge, MA: Harvard University Press.

Parsons, M. J. (1976). A suggestion concerning the development of aesthetic experience in children. *Journal of Aesthetics and Art Criticism, 34*(3), 305–314.

Parsons, M. J., Johnston, M., & Durham, R. (1978, January). Developmental stages in children's aesthetic responses. *Journal of Aesthetic Education, 12*(1), 83–104.

Plederer-Zimmermann, M. (1967). Conservation and the development of musical intelligence. *Journal of Research in Music Education, 15*, 215–223.

Probst, R. E. (1984). *Adolescent literature: Response and analysis.* Columbus, OH: Charles E. Merrill Publishing Company.

Purves, A. C. (1981). *Reading and literature: American achievement in international perspective.* Urbana, IL: National Council of Teachers of English.

Purves, A. C. (1988). The reader as cultural artifact. In C. Svensson (Ed.), *Litteraturen ach läsarna. Festskrift till Gunnar Hansson* (SIC 20). Linköping, Sweden: Tema Kommunikation, Universitetet i Linköping.

Purves, A. C. & Beach, R. (1972). *Literature and the reader: Research in response to literature, reading interests, and the teaching of literature.* Urbana, IL: National Council of Teachers of English.

Rabinowitz, P. (1987). *Before reading.* Cornell, NY: Cornell University Press.

Rosario, J. (1977). Children's conceptions of the arts: A critical response to Howard Gardner. *Journal of Aesthetic Education, 11*, 91–100.

Rosario, J. (1978). On the child's acquisition of aesthetic meaning: The contribution of schooling. In G. Willis (Ed.), *Qualitative evaluation, concepts and cases in curriculum criticism* (pp. 208–226). Berkeley, CA: McCuthran Publishing Corporation.

Rosario, J., & Collazo, E. (1981, January). Aesthetic codes in context: An exploration in two preschool classrooms. *Journal of Aesthetic Education, 15*, 71–82.

Rosenstiel, A. K., Morison, P., Silverman, J., & Gardner, H. (1978). Critical judgment: A developmental study. *Journal of Aesthetic Education, 12*(4), 95–107.

Shimron, J. (1980). Psychological processes behind the comprehension of a poetic text. *Instructional Science, 9*, 43–66.

Silverman. J., Winner, E., & Gardner, H. (1976). On going beyond the literal: The development of sensitivity to artistic symbols. *Semiotica, 18*(4), 291–312.

Steinley, G. L. (1982). Symbologizing: Recognizing and naming symbols. *College English, 44*, 44–56.

Svensson, C. (1985). *The construction of poetic meaning: A cultural-developmental study of symbolic and non-symbolic strategies in the interpretation of contemporary poetry.* Malmö, Sweden: Liber.

Svensson, C. (1987). The construction of poetic meaning: A developmental study of symbolic and non-symbolic strategies in the interpretation of contemporary poetry. *Poetics, 16*, 471–503.

Tajfel, H. (1969). Social and cultural factors in perception. In G. Lindzey & E. Aronson (Eds.), *The handbook of social psychology* (Vol. 3, pp. 315–379). Reading MA. Addison-Wesley.

Wollner, M. H. B. (1949). *Children's voluntary reading as an expression of individuality.* (Teachers College Contributions to Education, No. 944.) New York: Bureau of Publication, Teachers College, Columbia University.

7
Writing and Reasoning about Literature

James D. Marshall

How do the ways in which students write about literature help shape their understanding of literature itself? The last decade has provided a growing number of studies on the relationships between writing and learning in school, and several of these have examined the role of writing in the study of literature. On the one hand, this work has drawn on theoretical frameworks developed by Cassirer (1944), Vygotsky (1962), Bruner (1964), Langer (1967), and Britton (1970)—frameworks which view language, and especially written language, as a primary mode of representation that shapes thought and enables cognitive growth. On the other hand, research on writing and learning has been informed by empirical work in prose learning (e.g., Doctorow, Wittrock, & Marks, 1978; Peper & Mayer, 1978; Reder, 1980)—work which views writing as a means of processing information more deeply, thus enhancing the writer's memory for that information. Together, these two traditions of inquiry have furnished a promising conceptual base for studies of writing and learning across the disciplines (Weiss & Walters, 1980; Newell, 1984; Langer, 1986; Langer & Applebee, 1987) as well as in classrooms where literature is the major focus of instruction (Marshall, 1987, 1988; Newell, in press). And in general, these studies have concluded that writing is indeed a powerful instrument of thought, providing students with the opportunity to learn more about a subject in the very act of writing about it.

But while the work in this area has built a strong case for the positive effects of writing on learning, it has also raised new questions about the nature of writing and about the measurement of learning. In his review of the research, for example, Applebee (1984) suggests that "to the extent that writing is related to reasoning, the relationships will be complex rather than straightforward ..." (p. 594), and that research should "shift from a general focus on the effects of 'writing' toward a more rigorous conceptualization of the functions that writing can serve" (p. 594). Different writing tasks, in other words, may lead to different *kinds* of learning, and not simply to different *amounts* of learning, although our measures of what students may learn as a result of their writing have seldom been sensitive enough to capture the range of those differences. We have evidence, for example, that extended writing about texts enables students to remember information longer and more fully than restricted writing (Newell, 1984; Marshall, 1987; Langer & Applebee, 1987), and that some extended modes of writing about literature result in higher ratings than others (Newell, in press). But the very words we use to describe such findings ("longer," "more," "higher") suggest that research in the field has yet to move beyond a quantitative conception of learning toward a more qualitative analysis of the kinds of knowledge writing can produce. We have learned a great deal by measuring what students may know as a result of their writing, but we may learn even more by stepping back to ask what we mean by "knowledge" and by looking closely at the language students use to represent it.

Such a shift in focus seems especially critical for our discussions of writing about literature, for here we find little consensus about what knowledge of literary texts might be. The one point on which everyone might agree is that simple recalls of textual information—the measure most frequently used in studies of prose learning—are inappropriate to the study of literary understanding. Beyond this, however, one enters fully into a debate about legitimate sources of knowledge about texts that would seem to forestall any effort to measure such knowledge. Jonathan Culler's (1975) attempt to define literary competence as mastery of interpretive conventions provided one possible point of departure, but his argument left open the question of what those conventions might be. And recent arguments by Holland (1975), Bleich (1975), Rosenblatt (1978), Fish (1980), and Eagleton (1983) have made the conventions themselves the object of debate, proposing ways of reading texts that result in very different kinds of knowledge about them.

However, if we cannot agree on what knowledge of literary texts is, let alone how to measure it, we may at least examine the language students use to develop different kinds of knowledge about texts. We can ask, in other words, how the various forms of written discourse in which students engage when they study literature help shape their understanding of that literature—this, as a prelude to discussions of how that understanding might be enhanced. The following is an attempt to examine two kinds of knowledge that students may use and produce in their written discourse about literature.

TOWARDS A MODEL OF WRITING ABOUT
LITERATURE IN SCHOOL

Examining the role of written discourse in students' understanding of texts, however, requires first an adequate conceptual model of the kinds of writing about literature that students may be assigned in school. Such a model would not merely name the forms (book reports, journal entries, short-answer questions, extended arguments), but would attempt to organize those forms into a theoretically coherent set that would specify the relationship of one form to another and would additionally address the kinds of thinking each form required. We might, for example, categorize writing about literature simply in terms of its length (from short-answer questions, say, to more extended essays) or in terms of its formality (from journal entries to more structured analyses). These relatively straightforward models would allow us to place various kinds of writing along a continuum, thus providing one tool for organizing instruction. But while both of these may be practically useful, they focus primarily on the nature of the writing produced rather than on the kinds of thinking that inform the writing. And thus both are inadequate for the task of examining how writing may shape students' understanding of texts.

A more theoretically powerful model, addressing both the nature of students' written products and the nature of their thinking processes, organizes students' informational writing in school along a scale of abstraction, ranging from relatively simple records of events to analyses and theoretical speculations about why events occur as they do. Deriving from the work of James Moffett (1968), the model has been elaborated and employed in several major studies of school writing (Britton, Burgess, Martin, McLeod, & Rosen, 1975; Applebee, 1981, 1984). It has also achieved a fairly pervasive curricular authority, shaping the ways in which writing tasks are organized in textbooks (e.g., Winterowd & Murray, 1983; Farmer, Yesner, Zemelman, & Boone 1985), and often the ways in which writing tasks are sequenced in actual instruction (e.g., Marshall, 1984b).

As implemented in schools, the model often takes the form of a continuum that moves from personal narrative at one end to more public forms of analysis and argumentation at the other (Figure 7.1). Instruction, in the form of writing assignments, almost always proceeds from left to right along the continuum. This pattern obtains within particular classrooms (personal narratives come first as a way of building confidence and competence; public arguments are the goal, and come near the end of the instructional sequence) (Marshall, 1984b), across the grade levels (personal writing is more frequent in the early grades; public arguments in the upper grades) (Britton et al., 1975; Applebee, 1981, 1984), and even across ability

Personal   Public

Narrative   Analysis/
                                                         Argument

Figure 7.1.

levels (personal writing is preferred for the less able students; formal, public arguments for the college-bound) (Marshall, 1984a).

The model, as originally conceived and as implemented in schools, rests on two primary assumptions which, I would argue, are separable, though in practice they are often confounded. The first assumption is that narrative, in which chronology provides the principle of organization, is conceptually easier to sustain than analysis and argumentation—especially for younger or more inexperienced writers (Bereiter & Scardemalia, 1982; Durst, 1987). The second assumption is that students know more about themselves—their own experience, their own lives—than they do about the school subjects about which they are asked to write (Moffett, 1968; Britton, 1970; Graves, 1978, 1979). Taken together, these assumptions have provided a persuasive argument for beginning instructional sequences with a form of discourse and with a source of knowlege with which students are comfortable, moving only later toward more difficult forms and more distant sources of knowledge.

Though Moffett (1968) and Britton et al. (1975) have suggested that their models of discourse cannot be translated simply and directly into instructional practice, curricular versions of their models have been widely developed. And as developed, those models present some fairly serious problems when we consider the role of writing in students' understanding of literary texts. For by collapsing a form of discourse (narrative vs. analysis) with a source of knowledge (personal vs. public), such models assume that analyses of literature must proceed by reference to public (that is, more-or-less objective) sources of knowledge—and it is precisely that assumption that has become the focus of debate in recent discussions of literary theory. Whether the interpretation of literature should (or, indeed, *can*) take place without reference to personal sources of knowledge (however defined) has become so central to that debate that any model that finesses the issue underrepresents the very terms that need clarification.

To make room for a fuller examination of those terms, we might pull

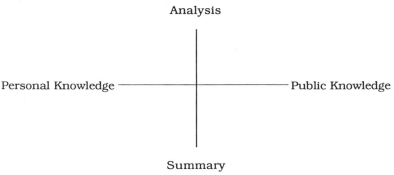

Figure 7.2.

the one-dimensional, linear model of written discourse into a two-dimensional version.

Within the larger model, it becomes possible to ask first what kinds of knowledge writers may employ when they write. They may, on the one hand, draw upon personal knowledge—knowledge which is shaped by culture, but which is finally their's alone. It is a knowledge that can be shared by a writer, but never truly verified by a reader, for it is primarily a knowledge of events as experienced, and not of the events themselves. On the other hand, writers may draw upon public knowledge—knowledge which is verifiable, which works from sources that are available to others— events, facts, and textual references that can be corroborated, argued about, and corrected if false.

We can make such a distinction about the sources of knowledge that writers employ without making a prior decision about the form their writing will take, for as suggested by Figure 7.2, writing which works from either kind of knowledge may be characterized as summary or analysis. We can summarize or narrate our experience of events or we can attempt to interpret that experience through a process of analysis and argumentation. And we can likewise summarize or analyze publicly available knowledge. Within the larger model, I would argue, it becomes possible to examine how writing may influence students' developing understanding of literary texts in terms that more adequately reflect the debates about appropriate sources of knowledge in recent discussions of literary theory.

In the following, I examine the personal and public sources of knowledge students drew upon in two forms of written discourse about literature: journal entries and stuructured arguments. The students' writing was collected during a larger study of classroom discourse about literature in an 11th grade, American literature class (Marshall, 1985, 1987, 1988). My method throughout is to attempt close readings of the students' writing about literature in order to understand the kinds of knowledge about texts that various writing tasks may elicit. I close with a discussion of how those kinds of knowledge may inform some of the curricular frameworks that govern our teaching of literature.

SOURCES OF KNOWLEDGE IN JOURNAL ENTRIES

Journals have recently become one of the most widely discussed and, perhaps, one of the most widely used features of writing instruction (Kirby & Liner, 1981; Fulwiler, 1987; Atwell, 1987). They have been proposed most often as a place for students to engage in expressive, first-draft writing that is not intended for a public, judgmental audience. In their journals, students are provided the opportunity to explore ideas freely and openly, to ask questions, to express doubts, to discuss what they know and believe about the topic at hand. Because they are relatively free of the constraints that govern other forms of school writing, journals are conceived usually as a place for students to *begin* the thinking that may result later in the more formal presentation of ideas. As Kirby and Liner (1981) put it, journals are "less structured and more subjective than most school writing assignments," and because of that, "many students find them instantly inviting, even seductive. . . . Because students use the journal to write about things *they* are interested in, they often write with clearer, more powerful language" (p. 46).

It is precisely because journals are a relatively open form of discourse that they provide a useful point of departure for our discussion of writing about literature. When students use journals as a place to think about literature, what kinds of knowledge do they use and produce? Let us examine two journal entries from two students in order to explore some of the possibilities.

The assignment was for students to keep a journal during their reading of Thoreau's *Walden*. There were no requirements as to length, purpose, or audience. The teacher simply asked students to "use the journal to think through what Thoreau was saying." The following is a excerpt from Rosemary's entries:

> Thoreau is certainly full of himself, isn't he? It's like little kids think they are the only real people in the world are themselves. He seems to be under the opinion that he is the only *truly* correct member of the human race. The rest of us are either blatently unhappy or disillusioned.
>
> What's all this about nature? Nature does not make me happy or a complete person. Granted, it's important to have around, but I feel and see no need to submerge myself in it. No way. Nature is not the bottom line of human souls, at least not mine.

Fashion! What's so bad about it? It makes people (some) happy to follow fashion. I may be brainwashed, but I generally like wearing "fashionable" clothes because they look good! Or if they don't, why bother?

I'm going to do this whole journal with this pen. It's great.

How much would his hut cost in today's world? It would depend on what materials were used. What about taxes? Would he have had to pay taxes? Is it illegal to not have a mailbox (or some mail service)? I wouldn't live in his hut. It isn't near enough to anywhere really. Well—maybe with a car. . . .

No letters? Didn't he care what people have to say to him? If someone is going to take the time and sit down to write a letter, put a stamp on it, address it, and mail it he might as well have the decency to see what they have to say! A letter, even junk mail, is a compliment.

I open everything. I love and appreciate mail. I'm on every mailing list I ever heard of.

He is such insufferable _____! Has he no indulgence? Has he no leniency? Talk about a closed mind. Doesn't he care about anyone but himself? No! I get livid just reading this book.

Ants?

The more I think and read, the more positive I am that Thoreau was either emotionally disturbed or just extremely immature. Well, maybe that's a little harsh. It's hard to tell.

I wonder why *Walden* is considered a classic. How did it happen that he became so well known? He doesn't seem to be that radically different from other writers of the period. His experiment on Walden Pond is not so unique. People had done it before and people still do. What about Grizzly Adams?

There isn't much more to say. I just remembered a portion at the beginning of the book where he wrote:

"As if you could kill time without injuring eternity."

I think this quote is wonderful. It's kind of clever and I like it. If it was at the end instead of the beginning then maybe I wouldn't feel so irate upon the completion of the reading.

It did impress me enough to earn a grudging place in my book of quotes however.

Thoreau is like that.

Perhaps the easiest way to begin a reading of Rosemary's journal is to ask what assumptions she has made about her purpose and audience. She has apparently taken the teacher at her word, choosing to "think through was Thoreau was saying" by offering both general statements about the author ("Thoreau is certainly full of himself, isn't he?") and more specific commentary on some of Thoreau's opinions ("Fashion! What's so bad about it?"; "No letters! Didn't he care what people had to say to him?"). She has organized her prose episodically, providing little or no transitions between paragraphs and little or no context for individual observations— a strategy that assumes that the reader (her teacher) has read the book and will know what sections of the text she is referring to. In a way, Rosemary has offered a kind of running dialogue with the text: She "answers" Thoreau when his views conflict with her own, and towards the end we see her moving toward a tentative and perhaps reluctant resolution of the conflict.

More interesting than Rosemary's organizational strategies, however, is the knowledge she draws upon in sustaining the dialogue. In almost every instance, she answers Thoreau by referring to her own experience or to contemporary circumstances. To Thoreau's criticism of fashion, for example, she replies, "I may be brainwashed, but I love wearing 'fashionable' clothes because they look good!". To his opinion of mail, she answers, "I open everything. I love and appreciate mail. I'm on every mailing list I ever heard of." Rosemary takes, in other words, a thoroughly ahistorical approach in her reading of Thoreau. She tests his opinions against her own, contemporary experience, using her own frame of reference as a context for interpreting and evaluating his work. The knowledge she uses and the knowledge she produces in her journal is primarily knowledge about herself—about her responses and the reasons for those responses. She has clearly "thought through what Thoreau was saying;" but she has done so by positioning herself within and working from a particular source of knowledge.

We can perhaps see the characteristics of Rosemary's journal more clearly if we contrast them with Tony's response to the same assignment:

> I have enjoyed reading *Walden* immensely. Thoreau is fun to read because his ideas go contrary to may of the ideas on which American society is based. Also, he frequently contradicts himself, or seems to. For example, on page 216 (Signet edition) Thoreau wrote, 'If a man does not keep pace with his companions, perhaps it is because he hears a different drummer." This seems contrary to the idea of an over-soul (or universal drummer). Thoreau didn't care about contradicting himself, though, for he was a believer in the views which Emerson expressed in his essay on self-reliance. Though I believe that a good deal of Thoreau's humor gets by me (whether beside or above me, I don't know), I am amused by the author's unashamed arrogance. In "Economy," Thoreau talks about his genius. On page 44, when criticizing the ancient pharohs of Egypt and the oppressed labor force, he says, 'I might possibly invent some excuse for them and him, but I have no time for it." Thoreau's arrogance, though, is in accordance with his transcendentalist ideas about individualism. Also in accordance with these ideas is the empirical fact of Thoreau's philosophy (p. 10): 'No way of thinking or doing, however ancient, can be trusted without proof.'

Tony has clearly taken a very different approach to the assignment. Though he too is "thinking through what Thoreau was saying," he has, unlike Rosemary, organized his observations in standard paragraph form and has provided his reader with textual references that sustain the flow of the argument. Though he knows that his reader knows the text, he has provided a context for his argument that can support the reader's progress through it.

More relevant than the obvious differences in style and organization, however, are the contrasting kinds of knowledge that Rosemary and Tony have brought to their efforts. While both comment upon Thoreau's apparent conceit (Rosemary thinks that Thoreau is "full of himself;" Tony is amused by the author's "unashamed arrogance"), Tony goes on to explain that conceit by reference to Thoreau's general philosophy ("Thoreau's arrogance . . . is in accordance with his transcendentalist ideas about individualism"). Whereas Rosemary employs a highly personal conceptual framework to respond to Thoreau, Tony attempts to understand and respond to Thoreau in Thoreau's own terms, viewing Thoreau's opinions within the historical and cultural context that helped shape them. Though Tony offers some personal reflections in the journal ("I have enjoyed reading Thoreau;" "I believe that a good deal of Thoreau's humor gets by me"), he elaborates upon those reflections in the direction of historical analysis and interpretation. If Rosemary's piece is primarily about herself and her own reactions to Thoreau, Tony's piece is primarily about Thoreau and *his* reactions to the historical circumstances in which he found himself. If these journal entries are both meant to be *beginnings* for the more extended or formal presentation of ideas, it seems clear that they are beginnings that proceed from contrasting assumptions about the proper *ends* of literary interpretation.

Rosemary's and Tony's journal entries, I would argue, represent two very different ways of knowing about texts, and I have discussed them at such length here because they exemplify some of the alternative strategies students may employ in reading and writing about literature. Before discussing the relative value of those strategies, however, we must first examine the knowledge students use and produce in more structured forms of written discourse about literature.

SOURCES OF KNOWLEDGE IN STRUCTURED ARGUMENTS

Students are not always or even usually free to choose the approach they will take when writing about literature in school. More often they must work within a set of conventions that are explicitly set by a particular assignment (length, form, time for completion) or that are implicitly understood by teachers and students as appropriate (clearly stating a thesis, for example, or employing evidence from the text to support an argument). It is these conventions of argumentative discourse that I would like to examine here, for embedded within them are theories of literary understanding that carry broad implications for the ways in which curricula in literature may be structured.

We can begin by looking closely at two essays written about the same text. The story is J. D. Salinger's "Pretty Mouth and Green My Eyes," in which Arthur, drunk and distressed about his wife's unfaithfulness, phones his friend Lee for advice. Lee, we find, is in bed with an unnamed woman, but he tries to calm Arthur down, assuring him that Joanie, Arthur's wife, will soon return home. Apparently succeeding in his efforts, Lee closes the conversation with Arthur and turns to the woman, only to have Arthur call again—this time to report that Joanie has indeed come home and that he has new hope for their relationship. At this point, Lee becomes visibly upset, claims a headache, and hangs up quickly. The story implies, of course, that the woman in bed with Lee is Joanie, but Salinger never states that directly, and the reader is left wondering why Arthur felt compelled to lie about Joanie's return.

Jake had read the story as part of a longer instructional unit on Salinger, and in one 90-minute block period he was asked to write on the following topic:

> In "Pretty Mouth and Green My Eyes" we are presented with three characters in a rather difficult relationship. Write an essay in which you explain how you personally feel about the characters and their relationship to one another.

The assignment would seem to push Jake in the direction we saw Rosemary taking in her journal on Thoreau. Here, however, he is to do more that simply "think through" what the author has said: He is to construct an argument, albeit a particular kind of argument.

Here is Jake's essay:

> Salinger's short story "Pretty Mouth and Green My Eyes" presents its characters in a rather precarious position. The story focuses on Lee and Joanie in bed together cheating on Lee's best friend Arthur who calls Lee in the middle of Lee's session to tell Lee about the fact that Arthur's wife has not come home yet. He thinks his wife is cheating on him. He has no idea that she is with Lee at the time which puts all of these characters in this predicament. The reader is subjected to this soap opera and has the opportunity to form personal views about each character. I, as the reader, found all of the characters to be weak and disgusting.
>
> Arthur, Joanie's husband, called Lee to cry and spill his guts out about how terribly his wife treated him, never giving thought to the fact that he

may not have deserved better treatment. When he called he was drunk and he went on to his "best friend" about how he would leave his wife and how she was no good. He was hysterical, he could not handle pressure, and in the end he went crazy. After he hung up with Lee he called back to say his wife had just walked in. His wife was with Lee and couldn't have walked in. Throughout the story, Arthur was a whimpering little worthless fool.

Lee disgusted me more than Arthur. Lee betrayed his best friend, he lied to him, he spat on him and mocked him. It's not that I particularly cared for Arthur, but Lee broke all of the codes of friendship and therefore I found him revolting. Lee got what he deserved, though, as after Arthur called a second time, Lee seemed to snap and join Arthur in never-never land.

Of all the characters, I despised Joanie the least. Anyone who was stuck with a man like Arthur would need to cheat on him. Still, she did cheat and therefore she was no better than a prostitute.

All of the characters were vermin. The story was entertaining because of its soap opera character.

Our first response in reading Jake's essay might be to admire its energy and vividness—even its apparent honesty—but to feel simultaneously a slight discomfort with the vehemence of its allegations. It doesn't look like school writing about literature; it looks, rather, like a passionate (and sometimes playful) reaction to the characters that is poorly informed by conventional forms of evidence. Though Jake recapitulates the major events of the story in his first paragraph ("The story focuses on Lee and Joanie in bed together cheating on Lee's best friend . . ."), he soon moves on to a colorful assault on each of the characters in turn, concluding with the less than dispassionate, "All of the characters in the story were vermin." He is so visibly stating his views that it is difficult to see the reasoning that sustains them.

A conventional mode of argumentation, however, does inform Jake's essay, although we must cut beneath his language to view it clearly. We can, for example, outline the basic skeleton of his argument, using Toulmin's (1958) model of informal logic. In that model, *claims* are "conclusions whose merits we are seeking to establish" (p. 97) and *data* are supports for the claim, consisting usually of facts not in dispute that are directly relevant to the claims made. Such an outline might look like this:

Major claim: All of the characters are weak and disgusting
    Minor claim: Arthur is weak
        Data: He cries to his friend
        Data: He is drunk
        Data: He loses control and tells a blatant lie
    Minor claim: Lee is disgusting
        Data: He betrays his friend

Minor claim: Joanie is despicable (but less so than Arthur and Lee)
Data: She cheats on her husband
Data: (But) Arthur's character makes this understandable

Thus stripped of its provocative language, Jake's argument comes to resemble a more conventional form of reasoning about literature. It makes a claim about the characters and then supports that claim with narrative data that describe what the characters do in the course of the story. We might quibble that his argument, in this version, is trivial, given the complexity of the story. We could not say, however, that it is absent of reason.

But, of course, Jake did not write the stripped-down version of the argument that our outline implies. His essay rests upon, but finally moves beyond the claims and data we have sketched. His purpose is not to conduct an analysis of how the text works, but to provide an explanation of how the text works *on him*. Thus, for example, though he cites Arthur's dependence on Lee as data, the data itself are embedded in language that is highly charged ("Arthur called Lee to cry and spill his guts out about how terribly his wife had treated him"). Or again, with Lee: "Lee betrayed his best friend, he lied to him, he spat on him and mocked him." Such statements do two things at once: They both cite data and react to it. They refer to the text, but they do so in a way that colors how the text is to be viewed. It is as if we see the text, but only as refracted by the emotional response it has elicited from Jake.

However we choose to describe Jake's reasoning, an important element is missing. Jake has not provided what Toulmin (1958) has called a *warrant* for his argument. In Toulmin's view, warrants are the bridges from data to claim:

> Rules, principles, inference-licenses or what you will instead of additional items of information. Our task is no longer to strengthen the ground on which our argument is constituted, but is rather to show that, taking these data as a starting point, the step to the original claim or conclusion is an appropriate and legitimate one. At this point, therefore, what are needed are general, hypothetical statements which can act as bridges; and authorize the sort of step to which our particular argument commits us. (p. 98)

What would warrant the kind of argument Jake has constructed? What hypothetical statements would authorize the mode of reasoning in which he has engaged? It seems clear that Jake himself has not taken responsibility for establishing the warrant: His essay proceeds under the unstated assumption that what he is doing is appropriate. The warrant, rather, is provided by the assignment itself, for by explicitly asking how Jake "personally feels" about the character, the assignment implicitly suggests that such responses constitute a legitimate form of evidence in discussions of literature. At the same time, however, the assignment does not encourage Jake to undertake an extended discussion of how the text itself works, and thus he does not explain how he knows that Joanie is the woman with Lee—even though it is that inference that elicits the powerful emotional reaction he is explaining. In a sense, Jake's warrant to explain how he personally feels overrides the need to explain how the text works. And such a warrant, I would argue, authorizes a kind of thinking about literature that differs, in nontrivial ways, from other avenues of approach.

We can perhaps see those differences more clearly by contrasting Jake's essay with Eric's response to a different assignment on the same story. Here the assignment read:

> In "Pretty Mouth and Green My Eyes" we are presented with three charac-
> ters in a rather difficult relationship. In a well-argued essay, use quotations
> and other evidence from the text to explain the nature and quality of that
> relationship.

This assignment would seem to push Eric in the direction taken by Tony in his journal entry on Thoreau. He is to focus on the text alone, drawing inferences that can be supported by "quotations and other evidence from the text."

Here is Eric's response to the assignment:

> During the story "Pretty Mouth and Green My Eyes," an old man, named
> Lee, talks on the phone with another man, Arthur. During the conversation
> one learns that Arthur's wife, Joanie, has not come home from a party that
> she and her husband attended that night. While the conversation is going on,
> a young woman who is with Lee silently listens. Evidence is presented in
> the story that that the two men are friends and the young woman with Lee
> is in fact Arthur's wife.
>
> The relationship between Lee and Arthur is simply that of two friends.
> This is shown by the fact that Arthur called Lee when Joanie did not return
> from the party to get advice on how to handle the situation. Another piece
> of evidence that the men are friends is that Arthur was very concerned about
> whether or not he woke Lee up when he called. In fact, the first thing that
> Arthur said during the conversation was, 'Lee? I wake you?' Also, Arthur told
> Lee several things about Joanie, such as his paranoia about his wife being
> unfaithful.
>
> In the story, it is hinted that the young woman with Lee is actually Joanie,
> Arthur's wife. The most obvious of these hints is that when Arthur wanted
> to go to Lee's house for a drink, Lee became frightened and then said that
> he thought it would be better for Arthur to "just sit tight and relax," which

could have been an attempt by Lee to keep Arthur from coming over and discovering Joanie. Also, he never mentioned to Arthur that he was with someone, who Arthur might have thought to be his wife, and Lee tried to assure Arthur that his wife was just with friends, which could have been a further attempt to throw suspicion off of himself.

The mode of reasoning that governs Eric's argument is more familiar than that shaping Jake's essay—familiar because he adheres more visibly to the conventions of textual evidence. Like Jake, Eric opens with a brief overview of the story ("During the conversation, one learns that Arthur's wife, Joanie, has not come home from a party …"), and like Jake, Eric closes his first paragraph with a statement that can serve as a thesis ("Evidence is presented in the story that the two men are friends and the young woman with Lee is, in fact, Arthur's wife"). But the data Eric employs to support his claims are strictly textual: It is embodied in language that remains cool and absent of first-person reactions. We can outline the argument, as we did Jake's, by employing Toumlin's system of claims and data:

> **Major claims:** (1) Arthur and Lee are friends; (2) The young woman is Joanie
> **Claim 1:** Arthur and Lee are friends
> Data: Arthur called Lee for advice
> Data: Arthur apologized for waking Lee
> Data: Arthur confided in Lee
> **Claim 2:** The young woman was Joanie
> Data: Lee is frightened when Arthur invites himself over
> Data: Lee never mentioned that he was with someone
> Data: Lee assures Arthur that Joanie is with friends

Like Jake, Eric employs textual evidence to support an argument about the characters, but unlike Jake, Eric stops with that evidence. The assignment from which he is working provides no warrant for personal reactions and thus he offers none—even though Lee's actions complicate one of Eric's claims (that Lee and Arthur are friends) and would seem to invite a response of some kind. In this case, though, the conventions governing Eric's writing (like those governing Jake's writing) override an invitation offered by the story itself. Working from textual evidence alone, he is authorized to say who the characters are and what they are doing, but he is not authorized to explain how he feels about the moral thicket in which they find themselves. His warrant encourages, in other words, a particular way of thinking about literature—of knowing about literature—that is very different from the approach that Jake felt authorized to take.

The point here, of course, is not that different kinds of assignments lead to different kinds of writing about literature. It is that different kinds of writing encourage students to use and produce different kinds of knowledge about literature. Rosemary, in her journal, and Jake, in his essay, I would argue, were not being *less* reasonable than Tony and Eric. Rather, they were reasoning about texts in different ways, drawing on different sources of knowledge that, in turn, enabled very different perspectives on the text itself. These differences are important enough, perhaps, to warrant a closer look at the curricular frameworks that govern the ways we use writing in classrooms where literature is taught.

A MULTIDIMENSIONAL VIEW OF WRITING ABOUT LITERATURE

I began this essay by reviewing some of the theoretical and empirical work that has enriched our understanding of the relationships between writing and learning. That work has enabled us to recast some of the assumptions that have guided our uses of writing in school, fostering a view of writing that emphasizes its heuristic powers for the writer. From such a perspective, writing becomes not just a measure of students' understanding, but a means of achieving it. It becomes an instructional tool that can shape at the same time that it deepens our students' conception of the subjects they address in their writing.

The student writing that we have examined here, I think, suggests that the effects of writing may be especially important when literature is addressed, for the ways in which students write about literature carry with them implicit theoretical assumptions about what it means to know a literary text. On the one hand, knowing a text may mean knowing how it works and why it works the way it does. Such a position might lead a reader to consider a text's images and thematic unity, to work toward inferences of authorial intention, to examine the cultural and biographical contexts out of which the text emerged. This position seemed to provide the warrant from which Tony and Eric were operating in their writing. On the other hand, though, knowing a text may mean knowing how it affects us. And such knowledge requires us to examine the cultural and autobiographical forces from which our reading has emerged. It was this position that warranted the kinds of thinking in which Rosemary and Jake engaged. While both ways of knowing began with the words on the page, the first may move us toward a fuller understanding of the text as written, the second toward a fuller understanding of the text as read. The differences between these ways of knowing about texts has informed much of the recent debates in literary theory, but they also carry some important implications for our teaching of literature.

Perhaps the most obvious of these is that choosing the ways in which students are to write about literature implies a theoretical position on the ways they are to think about literature. And to select one way over another is to suggest that one is better than another without adequately addressing the question: better for whom? or, better for what? The text-based, formal analysis of literature has for many years held a dominant position in academic classrooms (Squire & Applebee, 1968; Purves, 1981; Marshall, 1987), largely because of the broad influence of the New Criticism (Brooks & Warren, 1938). But that influence has been recently eroded by new developments in literary theory (Bleich, 1975; Rosenblatt, 1978)—developments which, in turn, have led to proposals for replacing the new critical approach in schools with one that features the kinds of reader-based, personal analyses that were exemplified in Rosemary and Jake's writing (e.g., Perl & Wilson, 1986; Atwell, 1987; Probst, 1988). While the effort to establish the legitimacy of such approaches seems important, however, the effort to establish a new orthodoxy of response might well impoverish our teaching by underestimating the valuable perspectives that a text-based, formal analysis can provide. Writing is a tool for thinking—different kinds of writing encourage different kinds of thinking—and it would make little sense to throw one tool away because we have found another with alternative purposes.

We may make another kind of mistake, however, if we attempt to include both approaches by organizing our instruction in such a way that students move consistently from reader-based, personal responses toward more public, formal, and text-based analyses. On the other hand, such a framework implicitly privileges the formal mode by suggesting that it is the goal of instruction, while the personal analyses in which students engage are only the means. On the other hand, however, such a framework suggests that we can work comfortably from the approach taken by Rosemary and Jake to the approach taken by Tony and Eric without fundamentally altering the assumptions that guide our reading and understanding of texts. It is not at all clear that the conventions shaping the two kinds of arguments are consonant, let alone that writing one would in some sense prepare students to write the other. The two pairs of students were working, rather, from very different theoretical positions on what constitutes legitimate knowledge about texts. To move from one to the other without acknowledging the shift in assumptions is to finesse in our teaching practice a problem that has thus far resisted theoretical solution: What and how does a text mean?

Since the problem will not go away, my suggestion is that we bring it directly into our classrooms: that in place of a unidiminsional concept of response (reader-based *or* text-based), or a developmental concept of response (from reader-based *to* text-based), we encourage a multidimensional, dialogic conception of response in which both forms of reasoning about texts are legitimized and their relationship itself becomes a focus of instruction. Such a suggestion echoes, of course, those recently made by Scholes (1985) and by Graff (1987) who have argued that we introduce students to a variety of interpretive strategies and at the same time help them to see the theoretical grounds from which those strategies derive. That such a proposal can be realized even with students who are largely innocent of theory is, I hope, evident from the writing we have examined here. For Rosemary and Jake, Tony and Eric, were working from clear theoretical positions even though they did not articulate those positions in their writing. Once different kinds of written response are elicited from students, I would argue, the next instructional step is to mirror the differences themselves back to the students, to encourage reflection on the source and value of their responses, and to orchestrate discussion, not only about texts, but about the ways in which we come to know texts. We can conceive, in other ways, of the teaching of literature as a dialogue in which different kinds of responses are not obstacles to be overcome by our instruction, but the means by which our instruction itself may proceed.

To accomplish these curricular goals, however, may require at least three changes in the way that we have come to view the teaching of English. First, we would need to see the relationships between the teaching of writing and the teaching of literature as both powerful and complex. Writing about texts does not merely enable students to process textual information more deeply: It invites students to take a stance with regard to the text, to look at it from a particular vantage point, to employ a set of argumentative conventions that themselves encourage a particular way of knowing the text. These two parts of our teaching, writing and literature, are so interrelated that we cannot alter our approach to one without fundamentally altering our approach to the other. To the extent that writing is a means of learning, our discussions of writing instruction need to address not only the kinds of writing we want our students to experience, but also the kinds of learning we want to them to achieve. To be fully understood, in other words, our teaching of writing must be placed within the larger instructional context of which it is, finally, only a part.

Second, a dialogic approach to the teaching of literature would require us to cultivate in our classrooms a multidimensional diversity of response—to elicit and encourage difference rather than consensus. Our purpose in such classrooms would be less to show students what texts mean than to introduce them to the variety of ways in which knowledge about texts may be made, and to help them become informed participants in the making of that knowledge. Such an approach would necessitate our relinquishing some of the authority we have, as teachers, traditionally held over the meaning of literary texts. And it would necessitate a greater self-consciousness on our part of the theoretical assumptions we bring to our own reading and interpretation of texts.

But finally, fundamental changes in the way we teach literature will require fundamental changes in the way we conceive of growth in students' ability to read and write. For as I've tried to suggest here, simple quantitative or linear models of development do not capture the complexity of what happens when students read and write about literature. We read and write from particular theoretical perspectives, and an alternative way to conceptualize growth is to think of it as the increasing ability to read and write from multiple perspectives. We can measure students' growth within particular theoretical frameworks, but we can perhaps also measure their growth by the flexibility and grace with which they can negotiate alternative frameworks—by their facility for and comfort with multiple ways of knowing texts. Revising our assumptions in these ways will of course be difficult. But in the end, such revisions might open our classrooms to the basic concerns of contemporary thought, and by so doing, increase our students' understanding of literature's power to engage us.

REFERENCES

Applebee, A. N. (1981). *Writing in the secondary school: English and the content areas.* Urbana, IL: National Council of Teachers of English.

Applebee, A. N. (1984). Writing and reasoning. *Review of Educational Research, 54,* 577–596.

Atwell, N. (1987). *In the middle: Writing, reading, and learning with adolescents.* Portsmouth, NH: Boynton-Cook.

Bereiter, C., & Scardamalia, M. (1982). From conversation to composition: The role of instruction in a developmental process. In R. Glaser (Ed.), *Advances in instructional psychology, Vol. 2* (pp. 27–63). Hillsdale, NJ: Erlbaum.

Bleich, D. (1975). *Readings and feelings: An introduction to subjective criticism.* Urbana, IL: National Council of Teachers of English.

Britton, J. (1970). *Language and learning.* London: Penguin Press.

Britton, J., Burgess, T., Martin, N., McLeod, A., & Rosen, H. (1975) *The development of writing abilities (11–18).* London: MacMillan Education.

Brooks, C., & Warren, R. P. (1938). *Understanding poetry.* New Haven, CT: Yale University Press.

Bruner, J. (1964). The course of cognitive growth. *American Psychologist, 19,* 1–15.

Cassirer, E. (1944). *An essay on man.* New Haven, CT: Yale University Press.

Culler, J. (1975). *Structuralist poetics.* Ithaca, NY: Cornell University Press.

Doctorow, M., Wittrock, M. C., & Marks, C. (1978). Generative processes in reading comprehension. *Journal of Educational Psychology, 70,* 109–118.

Durst, R. K. (1987). Cognitive and linguistic demands of analytic writing. *Research in the Teaching of English, 21,* 347–376.

Eagleton, T. (1983). *Literary theory: An introduction.* Minneapolis: University of Minnesota Press.

Farmer, M., Yesner, S., Zemelman, S., & Boone, B. (1985). *Composition and grammar 12: Steps in the writing process.* Irvine, CA: Laidlaw Brothers.

Fish, S. (1980). *Is there a text in this class?* Cambridge, MA: Harvard University Press.

Fulwiler, T. (1987). *The journal book.* Portsmouth, NH: Boynton-Cook.

Graff, G. (1987). *Professing literature: An institutional history.* Chicago: University of Chicago Press.

Graves, D. H. (1978). Research update: We won't let them write. *Language Arts, 55,* 635–40.

Graves, D. H. (1979). Let children show us how to help them write. *Visible Language, 13,* 16–28.

Holland, N. (1975). *Five readers reading.* New Haven, CT: Yale University Press.

Kirby, D., & Liner, T. (1981). *Inside/out: Developmental strategies for teaching writing.* Portsmouth, NH: Boynton-Cook.

Langer, J. A. (1986). Learning through writing: Study skills in the content areas. *Journal of Reading, 29,* 400–406.

Langer, J. A., & Applebee, A. N. (1987). *How writing shapes thinking: A study of teaching and learning.* Urbana, IL: National Council of Teachers of English.

Langer, S. K. (1967). *Mind: An essay on human feeling.* Baltimore: Johns Hopkins University Press.

Marshall, J. D. (1984a). Schooling and the composing process. In A. N. Applebee (Ed.), *Contexts for learning to write* (pp. 103–120). Norwood, NJ: Ablex.

Marshall, J. D. (1984b). Process and product: Case studies of writing in two content areas. In A. N. Applebee (Ed.), *Contexts for learning to write* (pp. 149–168). Norwood, NJ: Ablex.

Marshall, J. D. (1985). *Writing and learning about literature.* Unpublished doctoral dissertation, Stanford University, Stanford, CA.

Marshall, J. D. (1987). The effects of writing on students' understanding of literary texts. *Research in the Teaching of English, 21,* 30–63.

Marshall, J. D. (1988). Classroom discourse and literary response. In B. F. Nelms (Ed.), *Literature in the classroom: Readers, texts, and contexts* (pp. 45–58). Urbana, IL: National Council of Teachers of English.

Moffett, J. (1968). *Teaching the universe of discourse.* Boston: Houghton Mifflin.

Newell, G. N. (1984). Learning while writing in two content areas: A case study/protocol analysis. *Research in the Teaching of English, 18,* 265–287.

Newell, G. N. (in press). The effects of writing in a reader-based and text-based mode on students' understanding of two short stories.

Peper, R. J., & Mayer, R. E. (1978). Notetaking as a generative activity. *Journal of Educational Psychology, 70,* 514–522.

Perl, S., & Wilson, N. (1986). *Through teachers' eyes: Portraits of writing teachers at work.* Portsmouth, NH: Heinemann Press.

Probst, R. E. (1988). *Response and analysis: Teahcing literature in junior and senior high school.* Portsmouth, NH: Boynton-Cook.

Purves, A. (1981). *Reading and literature.* Urbana, IL: National Council of Teachers of English.

Reder, L. M. (1980). The role of elaboration in the comprehension and retention of prose: A critical review. *Review of Educational Research, 50,* 5–53.

Rosenblatt, L. (1978). *The reader, the text, the poem.* Carbondale, IL: Southern Illinois University Press.

Scholes, R. (1985). *Textual power.* New Haven, CT: Yale University Press.

Squire, J., & Applebee, R. K. (1968). *High school English instruction today.* New York: Appleton-Century Croft.

Toulmin, S. E. (1958). *The uses of argument.* Cambridge: Cambridge University Press.

Vygotsky, l. (1962). *Thought and language.* Boston: MIT University Press.

Weiss, R. H., & Walters, S. A. (1980). *Writing to learn.* A paper presented at the annual meeting of the American Educational Research Association, Boston, MA.

Winterowd, W. R., & Murray, P. Y. (1983). *English writing and language skills, 4th course.* New York: Harcourt, Brace, Jovonavich.

III
The Textual Stance

8
Writers, Judges, and Text Models

Alan Purves
Gail Hawisher

In this chapter, we shall undertake a reinterpretation of two studies that we have been involved in over the past eight years, both of which have examined the perceptions held by raters of compositions concerning the quality of the texts they have been reading. The first is the IEA Study of Written Composition in 14 countries and the second is a study of the ratings given to compositions written by national and international students applying to graduate schools in the United States. Both studies have led us to the conclusion that "good writing" is a culturally defined phenomenon, and that good academic writing has a particular definition within the academic circles of a culture. One implication of this assertion is that when we talk about "growth" or "development" in writing, we are disguising the fact that what we are referring to is acculturation and deliberate instruction. We shall begin by setting forth some general principles.

Two recent comparative studies of writing, Scribner and Cole's *The Psychology of Literacy* (1981), and Heath's *Ways with Words* (1983), examined the relation of culture to discourse and particularly to written discourse. Scribner and Cole studied the Vai of Liberia, among whom there are three types of literates as well as nonliterates (those literate in the indigenous Vai those literate in Arabic, and those literate in English). Heath examined two groups of poor Appalachians, one black and one white, and contrasted them with the urbanized middle-class black and white. Both studies point to the fact that written texts, and the ways in which they are used and perceived, vary according to the cultural group to which an individual belongs.

Together, the studies point to two aspects of that variation: The content that is written and the forms or structures used to encode that content constitute the surface manifestations of those cultural differences. In

Heath's study, the two Appalachian groups differ as to what should be included in a story. For one group, the story must contain only "true" events and should not have direct speech; for the other group, embellishment and fantasy are permitted and dialogue is a staple. The two groups differ as well as to the nature of the formulae used to open and close a tale. Scribner and Cole show the formulaic nature of Vai letters and how those letters differ from the formulae used by the English writers. The variations in content and form have been studied by many researchers in the areas of comparative literature and contrastive rhetoric.

Behind these surface manifestations of cultural differences, Heath and Scribner and Cole posit differences in three other aspects of discourse, and particularly in written language that Heath and Scribner and Cole also suggest. The first of these aspects is the relative stress given to the functions of discourse. If we adopt Jakobson's listing of functions: expressive, referential, conative, metalingual, poetic, and phatic, we see that in both of Heath's groups writing is seen as primarily referential, as it is among the Vai literates in Liberia. There is also some metalingual and phatic use of written language. These functions and the consequent stylistic characteristics differ from those of speech in the same communities. In the Qu'ranic writers, the use of literacy is primarily phatic. In the black Appalachian group of Heath, much oral discourse is poetic, but there is little poetic discourse among the white group. To a certain extent, these functional demands of discourse dictate both the content and the forms it will take, particularly with written discourse.

Closely connected with function, however, and perhaps influencing it, there exist two other aspects of written discourse that seem to vary according to culture and that seem to affect the content and form. One of these aspects we may think of as the cognitive demand of the discourse (Vähäpassi, 1988; Hairston, 1986), which is to say the degree to which the writer must "invent" either the content of the written text or the form of the text. Much writing is transcription, in which the writer is provided with predetermined content and the form to transcribe as is the case in copying from oral or written discourse or filling in forms. Much of the writing in all of the cultures these authors study is transcription. Another large segment of the writing involves the organization or reorganization of material that is known to the writer—shopping lists, brief reports such as directions, and the like. The form into which the material is to be placed may also be well known to the writer, but the writer has to select it from among a variety of forms. The demand, then, is to select an appropriate form and put the material into the proper places. A third kind of writing involves the invention or generation of both the content and the form or structure, although in many cases, that may be a conventional form such as the story or the rhyme or the proposal. Invention in this sense appears to play little part in the lives of any of the groups of writers studied by Heath or Scribner and Cole, although the black Americans do engage in invention in their talk and may even be inventive in their lexicon in early writing. It seems clear that Heath's townspeople are encouraged in secondary school to invent in their writing.

The last area in which cultural variation plays a part might be defined as the pragmatics of discourse. Written discourse, like oral discourse, occurs in a social setting, and there exist rules of behavior with respect to writing. In Heath's white Appalachian community, a child should write a thank-you note for a present; in the black community such an obligation does not exist. In the Vai community it was hard for the Vai language writers even to conceive of engaging in some of the tasks that Scribner and Cole asked them to do. Because they had difficulty conceiving of it, they did not know what to write or how to write it.

We may represent the interaction of these aspects of cultural variation as in the following diagram:

SOCIOCOGNITIVE INFLUENCES	TEXTUAL EFFECTS
PERCEIVED FUNCTION	
PRAGMATICS OF DISCOURSE	TYPE OF INFORMATION
COGNITIVE DEMAND	FORMAL CHARACTERISTICS

It is clear that the three cultural influences interact with each other. The particular situation in which a writer writes may also determine the pragmatics and the function, which may, in turn, affect the text produced. That is to say that writing in a business setting may become a different sort of activity than writing at home or in a community, differences constituted by differences in "institutional conventions."

We may extend this position from broad cultural groups such as those studied by Scribner and Cole to the narrower subcultures that constitute academic disciplines. The philosopher of science, H. Törnebohm (1973) has shown that the disciplines are "inquiring systems," or communities that have their own carefully defined ways of reporting to each other. Throughout school, students are taught to be members of rhetorical communities, both the specific disciplinary ones and the broader cultural ones (Purves, 1986). It is primarily in schools that students learn to write according to certain conventions, many of which have little to do with the structure of the language and more to do with the literary and cultural heritage of the society, or the academic subcommunity. That is to say that many aspects of texts are not bound by the morphology and grammar of a particular language, but by custom and convention.

In many academic disciplines, as well as in certain professions that demand a great deal of writing, individuals learn to write according to certain explicit and implicit conventions that affect patterns of organization, syntax, and phrasing, and even the selection from the lexicon. It is apparent that the scholarly article in a given academic discipline has properties demanded by the history of that discipline. In the humanities, references to previous research on the topic comes at the beginning of an article or are sprinkled throughout the text when needed; in psychology they always occupy the second of five sections of the article; and in the biological sciences they occur in separate articles from the report of a particular piece of research. In addition to structural conventions, disciplines differ in the degree to which they allow the writer to use the first person, the degree to which the passive is tolerated, and the degree to which interpretation or inference is permitted, to name but three instances. As we shall see, running across these disciplinary differences, there appear to be certain common strands which form a general type of academic discourse as it is construed by those who judge entrants into higher education.

This depiction of cultural variation suggests that written language and the activities involved in composing or reading and responding are highly conventional. Convention and need dictate the occasions for writing or reading and the functions of discourse appropriate to those occasions. From these two sources the writer or the reader then applies knowledge of both the content and form appropriate to a function on an occasion and conducts the appropriate search of the long-term memory. At that point, the writer then goes on to certain text-producing as well as discourse-producing activities (Takala, 1983). The text-producing activities include the more mechanical or physical; the discourse-producing activities include those related to the selection and arrangement of content. The reader goes on to certain decoding activities and certain types of response to the text material. Again these activities are bounded by convention (Purves, 1987), not unlike the conventions of response to literature set forth in Purves, Hansson, and Foshay (1973).

The reader, however, performs one additional and crucial act, and that act forms the basis for the argument of this chapter. The reader judges the adequacy of the text to the text model or models that exist in her head (Purves & Purves, 1986). Such a judgment may extend from whether the particular text is a good approximation to the model to whether the text indeed falls within the broad or narrow range of the model. The reader's judgment may range from "this is a good story," to "this isn't even a story." This judgment of value is and has been one of the most powerful forces to shape the nature of writing throughout history. The judgment may be based upon a variety of facets of the perceived text, but particularly the clarity—or type of information—and the effectiveness of the text—or formal characteristics—based on the reader's sense of appropriate function, cognitive demand, and pragmatics of the context for the writing. Judgments of texts based on mental models have informed rhetoric and poetics and continue to inform writing pedagogy and the various rhetorical communities of the world, be they religious, commercial, social, or academic. The use of these models can have a beneficial or a deleterious effect, they can serve to include or exclude people from rhetorical communities, and they are imperfectly understood.

These models are learned by student writers from the attitudes implied by their teachers' feedback. The result is that in various examination situations, including term papers and theses—when the writing counts—the students will use these models. It is the facile use of these models that determines such concepts as "writing skill" or "writing ability." It is to understand better the nature of these mental models that forms the focus of the discussion of the two studies.

THE IEA WRITTEN COMPOSITION STUDY

The IEA Study of Written Composition has in part been exploring what communal patterns of performance are learned as an individual becomes a literate member of a society. The study is looking at the writing of students in Chile, England, the Federal Republic of Germany, Finland, Hungary, Indonesia, Italy, Netherlands, Nigeria, New Zealand, Sweden, Thailand, the United States, and Wales.

Earlier studies in the field of contrastive rhetoric have concentrated primarily on people writing in a common second language or on literary styles as they change across linguistic or temporal boundaries. The IEA Study of Written Composition provides a way of examining the possibility of such differences by looking at a systematically drawn sample of writing in a number of rhetorical modes by an average school population writing in the language of instruction. It also examines the criteria used by teachers of writing in each of the countries in order to see if there are systematic differences that might help define rhetorical communities.

The first problem to be dealt with was that of creating a standardized set of neutral descriptors so as to portray these possible differences. There needed to be two sets of descriptors, one for the compositions themselves and one for the criteria used to judge the writing. The second of these shall receive the most attention in this section.

As an initial step, there were gathered a number of compositions written by small samples of students (approximately 100 per country or system of education) at or near the end of secondary school in several of the countries in the study and three countries no longer in the study (Australia, Japan, and Israel). The compositions were on the topics "My Native Town" and "What is a Friend?"—both thought to be relatively neutral topics that would not force a particular kind of pattern of organization or style on the students. If the compositions were not in English, they were translated by a literary translator and checked by bilingual teachers for their fidelity to the original. A team of three researchers then examined the whole group of compositions and found that they could place them into piles according to certain common characteristics (not including the content) and that the piles coincided with the country of origin. They then proceeded to define the characteristics that led to our selection. We found that the compositions tended to differ systematically by culture of origin along a number of continua, some of which matched those of earlier researchers, particularly Carroll (1960), Glenn and Glenn (1981), Hofstede (1981), and Kaplan (1966). The continua that emerged from our perceptions were the following (these terms define continua that raters agree upon as being culturally neutral):

- PERSONAL-IMPERSONAL: This continuum depends primarily on the frequency of references in the text to the writer's thoughts and feelings about the subject.
- ORNAMENTED-PLAIN: This continuum may also be defined as "figurative-literal" and depends on the frequency of use of metaphor, imagery, and other figures of speech.
- ABSTRACT-CONCRETE: This continuum is defined in terms of the amount of specific information and detailed references in the text as well as to the general level of abstraction.
- SINGLE-MULTIPLE: This continuum refers to whether the text focuses on one selected aspect of the subject or tries to cover a large number of aspects of the subject.
- PROPOSITIONAL-APPOSITIONAL: This continuum, which is similar to Glenn and Glenn's abstractive-associative continuum, as well as some of Kaplan's diagrams, refers to the types of connectives that hold the text together according to some clear order that follows one of a number of "standard" types of development (e.g., comparison-contrast); such a composition would be propositional. An appositional composition would use few connectives besides *and* or *but* and often omits cohesive ties other than idioms and repetitions.

These characteristics appear to distinguish the perceptions of writing by students in different cultures; from the initial research it appears that the characteristics form some of the dimensions by which the models of text are delimited in certain cultures (see Figure 8.1). The differences noted in Figure 8.1 are not inherent in the language but result from some

Country	FACTOR				
	Personal	Ornamental	Abstract	Single	Propositional
Australia	High	High	Low	High	Low
England	Medium	Low	Low	Low	Low
Federal Republic of Germany	High	Low	Low	Low	Low
Finland	Low	Low	Low	Low	Low
Israel	High	Medium	Low	High	High
Italy	High	High	High	High	High
Ivory Coast	Medium	Low	Low	Low	Low
Japan	High	Low	High	High	Medium
Netherlands	High	Low	Low	Low	Low
New Zealand	Low	Low	Medium	Low	Low
Nigeria	Low	Low	Low	Low	Low
Scotland	Low	Low	Low	Low	Low
Thailand	High	High	Medium	Medium	Low
United States	Low	Low	Low	Medium	High

Figure 8.1. FACTOR

form of cultural learning because the differences occur between students writing in the same language (such as English) but living in different cultures (Takala et al., 1982).

It is clear so far that the compositions of students in various countries can be classified according to the criteria that have been developed, although other differences emerge given other sorts of compositions (e.g., narratives or letters) (Söter, 1988). If the compositions by students from a particular country were consistently classified according to a certain set of dimensions (e.g., personal, figurative, single, appositional) one might proceed to ask whether such a style is desired by the educational system of that country. It is here that one turns to the question of criteria. In the pilot phase of the study a number of these compositions were given to a group of teachers from the countries in the study and they were asked to both rate and comment on the compositions. From a content analysis of the comments followed by a factor analysis, four factors emerged (apart from mechanics, spelling, and handwriting): (a) content, (b) organization and structure, (c) style and tone, and (d) personal response to the writer and the content (Purves, 1984). These "general merit factors" of judgment appeared in all countries, but the relative emphasis and interpretation varied systematically.

In order to check the teachers' criteria, students were asked to write a letter of advice to people younger than they who were about to attend the student-writers' schools. The letter was to suggest ways to succeed in school writing. A content analysis of the resulting compositions proved most revealing, although not necessarily complimentary to the schools. The resulting compositions were analyzed for the specific types of advice they gave; the advice being divided into the broad categories of content, organization, style, and tone (following the scoring scheme), presentation (including grammar, orthography, layout, and neatness), process, and classroom tactics (Takala, 1987).

Although the analysis for all countries is not complete, the results from a few of them strongly suggest that students within a country are aware of the existence of certain operating norms. There is variation within a country, of course, but nationally and internationally some patterns exist. Table 8.1 suggests some of those patterns.

The table reveals the general perception of students that their teachers are preoccupied with matters of "presentation." There are strong national differences in perception however, such as the relatively low emphasis on "organization" in Chile and on "style and tone" in the Netherlands. In New Zealand and Sweden, teachers appear to emphasize "process" more than in other countries, but in Sweden more of this emphasis concerns choice of topic than is the case in New Zealand.

There are differences within other categories as well. In the Nether-

Table 8.1. Summary Distributions of Student Advice in Five Countries Given in Percent of Total Items of Advice per Country.

	Chile	England	Netherlands	New Zealand	Sweden
Content	13.3	14.7	9.2	20.5	13.9
Organization	4.1	15.0	17.0	14.5	12.9
Style and Tone	13.0	13.0	7.8	13.5	13.7
Presentation	49.1	40.0	47.5	31.3	3.9
Process	11.4	13.0	11.0	18.5	19.6
Tactics	1.1	2.0	1.4	1.6	0.0
Unclassifiable	1.3	0.06	1.0	0.0	0.3

lands the emphasis under "presentation" is weighted more towards grammar than in the other countries, whereas in Chile the balance tips heavily to appearance and spelling. Under "organization" there is a strong concern in the Netherlands for using an organization set by the teachers, an issue which is of less importance in the other countries. In Sweden, teachers are seen to favor simple sentences, a feature not figuring much in the other countries. From this evidence it appears that students in particular countries see their teachers as favoring particular ways of preparing and presenting written discourse; as yet the analysis has not allowed a comparison of teacher and student views.

Each of the three aspects of the Written Composition Study (the examination of actual compositions, of the teacher questionnaires concerning criteria, and of the letters of advice) suggests that students in a particular educational system do indeed learn to become members of a rhetorical community. Students learn not only how to write in the sense of forming letters, words, and other units of discourse, but they also learn what aspects of their writing are valued in their society; they learn the appropriate models. At times there is direct instruction, at times it is implicit. In either case, the students learn that being able to write involves producing texts that match certain models and that these models serve as criteria for student and teacher.

THE GRE-TOEFL STUDY

Having established the principle that models exist in the heads of students and teachers and that these models can exert an influence on the writing performance of students and on writing instruction, one can then seek to make more explicit some of the operating models in the heads of those who control entrance into the academic rhetorical community. A group of us had that chance in the mid-1980s when we were asked to explore the reasons behind a particular series of findings on the part of those undertaking the Graduate Record Examination and the Test of English as a Foreign Language (Carlson, Bridgman, Camp, & Waanders, 1985; Carlson, 1988; Park, 1988)

An earlier study had tested two composition topics, one calling for the analysis of three graphs concerning the decline of farming in the United States, the other calling for an argument concerning the merits of spending funds on the explorations of space. These two topics were given to four groups of students—one: United States university students, the other three: applicants for graduate school in the United States from Latin America, China, and the Arab world. The groups were further divided into social science students and physical science/engineering students. The compositions were rated on a general impression scale by a team of experienced raters from the United States, a cross-section of college and university instructors of English either as a native or as a second language. This team consistently rated the national groups in the order given previously, with the United States students scoring best. Within each group, the social scientists were rated above the physical scientists.

Various teams were called upon to examine the texts and to examine the ratings. The general results of the study were reported by Carlson (1988), but we should like to focus on the activities of one team at the University of Illinois that we organized.[1] This team decided to examine the nature of the ratings in relation to the texts.

The first step we undertook was a repetition of the earlier IEA study. We used the same set of terms for the repertory grid and the results of the principal components analysis showed that our estimates of the compositions matched to a certain extent the results of the Graduate Record Scoring. We could predict by our mapping of the compositions where they might fall on the continuum of quality set by the United States markers.

Such an effort was only partially useful, however, for it did not elucidate the specific nature of the implicit criteria held by those markers. The group then set about an intensive study of the compositions, together with an a priori analysis of the specific attributes esteemed by the United States markers within the scoring scheme used in the IEA study. That study had confirmed the earlier Diederich study (French, Diederich, & Carlton, 1961), which showed that raters tended to focus on four aspects of the

---

[1] The team consisted of Donald Cruickshank and Susan Sullivan of the Division of English as a Second Language, Gail Hawisher then in the Department of English, and Anna Söter then of the Department of Elementary and Early Childhood Education at the University of Illinois, Urbana. The four of them helped in all phases of the rescoring and analysis, together with Myong Wan Noh and Young Mok Park of the Department of Educational Psychology, who ran the various analysis, and helped with the conceptualization of the study as well. Needless to say, we are grateful to them for their work in developing the scheme as well as doing the rating.

discourse level of a composition: content, structure, style or flavor, and wording. In the IEA study three of these four had been defined cross-culturally, that is to say, their general properties, or the aspects of a text to which they referred had been identified and isolated one from the other. The three aspects were, as we have set forth in the previous section: content, structure and organization, and style and tone; Diederich's wording was collapsed into these third (Gorman, Purves, & Degenhart, 1988). A fourth category of the IEA study, that of personal response of the rater, was omitted from the GRE-TOEFL exercise in part because we did not consider it germane, and in part because we thought it important to focus on common rather than idiosyncratic criteria.

These general categories did not suffice to delimit the specific criteria held by the ETS markers. The next step was to establish the specific aspects of the three categories that one could assert were United States norms against which the various compositions could be measured. The group then proceeded to examine textbooks on writing and the actual compositions. As a result of this exercise, the group arrived at 13 normative characteristics of United States academic writing against which to judge the compositions in the study. The results of this exercise produced the following scoring scheme.

Content. This dimension concerns the subject matter of the composition and the way it reflects the writer's manipulation of ideas, objects, and events. There are seven subaspects of content, which we might argue can be seen as fulfilling successively stringent criteria for academic writing:

1. *Adequacy of information.* There must be sufficient information to fulfill the assignment, which is to say the content must match the limits set by the assignment.
2. *Richness of additional information.* There may be additional information drawn from the writer's other reading or experience in the area. That information, however, must be clearly made relevant to the main focus of the assignment. Digression is not permitted.
3. *Relationships drawn among items of information.* The various discreet predications or subtopics must be shown to be related to each other according to an acceptable principle of grouping (see 9). There can be no outliers.
4. *Inferences made beyond the scope of information.* The text is not to be a catalogue of information, but there must be some inferences drawn from the various bits of data.
5. *Synthesis.* There should be drawing together of the inferences into a generalization. Taking 4 and 5 together, a composition should have an optimum of three levels of abstraction from specific to first-order inference to second-order generalization.

6. *Evaluation.* The paper should in most cases go beyond the reporting of data and should make a judgment, preferably on rational grounds, concerning the merits of the inferences and the generalization.
7. *Alternatives.* The composition should consider alternative explanations or generalizations and show why the one proposed is superior. The paper should give evidence of an open, but decisive, mind.

Organization. This dimension concerns the optimum structure for the composition as a whole text as well as the arrangement of its subunits. The organization can be modified according to the conventions of particular academic disciplines but those have the following common characteristics.

8. *Framing.* The composition needs to have a detectable beginning, middle, and end. Although the generalization need not be at the opening, it should be close to it and should be recapitulated near the end. The actual opening may take a number of appropriate forms. The development or middle must be longer than both opening and closing and may follow one of a number of acceptable formats for grouping.
9. *Grouping.* The information and ideas should be combined rationally, using a temporal, spatial, or classificatory structure. These three can be modified to form different complex structures such as cause-effect, comparison contrast, or hypothesis testing.
10. *Unity.* The writer has the obligation to indicate the relationship among the parts that have been grouped. The grouping structure should be signaled with the appropriate lexical items for the selected grouping, and these should be rather more present than absent.

Style/Tone. This dimension refers to the manner in which the composition is presented and particularly the degree to which the manner approximates the conventional uses of language in academic discourse.

11. *Objectivity.* The writer should use impersonal and detached language. There are some exceptions to this standard, particularly in the more "modern" subgroups of the humanities, but impersonality and detachment are still standard in the sciences and social sciences.
12. *Tentativeness.* There should be an ample number of semantic hedges and qualifiers to indicate that the composition is not dogmatic but a part of the academic scholarly dialogue.
13. *Metalanguage.* The composition should use an adequate number of markers to connect the propositions and the paragraphs. The text should in this sense make it easy for the reader to see the intended connections among propositions.

The team of markers then rescored the compositions using the 13 aspects of the scheme and a five-point scoring system for each of the aspects. The results of this exercise showed the following results. The reliability (Cronbach's alpha) of the scoring was .85 for one topic and .75 for the other. The correlation with the original general impression marking averaged .80. These two figures indicate that the more elaborated scoring scheme can be used reliably and can predict the unexamined general impression ratings of a group of trained United States academic raters.

What the study has revealed is that there appear to be a number of specific facets behind the ratings of American academic raters that international applicants have learned less well than their American counterparts. We know from previous rating studies that the content dimension is the most important (Freedman, 1981), which is to be expected given the fact that the compositions in our study as in most others were impromptu compositions done under timed test conditions. Such stringencies would seem to make the writer incapable of revising and polishing the composition, and the raters appear to recognize the limitation in the testing and adjust their ratings accordingly. Given the fact of a draft, the quality and development of the content would be the tacit compact for both writer and rater. Organization and style are important, but the expectations on the part of raters would logically be less stringent. In fact most scoring rubrics take this fact into account.

Despite this limitation, given the nature of the type of academic task, the scheme does tend to follow much of what is presented in textbooks on writing and various style manuals. One could argue that what we have listed are the desiderata of the infamous "five-paragraph theme," and to a certain extent we have done so, although we have never seen an apologia for or description of that supposed composition. The scheme represents a mental model of academic writing as raters think it should be practiced by students.

The scheme's various parts appear to derive from diverse origins. Within organization, for instance, the idea of framing, for example, appears similar to the strictures of classical rhetoric and poetics, and the idea of explicit grouping and unity is also classical in origin. Both of these traits are at variance with the Buddhist traits of a texts being a part of some hypothetical continuity and thus not needing internal framing nor connectives (Indrasuta, 1988). The ways by which these aspects of organization have come to be domesticated in academic writing results from some of the demands of commercial and technical writing so that the original classical impetus seems far distant from the present practice.

The stylistic aspects of the model come in part from a particular notion of what it is to be scientific. The objective or detached tone together with a tentative language bespeaks of models of the scientist-rationalist ready to be proved wrong by the next experiment and careful not to appear overly involved in the writing. The first person singular is permissible in hedges, we believe, but not as a part of the general discourse. This aspect of the model accounts for the reason that United States writing is relatively less figurative than that from other countries in the IEA study. Metaphor is generally to be eschewed. This scientific model of writing appears to come from certain European scientific communities. It is a style that encourages the passive voice, even though various composition teachers from Strunk to Flesch have urged that the passive be abandoned. The passive is useful to this model for it can keep the readers' attention on the study and not on the writer. There are no prima donnas in United States academic writing.

CONCLUSION

The preceding discussion clearly suggests that text models exist in readers' heads and that these models form the basis both for their acceptance of particular texts into an appropriate generic group ("this is an essay") and their evaluation of the sufficiency of the text to the model ("this is a good essay"). These text models appear to be culturally specific and they appear to affect the rating of particular student writing and to impose themselves as models on students. They are used in the gatekeeping role of academic assessment of writing and they exert an influence upon student beliefs and ultimately upon their actual writing performance. To some extent the text models are amplified by models of how to write in school as the data from the IEA content analysis suggest.

That these models affect the actual writing of people once they leave schools would appear to be evidenced by the uniformity of writing in certain contexts, but that uniformity may also result from the imposition of models by editors, supervisors in the workplace, or others in authority. Nonetheless, text models that are by their very nature culture-specific clearly have the effect of excluding people not from that culture. As the literary critic, Edward Said, has noted "culture is used to designate not merely something to which one belongs but something that one possesses, and along, with that proprietary process, culture also designates a boundary by which the concepts of what is extrinsic or intrinsic to the culture comes into forceful play" (Said, 1983, pp. 8–9). Said goes on to remark of the relationship between culture and the educational gatekeepers, "What is more important in culture is that it is a system of values *saturating* downward almost everything within its purview; yet paradoxically culture dominates from above without at the same time being available to everything and everyone that it dominates" (Said, 1983, p. 9).

The implication for the teacher of those both within and without the culture is to help make the student aware of the nature of the models held by the culture, to show that they are conventional and human and not divine, and that they may be violated with some attendant risk. We think that it is important for teachers to be honest with students about the nature of the conventions of writing that abound in the academic and nonacademic world. From our research it is clear that all students are well aware of the text-level conventions such as spelling, neatness, and grammar. Many students seem to think these are the only conventions that exist, that by attending to them, they will be good writers. Such is not the case in the world of school writing, and the higher up in the system one goes, the more discourse conventions become important.

It has been our experience that some of those who have attacked the idea of "product" and called for process, in fact have substituted a modified set of discourse conventions for those we have listed above. Often they have masked these with terms like "honest writing," and "your own voice," or "expressive writing." These get translated into specific conventions such as opening with a personal anecdote. The teachers are sometimes unaware that the have these conventional criteria, but students we have interviewed seem to be aware of them. Many students take some time to learn them; the research by Tibbetts, Baker, Noh, and Park (1986) suggests that it takes college-bound secondary school students two years of instruction and practice to master discourse conventions to the point where variance in scores virtually disappears. That time might be shortened were the teachers to be more honest about precisely what conventions are in their heads and what their criteria are. If the teachers are themselves unsure of their own conventional criteria, they should ask the students who have been under their tutelage for some time to define them. Teachers can then examine the criteria themselves and see if they really want to reject or rephrase some of them. Explicitness and honesty form, we think, the best policy—even for teachers.

REFERENCES

Carlson, S. B. (1988). *Relationships of reasoning and writing skills to GRE analytical ability scores* (GRE Rep. No. 84-23). Princeton, NJ: Educational Testing Service.

Carlson, S. B. (1988). Cultural differences in writing and reasoning skills. In A. C. Purves (Ed.), *Writing across languages and cultures: Issues in contrastive rhetoric.* (pp. 135–150). Newbury Park, CA: Sage Publications.

Carlson, S. B. Bridgeman, B., Camp, R., & Waanders, J. (1985). *Relationship of admission test scores to writing performance of native and nonnative speakers of English* (TOEFL Research Rep. No. 19). Princeton, NJ: Educational Testing Service.

Carroll, J. (1960). Vectors of prose style. In T. A. Sebeok (Ed.), *Style in language* (pp. 283–292). Cambridge, MA and New York: Technology Press and Wiley.

French, J. W., Diederich, P. B., & Carlton, S. (1961). *Factors in the judgment of written composition* (Research Bulletin RB61-15). Princeton, NJ: Educational Testing Service.

Freedman, S. (1981). Influences on evaluators of expository essays: Beyond the text. *Research in the Teaching of English, 15,* 245–255.

Glenn, E. S., with Glenn, C. G. (1981). *Man and mankind: Conflict and communication between cultures.* Norwood, NJ: Ablex.

Gorman, T. P., Purves, A. C., & Degenhart, R. E. (1988). *The IEA study of written composition 1: The international writing tasks and scoring scales* (International Studies in Achievement, Volume 5). Oxford: Pergamon Press.

Hairston, M. (1986). Different products, different processes: A theory about writing. *College Composition and Communication, 37,* 442–452.

Heath, S. B. (1983). *Ways with words.* New York: Cambridge.

Hofstede, G. (1981). *Culture's consequences.* Berkeley, CA: Sage.

Indrasuta, C. (1988). Narrative styles in the writing of Thai and American students. In A. C. Purves (Ed.), *Writing across languages and cultures: Issues in contrastive rhetoric* (pp. 206–227). Newbury Park, CA: Sage.

Kaplan, R. B. (1966). Cultural thought patterns in intercultural education. *Language Learning, 16,* 1–20.

Park, Y. M. (1988). Academic and ethnic background as factors affecting writing performance. In A. C. Purves (Ed), *Writing across languages and cultures: Issues in contrastive rhetoric* (pp. 150–156). Newbury Park CA: Sage.

Purves, A. C. (1984). In search of an internationally-valid scheme for scoring compositions. *College Composition and Communication, 35,* 426–438.

Purves, A. (1986). On the nature and formation of interpretive and rhetorical communities. In T. N. Postlethwaite (Ed.), *International educational research: Papers in honor of Torsten Husén* (pp. 45–60) Oxford: Pergamon Press.

Purves, A. (1987). Literacy, culture, and community. In D. A. Wagner (Ed.), *The future of literacy in a changing world* (pp. 216–232). Oxford: Pergamon.

Purves, A., Hansson, G., & Foshay, A. W. (1973). *Literature education in ten countries: An empirical study.* Stockholm: Almqvist and Wiksell.

Purves, A., & Rippere, V. (1968). *The elements of writing about a literary work* (Research Monograph No. 10). Champaign, IL: National Council of Teachers of English.

Purves, A., Söter, A., Takala, S., & Vähäpassi, A. (1984). Towards a domain-referenced system for classifying composition assignments. *Research in the Teaching of English, 18,* 385–416.

Purves, A., & Takala, S. (Eds.). (1982). *An international perspective on the evaluation of written composition: Evaluation in Education: An International Review Series* (Vol. 5, No. 3). Oxford: Pergamon Press.

Purves, A., & Purves, W. (1986). Culture, text models, and the activity of writing. *Research in the Teaching of English, 20,* 174–197.

Said, E. (1983). *The world, the text and the critic.* Cambridge, MA: Harvard University Press.

Scribner, S., & Cole, M. (1981) *The psychology of literacy.* Cambridge, MA: Harvard University Press.

Söter, A. (1988). The second language learner and cultural transfer in narration. In A. C. Purves (Ed), *Writing across languages and cultures: Issues in contrastive rhetoric* (pp. 187–205). Newbury Park CA: Sage.

Takala, S. (1983). *On the nature of achievement in writing.* Mimeo. Urbana, IL: IEA International Study of Written Composition.

Takala, S. (1987). Student views on writing in eight countries. In R. E. Degenhart (Ed.), *Assessment of student writing in an international context: Theory into Practice 9.* Jyväkylä, Finland: Institute for Educational Research.

Takala, S., Purves, A. C., & Buckmaster, A. (1982). On the interrelationships between language, perception, thought and culture, and their relevance to the assessment of written composition. *Evaluation in Education: An International Review Series, 5,* 317–342.

Tibbetts, C., Baker, M., Noh, M-W., & Park, Y. (1986). *The composition skills: Reality vs. perception* (Curriculum Laboratory Development Report No. 14). Urbana, IL: University of Illinois (mimeo).

Törnebohm, H. (1973). *Perspectives on inquiring systems* (Report No. 53). Department of Theory of Science, University of Gothenburg.

Vähäpassi, A. (1988). The problem of selection of tasks in cross-cultural study. In A. C. Purves (Ed.), *Writing across languages and cultures: Issues in contrastive rhetoric* (pp. 51–78). Newbury Park, CA: Sage.

9

The Development of Persuasive/Argumentative Writing*

Marion Crowhurst

Writing which argues a case is important both for academic success and for general life purposes. The coherent presentation of a well-argued case is required in university entrance exams, and in academic papers in a variety of disciplines. In personal disputes with business or bureaucracy, the ability to argue articulately and convincingly is an invaluable skill. The exercise of democratic rights and responsibilities requires citizens to look critically on society, and to try to influence, by persuasion, their fellow citizens and their law makers.

The importance of instruction in oral and written uses of argument has long been recognized in Western society. The argumentative composition, it is claimed, "lies at the very heart of education in general and of education in particular disciplines" (Connor, Gorman, & Vahapassi, 1987, p. 181). Recognition of the importance of written argumentation is reflected in the inclusion of persuasive/argumentative tasks in a wide variety of major assessments of writing in recent years, for example, in the National Assessment of Educational Progress (NAEP) in the United States, in assessments conducted by the Assessment of Performance Unit of the National Foundation of Educational Research (APU) in the United Kingdom, and in the study of written composition conducted in fourteen countries by the International Association for the Evaluation of Educational Achievement (IEA). In all three, the persuasive writing of both elementary and secondary students was examined.

A variety of terms is used for the kind—or kinds—of writing discussed

---

* Substantial use has been made in this chapter of Janet White's insightful discussions of persuasive/argumentative writing in national assessments in the United Kingdom as found in White (1989) and in Gorman, White, Brooks, MacLure, and Kispal (1988).

in this chapter. Applebee (1984), for example, uses the term *thesis/support essay* for that type of writing which has a hierarchical, analytic structure and which requires that arguments be systematically supported (p. 87); *persuasive writing* for him is that kind of writing "where the attempt to persuade overrides all other purposes (as in advertisements or propaganda)" (p. 14). Martin and Rothery (1980, 1981, 1986) use *exposition* for writing which has as its goal "persuad(ing) the reader of the truth or 'rightness' of a proposition" (1986, p. 72) and which has the structure: *Thesis* followed by a variable number of *Arguments* followed by *Conclusion*. The terms *argumentative, persuasive,* and *argumentative/persuasive* are used interchangeably both in descriptions of the IEA study (Connor, Gorman, & Vahapassi, 1987) and in reports of the APU assessments in the United Kingdom (Gorman, White, Brooks, MacLure, & Kispal, 1988). The IEA writers adopt a broad definition of the kind of writing they are discussing: "Written persuasive discourse is considered to be that which integrates the rational and affective appeals and the appeals to credibility . . . (A)rgumentation is a part of persuasion" (p. 185). *Persuasive writing* is consistently used in the most recent NAEP reports (Applebee, Langer, & Mullis, 1986a, 1986b). Bereiter and Scardamalia (1982) use the term *opinion essay*. The preceding list, while not exhaustive, indicates something of the variety both of terms and of definitions for the kinds of writing discussed in various articles reviewed in this chapter. The fact that there may be differences among studies in the type of writing being examined needs to be borne in mind. This chapter will examine the development of that kind of writing which takes a point of view and supports it with either emotional appeals or logical arguments.

STUDIES OF PERSUASIVE WRITING

Studies of argumentative/persuasive writing may be considered to fall into two major categories. In one category, students' performance in two or more kinds of writing tasks is examined. Such studies allow comparisons between students' performance in persuasive/argumentative writing and their performance in narration and, sometimes, in other kinds of writing as well. In the second category, persuasive/argumentative compositions written by students at various age levels are examined. These studies allow comparisons between younger and older students in the writing of persuasive discourse.

Studies of Performance

Reports of national assessments in the United States have consistently commented on poor performance in persuasive writing (Applebee et al.,

1986a; National Assessment of Educational Progress, 1980). Performance on persuasive writing tasks in the 1984 assessment are described as "dismaying" (Applebee et al., 1986b, p. 36). At all grade levels (4, 8, and 11), there was a high percentage of unsatisfactory responses and a low percentage that were adequate. Even on the easiest task, only 25 percent of fourth graders, 36 percent of eighth graders, and 28 percent of eleventh graders were able to write papers that were adequate or better; on the most difficult task, the percentage performing adequately ranged from 4 percent at grade 4 to 15 percent at grade 11.

In the United Kingdom, major assessments of writing were conducted annually from 1979 to 1983 by the Assessment of Performance Unit of the National Foundation for Educational Research (APU). In each assessment, a variety of writing tasks was assigned to national samples of 11- and 15-year-olds. For both age groups, performance on narrative writing was better than on persuasive writing, though differences between tasks on general impression scores were small (Gorman et al., 1988).

In Canada, the provincial assessment in British Columbia in 1978 allowed eighth and twelfth graders—but not fourth graders—to choose to write a story or to argue a point of view. Both eighth and twelfth graders performed poorly on argument. At grade 8, for example, 49 percent of students fell in the bottom one-third of the 9-point holistic scale, as against 28 percent in narrative (Conry & Rodgers, 1978).

In Ontario, Canada, Pringle and Freedman (1985) examined the ability of students in grades 5, 8 and 12 in two school boards to satisfy minimal criteria in writing narratives and arguments, "argument" being defined as "writing organized around a clear thesis ... which is substantiated logically and through illustration" (p. 26). At all grade levels, the number satisfying minimal criteria was substantially higher for narrative than for argument.

Several characteristic problems in writing argument are identified. One is inadequate content. Persuasive compositions have commonly been found to be shorter than narrative compositions (Bereiter & Scardamalia, 1982; Crowhurst, 1978, 1980a, 1986; Freedman & Pringle, 1984; Pringle & Freedman, 1985). Students often fail to support their points of view (Applebee et al., 1986b); content tends to be less original than for some other kinds of writing (Gorman et al., 1988). A second weakness is poor organization often associated with lack of knowledge of argumentative structure (Conry & Rodgers, 1978; Gorman et al., 1988; Pringle & Freedman, 1985). Even high-rated scripts by 15-year-olds in the APU study exhibited problems in managing argumentative structure due to such matters as "the sudden appearance of illogically placed information, gaps in knowledge, (or) wildly exaggerated statements ..." (Gorman et al., 1988, p. 146). A third noted weakness is stylistic inappropriateness, particularly the use of informal or familiar language, and the overuse of immature connectors such as "another thing" and "also," together with the failure to use connectors typical of argument (Crowhurst, 1987a; Gorman et al., 1988).

Argumentative Writing across Age Groups

Little research has compared argumentative writing across age or grade levels. A few studies have examined comparative use of such linguistic variables as measures of syntactic complexity (Crowhurst, 1980a, 1980b; Crowhurst & Piche, 1979) or cohesion (Crowhurst, 1987a). Others have attempted to quantify differences using such measures as language functions (Craig, 1986) or structural elements (McCann, 1989).

It is clearly established that syntactic complexity is greater in argument than in narrative or descriptive writing, and greater for older students than for younger (Crowhurst, 1980a, 1980b; Crowhurst & Piche, 1979). Moreover, Crowhurst (1980b) found a positive relationship between quality and syntactic complexity in argument (but not in narration) for tenth and twelfth graders, but not for sixth graders. Using compositions collected for an earlier study, she selected pairs of compositions by the same writer if one member of the pair was of high syntactic complexity and the other was of low complexity, and if the two were comparable in length. This study seems to suggest sharply different effects of complex syntax according to discourse type. Whereas effective narrative does not appear to require complex syntax, results of this study suggest a positive relationship between effective argumentative discourse and the ability to relate propositions syntactically, an ability that improves with age.

In a study of the use of different types of cohesive devices by grades 6, 10, and 12 in argument and narration, Crowhurst (1987a) found that older students used more synonyms and collocation signifying both more extensive vocabularies and a greater tendency to expand and elaborate their ideas. Grade 6 students used more causal conjunctives primarily because of their extensive use of the immature connective *so;* grade 12 students not only used fewer instances of *so* and more of other causative conjunctives (e.g., *therefore*), but were also more apt to express causal relationships by subordination. Twelfth graders were also more likely to use the kinds of conjunctives which appropriately signal the development of an argument (*first of all, next, for one thing, all in all, finally*), and used a range of adversative conjunctives (e.g., *however, rather, yet, on the other hand*) whereas sixth graders made little use of any adversative except *but.*

An early attempt to describe the argumentative writing of students at various age levels was made by Wilkinson, Barnsley, Hanna, and Swan (1980) who studied the writing of students aged 7 +, 10 +, and 13 +. Few of their 7-year-olds wrote more than two sentences; fewer than one third stated their position or gave even one reason; reasons, when given, were highly personal and context-bound. Of the 10-year-olds, three quarters stated a position and gave one or more reasons which were, again, usually personal; only 3 out of 31 had a generalized conclusion. Nearly all the 13-year-olds stated a position and supported it with a deductive sequence of reasons; two-thirds of their texts had concluding generalizations. Wilkinson et al.'s (1980) cognitive measures of *drawing inferences, generalizing, hypothesizing,* and *speculating* increased from age group to age group.

Crowhurst (1983a) used an adaptation of the cognitive measures of Wilkinson et al. (1980) in order to quantify differences in persuasive writing between grades 5, 7, and 11. The major difference between grades was on *reporting,* a category that reflected either narrative writing or reporting on "what is happening now." Grade 11 students used significantly less of this type of writing than students in grades 5 and 7. Seven out of 40 fifth-graders and four out of 40 seventh-graders wrote entirely in the narrative mode, and others did so partially. Eleventh graders also used more *generalizing* and *interpreting* than younger students, though differences were less than for reporting. *Speculating* was used scarcely at all at any grade level.

Craig (1986) examined the language functions used by grade 6 and grade 11 students in arguments written on two topics for two audiences (*teacher* and *best friend*). She found that grade 6 students used more of the *relational* and *informing and interpreting* functions whereas grade 11 students used more of the *theorizing* function. The heavier use of the relational function by grade 6 reflected higher use of the subfunctions, *asserting positive opinions* (e.g., "I think this is a great idea"), *rhetorical requests for opinion and direction* (e.g., "Don't you agree?" "Do you think so, Caitlin?"), and *incidental conversational expressions* (e.g., "So there!"). All three of these subfunctions are more characteristic of oral language and less characteristic of the more formal style expected in written argument. Heavier use of informing and interpreting by grade 6 reflected the fact that many grade 6 compositions were more informative than persuasive. This was especially true for one of the two topics which, briefly stated, was as follows: "Your class has $500.00 to spend. Decide how it should be spent and persuade your teacher to agree." This may be seen as an invitation to do two things: to *describe* how the money should be spent, and to *justify* the suggestions made. Younger students wrote more on the first part (i.e., describing), some of them to the exclusion of the second part (justifying).

Another line of investigation has focused on students' knowledge of appropriate argument structure. Two important recent reviews (Hillocks,

1986; Scardamalia & Bereiter, 1986) identify the study of discourse-schema-knowledge as an important emerging area of research in composition. Scardamalia and Bereiter believe that learning the essential form of various genres is "a major requirement for competence in writing" (p. 783), a point strongly argued also by Martin and Rothery (1980, 1981, 1986).

As noted above, student writing commonly fails to approximate conventional argument form (Pringle & Freedman, 1985). Yet even young students appear to possess knowledge of discourse elements found in argument. McCann (1989) found that when sixth-, ninth-, and twelfth-grade students and adults were asked to judge whether or not seven constructed prose passages were arguments, there was no difference between judgments made by the four groups. Bereiter and Scardamalia (1982) found that students aged 10 to 12 could identify a good number of the discourse elements of argument (e.g., statement of belief, reason, elaboration); they attribute this knowledge to students' knowledge of oral persuasion.

McCann (1989) compared arguments written by students at grades 6, 9, and 12 using a primary trait scoring system based on Hillocks' (1987) model of the structure of argument—a promising model that permits the differentiation of simple linear arguments from more complex recursive arguments. McCann found a steady improvement from grade to grade; sixth graders scored lower than ninth and twelfth graders in their use of *claims* (a generalization or assertion that something is true) and *warrants* (explanations of why data support the claim). Neither warrants nor *data* (grounds for stating the claim) were much used at any grade level.

Summary

Studies of persuasive/argumentative writing are not only few in number; they also exhibit substantial methodological differences. While some conclusions may be drawn, they must be tentative.

There is substantial evidence across studies that performance on persuasive writing is not as good as performance on narrative writing—though it is to be noted that neither on the NAEP in the United States nor the APU assessments in the United Kingdom was persuasive writing the lowest-scoring type of writing (Applebee et al., 1986b; Gorman et al., 1988). Persuasive compositions tend to be short and lacking in content, especially in the area of appropriate support for opinions. Persuasive essays often fail to exhibit appropriate structure, and are often marked by inappropriately informal and immature language, a fault not confined to argument but perhaps more acute in that kind of writing than in some others (Gorman et al., 1988). There is notable improvement in performance between elementary and upper secondary grades; however, performance by many twelfth graders remains poor.

The opinion is widespread, but not unanimous, that performance on persuasive writing taasks is unusually poor. While the NAEP report describes performance as "dismaying" (Applebee et al., 1986b), APU reports indicate little difference among writing tasks on general impression scores, and challenge the view that "argumentative/persuasive writing is an especially difficult, intractable genre for children" (White, 1989, p. 9). Whether the apparent difference of opinion between writers of the two different reports is due to methodological differences, different expectations, or differences in performance between students in the United States and those in the United Kingdom is not clear. Light may be shed on this question by the IEA study in which arguments were written by students in 14 countries with identical prompts and standardized scoring procedures. Early results seem to indicate disappointing results for argument in Finland, West Germany, and the Netherlands (Vahapassi, Lehmann, deGlopper, Lamb, & Langer, 1987), but final comparative results are not yet available.

DESCRIPTIONS OF EARLY ARGUMENTATIVE WRITING

Descriptive information contained in a variety of papers permits identification of characteristic patterns of persuasive writing by young students. A majority of 10- to 12-year-old students write recognizably persuasive pieces in response to assignments asking them to persuade. Some of them write well. However, many of their persuasive compositions deviate in characteristic ways from standard forms. In addition, there are some young writers who respond with kinds of writing which are not recognizably persuasive. Several of these characteristic patterns are described below together with illustrations selected from approximately 1200 persuasive compositions written on a variety of topics by grade 5, 6, and 7 students for several different studies (Crowhurst, 1978, 1980a, 1986, 1987b, in press).

Nonarguments

Narratives. A small number of young students write narratives when they are asked to persuade. Sometimes the response is entirely narrative. Sometimes narrative appears as a kind of framework for a segment of argumentative writing. Sometimes compositions seem to start as an argument, but then "drift" into narrative.

Script 1 is an example of a composition which is entirely narrative. The task assigned was for the student, as a member of the class disciplinary committee, to persuade the teacher that a certain kind of punishment was appropriate for a misbehaving classmate.

SCRIPT 1

One day while our teacher was showing us how to do our math, a boy shot an elastic band at me and I happen to be in a committee that decides what kind of punishments the children should get for breaking the rules of the class. I thought that he should get garbage duty for two weeks because that would teach him not to shoot elastic bands any more and besides, it hurts. The teacher is in the committee too except we had a substitute that day.

So I tried to convince her that my punishment would work, but she wouldn't hear of it. Finally I convinced her and the boy didn't shoot any more elastics. (At least not in school). (Grade 5)

While this composition contains an argument in embryo (a stated opinion and a reason), in form and function it is a narrative, an anecdote of an incident involving an attempt to persuade. Narratives were invariably of this kind. White (1989) also reports examples of narrative anecdotes describing moments of disagreement written by 11-year-olds in the APU study.

Sometimes the argument-in-embryo was more fully developed so that the narrative part seems to be a kind of framework for the argumentative writing as in *Script 2:*

SCRIPT 2

I am on the school committee and we decide punishments for kids who misbehave. One of today's decisions was to decide what should happen to Fred Jones because he was taking advantage of his substitute teacher and he was also shooting things around the class. The committee met in the library. I was first to talk so I stood up and said, I think Fred Jones should have his parents phoned and should have to write 250 lines telling why he shouldn't flick things at people and excluded from any activities he's in for 1 month. I think he deserves these punishments because he could of seriously hurt someone, and he knows he shouldn't take advantage of a substitute teacher. The rest of the committee agreed to my punishments and phoned his parents and enforce the punishments the next day. (Grade 7)

In this example, the student is, perhaps, easing his way into an unfamiliar kind of writing by starting in a more familiar mode.

Script 3 begins as an argument with a stated position supported by a reason, but drifts into narrative halfway through the second sentence.

SCRIPT 3

As a committee member I choose the punishment as followed: Make him sit in the office and do his work, have more homework, and have him in an isolated room for a week every month after school for an hour. After all he did take his eraser and fling it across the room when it hit Amy in the head and caused her to get a bump. Then it bounced back, hit the teacher, bounced up, and hit the clock; wich fell on the teacher. And the teacher's wig fell off! The eraser bounced and broke all the windows in the school! Also it bounced up and went in Mr. Stone's pants, then went down his pants leg, bounced up, went down Mrs. Smith's top, then Mrs. Smith had to put it on her desk. (Grade 5)

In this composition, the reason stated in the second sentence has such a strong narrative line, that the writer, perhaps, is sidetracked into pursuing the narrative, and abandoning the argument. Wilkinson et al. (1980) also found a number of compositions by 10-year-olds which alternated between stating opinions and lapsing into narrative anecdote.

Dialogues. A second kind of nonargument is the dialogue recording a conversational exchange between two people having a disagreement. *Script 5* is a response to an assignment asking the writer to persuade a friend to support a camping field trip:

SCRIPT 5

"You mean to say you don't like camping," I said.
"No I don't. I hate being outside."
"You must be crazy. The fresh air and sunshine is good for you."
"What I really hate is the bugs," she said.
"They aren't that bad if you put on repellant."
"Well, what if you tip over in the canoe."
"You'll live. You can swim."
"I guess it's okay. I'll give in. I'll go camping."
(Grade 6)

A particularly interesting example of dialogue-narrative writing is a composition written by a seventh grader who wrote a first draft as presented in *Script 6:*

SCRIPT 6

"I think the whole class should get to hit him with an elastic band." That was Gail's idea. Right now I'm in room 9 thinking of a punishment for Billy Jones. In our class we have a system where if a kid disobeys, our "crime committee" must find a punishment for him or her. So many ideas were floating around the room and here I am thinking for an appropriate punishment. Then suddenly it dawned on me. I put up my hand for about five minutes before I was noticed. "Mrs. Smith I think we should send Billy to work in a grade 2 class for a day" I started. "No I don't think so, what good would that do?" She tried to make me forget it but I wouldn't give up. "Mrs. Smith what age level do you think shooting elastics around the room is?" She answered me quickly with a "that's not the point" routine, but she's not going to get me to give up that easy. "Mrs. Smith if I got caught shooting elastics and my punishment was cleaning the board it wouldn't stop me." I thought I was putting up a good fight so far. "Well that just goes to show what kinda person you are but we are talking about Billy." I was fuming now someone who shoots elastics around like him wasn't gonna get off that easy if I could help it. "If we are gonna let everybody get off that easy then I don't want to be a part of the committee." I know that sounded kinda harsh but I didn't think you could let someone off that easy. All Mrs. Smith answered with was "I get your point and I will certainly think about it." I thought I deserved at least a maybe.

Three days later, when the composition was returned for revision—without teacher response, or intervening writing instruction—the student produced the composition presented in *Script 7:*

SCRIPT 7

Mrs. Bernard and members of the crime committee we are here to find a suitable punishment for those who deserve to be punished. I think I have a suitable punishment for those who have done something wrong. If they have done something that a grade 2 would do they should have to spend a day in a grade 2 room if that doesn't work grade 1 if not that kindergarten if that doesn't work they must be a juvenile delinquent on your hands. I feel that having to spend a day in a primary classroom would be more than enough of a punishment and that person would not be a bother anymore. The embarrassment would probably be too much to be able to face those of a grade 2 room to have to be sent there again. I am very confident that this punishment will be suitable.

The student wrote first an able, appealing composition in a well-practiced form of discourse. Having generated content by this means, she seems to have turned to the business of transforming it into the less familiar argumentative mode required by the assignment, a mode, it is to be noted, which she does not carry off with quite the panache of the original narrative.

Other researchers have also reported dialogue structures in response to persuasive assignments (Fowler & Glynn, 1983; Gunderson, 1981; White, 1989). The influence of children's experience of spoken language on such dialogue compositions is clear: A persuasive composition is like an oral persuasive exchange in written language.

Informative compositions. Compositions which inform or describe rather than trying to persuade are reported by Craig (1986),

Crowhurst (1983b), and Gorman et al. (1988). Some tasks, in particular, seem likely to produce this kind of writing. One of the three assignments used by Crowhurst (1978, 1980a, 1983a) asked students to decide how a misbehaving classmate should be punished and to persuade the teacher to agree. Several grade 5 and grade 6 compositions in those studies concentrated heavily—and some of them exclusively—on the first part of the task, as in the following example:

SCRIPT 8
I think the punishment would be is he should stay after school for 1 hour every day for a month or three weeks. I would let the committee decide when he could leave. I would give him extra homework, give him lines, and to clean up the school yard. I would give him extra homework so he wouldn't do that again. I would give him lines that says I will not shoot elastic bands again and I would tell him to pick up the garbage after school. (grade 5)

Students may respond in this manner because describing comes more easily to them than giving reasons. It is also possible that report writing (i.e., informative writing) is a more common kind of writing for elementary students than is persuasive writing. However, students' difficulty may also be due to the constraints of a two-part writing task. Wilkinson and his colleagues (1980) found that comparatively few 10-year-olds attempted to respond to both parts of their writing task: "Would it work if children came to school when they liked and could do what they liked there?"

Wishes. White (1989) reports a small number of compositions which she calls "wishes." These compositions communicated personal likes and dislikes (e.g., I would like to be a karate expert) but lacked any sign of trying to persuade others to share their points of view.

Characteristics of Early Arguments

Examples of responses such as those described above have been found in studies in various countries. They do, however, comprise a comparatively small proportion of responses to persuasive assignments. Most young students do write compositions which are recognizably persuasive. However, a considerable number of them deviate in characteristic ways from expected forms.

Arguments written by young writers, for example, are relatively brief. Opening position-taking statements are usually of the "I think ..." or the "No, I don't think ..." variety with little elaboration of the topic and baldly stated, unelaborated reasons. Sometimes a number of unelaborated reasons are given resulting in a composition that reads like a list, as in *Script 9:*

SCRIPT 9

No, I don't think this would be a very good trip for my class because some people cannot canoe, and some people might drown. There would be too many rocks to carry your canoe over. There wouldn't be enough canoes.

It would be better if it was in a semi-wilderness environment. They don't have enough food supply for all of them. They wouldn't be any place to put up their tent. They would have to take warm clothes or they might freeze in the night. There wouldn't be any bunk houses. (Grade 6)

Compositions often lack any kind of concluding statement, as illustrated in *Script 9* above. Where there is a conclusion, it is most likely to be either some kind of appeal or hope ("So please stop homework!" "I hope I have persuaded you to NOT cut our homework." "So please let us have pools. DECIDE QUICK.") or a single statement repeating the writer's opinion ("That's why homework should be cut off." "And that's why I think Ross Road (school) should have lockers.")

Sometimes compositions present a set of opinions on different, though related, matters. This kind of multistatement response is reported by Gorman et al. (1988) for their topic which asked students to think of a subject on which they had a strong opinion and to persuade somebody else who did not share that opinion; such responses were also found by Crowhurst (1987b) for one of the four topics used, a topic which asked students to think of one thing about their school that should be changed and to try to persuade the principal to change it. Instead of choosing one unsatisfactory aspect, they wrote about three or four. Such multitopic responses did not occur when students were asked to persuade the principal on specifically identified questions such as whether homework should be eliminated.

Comparatively few compositions are organized into paragraphs (Gorman et al., 1988). Rather than logical organization based on separate but related points, appropriately elaborated and illustrated, young writers frequently engage in associative writing (Bereiter, 1980) where each successive sentence relates to the one immediately preceding. Freedman and Pringle (1984) report that 50 percent of the arguments of their seventh and eighth graders were of this kind.

Younger writers also differ from older writers in their language use. Young writers use less diverse, less precise, less interesting vocabulary. They make monotonous use of a small number of connectives (*so, but, another thing, also*). Sentences are shorter and simpler—perhaps significant in that syntactic complexity has been found to be related to quality for older students in argumentative writing, though not in narrative writing (Crowhurst, 1980b). Expressions and structures reminiscent of spoken language are common, like the appeals with which younger writers frequently conclude. Students sometimes attempt to capture the prosodic features of spoken language by using graphic features such as capitals, underlining and exclamation marks (White, 1989).

Not all the spoken-language features of young students' writing are interpreted negatively. Indeed White (1989) points out that "much of the best writing from 11-year-olds gains force and immediacy from the adaptation of spoken language exchanges" (p. 20). She points out, however, that the difference between good writing at age 15 and good writing at age 11 is clear. Whereas much of the best writing at age 11 reflects the conventions of speech—as, indeed, does weaker writing by 15-year-olds—able 15-year-olds have learned a good deal more both about written argument and about the text-forming devices of language. They have a variety of linguistic means at their disposal for conveying urgency and emphasis and have less need for the passionate personal statements and rhetorical questions of younger children.

QUESTIONS OF DEVELOPMENT, DIFFICULTY, AND TEACHABILITY

The above descriptions of young writers' responses to persuasive topics invite speculation about the processes by which young students construct arguments. They also invite discussion of the comparative difficulty of argument and narrative, and of appropriate methods of instruction and assessment.

Development

One suggested reason for young students' comparatively poor performance in argument is that their schema for written argument—indeed their schemata for written forms in general—is derived from the textual structures of speech with which they become acquainted first (Bereiter & Scardamalia, 1982; Kress, 1982). Structures, like argument, which are heavily dependent, in spoken language, on the input of an interlocutor do not transfer as easily from spoken to written language as narrative structure and may therefore be expected to be acquired later.

Certainly the influence of spoken language on the persuasive writing of young students is clear. Some compositions—dialogue compositions—are direct representations of spoken persuasive exchanges. A large number of compositions which conform more closely to the expected form of argument show the influence of spoken language in the direct, colloquial forms of language used, and in the strategies used to persuade—direct appeals and imperatives, for example.

Narrative compositions written by some students in response to persuasive tasks also reveal strong evidence of spoken persuasive discourse. *Script 2* above, an example of an argument set in a narrative framework, contains what is, in fact, the record of a persuasive speech delivered to the punishment committee. When the writer of *scripts 6* and *7* rewrites the narrative-dialogue of *script 6* as the more formally persuasive composition of *script 7*, she writes what sounds like a formal persuasive speech. The first and last sentences, in particular, sound like the opening and closing of a speech: "Mrs. Bernard and members of the crime committee we are here to find a suitable punishment. . . . I am very confident that this punishment will be suitable." These examples suggest the influence not so much of informal conversational exchanges, but of more formal speeches delivered, perhaps, to the class. The conclusion must be drawn that the influence of spoken language—perhaps in a variety of forms—on written persuasive pieces is substantial and pervasive, that when young students write, the structures and language of oral persuasion are readily available and freely used.

Narrative writing in response to a persuasive task is attributed by White (1989) to lack of knowledge of the functions of language. She suggests that students may not know "how to use (written) language for anything other than an informal anecdotal/informative function" (p. 19). Scardamalia and Bereiter (1986), on the other hand, suggest that deviations from argumentative forms are "more likely attributable to losing hold than to lack of the appropriate schema" (p. 784). Some examples seem to illustrate such "losing hold"—compositions that begin as arguments but then drift off into narrative (like *script 3* above), for example, or into excessive illustrative material (see *script 5* in White, 1989), and never come back to the argument. Such drifting off probably results from the use of a "what next" strategy resulting in "associative writing" in which the sentence just written, rather than an overall plan, triggers what comes next (Bereiter, 1980; Bereiter & Scardamalia, 1982; Bereiter & Scardamalia, 1987).

However, arguments set in a narrative framework (see *script 2* above) fit this explanation less well. They appear, rather, to indicate uncertainty about how to get started on a persuasive piece, and to reflect lack of clear, accessible knowledge of argument structure.

It is sometimes suggested that narrative writing should be considered appropriate as a response to argument assignments because arguments frequently make use of narrative and anecdotal illustrations to make a point, and because certain kinds of narratives function, in their entirety, as persuasive pieces. It is difficult, however, to justify such an argument. The anecdotes of young writers do not usually make points or illustrate points being made. In our research we have occasionally found a narrative by an older student which functions in this way. We have never found such an example in responses by fifth, sixth, or seventh graders.

Difficulty

Poor performance in argument as against narrative has commonly been attributed to its greater cognitive difficulty (Bereiter, 1980; Crowhurst, 1983a; Freedman & Pringle, 1984; Moffett, 1968; Scardamalia, 1981; Wilkinson, Barnsley, Hanna, & Swan, 1980), such views deriving largely from Piagetian psychology. Moffett, for example, describes discourse as an abstractive hierarchy, beginning, at the lowest level, with narrative, followed by generalizing and theorizing. Narrative, which closely resembles the chronological structure of external reality, is, he believes, the easiest and most natural form of discourse for children.

There is undoubtedly some validity in the suggestion that writing a formal argument is a demanding cognitive task. It requires an ability to abstract and conceptualize, to deal in generalizations—particularly for certain topics and for generalized or universal audiences. Appropriate organization—critical for effective argument—is more difficult than the chronological ordering of information which is typical of narrative. Not only the production of chronologically ordered text, but also the generation of usable content is an easier task for the story writer than for the persuader. Their whole world of experience is available to story writers who may take their narratives in any direction they choose, selecting from well-known material appropriate content from which to fashion their stories. However once a topic is chosen by or assigned to a persuader, relevant material is considerably more limited. Information, moreover, is likely to be less accessible, stored in scattered nodes in memory. Generating content, always a difficult task for young writers, is especially difficult for universal topics or issues of public policy requiring, as they do, information—and even vocabulary—somewhat removed from students' usual experience. Thus writing arguments presents both cognitive difficulties and difficulties associated with lack of experience and lack of knowledge.

Arguments, moreover, appear to require linguistic resources not readily available to young students. Argument characteristically has longer clauses and T-units than narration, is typified by more complex constructions such as nominalizations, and is heavily dependent on logical connectives to signal relationships between sentences. Ability in all of these areas increases with age, though the interrelationships between cognitive development, sociological factors, and language development are, as always, not easily determined.

Discussions of the difficulty of argumentative writing must address also the fact that there are obvious differences among persuasive assignments. As noted in the discussion above, some assignments are more apt than others to lead some children into different and inappropriate forms of writing. Assignments which ask students to find a topic about which they feel strongly seem more likely to produce multistatement responses as reported by Gorman et al. (1988) and Crowhurst (1987b). Two-part tasks are less well done; in particular, when a two-part task asks children to decide what should be done (e.g., about how to spend money or how to punish a misbehaving classmate) and then to persuade, more children are likely to write descriptively informative compositions without giving reasons or otherwise trying to persuade. In our research, when assignments were presented in conjunction with a color slide—for purposes of controlling topic across different modes of discourse—there were more instances of narrative writing than in other kinds of assignment presentation.

Then, again, persuasive/argumentative writing comes in many forms and degrees of difficulty ranging from formal to informal. Not all forms of argument are equally difficult. In the 1983 National Assessment for example, 25 percent of fourth graders managed to write an adequate letter persuading Aunt May on an issue of personal concern, but only 4 percent produced "adequate" texts when the task was to convince the principal to change a school rule—a topic that required more general arguments than the personal opinions and examples that were appropriate for Aunt May. Miller (1980) found that her freshman students were well able to persuade an immediate audience on a personally important topic but that they could not write effectively on a universal topic for a general audience.

Given the reasonable assumption that an attempt to persuade implies both a commitment to a position and a desire to convince an other or others, one may well question the appropriateness of any assigned topic as a stimulus for effective persuasive writing. Assigned tasks to persuade make-believe audiences on topics of peripheral interest to the writer seem to involve special difficulties. The problems and limitations of all testing are to be kept in mind in making judgments about students' ability. Large-scale assessments and controlled research studies are inevitably a-rhetorical and a-contextual. They give limited information on carefully limited questions. The information thus acquired is useful in certain ways. But the writing tasks and assessment measures used in such studies must not be assumed to be appropriate models for instructional purposes.

Teaching Persuasive Writing

Elementary students have little opportunity to become acquainted with written argumentation either in their reading or in their writing. Even the easier kinds of persuasive writing receive little attention during the middle school years. Educators have continually noted the discontinuity between writing in the elementary school where the most common kind of writing is the "story"—a catch-all term that covers many kinds of writing—and the high school where argument becomes the required and valued form (Martin & Rothery, 1981; Newkirk, 1987; White, 1989). Yet, persuasion, as any parent can testify, is a form of discourse that develops early in the oral mode. Wilkinson (1986) calls argument "a primary act of mind." Interesting evidence emerging from the primary grades suggests that precursors of exposition and argument also appear early in writing (Martin & Rothery, 1981; Newkirk, 1985, 1987). Newkirk argues persuasively against theorists who claim that children first produce expressive or narrative writing (e.g., Moffett, 1968; Britton, Burgess, Martin, Mcleod, & Rosen 1975), and gives many examples of nonnarrative writing by children in primary grades, including the writing of incipient arguments. A case in point is the argument made by 6-year-old Sarah in a sign for a booth at a lawn fair where children could make their own pin-on buttons:

> Desin-a-button
> only 75 cents   the desins
> cuck.E.Cheese
> Unicons rainbows
> and much much
> more
> its's better pric
> than last year
> 75 cents

The argument is quite complex:

> Major Assertion: Buy a design-a-button (implied).
> Major Reason: Low cost.
> Evidence: The cost is 75 cents.
> Evidence: The cost is lower than last year.
> Major Reason: The many designs (implied).
> Evidence: Chucky Cheese, Rainbows, Unicorns and more.
> (Newkirk, 1985, pp. 297–298)

This text illustrates what other writers assert: that non-narrative writing occurs early and naturally in the first years of school (Martin & Rothery, 1981). However, the value and importance of non-narrative writing are sometimes not recognized. Rather, teachers value and encourage expressive and narrative writing either because they are influenced by a strong romantic tradition deriving from the nineteenth century or because they believe that children are not cognitively ready for what they see as a more difficult kind of writing (Martin & Rothery, 1981; Newkirk, 1985, 1987).

Influential voices urge the importance of teaching argumentative writing (Dixon & Stratta, 1986; Kress, 1982; Martin & Rothery, 1980, 1981; White, 1989). Given the importance of argumentative/persuasive writing in a wide range of life situations and evidence that elementary students have at least rudimentary knowledge of the genre, White believes that to exclude them from practice in this form of writing "amounts to a form of linguistic disenfranchisement" (1989, p. 9).

However, little writing instruction occurs in schools, particularly in persuasive writing (Applebee, 1981, 1984; Martin, 1980; Wignell, 1987). Applebee found that writing instruction was rarely given either prior to or during writing, that assignments consisted of little more than the presentation of a topic, a length, and a due date, findings echoed by Wignell (1987) in Australia. Insofar as it occurs at all, writing instruction comes after the writing is finished, and is delivered by means of written teacher comments and corrections. Such response is more often negative than positive, and is often vague with no indication of how to improve.

Martin (1980) believes that teachers make vague comments because they lack explicit knowledge about genres. They have good intuitions about whether writing is good or bad because they have an *implicit* knowledge of the requirements of various genres which enables them to recognize when things go wrong. But they cannot give concise, descriptive, "reader-based" feedback because they lack explicit knowledge. Such full and explicit knowledge might enable teachers to take what Newkirk calls another angle of vision which would uncover the competence of children writing argument. Instead of "a 'deficit' model which views children's writing as deficient adult writing, as writing which suffers from various cognitive overloads or breakdowns," a more precise understanding of what is involved in writing argument may permit "an incremental viewpoint which examines the approximations children *successfully* attempt" (Newkirk, 1987, p. 142). Such a viewpoint would allow teachers to recognize the beginnings of argument in writing which does not conform to conventional expectations but which yet reveals some understanding of what argument involves.

Talk of "teaching" argument does not, of course, mean only or mainly instructing students in the structure of argument. "Since text and context are in a deterministic relation, various techniques can be used to improve a student's writing without him ever knowing what schematic structure . . . (is)" (Martin, 1980, p. 28). What *is* important is for the teacher to know enough about the genre to organize writing situations so that students will master the genre. "In order to get good writing, a good writing context must be effected . . . That is, students must be clear about what they are writing about (the topic), who they are writing to (the addressee), . . . and why they are writing (what their purpose is)" (Martin, 1980, p. 27).

No kind of writing provides more opportunities for writing about real issues for real audiences than does argument. Issues constantly arise in classrooms and schools about which students are likely to have firm personal opinions. Alert teachers can easily channel the interest thus aroused into productive writing, addressed, for example, to teachers or principal. Opportunities for discussion and argument are also presented by a constant stream of controversial topics in the public arena which students can easily relate to. Topics widely and hotly debated in my region in the recent past have included the following: capital punishment (occasioned by a free vote in the federal parliament on the possible reintroduction of the death penalty); immigration policy (occasioned by the arrival off the coast of eastern Canada of a boat load of illegal immigrants); wolf kills authorized by the provincial government as a measure of wildlife management; whether or not the provincial government should pay for lunches for hungry school children and expensive drugs for AIDS victims. These subjects—and many others—were widely discussed on radio and television talk shows, and in newspaper editorials and letters to editors. To take up such matters in school allows opportunity for students to read examples—good and bad, emotional and rational—of persuasive writing in the world around them. It also allows classroom discussion, an important support for writing which may follow. Finally, there is ample opportunity for writing for real purposes to newspapers and to members of parliament and other public figures on topics of current public interest. Teachers interested in contextually situated writing will find rich opportunities in persuasive writing. Argumentation need not be the sterile exercise on topics far removed from students' interest which Dixon and Stratta have criticized so eloquently (e.g., 1986).

CONCLUSION

Existing evidence suggests that students do less well writing argument than writing narrative, or descriptive reports. Reasons for poorer performance in argument are complex and interactive.

In some ways argument is more cognitively demanding—in the location of relevant content, for example, and in the organization and logical use of that content. It characteristically uses linguistic forms not mastered early. Again, many young students do not appear to have an appropriate schema for written argument. Compositions start and end abruptly; reasons are often not elaborated; some students respond with unexpected kinds of writing—narratives, dialogues, descriptions.

While cognitive difficulty undoubtedly plays a role, difficulties of other kinds must also be considered. One such difficulty is lack of experience. Young students lack two kinds of experience: First, they often lack experience of the kind that would give them information and vocabulary to discuss topics of interest; they lack experience with written argument. They do not *read* argumentative writing and therefore have little opportunity to acquire either the organization structures or the linguistic structures that typify formal argumentation. Further, they are not usually encouraged to *write* argument, either because it is judged too difficult, or because expressive writing is more highly valued.

Another source of difficulty arises from the interrelated matters of the writing situation and the assessment situation. Persuasive strategies cannot be judged except in the context of the audience to whom the persuasive writing is addressed. What persuades me may not persuade you. A teacher-reader is not necessarily well equipped to judge the effectiveness of language and arguments addressed to the make-believe peer of a 12-year-old. Highly personal reasons may be inappropriate for some topics and some audiences, but they are not inappropriate for all. There are, then, some problems with assessment when the assessor is not the intended audience, or when writing is addressed to no real audience at all, as is usually the case in assessments and controlled research studies. Appropriate uses and forms of language are learned when language is used for real purposes in interactive situations. Despite the considerable advances in recent years in devising more valid tasks in writing assessments, contextually relevant writing will remain difficult, especially for persuasive writing since the audience is critical to the means and to the language of persuasion. The classroom teacher, however, need not be inhibited by the constraints faced in assessments. The classroom provides rich opportunities for contextually situated persuasive writing.

Several lines of evidence suggest that persuasive/argumentative writing should not be neglected in the middle school years: (a) persuasive uses of language appear early in spoken language, (b) precursors of argument appear in the writing of very young children in the early years of schooling, (c) even poor persuasive writing in the pre-teen years presents knowledge of and embryonic forms of argument, and (d) there are abundant opportunities for contextually relevant writing.

Useful procedures for developing persuasive writing ability include the following:

1. Topics should always be issues important to students.
2. Even in the early school years, individual students should be encouraged to engage in persuasive writing to teachers, classmates, principals, and others when they feel strongly on issues. Such writing, of course, should be sent to the intended audience.
3. Large and small group discussions of issues are invaluable, not only for developing oral skills, but also for identifying relevant content and

for the clarification of individual stances on matters under discussion.
4. Dixon and Stratta (1981) suggest the "ruminative essay" as an impor-
    tant bridge to argumentative writing. The purpose of such essays is to
    think around or mull over an issue, to sort out for oneself what one
    thinks.
5. In addition to writing, students in the upper elementary years and be-
    yond should read persuasive/argumentative writing. The linguistic
    forms and the structures of argumentative writing are less likely to be
    acquired unless students are exposed to good models of various kinds.
    Discussion of such readings should cover both content and structure.

Attempts to persuade occur early in the life of a child. Argument, Wilkinson (1986) claims, is one of two "natural or universal genres rooted in
the human psyche" (p. 137)—the other being narrative. There is no good
reason why this kind of writing should be regarded as a difficult form to
be attempted only by older and brighter students.

REFERENCES

Applebee, A. N. (1981). *Writing in the secondary school* (Research Monograph No.
    21). Urbana, IL: National Council of Teachers of English.
Applebee, A. N. (1984). *Contexts for learning to write: Studies of secondary school
    instruction.* Norwood, NJ: Ablex.
Applebee, A. N., Langer, J. A., & Mullis, I. V. S. (1986a). *Writing: Trends across the
    decade, 1974–1984.* Princeton, NJ: The National Assessment of Educational
    Progress.
Applebee, A. N., Langer, J. A., & Mullis, I. V. S. (1986b). *The writing report card:
    Writing achievement in American schools.* Princeton, NJ: The National As-
    sessment of Educational Progress.
Bereiter, C. (1980). Development in writing. In L. W. Gregg & E. R. Steinberg (Eds.),
    Cognitive processes in writing (pp. 73–93). Hillsdale, NJ: Lawrence Erl-
    baum.
Bereiter, C., & Scardamalia, M. (1982). From conversation to composition: The role
    of instruction in a developmental process. In R. Glaser (Ed.), *Advances in
    instructional psychology* (Vol. 2, pp. 1–64). Hillsdale, NJ: Erlbaum.
Bereiter, C., & Scardamalia, M. (1987). *The psychology of written composition.*
    Hillsdale, NJ: Erlbaum.
Britton, J. N., Burgess, T., Martin, N., McLeod, A., & Rosen, H. (1975). *The develop-
    ment of writing abilities (11–18).* London: Macmillan Education.
Conry, R., & Rodgers, D. (1978). *B.C. assessment of written expression: Summary
    report.* Vancouver, B.C.: Ministry of Education.
Connor, U., Gorman, T., & Vahapassi, A. (1987). The argumentative/persuasive task.
    In T. P. Gorman, A. C. Purves, & R. E. Degenhart (Eds.), *The IEA study of*

written composition. Volume 1. The international writing scales and scoring scales (pp. 181–202). Jyvaskyla, Finland: Institute for Educational Research.

Craig, S. G. (1986). *The effect of audience on language functions in written argument at two grade levels.* Unpublished doctoral dissertation, University of British Columbia.

Crowhurst, M. (1978). The effect of audience and mode of discourse on the syntactic complexity of the writing of sixth and tenth graders. Unpublished doctoral dissertation, University of Minnesota, 1977. *Dissertation Abstracts International, 38,* 7300A.

Crowhurst, M. (1980a). Syntactic complexity in narration and argument at three grade levels. *Canadian Journal of Education, 5*(1), 6–13.

Crowhurst, M. (1980b). Syntactic complexity and teachers' quality ratings of narrations and arguments. *Research in the Teaching of English, 14,* 223–242.

Crowhurst, M. (1983a). *Persuasive writing at grades 5, 7, and 11: A cognitive-developmental perspective.* Paper presented at the Annual Meeting of the American Educational Research Association, Montreal. (ERIC Document Reproduction Service No. ED 230 977)

Crowhurst, M. (1983b). *A developmental perspective on persuasive writing.* Paper presented at the Annual Meeting of the Conference on College Composition and Communication, Detroit, MI.

Crowhurst, M. (1986). Revision strategies of students at three grade levels. *English Quarterly, 19*(3), 217–226.

Crowhurst, M. (1987a). Cohesion in argument and narration at three grade levels. *Research in the Teaching of English, 21,* 185–201.

Crowhurst, M. (1987b). *The effect of reading instruction and writing instruction on reading and writing persuasion.* Paper presented at the Annual Meeting of the American Educational Research Association, Washington, DC.

Crowhurst, M. (in press). Reading/writing relationships: An intervention study. *Canadian Journal of Education.*

Crowhurst, M., & Piche, G. L. (1979). Audience and mode of discourse effects on syntactic complexity in writing at two grade levels. *Research in the Teaching of English, 13,* 101–110.

Dixon, J., & Stratta, L. (1986). Argument and the teaching of English. In A. Wilkinson (Ed.), *The writing of writing* (pp. 8–21). Milton Keynes: Open University Press.

Dixon, J., & Stratta, L. (1982). *Teaching and assessing argument.* Southampton: Southern Regional Examinations Board.

Fowler, L. M., & Glynn, S. M. (1983). *Descriptive and persuasive writing skills of children.* Paper presented at the Annual Meeting of the American Educational Research Association, Montreal, Canada.

Freedman, A., & Pringle, I. (1984). Why students can't write arguments. *English in Education, 18* (2), 73–84.

Gorman, T. P., White, J., Brooks, C., MacLure, M., & Kispal, A. (1988). *A review of language monitoring 1979–83.* London: Assessment of Performance Unit, HMSO.

Gunderson, L. (1981). *Developmental characteristics of the writing of urban students at grades 2, 5, and 11.* Paper presented at the Annual Meeting of the National Council of Teachers of English, Boston, MA.

Hillocks, G., Jr. (1986). *Research on written composition: New directions for teaching.* Urbana, IL: ERIC Clearinghouse on Reading and Communications Skills and the National Conference on Research in English.

Hillocks, G., Jr. (1987). *Analyzing the structure of written arguments.* Paper presented at the Annual Meeting of the American Education Research Association, Washington, DC.

Kress, G. (1982). *Learning to write.* London: Routledge & Kegan Paul.

Martin, J. R. (1980). Exposition: Literary criticism. In J. R. Martin & J. Rothery (Eds.), *Working papers in linguistics. No. 1 Paper 2.* Sydney, NSW: Linguistics Department, University of Sydney, Australia.

Martin, J. R., & Rothery, J. (1981). The ontogenesis of written genre. In J. R. Martin & J. Rothery (Eds.), *Working papers in linguistics. No. 2* (pp. 1–59). Sydney, NSW: Linguistics Department, University of Sydney, Australia.

Martin, J. R., & Rothery, J. (1986). *Working papers in linguistics. No. 4.* Sydney, NSW: Linguistics Department, University of Sydney, Australia.

McCann, T. M. (1989). Student argumentative writing, knowledge and ability at three grade levels. *Research in the teaching of English, 23,* 62–76.

Miller, S. (1980). Rhetorical maturity: Definition and development. In A. Freedman & I. Pringle (Eds.), *Reinventing the rhetorical tradition* (pp. 119–27). Conway, AK.: L&S Books for the CCTE.

Moffett, J. (1968). *Teaching the universe of discourse.* Boston: Houghton Mifflin.

National Assessment of Educational Progress. (1980). *Writing achievement: Results from the third national writing assessment* (Vols. 1–3). Denver, CO: Education Commission of the States. (ERIC Document Reproduction Service No. ED 196 042, 043, 044)

Newkirk, T. (1985). The hedgehog or the fox: The dilemma of writing development. *Language Arts, 62,* 593–603.

Newkirk, T. (1987). The non-narrative writing of young children. *Research in the Teaching of English, 21,* 121–144.

Pringle, I., & Freedman, A. (1985). *A comparative study of writing abilities in two modes at the grade 5, 8, and 12 levels.* Toronto: Ministry of Education.

Scardamalia, M. (1981). How children cope with the cognitive demands of writing. In C. F. Frederiksen & J. F. Dominic (Eds.), *Writing: The nature, development and teaching of written communication* (Vol. 2, pp. 81–103). Hillsdale, NJ: Lawrence Erlbaum.

Scardamalia, M., & Bereiter, C. (1986). Research on written composition. In M.C. Wittrock (Ed.), *Handbook of research on teaching* (3rd ed., pp. 778–803). New York: MacMillan.

Vahapassi, A., Lehmann, R., deGlopper, K., Lamb, H., & Langer, J. (1987). *The IEA study of written composition: Reports from four countries—Finland, Federal Republic of Germany, The Netherlands, New Zealand.* Symposium presented at the Annual Meeting of the American Educational Research Association, Washington, DC.

Wignell, P. (1987). In your own words. In S. Eggins, J. R. Martin, & P. Wignell (Eds.), *Working papers in linguistics, No. 5* (pp. 1–24). Sydney, NSW: Linguistics Department, University of Sydney.

White, J. (1989). Children's argumentative writing: A reappraisal of difficulties. In F. Christie (Ed.), *Writing in schools: Reader* (pp. 9–23). (ECT418 Language Studies Course). Geelong, Victoria: Deakin University Press

Wilkinson, A. M. (1986). Argument as a primary act of mind. *Educational Review,* *38*(2), 127–138.

Wilkinson, A. M., Barnsley, G., Hanna, P., & Swan, M. (1980). *Assessing language development.* Oxford: Oxford University Press.

10
Adolescents' Uses of Intertextual Links to Understand Literature

Richard Beach
Deborah Appleman
Sharon Dorsey

In reading a mystery story, a reader encounters the words, "Without a touch, the huge, heavy door to the house slowly squeaked opened, but there was no one there." To most readers of mystery stories, this is familiar stuff. Drawing on her knowledge of mystery stories, the reader infers that she is about to enter a haunted house fraught with further mysteries. This reader is linking the current text to a reservoir of literary know-how regarding mystery stories.

In this chapter, we will argue that readers understand texts not as discrete, autonomous entities but as further extensions of their own previous literary experiences. Developing a "textual" stance therefore entails learning to infer intertextual links between past knowledge and current texts.

While literary critics have recently been interested in how authors use of intertextual links with their own or others previous texts (Valdes & Miller, 1985), we know little about the processes by which readers define intertextual links.

As many of the chapters in this volume argue, the kinds of discourse practices readers acquire depend on the nature of their instruction. Much of secondary literature instruction is "text-based" in that it focuses on factual knowledge about or interpretation of specific texts (Bernstein, 1984). For example, reflecting the evaluation techniques that drive much of literature instruction, recent assessments of students' knowledge of literature has focused primarily on students' knowledge of particular texts or authors (Applebee, Langer, & Mullis, 1987; Ravitch & Finn, 1987). This "text-based" conception assumes that texts are known as autonomous entities, an assumption derived from the New Critical approach that priveledges analysis of the features unique to that particular text.

AN INTERTEXTUAL CONCEPTION OF LITERARY UNDERSTANDING

Treating texts as distinct entities assumes that readers understand texts in a conceptual vacuum. However, we believe that readers understand texts as extensions of their previous reading experience.

In contrast to a "text-based" conception of literature, an "intertextual" conception assumes that the meaning derives from a readers' transaction with the text (Rosenblatt, 1978) in which readers apply their knowledge of literary and social conventions to that text (Beach, 1985; Beach & Brown, 1987). The text evokes or invites (Smith, 1968) a reader to conceive of a text as representative of certain generic or conventional ways of knowing literature (Mailloux, 1985; Rabinowitz, 1987; Ricoeur, 1985).

With each new text, readers become more proficient in applying their evolving literary know-how to understand texts by attending to relevant information, explaining, predicting, interpreting, and, most importantly, relating or connecting each new text to evolving knowledge (Beach & Appleman, 1985). Roland Barthes (1980), a strong proponent of an intertextual perspective, argues that "the Text is experienced only in an activity, a production . . . the constitutive movement of the Text is a traversal; it can cut across a work, several works" (p. 75).

Acquiring the ability to define relationships between current texts and past knowledge or texts is particularly important for learning to respond to computer "hypertext" (Barrett, 1988; Tchudi, 1988). Computer "hypertext" based on multidimensional databases allows the computer users to mesh categories of information in order to develop unique combinations of information. In order to create their own "hypertext," students need to be able to connect disparate texts according to a range of different categories. For example, in reading a series of historical documents stored in the computer, students need to define the similarities between the documents and their purposes for combining those documents in order to extract relevant knowledge.

DEFINING LINKS AS A SOCIAL ACTIVITY

Readers acquire the practice of defining connections from engaging in everyday social conversation in which conversants are constantly recalling related experiences, or texts, ideas pertinent to the topic at hand. If the topic of conversation is restaurants, then people may recall experiences of eating at various restaurants, with one anecdote triggering a related anecdote.

These social recollections are often driven by knowledge of genres or prototypes related to certain topics: restaurants, births, deaths, travel, and so on. Similarly, the more familiar readers are with certain genres, the more likely they are to recall prototypical characters, settings, or storylines associated with that genre.

Readers are often motivated to share their responses in order to develop social relationships or membership in groups. As "mystery buffs," "science-fiction freaks," or avid romance novel readers, they seek out other readers with similar reading interests, creating a community of readers. They establish membership in these communities by contributing their knowledge and understanding of previous texts, defining those links relevant to the membership's interests. This means that interpreting texts, as Paul Gee (1988) argues, is an acquired social practice: "One always and only learns to interpret texts of a certain type in certain ways through having access to, and ample experience in, social settings where texts of that type are read in those ways" (p. 309).

As readers learn to apply past knowledge to current texts, they are also using their experiences with current texts to revise their knowledge of past texts. Having read *Hamlet*, and having been puzzled by Hamlet's indecision in killing Claudius, they may then think about *Oedipus Rex*, and Oedipus's own relationship with his father. They are then applying insights from the current text to revise their conceptions of past texts.

For example, in a newpaper editorial, Amy Schwartz (1988) of *The Washington Post*, noted that Toni Morrison's *Beloved* reminded her of *Exodus:*

> Reading "Beloved" instantly called "Exodus" to mind: the sweeping historical plot, the many characters (some historical) with their differing experience of the central horror; the way their imagined stories gave historical memory an anchor. Most strikingly similar are the points when the narrative halts momentarily for a cry of rage and suffering.

Comparing these two novels helps Schwartz define the similarities between the suffering of the slaves and of the Jews during the Holocaust. She enriches her understanding of *Beloved* by applying her literary knowledge to that novel. At the same time, in adding *Beloved* to her knowledge, she reshapes her literary knowledge, retroactively broadening her understanding of *Exodus*.

By applying their literary knowledge, readers are drawing on knowledge of a vast, multiple-dimensional, hierarchical databank of cognitive categories and scripts. Story comprehension research in the fields of reading comprehension and artificial intelligence posit various models of readers' knowledge of narratives. In Roger Shank's model of memory (1982), the level of one's inferences about the current experience or text is related to the level at which one recalls prior experiences or texts. Shank argues that our memory is organized in a hierarchical manner, with certain low-level phenonmena—sequences of actions which are subsumed under goals, which are, in turn, subsumed under themes. The "highest" level consists of knowledge of global themes such as "might makes right" or "hard work pays off." Embedded within these global themes are knowledge scripts for characteristic plots, characters' goals, beliefs, and traits.

For example, in going to a restaurant, a person may recall previous experiences of going to restaurants in terms of what one does in ordering from a menu. That may then remind them of larger goals or purposes for ordering: satisfying one's craving for a certain type of food. This, in turn, may remind them of certain larger themes, for example, the value of nutrition. Shank's model therefore suggests that the level of one's inference about a current experience or text triggers recollections of prior experiences or text at a similar level.

Certain aspects of texts also trigger recollections. In responding to current texts, reader may be most likely to attend to instances that deviate from their expectations. Once they experience that deviation, they search their memory schema for instances that match that deviation. If they do not find any similar matches, then they revise their schema, adding new instances. For example, at the Legal Seafood restaurant in Boston, one pays the check before eating. That constitutes a revision of one's typical previous experience, requiring a revision of one's knowledge about "ordering in restaurants" (Schank, 1982).

Readers define these deviations by applying their knowledge of social conventions constituting appropriate behavior (Beach & Brown, 1987). For example, in responding to *Pride and Prejudice*, a reader knows that certain conventions constitute appropriate courting behaviors. Knowing those conventions means that a reader can readily detect instances of violations of those conventions.

Once readers conceive of a text as constituted by certain types of conventions, they can then search back through their knowledge base or "literary databank" to define certain relevant concepts or categories about characters or events. For example, if they infer that a story is about "a betrayed lover seeking revenge," they may then apply their knowledge of categories having to do with "betrayal," "revenge," or "love relationships." By inferring more specific categories: traits, beliefs, knowledge, needs, goals, themes, settings, and so on, readers further refine the scope of their review. For example, by inferring that a character's goal is to "seek revenge," they may recall related character traits and beliefs—that characters seeking revenge are typically persistant and believe that they are "in the right." Readers are, therefore, recalling knowledge of relationships between categories.

As Shank's model suggests, the relationships between these categories are organized hierarchically with certain "larger" categories (genre types or themes) containing more "specific" categories (character types or settings typical of certain genres or themes), which, in turn, contain specific categories (character traits, beliefs, or goals typical of certain character types).

Readers also draw on their social attitudes to define links within and across texts. A reader who evaluates a character's action positively may link that act to a positive story resolution (Golden & Guthrie, 1986) or to instances of "positive" actions in other texts. In Dorfman's (1985) "just ending" model of story understanding, readers may judge the plodding, persistent tortoise in "The Tortoise and the Hare," in a positive light and the hare in a negative light. These readers may also judge the story resolution—the tortoise winning the race in a positive light. By relating their positive character evaluation with their positive evaluation of the story resolution, they may then infer the theme, that characters with certain positive attributes—"hard work/persistence"—are rewarded accordingly in a "just-ending." From learning to apply their attitudes to define character attributes, students develop a set of categories for linking texts.

In the literature classroom, students learn to define these links by engaging in what Dennie Wolf (1988, p. 30) describes as "reading with memory" or "reading resonantly"—the ability to "remember what they read and reflect on their own histories as readers" involving "the willingness to think back on what you read in September, last year, or in some other class." As Wolf found in a study of literature instruction, teachers noted that students' often have difficulty remembering prior reading experiences. Wolf cites one teacher who noted that " 'School can be a hard place to do it. It is a place with no memory. First period, second period; Monday, Tuesday; ninth grade, tenth grade. Very little lasts or looks back' " (1988, p. 30).

Wolf argues that "looking back might allow students to have a sense for their autobiographies as readers—just as an artist might when paging through her portfolio," and she quotes a teacher who notes:

> Think what it would be like if students read *Lord of the Flies* as ninth graders, and then they read it again as seniors. What if they kept their journals, or papers, and could look back? What if I asked them to write about their development as reader—of if they did that for each other? (1988, p. 30)

Unfortunately, teachers often do not encourage students to define links between texts. In an analysis of the ninth-graders' open-ended "think-aloud" responses, Rogers (1988) found that only one percent of the students' responses were devoted to intertextual links. Interviews with the students indicated that they were rarely asked to infer such links. She also found that unless students perceived texts to be carbon-copy, exact matches, they were reluctant to define links.

DEVELOPMENTAL DIFFERENCES IN LITERARY INFERENCES

Students' ability to define links also varies according to readers' level of cognitive development (Applebee, 1978; Fusco, 1983) or cognitive complexity (Hynds, 1985). By attaining the level of formal operations, or the ability to engage in propositional thinking (Applebee, 1978), what Elkind (1984) has aptly called "thinking in a new key," adolescents begin to experiment with defining connections in their lives. No longer bound by the constraints of the immediate physical world, adolescents are able to think of possibilities, to dwell in the world of what might be rather than what is. Because they can imagine optional possibilities, adolescents are better able to hypothesize about characters' motives, predict plots, or speculate about abstract themes and symbols.

And, rather than responding to each literary work as a discrete text, the adolescent is able to begin to formulate categories and generalizations about a particular author's work, characteristics of a genre, character stereotypes, and other literary conventions. Because they can categorize and analyze characters' actions, they can then connect the current text to an abstract network of knowledge about other texts, thus facilitating the possibility of intertextual links.

For example, in his study of developmental differences in adolescents' responses, Thomson (1987) found that early adolescent readers were more likely to respond with "unreflective interest in action"—by defining mental images or making short term predictions, "empathizing—by noting feelings or defining expectations about characters, or "analogising" by connecting autobiographical experiences to the text. In contrast, older adolescents were more likely to reflect on the significance of events and behavior by defining long-term predictions, reviewing the text as the author's creation, or comparing one's own representation with that of the author's representation. This suggests that readers who have read more literature may be more likely to conceive of intertextual connections in terms of literary categories, while less knowledgable readers may be more likely to define links in terms of similar autobiographical experiences.

Adolescents' cognitive and social development may also influence their ability to elaborate on their links, particularly in terms of similarities in characters' attributes or motives. Because some early adolescents are still operating at the initial formal operations stages, they may define links in terms of surface physical description of character traits rather then in terms of abstract prototypical categories (Applebee, 1978; Petrosky, 1977). In Hynds' research (1985), adolescent students with higher degrees of cognitive complexity were more likely to elaborate on a range of different character attributes or motives than low-cognitive complexity students, elaboration that contributed to their ability to explain the characters' actions in terms of external influences.

In a comparison of eighth graders, 11th graders, college freshmen, and college juniors' character inferences were rated according to a scale for degree of abstraction (Beach & Wendler, 1987). The eighth graders differed significantly from 11th graders, who, in turn, differed from the college students in terms of the level of abstraction. The eighth graders' inferences, consistent with cognitive developmental research, focused more on surface, physical behaviors, while the older students focused more on social and psychological aspects.

However, as Svensson's research (1985; see also Chapter 6, this volume) indicates, development is also influenced by variations in readers' prior reading and instructional experiences. The fact that he found a significant relationship between amount of prior literary experience and level of interpretation suggests the limitations of explaining differences in level of response simply in terms of level of cognitive development.

In one of the few studies on developmental differences in intertextual links (Lehr, 1988), kindergarten, second-grade, and fourth-grade students were asked to match up sets of realistic and folklore books according to similarity in the themes. As part of the interviews, the students were also asked to summarize the books using drawings of the story content. The students were more likely to match thematically the realistic books than the folktales, possibly because they were more familiar with the material in the realistic stories than the material in the folktales. Moreover, students who scored higher on the Huck Literature Inventory, a measure of familiarity with literature, were more likely to make thematic inferences than low-scoring children.

The very fact that the students were asked to summarize the books as well as draw pictures of the books may have helped them define some concrete similarities between stories, which, in turn, contributed to their ability to infer thematic meanings.

This study indicates that differences in prior experiences or knowledge of literature contribute to differences in students' ability to define intertextual links. To some degree, the more students know, the more relevant knowledge they can apply to the current text. This research also suggests that the more students elaborate about aspects or meanings of the current text, the more likely they are to recall related past texts or knowledge.

In a related study, Beach (in press) analyzed the degree of elaboration of autobiographical responses as related to college students' ability to interpret stories. Students' autobiographical journal responses to stories were analyzed in terms of the degree of elaboration of their narratives, the extent to which students extended their autobiographical narratives beyond statements such as, "this story reminds me of the time my own family's house caught on fire," to include specific details. By recounting specific details of the event and reflecting on the meaning of that event, students were able to define the point of that event. By defining the point of their own experience, they were then able to apply that point to the story, enhancing their interpretation of the story. The degree to which students elaborated on their narratives was positively and significantly correlated with the level of interpretation of the story. Similarly, by elaborating on specific aspects of a text, a reader moves from more global, prototypical conceptions of characters, events, and settings to more specific, concrete traits that serve to interpret characters actions (Hynds, in press). For example, a character may initially remind them of prototypes such as the "hero," "villian," "tyrannical leader," "controlling husband," etc. Then, as students refine these conceptions to incorporate new information from the text, they discover certain complexities in these characters that defy their initial prototypes.

THE PHASES OF DEFINING INTERTEXTUAL LINKS

As illustrated in Figure 10.1 below, theory and research suggests that readers are engaged in the following phases.

We want to emphasize that readers need not proceed with these phases in a linear, chronological order; they may recursively move from one phase to the next.

This model suggests that the level of response to the current text may be related to the level of response to past texts. That is, if readers are able to abstract about the current text, they may be more likely to abstract about past texts. And, the degree to which they elaborate about specific aspects of the current and past texts may be related to their ability to define similarities between past knowledge and the current text. If, for example, readers infer a range of different character elements: traits, roles, beliefs, goals, and so on, then they may be more likely to evoke their prior knowledge of prototypical character elements. They may be better able to

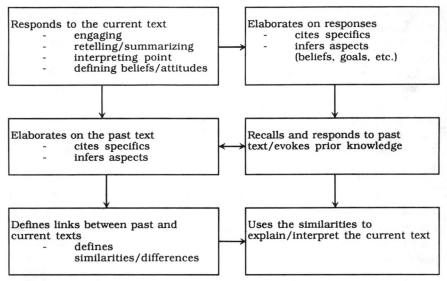

Figure 10.1. Phases of Defining Intertextual Links.

formulate a valid explanation or interpretation of the current text than if they apply only a limited range of elements.

In order to examine readers' use of these processes, we conducted two studies of readers' responses, a large-scale empirical study and a small-scale interview study. In designing these studies, we wanted to examine the following processes illustrated above:

• the relationship between the level of readers' response to a current text and a past text
• the relationship between level of response and degree of elaboration about text elements
• the relationship between degree of elaboration and level of explanation or interpretation of the current text
• the influence of individual differences in background leisure-rading experiences and prior knowledge of literature on the ability to define intertextual links.

Study 1

Subjects. The subjects in this study consisted of 119 eighth grade students in schools representing three different social and economic backgrounds: a junior high school in a middle class suburb of Minneapolis,

Minnesota; a private school in St. Paul, Minnesota with predominately middle- to upper-middle-class students, and three junior high schools in Columbus, Ohio with population representing a relatively high percentage of minority students.

Materials. The text employed in this study was "Priscilla and the Wimps," by Richard Peck (1984), a short story geared primarily for junior high students. In this story, a gang of high school students, the Kobras, headed by Monk, continually harass Melvin and his friends in the school hallways. However, Priscilla, a relatively large female student, confronts Monk, stuffs him in a school locker, and locks the door.

In order to elicit responses to this story, a guided response form was developed that contained the following steps:

1.   After reading the story, students were asked to "freewrite about one or more characters and/or the story situation—what the story was about—for six minutes." Previous research indicates that freewriting serves to foster elaboration of ideas (Hilgers, 1980). Students were then asked to draw a "circle map" of the story in order to help them "visually 'map out' your thoughts about the character(s) and/or the situation. In drawing your map, whenever you think of something, draw a circle and write that thought in the circle. If you think of something else connected to the first circle, draw a line or "spoke" to other new circles from the smaller circles." An example of a map for the fable "The Tortoise and the Hare" was provided as an illustration.

Mapping has been recently introduced in language arts classes as a prewriting device to encourage students to cluster their ideas and consider associations between concepts before generating a draft. This technique enables students to create a visual representation of the central themes of their papers and helps them generate supporting ideas by adding nodes and spokes to their main ideas.

This prewriting technique, which was adapted for this study as a post-reading activity, has its roots in cognitive psychology. Mapping has been viewed as a useful way to represent knowledge (Rumelhart & Norman, 1985). While debate continues regarding the different ways in which knowledge can be represented as well as what is actually being depicted in cognitive models, recent developments in cognitive psychology have suggested that mapping can enhance comprehension by making explicit to students the structure of their representational system as well as connections that exist within that system (Perfetti & Curtis, 1986). That is, in drawing maps of their interpretation of the story and the intertextual links the story evokes, students are visually portraying a representation of their underlying knowledge by depicting a propositional network (Gagne, 1985). As their knowledge increases and the ability to create intertextual links improves, their maps become increasingly complex.

Several researchers have discussed the usefulness of directly teaching mapping to improve reading comprehension (Perfetti & Curtis, 1986; Rumelhart & Norman, 1985). Other studies have indicated that exercises in mapping may help readers infer analogies between stories (Gick & Holyoak, 1985). For example, Gick and Holyoak found that by mapping two stories and making their component parts explicit, subjects were better able to make analogies between specific aspects of both stories. This suggests that mapping may increase students' inclinations to make intertextual links, as their maps graphically underscore those elements that several literary works may share.

Representations such as mapping can also be useful in explaining differences between better and poorer readers. Less elaborate maps may help indicate an impoverished network of prior knowledge of story schema (Just & Carpenter, 1987). Similarly, the more elaborate maps generated by more skilled readers provide a graphic indication of the kind of organizational network the reader has constructed.

2.   Students were then asked to freewrite about "any other characters and/or situations you've read about in other stories, novels, or plays." Then, based on the past text recalled, students completed the same mapping activity for the past text, followed by drawing lines between the aspects of the map that are similar.

3.   Based on the connecting lines between the two maps, students were then asked to list and describe the similarities between the current and past texts.

4.   For the final step, students were asked to review their list of similarities and to "write four or five sentences explaining why the main character acted the way s/he did."

In order to determine the amount of previous reading, scales employed in the Svensson (1985) study were incorporated into a reading inventory questionnaire. And, in order to determine students' propensity to empathize with or to relate their own experiences to literature, scales from the "Transfer" scales employed in the International Education Assessment of Literature were employed (Purves, 1973).

Procedures. Students were asked to read the story, "Priscilla and the Wimps," and to complete the guided response from within one class period. They then completed the reading inventory questionnaire in a subsequent class period.

Analysis. Two judges rated the freewrites for the current and past stories according to degree of "focus," "abstraction" and "specificity" on scales of "1" to "4" and "level of thematic inference" on a scale from "1" to "3." Their percentage of agreement across all ratings was .82. They also analyzed the maps according to the number of references to roles, attributes, actions, beliefs, goals, plot, and theme for each of two characters for both the "Priscilla" and the recalled text. And, they determined the number of defined links between the maps and the number of similarities listed. And, finally, they rated the final explanation of Priscilla's behavior on a scale from "1" to "4" for the quality of the explanation and a scale from "1" to "3" for "level of thematic inference."

Results. (These results are presented only in summary form; for a description of specific results, contact the authors.)

The results of the reading inventory indicated that, for these 119 eighth graders:

- 60% watch television and 72% listen to the music "nearly every day"
- 40% read magazines "nearly every week"
- 67% "never" or "now and then" read stories, while only 10% read stories "often"
- During the past year, 60% read only one or two novels for pleasure.
- when they read, 50% read for a half an hour or less.
- 40% "occaisionally" or "often" compare a "real life" person to a character.

In drawing their maps, the students had an average of 5.0 aspects for the first character and 4.7 aspects for the second character in "Priscilla;" 4.3 for the first character and 3.2 for the second character in the recalled text. The most common type of aspect consisted of character attributes, followed by actions and roles. There were few if any references to beliefs, goals, plot, or theme. In connection the two maps, students were most likely to connect the stories in terms of attributes.

Several different stepwise regression analyses were conducted in order to determine the extent to which the inventory items and the initial linking processes (as illustrated below) served to predict subsequent processes.

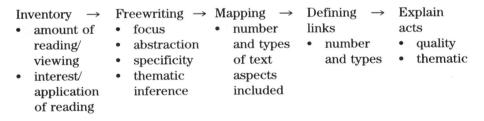

Inventory → Freewriting → Mapping → Defining → Explain
- amount of reading/viewing
- interest/application of reading

- focus
- abstraction
- specificity
- thematic inference

- number and types of text aspects included

links
- number and types

acts
- quality
- thematic

More specifically, the regression analysis determined which of the writing and mapping variables (independent) best predicted the total number of items on the map and the number of links defined (dependent). And, further analyses determined which of the inventory and which of the writing and mapping variables as well as the number of similarities defined variable (independent) best predicted the final quality and "level of thematic inference" for the final explanation (dependent).

Factor analysis of the combined Svensson/Purves inventories generated five factors: (a) Amount of literary reading, (b) Application of literature to life, (c) Involvement/empathy with reading, (d) Comparison of reading and life, and (e) Amount of fantasizing/media use (music, newspapers, magazines).

To summarize the results of the regression analyses, these eighth graders' leisure media use and ability to use freewriting to define thematic meanings were significant predictors for the degree of elaboration of their mapping. Then, as can be expected, the total number of aspects included on the maps as well as the media-use factor was a significant predictor for the similarities listed. The level of specificity of the freewriting and the amount of literature reading were significant predictors for the range of similarities. And, the level of abstraction for the freewriting, the total number of map aspects for the first character, and the number of similarities defined were significant predictors for the quality of the final explanation.

Analysis of specific story elements indicated that students were most likely to focus on character attributes, with few references to belief or goals. However, the degree to which students did include aspects of beliefs and goals influenced the final quality of their explanations.

All of this suggests that initial phases of the process influenced subsequent phases, with students discovering thematic meanings as they moved through the process. For example, dealing with thematic matters in the freewriting helped students develop ideas for their maps. The degree to which they developed their maps and specified their freewriting influenced their ability to list similarities. And, the level of abstraction of the freewriting and the range of similarities, particularly in terms of roles, beliefs, and goals influenced the final quality of the explanations.

Thus, the degree of elaboration and abstraction seem to be crucial factors in determining students' success in using the freewriting and mapping. In the freewriting, many of the students simply retold the story, without inferring any thematic meanings.

As illustrated in the map in Figure 10.2 one student linked "Priscilla and the Wimps" to the S. Scott Fitzgerald story, "Bernice Bobs Her Hair." In that story, which takes place in the 1920s, Marjorie teaches her shy cousin, Bernice, techniques for becoming popular with boys. However, when Bernice becomes so popular that the boys prefer Bernice to Marjorie, Marjorie bates her into cutting off her hair on a bet. After she does so, losing her popularity, Bernice seeks revenge by cutting off Marjorie's hair as she is sleeping. This student was able to define a range of different character attributes, actions, and goals that help her define the similarities between the "good" characters, Priscilla and Bernice, and the "bad" characters,

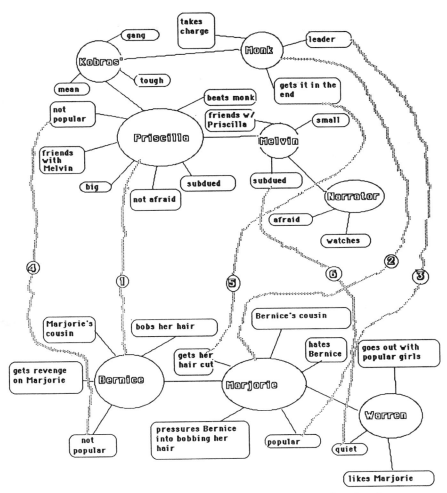

The images contain the following labels:

- gang
- takes charge
- Kobras'
- Monk
- leader
- tough
- mean
- beats monk
- gets it in the end
- not popular
- friends w/ Priscilla
- small
- Priscilla
- Melvin
- friends with Melvin
- big
- subdued
- subdued
- Narrator
- not afraid
- afraid
- watches
- ④
- ①
- ⑤
- ⑥
- ②
- ③
- Marjorie's cousin
- bobs her hair
- Bernice's cousin
- hates Bernice
- goes out with popular girls
- gets revenge on Marjorie
- gets her hair cut
- Bernice
- Marjorie
- Warren
- not popular
- pressures Bernice into bobbing her hair
- popular
- quiet
- likes Marjorie

Figure 10.2.   Student's Map of the Links between the Stories: "Priscilla and the Wimps" and "Bernice Bobs Her Hair."

Monk, the gang leader, and Marjorie. From defining these similarities, the student then went on to list similarities having to do with Priscilla's and Bernice's goal of seeking revenge for wrongdoing.

The amount of leisure reading of literature was a significant predictor of the ability to infer a range of different similarities. As Svensson's research (Chapter 6) suggests, by reading literature, students acquire inference strategies necessary for making symbolic inferences about texts, including the strategy of connecting texts. Thus, growth in strategic know-how of understanding texts is related to reading experience. However, as the survey results indicate, most of these eighth graders devoted little, if any, of their leisure time to reading literature.

Study 2

In the second study, we interviewed 20 high school juniors enrolled in the same college preparatory English class in a Minneapolis, Minnesota high school. The purpose of this study was to determine differences in students' ability to use intertextual links to interpret texts.

Students were asked a series of questions about a group of core works that had been assigned and taught in class. The works included *The Grapes of Wrath, The Scarlet Letter, King Lear, Things Fall Apart, Oedipus Rex, A Doll's House, Miss Julie,* selected Shakespearean sonnets, and selected poetry of Emily Dickinson. Because the students had all read the same core works, they were drawing on the same potential pool of texts for making connections.

Analysis of the interview transcripts indicated that students, regardless of their ability, were consistently more likely to recall certain texts than others. They were much less likely to recall the African novel by Chinua Achebe, *Things Fall Apart*, the Shakespearean sonnets, and the Emily Dickinson poetry than the other texts, possibly due to the difficulty level of these texts.

Students were most likely to recall *The Grapes of Wrath* and *The Scarlet Letter*. The strength of individual characters, the dramatic yet plausible plot structures, and the comparative familiarity of the language all contributed to the degree to which these works were etched in the students' reading memories. Not surprising, another important factor in the availability of specific texts had to do with the amount of class time that had been devoted to each literary work. Obviously, works that had been the focus of extended class discussion and/or writing assignments were most available to students. Even for the most able students, individual reading with no classroom discussion resulted in little more than a superficial understanding of the work and seriously affected students' ability to recall specific characters and events. Articulating their responses to the texts may have helped students store those responses into their "literary databank."

Another related factor influencing differences in students' recollection of texts was their knowledge of categories about literature acquired from instruction. The students who more readily referred to these categories were also more likely to use those categories to retrieve information about texts.

Most students had developed genre categories, into which they had filed similar works. Therefore, they were more likely to connect examples of poetry to one another, rather than connect a theme that emerges in a poem to a novel. The students therefore had little difficulty linking Oedipus Rex and King Lear. Students were able to connect Lear and Oedipus because they had labeled them both as "tragic heroes."

Consistent with the findings of Study 1 and Rogers' (1988) study, students defined links primarily in terms of character traits. The students made frequent reference to categories such as "protagonist" or "villain," suggesting that their categories for characters were more fully developed than their thematic categories. Many students, in a clear example of a teacher-initiated category, defined links according to the broad category of symbol, in which scarlet A's, fierce winter storms, and dust bowl turtles appeared to keep company.

Despite these similarities in their use of categories, the students also differed in their ability to define links due to differences in literary know-how. Based on independent judges' ratings of the students' interpretative ability, the students were rank-ordered into those considered "more" versus "less" able interpreters.

More able students tended to define links in terms of more specific themes such as the effect of being isolated or shunned from society, or the degree to which we are responsible for our fate. Less able students tended to make more intertextual links between character traits or plot than between themes. Less able students' thematic links were more broadly structured, in terms of, for example, love or death.

Less able students were more likely to define links into terms of autobiographical associations, while more able students made more literary associations, a finding consistent with Thomson (1987).

More able students spontaneously compared form (such as in the sonnets or Emily Dickenson's poetry) or genre (in comparing the elements of tragedy found in *King Lear, Oedipus Rex* or *Things Fall Apart).* Less able students were generally able to make those connections when they were pointed out, but did not initiate them.

While the less able students tended to move methodically in their discussions from one consideration of the text at a time (e.g., first plot, then character, then theme), more able readers were more likely to simultaneously consider a multiplicity of factors in their discussion, for example, connecting several aspects of *King Lear* to *Things Fall Apart.*

Finally, the more able students seemed to be more socially confident about mutually exploring links with the interviewer than the less able students. For example, these students were more likely to pick up on and extend the interviewer's own implied cues for making links. This suggests that these students may have had more previous social experience in defining links in everyday conversations. In contrast, the less able students often mechanically searched through their file of texts with less mutual involvement with the interviewer.

In order to illustrate these differences in linking processes, we will compare the responses of two readers, the reader ranked highest (Student A) and the reader ranked lowest (Student B).

One of the differences between these students was the length and degree of elaboration of these students' responses. Student A's responses often extended to paragraph length, while Student B's responses averaged about two sentences in length. Consequently, the interviewer asked Student B many more questions, while Student A offered extended responses, thus requiring fewer questions. Student A and the interviewer were therefore more likely to engage in a mutual, dialogic exploration of links.

Student A initiated several intertextual links without invitation. For example, when asked if Lear is responsible for his fate she responds in the following manner:

> Well, I think he and Oedipus are kind of the same because the reason Oedipus is doomed was because of himself. He acted really quickly and didn't think about what he was really doing all the time and he was—I don't know how to put it—very prideful, put up kind of a big front and Lear was like that in the beginning too. So I guess they were kind of doomed in the same way.

In contrast, Student B never initiates any links between texts and offers less-elaborated explanations. When asked to make parallels between texts, they are neither structural (as in "they're both tragedies") nor thematic ("they show that if you're too ambitious, you fall"), but are simply emotional reactions. For example, she connects Oedipus to the idea of pain because he "probably felt gross. He slept with his mom and stuff." While Student A provided a fairly involved explanation of what happened to Lear, Student B explains simply that "he cracked. His mind just went somewhere and he was gone."

Student A was more likely to make thematic links as well as links about several different character traits within each text. Student B, who could not recall as many of the details of the works, was more likely to cite autobiographical experiences. Instead of comparing characters' behavior to some generalized standard, she tended to judge the characters according to her own attitudes. For example, she judges Hester Prynne to be "stupid" because "she should have been stronger . . . she should have made him (Dimmesdale) pay." In contrast, rather than conceiving of Hester in terms of her own code of behavior, student A infers that she is "strong" because she views her in the context of the prevalent sex roles of the novel: "Women weren't supposed to be strong." Similarly, in discussing

Cordelia, Student B insists on explaining what she would have done in the same situation: "I would have made him understand what I was talking about. . . . I wouldn't have let my sisters take advantage of him like that." Student A does not compare her own inclinations to Cordelia's; she develops a rather elaborate character analysis to help explain her actions and compares her to Hester Prynne: "She isn't like Hester where she can't just say what she means. . . . she was very honest but she wasn't strong enough to go and tell him . . . she could only say it to herself."

Viewed in terms of Thomson's (1987) developmental scheme, Student B, tended to empathize (stage 2) or analogize (stage 3), while Student A displays evidence of reflection (stage 4), reviewing the text (stage 5), and defining one's relationship with the author (stage 6). While Student B generally relates all questions to her own "personal construct" of values, situations, and events, Student A not only reflects on her own experience but also applies knowledge of the nature and function of literature itself. When asked what Hester Prynne might have done to alleviate her pain, Student A suggests, "Well, maybe if she had written or something . . ."

In summary, the results of Study 1 indicated that the degree to which eighth grade students specified and elaborated on links between texts was related to their ability to use links to explain characters' actions. In Study 2, some students developed more proficient strategies for defining links than other students, differences due to differences in prior reading and classroom experiences. All of this suggests that, in addition to the amount of leisure literature reading, learning to define intertextual links is a learned discourse practice that contributes to understanding texts.

IMPLICATIONS FOR TEACHING

These results suggests that instructional activities can influence students' ability to define links. Rather than organizing the literature curriculum simply in terms of historical periods, teachers may also foster intertextual links by organizing literature units and courses around thematic, topical, cultural, historical, archetypal, or genre connections between texts. Teachers also need to encourage students to reach beyond the scope of their own units or courses to draw on their own unique prior reading experiences. Rather than simply mimicing the implied connections of a teacher-designed unit or course, students need to learn to make their own connections based on their own prior reading experiences.

And, within these units or courses, teachers could employ writing and mapping activities to help students articulate and elaborate on their responses. As suggested by Marshall's discussion (see Chapter 7, this volume) of informal writing about literature, by elaborating on their written responses through informal, dialogic writing in terms of the categories in characters' roles, traits, beliefs, plans, and goals, students may be more likely to store or "instantiate" responses to each text in their memory according to these categories than if they simply read the text.

The interview data also suggest that relying exclusively on autobiographical rather than literary links may limit students' learning to apply their prior literary knowledge. While autobiographical responses can enhance students' understanding of texts (Beach, in press), students also need to learn to define literary links.

Teachers also need to demonstrate ways of defining connections between texts and elaborating on those connections. By socially collaborating on their recollection and elaboration of links with students, teachers can demonstrate that through sharing responses, students establish and build social relationships. Given adolescents' primary concern with their peer relationships, awareness of the value of social exploration of response serves as a strong incentive to contribute their own experiences to a discussion (Hynds, in press).

Teachers could use computer "hypertext" programs (Barrett, 1988; Tchudi, 1988) to provide students with open-ended tools to help them develop their own connections. As the use of computer database software becomes more commonplace, students could store their own responses onto databases using a range of different categories: topic, character type, storyline, setting, themes, period, author, techniques, and so on. They could then create their own personal database, or build onto preexisting databases created by the school librarian, a teacher, a class, or publishers. By using multidimensional databases such as the Macintosh Hypercard system, students can make multiple links between these categories, so that texts representating any combination of these categories can be linked with texts with any other combination. The very activity of having students as a group or class construct the own program and develop categories used to store knowledge may itself create a sense of social community built on a shared knowledge base.

The fact that the eighth graders in Study 1 devote little leisure time for reading literature may be a function of their attitude toward reading literature as an enjoyable leisure-time activity. Some research (Abrahamson & Tyson, 1986) indicates that individualized reading programs enhance students' attitudes towards reading. By encouraging students to select their own texts, thus enhancing their motivation to read those texts, these programs may encourage leisure-time reading.

The results also indicate that amount of leisure-time reading of literature, magazines, and newspapers was a significant predictor of the ability to make intertextual links. Given the increasing percentage of students in disadvantaged homes in which students may have little or no access to books, magazines, or newspapers, these students may devote little time to leisure-time reading. Books and magazines in the home is one of the strongest predictors of students' leisure time reading and reading interests (Purves, 1981, 1973). Disparities in the amount of reading material in the home may only perpetuate a two-tier cultural split between the haves and the have-nots. In order to enhance the availability of books and magazines in the home, which, in turn, may enhance leisure-time reading, students from disadvantaged homes should be provided with free books and magazines of their choosing or and/or access to library materials for use in the home.

Ultimately, by exploring mutual knowledge of literary experiences, students are participating in defining and extending the literary culture, not as an elitist, institutional fixture, but as a socially constituted phenonena requiring participation of readers as active, engaged members.

REFERENCES

Abrahamson, D., & Tyson, E. (1986). What every English teacher should know about free reading. *The ALAN Review, 14,* 54–58.

Applebee, A. (1978). *The child's concept of story.* Chicago: University of Chicago Press.

Applebee, A., Langer, J., & Mullis, I. (1987). *Literature and U.S. history: The instructional experience and factual knowledge of high school juniors.* Princeton, NJ: Center for the Assessment of Educational Progress, Educational Testing Service.

Barrett, E. (Ed.). (1988). *Text, context, and hypertext.* Cambridge, MA: MIT Press.

Barthes, R. (1980). From work to text. In J. Harari (Ed.), *Textual strategies: Perspectives in post-structuralist criticism* (pp. 124–162). London:

Beach, R. (1985). Discourse conventions and researching response to literary dialogue. In C. Cooper (Ed.), *Researching response to literature and the teaching of literature* (pp. 103–127). Norwood, NJ: Ablex.

Beach, R. (in press). The creative development of meaning: Using autobiographical experiences to interpret literature. In S. Straw & D. Bogdon (Eds.), *Beyond comprehension and communication to response.* Portsmouth, NH: Boynton Cook.

Beach, R., & Appleman, D. (1984). Reading strategies for expository and literary text. In A. Purves & O. Niles (Eds.), *Becoming readers in a complex society* (pp. 115–143). Eighty-third Yearbook of the National Society for the Study of Education. Chicago: The National Society for the Study of Education.

Beach, R., & Brown, R. (1987). Discourse conventions and literary inference: Toward a theoretical model. In R. Tierney, P. Anders, & J. Mitchell (Eds.), *Understanding readers' understanding* (pp. 147–174). Hillsdale, NJ: Erlbaum.

Beach, R., & Wendler, L. (1987). Developmental differences in response to a short story. *Research in the Teaching of English, 21,* 286–297.

Bernstein, H. (1984). What literature should adolescents be reading. *ASCD Curriculum Update,* 1–9.

Elkind, D. (1984). *All grown up and no place to go.* Reading, MA: Addison-Wesley.

Dorfman, M. (1985, August). *A model for understanding the points of stories: Evidence from adult and child readers.* Paper presented at the Seventh Annual Conference of the Cognitive Science Society, Irvine, CA.

Fusco, E. (1983). The relationship between children's cognitive level of development and their response to literature. *Dissertation Abstracts International, 45,* 5A. (University Microfilms #84-10, 959).

Gagne, E. (1985). *The cognitive psychology of school learning.* Boston: Little, Brown.

Gee, J. P. (1988). The legacies of literacy: From Pluto to Freire through Harvey Graff. *Harvard Educational Review, 58,* 200–212.

Gick, M., & Holyoak, K. (1985). Analogical problem solving. In A. Aitkenhead & J. Slack (Eds.), *Issues in cognitive modeling* (pp. 279–306). Hillsdale, NJ: Erlbaum.

Golden, J., & Guthrie, J. (1986). Convergence and divergence in reader response to literature. *Reading Research Quarterly, 21,* 408–421.

Hilgers, T. (1980). Training college composition students in the use of freewriting and problem-solving heuristics for rhetorical invention. *Research in the Teaching of English, 14,* 293–307.

Hynds, S. (1985). Interpersonal cognitive complexity and the response processes of adolescent readers. *Research in the Teaching of English, 19,* 386–404.

Hynds, S. (in press). Reading as a social event: Comprehension and response in the text, classroom, and world. In S. Straw & D. Bogdan (Eds.), *Beyond communication: Comprehension and criticism.* Portsmouth, NH: Boynton Cook.

Just, W., & Carpenter, P. (1987). *The psychology of reading and language comprehension.* Newton, MA: Allyn & Bacon.

Lehr, S. (1988). The child's developing sense of theme as a response to literature. *Reading Research Quarterly, 23,* 337–357.

Mailloux, S. (1982). *Interpretive conventions.* Ithaca, NY: Cornell University Press.

Peck, R. (1984). Priscilla and the wimps. In D. Gallo (Ed.), *Sixteen.* New York: Dell.

Perfetti, C., & Curtis, M. (1986). Reading. In R. Dillon & R. Sternberg (Eds.), *Readings in cognition and instruction* (pp. 13–57). Orlando, FL: Academic Press.

Purves, A. (1973). *Literature education in ten countries, an empirical study.* Stockholm: Almqvist and Wiksell.

Purves, A. (1981). *Reading and literature: American achievement in international perspective.* Urbana, IL: National Council of Teachers of English.

Rabinowitz, P. (1987). *Before reading.* Ithaca: Cornell University Press.

Ravitch, D., & Finn, C. (1987). *What do our 17-year-olds know?* New York: Harper & Row.

Ricoeur, P. (1985). The text as dynamic identity. In M. Valdes & O. Miller (Eds.), *Identity of the literary text* (pp. 175–188). Toronto: University of Toronto Press.

Rogers, T. (1988). *Students as literary critics: The interpretive theories, pro-*

cesses, and experiences of ninth grade students. Doctoral dissertation, University of Illinois.

Rosenblatt, L. (1978). *The reader, the text, and the poem.* Carbondale, IL: Southern Illinois. University Press.

Rumelhart, D., & Norman, M. (1985). Representations of knowledge. In A. Aitenhead & J. Slack (Eds.), *Issues in cognitive modeling.* Hillsdale, NJ: Erlbaum.

Schank, R. (1982). *Dynamic memory.* New York: Cambridge University Press.

Schwartz, A. (1988). Pain of slavery touches readers of *Beloved. Minneapolis Star and Tribune,* April 11, 1988.

Smith, B. H. (1968). *Poetic closure.* Chicago: University of Chicago Press.

Svensson, C. (1985). *The construction of poetic meaning.* Malmo, Sweden: Liber.

Tchudi, S. (1988). Invisible thinking and the hypertext. *English Journal, 77*(1), 22–30.

Thomson, J. (1987). *Understanding teenage readers.* New York: Nichols.

Valdes, M., & Miller, O. (Eds.). (1985). *Identity of the literary text.* Toronto: University of Toronto Press.

Wolf, D. (1988). *Reading reconsidered: Students, teachers, and literature.* Princeton, NJ: Report to the College Board.

11
Verbocentrism, Dualism, and Oversimplification: The Need for New Vistas for Reading Comprehension Research and Practice

Robert J. Tierney

What are the challenges facing reading comprehension research and practice? Over the past 20 years, research and practice in the teaching of reading comprehension has received a great deal of attention. In conjunction with a schema-theoretic view of meaning making and metacognitive tenets of learning, our understanding of the nature of reading comprehension has expanded at the same time as explorations of the viability of teaching practices increased. But, nowadays, these views are being criticized. It has been suggested, for example, that researchers and practitioners have been quick to simplify as they indulge in ideological stances which tend toward verbocentricism and dualistic notions of the nature of knowledge.

It is my thesis that such criticisms represent important challenges which researchers and practitioners should examine as they consider an agenda for the future. It is toward addressing some of these key issues and a possible agenda that the present chapter is directed.

VERBOCENTRISM, DUALISM, AND OVERSIMPLIFICATION

In her chapter on reading research in the affective domain, Athey (1984) lamented the state of research in that area. She stated:

> There is probably little disagreement today, even among the most fervent advocates of a cognitive-linguistic view of reading, that affective factors play

246

a role both in reading achievement and reading behavior. Given this fact, it might be expected that theoretical models of the reading process would incorporate components that reflect motivational or attitudinal variables and would give them due emphasis in recognition of the presumed importance; and, indeed, some models have been constructed in such a way as to draw attention to the significance of affect in a comprehensive view of the reading process.

Having said that, it must be acknowledged that, beyond appearing as a "box" in the future depicting the model, affective factors receive little elaboration or explication.

Unfortunately, modern day schema theorists have focused upon a reader's retrieval of content rather than affective dimensions of a reader's experience including feelings of immersion, imagery, and character identification. As Spiro (1980) commented, the work in the schema-theoretic tradition has focused on "the structure of knowledge that must be analyzed rather than on the text that must be felt" (p. 273). Or, as Brewer and Nakamura (in press) commented:

> The main focus of information processing psychologists was on unconscious mental processes. Therefore, they tended to ignore the data of phenomenal experience, or to argue that the experience itself was of little interest to information processing psychology as compared to the underlying unconscious cognitive processes.... Schema theorists have also focused on the unconscious mental processes of the schema and ignored the problems of consciousness and phenomenal experience. Minsky (1975) discusses the problems of imagery and consciousness at various points in his frame paper, but never explicitly relates these issues to the frame construct.

Brewer and Nakamura go on to argue

> that an ultimate scientific psychology *must* account for the data from phenomenal experience. Just as it must account for the data of performance. If, for example, the data from experience and performance on some task are "inconsistent" one does not throw out the phenomenal data because it is somehow less scientific. Instead the science of psychology must aspire to explain all of the data ...

Two questions that are important to address are: What is the nature of the reader's affective experience? What is its role in comprehending?

A reader's affective response often takes the form of what Rosenblatt (1985) has described as a lived-through experience. Readers say that a story "caught their imagination" or that they were "lost in the book." They also talk about "being in another world." Metaphors such as these suggest that readers feel as if they are experiencing a shift in space and time where the separation of oneself from the world of the text became blurred. Slatoff (1970) described the experience in these terms:

> As one reads one has the feeling one is moving into and through something and that there is movement in oneself—a succession of varied, complex, and rich mental and emotional states usually involving expectancy, tensions and releases, sensations of anxiety, fear, and discovery, sadness, sudden excitements, spurts of hope, warmth, or affection, feelings of distance and closeness, and a multitude of motor and sensory responses to the movement, rhythm, and imagery of the work ... (pp. 6–7)

Unfortunately, researchers, while they recognize these experiences as important have tended to be resistant to consider them fully, or on their own terms. For example, reading researchers have been satisfied with relegating affective factors (such as emotional response, imagery, identification) to being an adjunct for learning or to describe it in such vague, incidental or broad terms as to lack any explanatory power. It is interesting to note that in a recent review of research exploring the effects of attempts to enhance imaginative expression, Wagner (in press) suggested that the majority of studies measured success in terms of whether or not such experiences contributed to "the sterner stuff."

The research on imagery is a case in point. With few exceptions, the research on helping students to image has been examined in terms of whether recall or memory for content are facilitated; imagery effects in their own right have tended to be overlooked. In the typical study, students have been encouraged to evoke images based upon what they have read. Rather than explore what their images themselves engender, researchers have examined the effects in terms of the content recalled.

In a similar vein, studies and theories which refer to a reader's engagement in rather broadly defined terms such as spectator and participant (Britton, 1982) represent a similar preoccupation with content. Analyses of these notions tend to overstate the pitfalls of affective involvement without regard to any benefits which might be accrued. Emphasizing the role of spectator as interpreter represents an inaccurate portrayal of the nature of readers involvement and the functions served. For example, a reader's participation involves complex perspective-taking processes that transcend the either/or dualistic notions of spectator and participant.

In work with which Edmiston and myself are involved, readers use cutout shapes of characters and themselves as readers to portray their involvement (placement, transactions, movements) in a story. As a reader reads the story he moves the characters to reflect his view of the plot as it unfolds. Alongside the characters, narrator or others, the reader moves a cutout or symbol which represents himself or herself. A reader will sometimes place himself or herself beside a particular character, sometimes distanced from the action, sometimes amidst a conversation and so on. It is apparent from their movements that readers pursue various idiosyncratic transactions with characters and events as well as adopt various perspectives both within this secondary world as well as distanced from it. To describe their journey through texts in terms of spectator and participant roles grossly oversimplifies their experiences as onlooker amidst the "world of the text" and active agent transacting with characters. To suggest that there is a preferred orientation based upon such global descriptors as spectator and participant detracts from just how these various and sundry involvements heightens a reader's understanding of characters and plot (including sensitivity to the values of characters, narrator and author) in different ways.

BIASES IN RESEARCH AND TEACHING

Reading research is often limited by implicit assumptions or standards for interpretation reflecting unstated biases that constrain ongoing research pursuits and their interpretation. Siegel (1984) contends that research in reading comprehension has been biased toward a view of comprehension tied to verbocentrism and duplication of an author's message. That is, research on reading comprehension has tended to be preoccupied with defining learning from text purely in terms of the content which is learned. Again, other dimensions related to the experience of meaning making such as imagery have been relegated to serving a secondary role or to function as an adjunct. Rather than embrace comprehension as a creative enterprise, researchers tend to use as yardsticks the amount of ideas recalled and other measures which support a truncated view of meaning making. Spiro, Vispoel, Schmitz, Samarapurgavar, and Boerger (1987) contend that such biases are tied to a conspiracy of convenient—" 'simplifying assumptions' that would have us understand things are simpler and more regular than they in fact are." Furthermore, as they stated:

> The simplifying assumptions of cognitive science apply as well to the dominant models of education. Simplification of complex subject matter makes it easier for teachers to teach, for students to take notes, and prepare for their tests, for test-givers to construct and grade tests, and for authors to write texts. The result is a massive 'conspiracy of convenience.' (p. 180)

As a result, research and practice of reading comprehension has often adopted a neat versus a complex view of reading and learning. The pervasive simplification of reading comprehension undergirds current thinking about reading comprehension. For example, researchers have tended to approach the construction of meaning as if all knowledge were neatly structured in terms of straightforward hierarchies or scripts. Furthermore, they assume that understandings were of necessity coherent, singular and unidimensional. As Spiro et al. (1987) have argued, many content domains may be more irregular, ill-structured, complex, and less fixed than assumed by current models of knowledge. Furthermore, reading comprehension may be more impressionistic, multifaceted, and variable than implied by the slot-filling metaphors used to describe comprehension by some schema theorists (Beers, 1987).

The impact of the artificial simplicity of past concepts of comprehension is evident in the definition of reading suggested in *Becoming a Nation of Readers* (Anderson, Hiebert, Scott, & Wilkinson, 1985). As was stated:

> Reading is the process of constructing meaning from written texts. It is a complex skill requiring the coordination of a number of interrelated sources of information.... Reading is a process in which information from the text and the knowledge possessed by the reader act together to produce meaning. Good readers skillfully integrate information in the text with what they already know. (Anderson et al., 1985, pp. 7–8)

Their definition is devoid of any mention of the functions that reading serves, fails to consider that readers may acquire several meanings from the same text, and tends to tie meaning making to purely informational sources rather than affective dimensions or social sources.

I am not suggesting that there exists no research which explores reading comprehension in terms of factors other than informational sources. A number of studies (e.g., Bleich, 1986; Bloome, 1983; Fish, 1980; Rowe, 1987; Short, 1986) employing more ethnographically oriented methodologies to describe reading in more collaborative contexts have incorporated a consideration of such factors. But, more important than acclaiming some studies over others, at the heart of my concern is the need to examine our biases (that is, attain some perspective upon our perspectives) and pursue research which ensures that we consider more than one stance.

In most classrooms there is a tendency to perpetuate a unidimensional view of comprehension tied to a single correct meaning for a text. Most instructional procedures, textbooks and study guides have had a tendency to guide readers through a single reading of a text rather than helping readers achieve their own purposes through self-initiated explorations of topics across multiple texts and media. For example, in a replication of Guszak's study of teacher questioning during reading, O'Flahavan, Hartman, and Pearson (1988) found teaching behavior in the 1980s reflected similar patterns to teaching patterns in the 1960s. Students' ideas rarely directed discussions, and student ideas were rarely expanded upon. Teachers maintained control of the floor 60 percent of the time and in less than 10 percent of the cases were students' ideas the basis for discussion. In the majority of cases, lines of thought were kept to less than a minute. Essentially, the students task tended to be to respond to a set of questions offered by the teacher.

In a study exploring the literary theoretic orientation of advanced high school students, Rogers (1988) reported an attitude to interpretation which was framed by what the students sensed the teachers expected. As she stated:

> It was evident from the students' interviews that they were then expected to reiterate the teacher's interpretation (or "class theme") on tests, using either the same or novel textual evidence to support or justify that interpretation.
>
> Many students seemed to equate, if not the right interpretation, at least the appropriate interpretation with the one sanctioned by the teacher and therefore expected on a test. As Karl said, "if a teacher tells me something that he is going to put on a test, that is what I end up accepting as right even if that's not what I agree with." Gary described the "class theme" which, he explained, all the students come to agree with.
>
> Even Pam, who seemed so self-reliant in evaluating her own interpretations, said she writes something that is "unanimously justified" on the tests. (Rogers, 1988, p. 136)

Such authoritarian views of response extend to how both researchers and teachers have operationalized the teaching of comprehension—at least in terms of the initial introduction of skills and strategies. The teaching rubrics of direct teaching, explicit teaching, and reciprocal teaching are tied to teacher modelling followed by guided practice—that is, a view of learner initiative with a high degree of teacher control. Black (1967) discussed the inherent danger with such bridled learning in his discussion of rules and routines. As he stated, "when a man's behavior is blind routine, there is an important sense in which he does not know what he is doing, or why he is doing it" (p. 97). Consistent with Black's view, Shannon urged the need for a child to have his or her own authority with fewer, if any, strings attached. As he stated:

> Clearly, the aid with the most strings of dependence for both teachers and students comes from the University of Oregon's Direct Instruction Model because it makes the teacher rely completely on curriculum programmers; it ignores the experience and knowledge of students altogether with its standardization of methods, making students dependent on lessons to learn to

read; and it analyzes actual acts of literacy use into numerous preliteracy skills, having students wait to use literacy for their own purposes. However, the aid offered in less standardized forms than Direct Instruction also includes strings of dependence. For example, reciprocal teaching (Palincsar & Brown, 1984), which has students model teachers' questioning behaviors in order to develop a greater understanding of text, does not promote independence in reading—at best it perpetuates the status quo in which someone asks others known fact questions (see Weber, 1986, for a full explanation of this point). I do not dispute that students can learn such things, but this is not an independent use of literacy. Independence in questioning is the courage to ask the questions for which you do not know the answers. Such questions are not a request for direct instruction, rather, they are a sign of trust: the questioner trusts the person asked enough to spend time with them while trying to develop answers through reading and other means in order to promote the questioner's goals. Advocates of direct instruction in any of its forms seem to have little to say about this type of independence. (Kameenui & Shannon, 1988, pp. 36–37)

In a similar vein, Scollon (1988) argued that our approaches to literacy tend to perpetuate a political stance more in line with entrapment rather than empowerment and, as a result, engender some suspicion of the purposes of literacy. As he stated:

There is wisdom in this deep suspicion of literacy that we would do well to remember in our enthusiasm to find improved methods for teaching reading and writing. The choice not to read may be a choice to avoid an all too easy entrapment in the forced agendas of literacy. If we genuinely believe that literacy is empowering, we owe it to ourselves to ask first about the power relationships between authors and readers. We cannot just assume that it will all work out well in the end. (p. 32)

How can reading researchers and practitioners address these challenges? I contend that one of the key issues facing reading comprehension is the obvious and sometimes subtle ideological messages inherent in our teaching practices. Many of our teaching practices relegate students to that of a performer—a respondent rather than initiator. Readers are expected to respond to somebody else's choice of music and perform in accordance with someone else's interpretation.

In the traditional classroom, students are the recipients; students pursue answers to predetermined questions and their responses are assessed as either right or wrong by others. In a more ideal situation, the student initiates his or her own goals, orchestrates his or her own research directions using multiple texts, and self-examines his or her understanding as well as routes to achieving them. This use of more than one text moves the student away from a single correct interpretation to multiple perspectives which may be less well-defined, but are apt to be more generative and thoughtful.

In many ways, the research and practice on teaching reading comprehension over the past 20 years has become bogged down in rather absolute views of literacy and assumptions tied to efficiency vis-à-vis teacher dominated delivery systems. In addition, they have been quick to adopt a restricted view of comprehension development. Studies examining differences between good and poor readers prompted educational researchers to suggest and study the effects of a variety of interventions. In particular, numerous studies were carried out with the goal of improving comprehension abilities which might transfer to new situations. The underlying tenet was that improvement in comprehension was tied to differences between good and poor readers in their metacognitive awarenesses (see Tierney & Cunningham, 1984; Brown, Armbruster, & Baker, 1986).

Unfortunately, questions pertaining to comprehension development took a back seat to metacognitive training studies. The metacognitive research was based upon an explicit reading model which assumes that we know what to teach, when, and how. Furthermore, researchers using this model further assume that we know how we might specify how to use the particular strategies. The problem arises that certain strategies, if not most, are difficult to describe in words. When described or explained they tend to overwhelm or constrain the naive reader rather than inform and empower flexible use.

As described by Pearson and Gallagher (1983) explicit teaching assumes a gradual release of responsibility from teacher to students (see Figure 11.1). The initial teaching of skills includes demonstration and modeling followed by guided practice and eventually independent application. As I have suggested, the model perpetuates the use of delivery systems based upon transmission of information. Students tend to be excluded from directing their own learning, instead, they are expected to aspire to the rules and routines modeled by the teacher and student. To date, the model lacks a research base. Those studies which have examined the utility of explicit teaching in reading comprehension have not achieved enduring gains. Moreover, the model lacks a strong basis in development. The model assumes a progression from novice to expert without a careful study of such transitions. Indeed a recurring problem in research on teaching reading comprehension is a lack of development studies.

The problem of an incomplete model of development is tied to a major drawback in comprehension research which persists today—namely a lack of longitudinal studies of comprehension from which a model or models of comprehension development beyond the early years might be formulated. There is a dearth of studies describing the repertoire of strategies that students acquire and enlist to make and assess meaning. What can be said about development? Apart from some general principles or state-

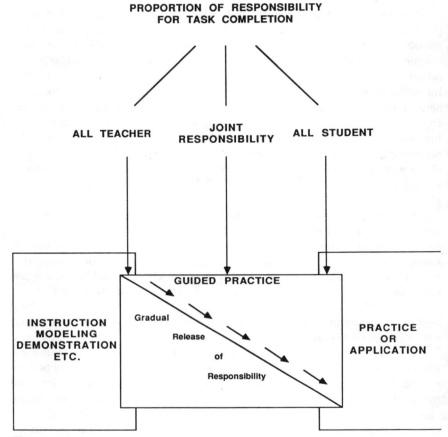

Figure 11.1.

ments of development which can be drawn from emergent literacy studies and studies looking for differences between good and poor readers, discussions of development are few in number.[1] To my knowledge, a theory of reading comprehension development, from which teaching-learning algorithms might emerge, is nonexistent.

---

[1] Statements which can be made about comprehension development seem to be as follows:

- Readers generate, refine, and restructure strategies, knowledge, and principles about language as they strive to use language to achieve different functions.
- Sophisticated readers and older readers appear to be more sensitive to: how a text is organized; the relative importance of different ideas; the nature of task demands; and how to use strategies flexibly for different purposes and text. In addition, they also seem more likely to offer elaborations, self-correct without prompting, have more strategies by which to glean meanings, and are more apt to use what they know.
- When students become aware of strategies they might use, improvement in comprehension is sometimes achieved.

THE ROLE OF TESTING

Testing practices are often cited as being impediments to changing reading comprehension practices. The criticisms seem quite deserving. Tests perpetuate the misnotion of a single correct response, a view of being right or wrong. That is, most tests (even informal inventories) used in schools assume that responses to questions (or other test probes) from recall can be scored in absolute terms as either right or wrong. Partial understandings rarely receive any credit and divergent understandings are dismissed.

This simplistic measurement ethic extends to overall assessment of abilities. In most testing situations, accuracy of understanding for a single passage or several passages is summed as a means of summarizing performance. The problem arises that the sum total perpetuates other distorted notions of reading comprehension. First it assumes reading comprehension can be summarized by a single score when reader's responses across a single passage or several passages vary so much as to diminish the luster or predictability of a single score. Second, the use of sum totals compounds the problems associated with a preoccupation with a predetermined set of correct responses, especially for divergent or partial responders. The sum total of partial understandings of a poorer student is zero. If this is not sufficiently problematic, indices are usually enlisted which tend to exclude items which might favor the poorer student—namely, items will usually be dropped from a battery if they do not differentiate poorer students from good students. In other words, test developers have a tendency to exclude from their batteries items to which less able students respond correctly. The end result is that those students who perform poorly have less chance to be viewed as if they are achieving.

Another problem is that tests do a poor job of sampling meaningful prose selections. In their review of tests, Nystrand and Knapp (1987) found that most tests were devoid of "authentic discourse written to communicate to actual readers with real needs to know" (p. 25). The authors explained:

> Many items involve texts and passages composed especially for the tests. . . .
> that exists nowhere but in the . . . when students are required to read text
> which have been shorn of their rhetorical contexts.

Furthermore, tests relegate students and the teacher to being respondents rather than initiators, assuming a lowest common denominator view of readers and a belief in either mandates or "trickle-down" curriculum. Rather than placing faith in either the teacher's ability to negotiate learning based upon the idiosyncratic needs of students or the need for students to learn to assess themselves, there is an attempt by states, districts, and now the federal government, to dictate performance through standards as defined by the test's content. The federal government, states, and districts seem intent on arranging a marriage between teaching, learning, and testing with little regard to empowering teachers and students to be effective decision makers. As a result, there is a mismatch between what teachers and students should be pursuing and what they are mandated to do by tests. For example, in many school districts, time is put aside just to prepare students for these tests; likewise, publishers include sample activities to ensure that students involved in their programs have practiced certain types of test items. In a recent article on writing instruction and assessment, appearing in *College Composition and Communication,* a contributor concluded with the following admonishment:

> Thus, what ever strategies we use, we must help our students apply our teachings not only to the compositions they write outside of class, but also to the essays they prepare under assessment conditions.... We must show our students how to employ pre-writing techniques as tools for generating ideas in timed situations. We must help them to understand the concepts of audience and aim as they relate to examination topics or to the focus and organization of the essay test itself. Finally, we must help our students see that revision, limited though it must be in testing situations, is both possible and necessary. (Wolcott, 1987, p. 45)

This suggestion should not be trivialized for such is the plight of teachers and students and maybe the course of classroom learning.

On the positive side, there is a great deal of research and development currently being directed at exploring alternative assessment practices. In Illinois and Michigan, major efforts were launched in hopes of developing more viable statewide assessment practices. On the positive side, these statewide initiatives have prompted the development of alternative item formats as well as the use of extended reading selections. On the negative side, they have been hamstrung by some of the restrictions associated with large scale assessments—in particular, uniform items types, ease of administration, and summative data. Unfortunately, these restrictions often override other features of the tests.

On a smaller scale, a number of innovative assessment practices are being developed and tested by a variety of individual groups. In Columbus City Schools, primary-trait scoring procedures are being used to describe students' responses to open-ended comprehension probes. The advantage of this approach is that it supports a description of the distinguishing features of a variety of responses including those responses which are partial or divergent. In addition, portfolios are being explored as vehicles for helping students sample their achievements in reading to assess their strengths, weaknesses, and growth. As teachers and administrators search for a marriage between teaching, learning, and assessment, portfolios and other dynamic testing practices seem to hold more promise than importing assessment practices from published sources which detract from rather than complement classroom learning goals.

NEW VISTAS FOR RESEARCH AND PRACTICE

In his book, *The Mind's New Science*, Howard Gardener contended that there was a cognitive revolution that took place in the 1970s. Brewer and Nakamura (in press) suggested the mid-1970s saw the emergence of schema theoretic notions as the turning point for cognition. In terms of literacy, schema theory prompted a major shift in the field toward studies of comprehension and a minor revolution of sorts in thinking about the reader's role as an active meaning-maker.

In my opinion, the revolution in comprehension together with its grounding in sociolinguistic views of reading achieved a great deal. It focused attention upon reading comprehension and established key tenets about the nature of reading comprehension which are still being used to scrutinize and challenge teaching practice.[2] At the same time, the revolu-

---

[2] Key tenets about comprehension might include:

a. The reader's desire to make sense drives their processes.
b. Understandings are essentially inferential—readers use their background knowledge in conjunction with their expectations.
c. Undergirding these inferential operations is a gestalt-like tendency—that is, readers instantiate a sense of the whole or a scenario which they refine. It is as if they acquire a view of the forests prior to seeing the trees.
d. Influencing the focus of these scenarios is the stance a reader adopts. These stances direct a reader's attention and, in turn, are influenced by the understandings which are developed.
e. A reader's background of experiences with topics, different text genres, written language conventions and so on has been shown to inform the meanings which readers glean.
f. These various processes and operations are ongoing and ... meanings are subject to refinement and reconstruction as readers elaborate scenarios, extend interconnections and fill slots, adopt different perspectives or retrieve these at some later time.
g. Different texts and different readers will prompt a different array of strategies and different outcomes.
h. Reading is quite individualized and idiosyncratic from the reading to the text, one text to the next, one individual to the next.
i. A reader's purposes (goals, questions) as well as perspective [stance (critic, collaborator), identification with characters, etc.] focus the reader's attention and energies.
j. Situational factors including the reader's view of the author, themselves, and those who share in the interpretative experience extend the ideas which are considered and foci adopted.

tion may have stalled as research and theory failed to expand its agenda and face the challenge of complexity.

Perhaps the problem can be tied to ideology. Indeed, the verbocentricism of researchers and their concern with what is remembered seems more consistent with dualistic rather than relativistic notions of meaning making. Whereas schema theory might support the view that accuracy of understanding is relative, much research has been done in a tradition which is antithetical. Student's understandings were often measured against expected responses to questions or a detailed template of the text. For example, in most studies, individuals were asked to read and either recall as much as they can or answer a prescribed set of questions. Their recalls were then examined against a fixed determination of what was allegedly the text's intended message; likewise, their responses to questions were checked against some presupplied responses. It is as if researchers may claim comprehension is a creative enterprise, but used as their yardsticks measures which are fixed. While research in reading comprehension may have leanings which see-saw between dualism and relativism, classroom practices seem tied to unabridged dualism or what might be termed reader-detached relativism. In conjunction with testing and teaching, students expect either a "right" or "wrong" answer or some authority (e.g., test-maker or teacher) to deem what are acceptable responses.

Obviously, my view may be somewhat egocentric. Indeed, a paper claiming to deal with new vistas seems quite self-indulgent. To suggest new vistas presumes a knowledge of what has preceded and recognition of the forces shaping the future. Perhaps vistas takes more the form of a "wish list" or a personal agenda. If so, my list would include some obvious areas for research (comprehension development, alternative instructional and assessment practices, longitudinal studies, studies focusing upon affect including imagery, and so on) as well as some consideration for the view that reading should be viewed as more complex, multifaceted, and multidimensional than it has been.

REFERENCES

Anderson, R. C, Heibert, E. F., Scott, J. A., & Wilkinson, I. G. (1985). *Becoming a nation of readers.* Washington, DC: National Institute of Education.

Athey, I. (1985). Reading research in the affective domain. In H. Singer & R. Ruddell (Eds.), *Theoretical models and processes of reading* (3rd ed., pp. 527–557). Newark, NJ: International Reading Association.

Beers, T. (1987). Commentary: Schema-theoretic models of reading: Humanizing the machine. *Reading Research Quarterly, 22*(3), 369–377.

Black, M. (1967). Rules and routines. In R. S. Peters (Ed.), *The concept of education.* London: Routledge and Kegan Paul.

Bleich, D. (1986). Intersubjective reading. *New Literary History, 17*(3), 401–421.

Bloome, D. (1983). Reading as a social process. In B. Hutson (Ed.), *Advances in reading/language research* (Vol. 2, pp. 165–193). Greenwich, CT: JAI Press.

Brewer, W. F., & Nakamura. (in press). The nature and functions of schemas. In R. S. Wyer & T. K. Srull (Eds.), *Handbook of social cognition.* Hillsdale, NJ: Erlbaum.

Britton, J. (1982). Response to literature. In G. M. Pradl (Ed.), *Prospect and retrospect* (pp. 32–37). London: Heinemann.

Brown, A., Armbruster, B. B., & Baker, L. (1986). The role of metacognition in reading and studying. In J. Orasanu (Ed.), *Reading comprehension from research to practice* (pp. 49–75). Hillsdale, NJ: Erlbaum.

Fish, S. (1980). *Is there a text in this class?* Cambridge, MA: Harvard University Press.

Gardener, H. (1985). *The mind's new science.* New York: Basic Books.

Holmes, J. A. (1976). Basic assumptions underlying the substrata-factor theory. In H. Singer & R. B. Ruddell (Eds.), *Theoretical models and processes of reading* (2nd ed., pp. 597–618). Newark, DE: International Reading Association.

Kameenui, E. I., & Shannon, P. (1988). Point/counterpoint: Direct instruction reconsidered. In J. Readence & S. Baldwin (Eds.), *Dialogues in literacy research* (pp. 35–44). Thirty-seventh Yearbook of the National Reading Conference. Chicago, IL: National Reading Conference.

Minsky, M. (1975). A framework for representing knowledge. In P. H. Winston (Ed.), *The psychology of computer vision* (pp. 211–277). New York: McGraw-Hill.

Nystrand, M., & Knapp, J. V. (1987). *Review of selected national tests of writing and reading.* Report for Office of Educational Research and Improvement (Grant No. OERI-6008690007).

O'Flahavan, J., Hartman, D., & Pearson, P. D. (1988). Teacher questioning and feedback practices: A twenty year retrospective. In J. Readence & S. Baldwin (Eds.), *Dialogues in literacy research* (pp. 183–200). Thirty-seventh Yearbook of National Reading Conference, Chicago, IL.

Palincsar, A., & Brown, A. (1984). Reciprocal teaching of comprehension-fostering and comprehension-monitoring activities. *Cognitive and instruction, 1,* 117–125.

Pearson, P. D., & Gallagher, M. C. (1983). The instruction of reading comprehension. *Contemporary Educational Psychology, 8,* 317–344.

Rogers, T. (1988). *Students as literary critics: A case study of the interpretative theories, processes and experiences of ninth grade students.* Unpublished doctoral dissertation, University of Illinois.

Rosenblatt, L (1985). The transactional theory of the literary work: implications for research. In C. Cooper (Ed.), *Researching response to literature and the teaching of literature: Points of departure* (pp. 33–53). Norwood, NJ: Ablex.

Rowe, D. W. (1987). Literacy learning as an intertextual process. In J. E. Readence & R. Scott Baldwin (Eds.), *Research in literacy: Merging perspectives.* Rochester, NY: National Reading Conference.

Scollon, R. (1988). Storytelling, reading and the micropolitics of literary. In J. Readence & S. Baldwin (Eds.), *Dialogues in literacy research* (pp. 15–34). Twenty-seventh Yearbook of the National Reading Conference, Chicago, IL: National Reading Conference.

Short, K. G. (1986). *Literacy as a collaborative experience.* Unpublished doctoral dissertation, Indiana University, Bloomington, IN.

Siegel, M. G. (1984). *Reading as signification.* Unpublished doctoral dissertation, Indiana University, Bloomington, IN.

Slatoff, W. (1970). *With respect to readers: Dimensions of literary response.* Ithaca, NY: Cornell University Press.

Spiro, R. J. (1980). Cognitive processes in prose comprehension and recall. In R. J. Spiro, B. C. Bruce, & W. F. Brewer (Eds.), *Theoretical issues in reading comprehension* (pp. 245–278). Hillsdale, NJ: Erlbaum.

Spiro, R. J., Vispoel, W. L., Schmitz, J. B., Samarapurgavar, A., & Boerger, A. E. (1987). Knowledge acquisition for application: Cognitive flexibility and transfer in complex content domains. In B. C. Britton & S. Glynn (Eds.), *Executive control processes.* Hillsdale, NJ: Erlbaum.

Tierney, R. J., & Cunningham, J. W. (1984). Research on teaching reading comprehension. In P. D. Pearson (Ed.), *Handbook of reading research.* New York: Longman.

Wagner. B. J. (in press). Imaginative expression. In J. Squire (Ed.), *Handbook of research on the teaching of language arts.* New York: Macmillan.

Weber, R. M. (1986). *The constraints of the questioning routine in reading instruction.* Paper presented at American Educational Research Association, San Francisco, CA.

Wolcott, W. (1987). Writing instruction and assessment: The need for interplay between process and product. *College Composition and Communication, 38*(1), 40–46.

IV
The Institutional Stance

12
Developing Reflective Thinking and Writing

Mark L. Davison
Patricia M. King
Karen Strohm Kitchener

Writings on elementary, secondary, and postsecondary curricula often refer to the development of higher-order cognitive skills, such as critical thinking, inquiry, problem solving, reasoned judgment, reflective thinking and reflective processes (Anderson, DeVito, Odvard, Kellogg, Koch, & Weigand, 1970; Banks, 1977; Dunfer, 1978; Edwards & Fisher, 1977; Esler, 1973; Jarolimek, 1977; Kaltsounis, 1979; National Council for the Social Studies, 1971; Rowe, 1978). School district mission statements also commonly refer to the development of such skills. More recently, authors have suggested that higher-order thinking is necessary for effective argumentative writing, and the poor argumentative writing skills of many students may be partially a function of undeveloped thinking skills (Applebee, Langer, & Mullis, 1986; see also Chapter 9, this volume). For educators, the development of higher-order reasoning is made difficult, in part, because the goal itself is unclear. The reflective judgment model, proposed by King (1977) and Kitchener (1977/1978) and elaborated most recently by Kitchener and King (in press) and Kitchener (1986), offers one vision of higher order reasoning, reflective judgment, and how it develops.

The reflective judgment model attempts to describe a series of changes that occur in the ways adolescents and adults understand the nature of intellectual problems and judge the adequacy of alternative solutions. While a developmental perspective is not new to research on writing (Beach, 1987; Beach & Anson, 1988), reflective judgment involves a very particular developmental progression which, theoretically, enables a person to better evaluate, explain, and defend a point of view on controversial issues. Specifically, the model describes the shifts that occur in assumptions about knowledge and in the way a person justifies his or her beliefs or decisions.

As has been noted by others (Applebee et al., 1986; see also Chapter 9, this volume), it is difficult to separate the development of writing and thinking. Rather, the development of one is aided by the other in a reciprocal way. Writing can enhance reflective judgment by providing students with the opportunity to engage in higher-order reasoning. Where confused writing reflects muddled thinking, not poor expression, the development of reflective judgment can lead to clarity in the student's written word. Our purpose is to outline a theory of and research on reflective judgment, a type of higher-order reasoning which can enhance and be enhanced by writing.

This chapter begins by describing the type of intellectual issues with which the reflective judgment model is concerned. Next we will discuss the reflective judgment model, the measurement of reflective judgment, and selected research on the topic. Our discussions of the reflective judgment model and research are taken from Kitchener (1986) and Kitchener and King (in press). Finally, we will summarize our ideas about the use of writing throughout the curriculum to enhance both writing and reflective judgment. Other discussions relevant to the relationship between reflective judgment and writing can be found in this volume: Kroll (see Chapter 13, this volume) describes a course which embodies the components needed to enhance writing and reflective judgment. Crowhurst (see Chapter 9, this volume) discusses argumentative writing, the type of writing to which reflective judgment seems most closely linked.

ILL-STRUCTURED PROBLEMS

Reflective judgment is probably most important for argumentative writing because reflective judgment involves judgments about "ill-structured" problems. Authors in various fields have noted that some questions are structured so as to be more amenable to solution (MacDonald, 1987; Scarr & Vander Zanden, 1984). For example, a story problem in arithmetic and the issue of how to reduce pollution differ in the completeness with which they can be described and the certainty with which a solution can be identified as correct. Churchman (1971) labels the first problem type a "puzzle" and suggests that puzzles are of limited interest in either measuring or in describing the problem solving required in the daily decision making of adults. The "real world" problems often faced by adults, such as who will make the best senator or how to protect one's savings from inflation, can rarely be constructed as puzzles since one of the biggest difficulties is to determine when and whether a solution has occurred. The second kind of problem has been labeled an "ill-structured" or "wicked" problem (Churchman, 1971).

Wood (1983) has elaborated on the concept of "ill-structured problem." According to Wood, an ill-structured problem results when one of the following is unknown or not known with a high degree of certainty to even an expert decision maker: the acts open to the decision maker, the states of nature (i.e., the relevant facts), the potential outcomes, and the utility of potential outcomes.

For example, at the time this chapter was being written, one of our communities was considering whether to build a controversial garbage-burning facility. The problem was ill-structured, because the potential outcomes and the utility of potential outcomes was unknown. There was disagreement with respect to at least one outcome, the amount of ash that would be emitted by the plant. Furthermore, the health risks associated with various levels of ash had not been firmly established, so the utility of various possible "ash outcomes" was uncertain.

Many examples of ill-structured problems are broad societal issues: pollution, nuclear energy, poverty, or alcoholism. Many personal issues are also ill-structured. For example, consider a young couple's decision about whether both parents should work full-time before the child enters kindergarten. The decision must be made in the face of uncertainty about the day care facilities which will be available now and in the future, uncertainty about the cost of those facilities now and in the future, and disagreement among child care experts about the effects of day care on the intellectual and emotional development of children.

The reflective judgment model is concerned with how people reason about "ill-structured" problems. It is *not* a model of how people reason about well-structured problems, such as an arithmetic story problem in which all of the information needed to solve the problem is given and the correctness or incorrectness of an answer is known with certainty by any knowledgeable problem solver. Writing designed to develop reflective judgment would center around ill-structured problems. Such problems are more likely to arise in argumentative writing than in purely descriptive or narrative writing. By argumentative writing, we mean writing in which the author states a thesis and supports it with logical arguments. A teacher who wishes to develop reflective judgment needs illustrative ill-structured problems to use as class examples and as foci for writing assignments. Kroll's (Chapter 13, this volume) use of readings about the battles of Hue and Ap Bac provide excellent illustrations of suitable readings and their use in a college composition course. Suitable ill-structured problems can be found in personal issues (e.g., Should I go on to college?), academic material (e.g., issues of literary or historical interpretation), and current events (e.g., Should the highway speed limit be lowered to 55 mph?). Clearly ill-structured problems do not belong to one subject matter area. They arise in fields as diverse as science, social studies, literature, and journalism. While writing can be used to develop reflective thinking and vice versa, the development of reflective thinking through writing cannot be viewed as the sole province of the rhetoric or composition faculty.

THE REFLECTIVE JUDGMENT MODEL

The reflective judgment model has many intellectual roots. It was heavily influenced by the educational writings of Dewey (1933, 1960), the works on intellectual development by Broughton (1978), Harvey, Hunt, and Schroder (1961), and Perry (1968), and the developmental stage conceptions of Piaget (1965), Kohlberg (1969), and Rest (1979). Dewey (1933) initiated the discussion of reflective thinking and the theoretical arguments for it. In specifying reflective thinking as an aim of education, Dewey acknowledged the existence of qualitative differences in reasoning. For Dewey, it was uncertainty that made intellectual questions truly problematic and which, therefore, initiates true inquiry. Reflective thinking, Dewey argued, is uncalled for in situations in which there is no controversy or doubt, no concern about current understanding of an issue, or in which absolute, preconceived assumptions dominate.

Perry (1968) presented a theory of intellectual and ethical development in the college years. His descriptions of dualistic and relativistic thinking closely parallel descriptions of the early and middle stages in the reflective judgment model. Whereas Perry's theory mixes strands of intellectual and ethical development, the reflective judgment model concerns only intellectual development, and it identifies aspects of dualistic and relativistic thinking as precursors to the development of reflective thinking.

The reflective judgment model describes changes which take place between adolescence and adulthood. These changes involve students' assumptions about knowing and corresponding beliefs about the nature of problems and how to solve them. The changes form a sequence of seven qualitatively different sets of assumptions about what can be known, how certain we can be about knowing, and the role of evidence, authority, and interpretation in the formation of a solution for a problem. Initially, beliefs are characterized by the view that knowledge can be had with absolute certainty via direct experience of the world. Such a view assumes that all problems are of the puzzle variety. As thinking evolves, individuals develop the ability to differentiate between puzzles and ill-structured problems. Students at this middle level recognize that while the answers to puzzles can be known with certainty, in the case of ill-structured problems, knowledge must be constructed. At the most advanced level, individuals use a form of problem solving similar to what Dewey

(1933) characterized as reflective thinking. While these individuals acknowledge the uncertainty of knowing and the ill-structured nature of many problems, they also suggest that knowledge must be understood as a reasonable conjecture about the world or a reasonable solution to the problem at hand. They suggest that knowledge about ill-structured problems is constructed via the process of inquiry or by integrating and synthesizing different perspectives into a solution. Forms of knowing which develop later in the sequence are better because they allow well and ill-structured problems to be differentiated and because they require diverse perspectives to be considered and evaluated prior to constructing a solution.

The following stage descriptions are based on the Reflective Judgment Scoring Rules (Kitchener & King, 1985) as well as other recent formulations (Kitchener, King, Wood, & Davison, in press). They illustrate more specifically the relationship between assumptions about knowledge and the nature of justification at each developmental level.

At the first stage, knowing is characterized by a concrete, single category belief system: What I observe to be true is true. Students appear to assume that knowledge exists absolutely; therefore, beliefs do not need justification. One must just observe to know. Ill-structured problems are not acknowledged since such an acknowledgement would imply that direct observation would not reveal "truth;" therefore, judgments which presume uncertainty are not made nor are they necessary.

At the next stage, Stage 2, knowing is characterized by the belief that while truth is knowable, it may not be directly and immediately known by everyone. In other words, the individual moves beyond an egocentric, single-category belief system, "What I observe is true," to a belief system in which single instances can be differentiated and related: Some beliefs are right and others are wrong. On the other hand, those who hold these assumptions maintain the belief that all variables can be known completely and with certainty. Thus, ultimately they reduce all problems to well-structured ones; that is, ones that have right answers. They assume the knower's role is to find the right answer and they assume authorities have the answer.

In response to a question about the safety of chemical additives in food, one person whose responses were scored at Stage 2 stated:

> If scientific studies say these chemicals cause cancer, then, yes, they cause cancer.

Another example of a Stage 2 response is the following:

> Mostly, I hear it and believe it because I figure if it's on the news, it's got to be true or they wouldn't put it on.

At Stage 3, individuals acknowledge that in some areas truth is temporarily inaccessible even for authorities, although they maintain the belief that absolute truth will be manifest in concrete data sometime in the future. They claim that since evidence is incomplete, no one can claim to "know" beyond her/his own personal impressions or feelings. Beliefs are justified only on the basis of what "feels" right or what one wants to believe at the moment. Stage 3 expands the categories of knowing into those that are right, those that are wrong, and those that are temporarily uncertain. Alternative interpretations, theories, and beliefs are assimilated into areas of uncertain knowledge. Implicitly, however, individuals maintain the assumption that all problems are ultimately reducible to well-structured ones since they continue to believe that truth will be known at a future date. Individuals with such a frame of reference would have difficulty with persuasive writing where they are called upon to marshal evidence and opinion for their viewpoint. Since, without certainty, they believe that individual feelings about an issue are the only justification for beliefs.

Knowing at Stage 4 is characterized by uncertainty and, frequently, skepticism in light of that uncertainty. Individuals claim that knowledge cannot be externally validated, thus they suggest it is idiosyncratic. They appear confused about how to make knowledge claims in light of uncertainty and without authorities to provide the answer. For example, one person, when asked about how to sort out the claims about creationism and evolution, said;

> I'd be more inclined to believe in evolution if they had proof. . . . I don't think we'll ever know because people will differ. Who are you going to ask? No one was there.

The uncertainty can take the form of arbitrary or partially reasoned decisions. For example, when asked whether the ancient Egyptians could have built the pyramids, one person responded;

> I've had several anthropology courses and all the cultures we studied are more advanced than the Egyptians. I read *Chariot of the Gods*. Some people say 'ah-oh!' but I'm more scientific than mystical; I tend to look at facts rather than other evidence.

Reasoning at this stage does, however, acknowledge that uncertainty is a legitimate and necessary aspect of knowing. By acknowledging uncertainty, ill-structured problems are afforded legitimacy, and therefore they can be differentiated from well-structured ones.

At Stage 5, knowing is distinguished by the belief that knowledge must be understood within a context, a belief occasionally labeled "relativism." The logic is that everything that is known is known via perceptual filters;

thus, we can only know others' and our own interpretations of the world. However, individuals move beyond the idiosyncratic justifications of Stage 4 and see justification as involving interpretation of evidence within a particular perspective. Justification remains context specific, however, and individuals appear hampered by their inability to compare and evaluate two different interpretations of the same issue or problem. As we have noted elsewhere (Kitchener & King, in press) when faced with ill-structured problems, this limitation offers the individuals no way to integrate perspectives and draw conclusions beyond limited relationships.

On the other hand, individuals whose thinking is characterized by Stage 5 assumptions do acknowledge and appreciate multiple perspectives on an issue, which is clearly a critical element in adapting writing for specific audiences. If writers cannot acknowledge that multiple perspectives on an issue exist, they cannot adapt their writing for an audience whose viewpoint may be different from their own.

Stage 6 knowing acknowledges both the uncertainty of knowing absolutely and that knowledge must be understood in relationship to context and evidence. It moves beyond Stage 5 belief systems by further claiming that, despite these limitations, some judgments or beliefs may nevertheless by judged as better than others. Beliefs are justified by evaluating and comparing evidence and opinion on different sides of an issue across contexts. In other words, students can compare the properties of two contexts and combine them into a system that allows for simple judgments about solutions for ill-structured problems or for an evaluation of two writers' perspectives on the same issue. Stage 7 knowing is comparable to what Dewey (1933) would call "reflective thinking." It is characterized by the belief that while uncertainty is an essential aspect of the knowing process, evidence and interpretations can be synthesized into epistemically justifiable claims about the best solution for the problem under consideration. Individuals appear to construct points of view about problems via critical inquiry or through the synthesis of existing views and evidence into a coherent or meaningful solution. Using these processes, it is possible for individuals to claim that given current evidence or knowledge, some judgments or interpretations of ill-structured problems have greater truth value than others and/or to suggest that a given judgment is a reasonable current solution to a problem. As one person said:

> One can argue here that one is a better argument than the other. One is more consistent with the evidence. What I am really after is a story that is in some sense intelligible and as intelligible as possible. . . . So it's very much a—I don't think it's as much of a puzzle solving as it is trying to get the narrative straight.

This person seems to understand that the ideas which form a reasoned judgment must be consistent with each other and with the evidence.

As with Dewey's reflective thinking, knowing in Stage 7 begins with an acknowledgement that a situation is truly problematic and that it is marked by uncertainty. It ends with a judgment or "grounded assertion" which at least temporarily closes the issue. Such reasoning is critical to good argumentative writing.

MEASURING REFLECTIVE JUDGMENT

Reflective judgment stage is assessed with the Reflective Judgment Interview (RJI) (King, 1977; Kitchener, 1977/78). In the interview, the interviewees are individually presented with four ill-structured problems, called dilemmas, drawn from the domains of physical science, social science, history, and biology. An example follows:

> Some people believe that news stories represent unbiased, objective reporting of news events. Others say that there is no such thing as unbiased, objective reporting and that even reporting the facts, the news reporters project their own interpretations into what they write.

The task for respondents is to explain and defend their judgment about the issue and to explain in what way they know their belief to be true. Responses to these issues are elicited through six semistructured probe questions; for example, can you say you know for sure your position is correct or true? If individuals do not have a judgment about the issue, six parallel probe questions are used to elicit their rationale for not taking a point of view and their assumptions about knowing. Interviewers also ask respondents to elaborate their ideas and offer explanations of word use; for example, what do you mean by "right"? The probing is designed to clarify the nature of assumptions currently being used and encourage the interviewee to take the interview seriously.

Responses to probe questions are scored by stage using reflective judgment scoring rules (Kitchener & King, 1985). Responses are scored by evaluating respondents' assumptions about knowledge, use of evidence, certainty of knowledge, and nature of justification. Scoring is usually done by two certified raters.[1] Responses to each of the interview questions are scored and then summarized into a 3-digit code. The first score represents the dominant stage used. The second score represents the subdominant

---

[1] A certification procedure has been established for both interviewers and raters in order to increase the comparability of data gathered by different researchers. Permission to use the copyrighted RJI interview is dependent on using certified raters and interviewers. For more information, contact Dr. Karen Kitchener, School of Education, University of Denver, Denver, Colorado 80208 or Dr. Patricia King, 330 Education Building, Bowling Green University, Bowling Green, Ohio 43403.

stage. A third score is given either if there is evidence of a third stage (which has occurred in less than 1% of the dilemmas) or to weight the dominant stage; for example, dominant Stage 3, subdominant Stage 2 is scored "323". For purposes of making group comparisons, a mean score for each person is derived by averaging scores across all dilemmas and both raters (i.e., 4 dilemmas x 2 raters x 3 scores per dilemma by rater = 24 scores). Several characteristics of the RJI should be noted. The ill-structured problems used in the interview were written about content with which people in the United States would be familiar, so that a knowledge of content would not unduly influence stage scores. In order to evaluate the generalizability of reflective judgment scores across ill-structured problems, four content areas are sampled. Reading level was designed so that most people with more than a junior high school education could comprehend the dilemmas. Since the interviewer reads the dilemma out loud while the interviewee reads his/her copy silently, comprehension is not a problem with many younger students. In fact, the interview has been used successfully with over 1,000 people ranging between 14- (McKinney, 1985) and 55-years-old (Glatfelter, 1982); with undergraduate and graduate college students (Brabeck, 1983; Hayes, 1981; Mines, 1980/1981; Schmidt, 1983; Shoff, 1979; Strange & King, 1981; Welfel, 1982); with nonstudent adults (Glatfelter, 1982; King, Kitchener, Davison, Parker, & Wood, 1983; Lawson, 1980; Schmidt, 1983); and with German university students (Kitchener & Wood, 1987).

The psychometric properties of the RJI have been reviewed by Mines (1982). In general interrater agreement has been moderate to high, ranging from 70% to 80% in most samples. Coefficient alpha, an estimate of the extent to which dilemmas are measuring the same construct, has generally been in the mid-to high-.90's (King et al., 1983). On a small sample, Sakalys (1982) reported that the three month test-retest reliability was .71.

SELECTED RESEARCH

In the reflective judgment research, there are three lines of research with particularly important educational implications: research on stage consistency, longitudinal and cross-sectional studies of development, and studies relating area of concentration to development. This research has been done primarily with college undergraduate and graduate students.

Stage Consistency

One appeal of stage theories to educators is their potential usefulness in individualizing instruction. If a person can be categorized as Stage X and people at Stage X best benefit from educational intervention Y, then a student reasoning at Stage X should have an individual instructional plan which includes intervention Y. This logic assumes reasoning is so highly structured that students' responses can legitimately be assumed to fall in one and only one stage. Is this a legitimate assumption with the reflective judgment stage model?

Student responses do not appear to be so highly structured. The structuring is certainly not as extensive in terms of horizontal generalizability as Piaget had in mind by the term "structure d'ensemble." Stage responding is not an all or nothing matter. A better description is that individuals hold a loosely related network of assumptions about knowledge, some of which are more closely associated than are others. While epistemological assumptions may change, the implications for related beliefs may not be understood immediately nor generalized to all content areas at the same time. Thus development does not appear to be abrupt nor show total synchrony. On the other hand, individuals' reasoning is quite consistent on ill-structured problems even when they are drawn from different domains.

Consistency across tasks has been evaluated several ways. First, inter-dilemma correlations, one indicator of the similarity of scores across dilemmas which differ in content, have been moderate to high in most reflective judgment studies (ranging between .65 and .92) depending on the heterogeneity of the sample (Mines, 1982). Second, when interviewees' scores are evaluated across tasks, they show a strong modal tendency. Usually the distribution of scores ranges across three stages or less. Specifically, Kitchener et al. (1989) reported that 60% of their interviewee's scores fell in their modal stage. Further, the modal stage agreement by problem was 75%. In other words, when a person's modal score was identified for each of the four problems in the RJI, the modal scores were identical in three of the four cases. On the other problem, modal score was discrepant by more than one stage only 4% of the time. These findings were consistent with prior research (King et al., 1983; Kitchener & King, 1981). These data do *not* support a simple stage model in which a given student's various responses all conform exactly to the thinking of a single stage. Rather, as already noted, they suggest individuals' thinking is moderately consistent.

In a related study, Hayes (1981) evaluated whether familiarity with content would significantly affect reflective judgment scores. Using two ill-structured problems from education and two standard dilemmas with teacher trainees, he found only about one-quarter of a stage difference. While he concluded that content made some difference in reflective judgment scores, the difference was quite small.

Taken together, these data suggest that one cannot say a person's reasoning is "in" a given stage. On the other hand, a mean or modal score from the RJI characterizes ill-structured problem solving across different domains better than one might expect considering the dissimilarity of the RJI domains (e.g., history and science) and provides a reasonable estimate of the assumptions with which an individual will approach and understand a variety of problems. This is especially true since the assumptions of adjacent stages in the model are not as discrepant as are the assumptions that are two-stages discrepant. For example, if a person scores as dominant Stage 4, subdominant 5 we can conclude that he/she will see knowledge as ultimately uncertain since this is a characteristic of both stages. Further, in most cases, he/she is probably skeptical about the ability of people to know anything via reason, but is learning to use evidence to make reasoned judgments in some cases. As explained in our section on educational implications, this type of moderately structured stage information allows a greater diagnostic clarity about reasoning errors and potential areas for educational intervention than, for example, do intelligence test scores.

Cross-sectional studies

There are some educational goals which can be viewed as "short term" in that it is reasonable to expect the outcome to occur in a relatively short period of time. The appropriate intervention operates on a malleable aspect of the student. Memorizing a delimited set of facts is one such short term educational goal. One can assign third graders a list of 20 spelling words on Monday and expect students to have learned most of them by Friday. Or one can reasonably expect first graders to learn the basic addition facts over two semesters.

Other educational goals must be viewed as long-term goals. Interventions designed to foster those goals operate on an aspect of the student that is more stable and requires more time to change. The longitudinal and cross-sectional studies of reflective judgment suggest that reflective thinking develops very slowly over many years.

Table 12.1[2] shows the mean Reflective Judgment scores by educational level for 14 studies using over 800 traditional age students. Mean scores correspond to stages: A mean score of 2.0 indicates that the average score for a given sample was Stage 2.

If one looks closely at Table 12.1, it becomes apparent how slow devel-

---

[2] Our thanks to Michael L. Commons for permission to reprint Table 12.1 from Kitchener, K. S. & King, P. M. (in press). The reflective judgment model: Ten years of research. In M. L. Commons, C. Armon, L. Kohlberg, F. A. Richards, T. A. Grotzer, & J. D. Sinnott (Eds.), *Adult development, 2, Models and methods in the study of adolescent and adult thought.* New York: Praeger.

Table 12.1. Mean Reflective Judgment Scores by Educational Level for Traditionally Aged Students Across Fourteen Studies

Reflective Judgment Mean Score	High School			College				Graduate	
	Freshmen	Junior	Senior	Freshmen	Sophomore	Junior	Senior	Beginning	Advanced
2.0[a]									
2.5									
3.0	2.79(14)	2.77(1)[b]	2.94(14)						
3.5			3.40(8)	3.23(10)	3.40(8)	3.54(11)	3.56(10)		
				3.31(5)					
				3.35(11)					
				3.62(9)		3.65(1)	3.63(12)		
				3.74(6)		3.73(7)	3.70(8)		
4.0				3.81(13)		3.93(2)	3.78(3)	4.00(8)	
							3.97(7)		
							4.00(9)		
							4.08(5)		
4.5							4.27(6)	4.60(4)	
5.0							4.98(13)		
5.5									4.76(5)
6.0									4.96(4)
6.5									5.67(1)
7.0									
Overall									
Mean	2.79	2.77	3.18	3.60	3.40	3.68	3.99	4.24	5.04
N	23	20	58	216	30	100	257	49	80

276

[a]A mean score of 2.0 includes the range of 1.75 – 2.24; 2.5 includes 2.25 – 2.74, etc.

[b]Numbers in parentheses correspond to studies, listed below.

Sample Source

(1) Kitchener & King (1981), n = 20 per group, Minnesota high school and University of Minnesota.

(2) King & Parker (1978), n= 20. Sample is matched to the Kitchener & King (1981) sample of college juniors.

(3) Shoff (1979), n = 14, University of Utah.

(4) Lawson (1980). n = 20 per group, University of Minnesota.

(5) Mines (1980/1981), n = 20 freshmen, 40 seniors, 40 advanced doctoral students, University of Iowa.

(6) Strange & King (1981), n = 16 per group, University of Iowa.

(7) Hayes (1981), n = 30 per group, University of Utah.

(8) Braback (1983), n = 30 high school seniors, 30 college sophmores, 30 college seniors, and 29 beginning graduate students, private Catholic high school and college.

(9) Welfel (1982). n = 32 per group, University of Minnesota

(10) Glatfelter (1982). n = 16 per group, Utah State University.

(11) Schmidt (1985). n = 40 per group, University of Minnesota.

(12) Sakalys (1982). n = 50 senior nursing students, University of Colorado.

(13) Griffith (1984). n = 92 freshmen, 29 seniors, Davidson College.

(14) McKinney (1985), n = 28 freshmen, 28 seniors, Colorado high school.

Note. From K. S. Kitchener & P. M. King, in press, "The reflective judgment model: Ten years of research," In *Adult development. 2. Models and methods in the study of adolescent and adult thought,* edited by M. L. Commons. C. Armon. L. Kohlberg. F. A. Richards, T. A. Grotzer, & J. D. Sinnott, New York: Praeger. Reprinted by permission.

277

opment is. Note that, in Table 12.1, all four high school samples score between 2.77 and 3.40. That is, their typical thinking is best characterized by Stages 2 and 3. In Stage 2 and 3 thinking, the ill-structured nature of problems is not really recognized. If there are alternative views, it is because some of them are wrong or because truth is temporarily inaccessible.

In Table 12.1, the means for college samples range from 3.23 to 4.98, indicating that Stages 3 and 4 best characterize their thinking. In Stage 3 thought, the ill-structured nature of problems is denied because truth is temporarily inaccessible. Stage 4 thought gives ill-structured problems a legitimacy by granting that truth is unknowable in some areas. Since the role of evidence is not understood, individuals using Stage 4 reasoning do not understand how to validate knowledge or interpretations against reality; consequently knowledge or interpretation is idiosyncratic.

The graduate student means range from 4.00 to 5.67, indicating that their responses were best characterized by Stages 4 and 5. As stated above, Stage 4 thought gives ill-structured problems a legitimacy by granting that truth is unknowable in some areas, but it provides no means of validating interpretations against reality. Stage 5 does allow evidence-based validation of interpretations within a given perspective, but provides little or no basis for comparing perspectives.

While Table 12.1 indicates that development is typically slow, it also indicates that students at different educational levels will struggle with different developmental issues. That is, most high school students are still developing an awareness that some issues are ill-structured problems for which absolute certainty is impossible. Some college students are still developing this awareness. Other college undergraduates and most graduate students understand the difference between puzzles and ill-structured problems and can begin to develop ways of thinking that allow them to validate interpretations using evidence and data, first only within a context and later across contexts.

Area of concentration

Several studies have examined the relationship between college experiences and reflective judgment scores. King and Parker (1978), King, Wood, and Mines (1990), Schmidt (1985), and Welfel (1982) started with the hypothesis that liberal arts classes more frequently bring students into contact with ill-structured problems than do classes in technical majors. King and Parker (1978) compared the reflective judgment scores of juniors in liberal arts and agricultural majors and found no significant difference in their scores. Welfel's cross-sectional study and Schmidt's longitudinal study compared the difference between freshmen and seniors in liberal arts and engineering majors. If a liberal arts education better promoted growth, one might expect the freshman-senior difference to be greater for the liberal arts majors. However, from freshman to senior years, the liberal arts students did not change significantly more (or less) than did the engineering majors. King et al. (1990) found higher scores among graduate social science students than among graduate mathematical science students, but they did not find differences between undergraduate social science and undergraduate mathematical science students.

Upon hearing that the data do not suggest a difference between undergraduate liberal arts and undergraduate science or technical students, professors in technical fields have seemed unsurprised. Some have pointed out that undergraduates in technical majors take a substantial number of liberal arts courses to fulfill distribution requirements. Others have argued that the technical fields do indeed confront students with ill-structured problems. In any case, the research to date has uncovered no evidence to suggest that some undergraduate college majors promote reflective thinking more than do others.

EDUCATIONAL IMPLICATIONS

While there has been no research on the relationship between writing and reflective judgment, Hays, Brandt, and Chantry (1988) did find a relationship between scores on argumentative essays and Perry's (1968) measure of development. The theory and research presented above suggest several implications regarding the development of reflective judgment through writing. Our conjectures below represent just that—conjectures—rather than empirically tested conclusions. While our suggestions are rather general, Kroll (see Chapter 13, this volume) presents an excellent, concrete illustration of a college composition course designed to promote reflective thinking.

It seems reasonable to conclude that reading will play a role in the development of reflective judgment and related writing skills. Applebee et al. (1986) have noted a relationship between reading skill and writing proficiency. Before asking students to write, interventions designed to promote reflective thinking, such as Kroll's (see Chapter 13, this volume), often ask students to read essays presenting alternative points of view. By reading the essays of others, students in the early stages (i.e., Stages 1–3) may come to better understand that different perspectives exist on issues, even among legitimate authorities. In the middle stages, such reading can help students understand the role of evidence (ranging from formal data to anecdotal experience), appeals to authority, assumptions, values, and interpretation in drawing conclusions about ill-structured problems. And they may come to better understand the structure of written arguments, a structure with which many students seem unfamiliar (Applebee et al., 1986; see Chapter 9).

Developing reflective judgment involves an evaluation of assumptions regarding ill-structured problems. Teachers can promote such cognitive evaluations with suitable educational challenges and supports (Sanford, 1966). Challenge derives from presenting problems for which the student's current assumptions are insufficient and which cause the student to seek more adequate ways of thinking about a problem. In the early stages, the challenge arises when the student realizes that simply looking to authorities will not suffice, because the authorities disagree and for good reason. Once the student understands the nature of ill-structured problems, the challenge comes from the complexity of developing a well-reasoned argument which starts from reasonable assumptions and contains ideas which are consistent with each other and with the evidence.

Along with the challenge, students need appropriate support. Exercises designed to promote reflective judgment need to be interesting and engaging to students, but they cannot be so emotionally involving as to preclude clear thinking by invoking an emotional or reflexive response. Teachers need to create an atmosphere of thoughtful reasoning, and the content of the exercises needs to be content which brings out a reflective, reasoned response from the student. Further, teachers need to acknowledge that the revolutions in thinking that are implied by the reflective judgment model are frequently disturbing, frustrating, and even frightening. Students' frustrations need to be, at minimum, acknowledged.

Reflective judgment is most closely linked to writing which involves ill-structured problems. While most types of writing can involve ill-structured problems, such problems are often used in argumentative writing which uses an analytic structure and which requires systematically supported arguments. Such writing is somewhat distinct from purely persuasive writing, such as advertising copy, where the goal is to persuade (logically or otherwise) and emotional appeals play a large role. Writing about ill-structured problems involves more than correct grammar, clear organization, interesting prose, and clarity. It also requires developing a well-reasoned thesis about a controversial topic. This involves becoming familiar with the positions taken and arguments used to support these positions, weighing and interpreting the evidence for each position, deciding which position to endorse, choosing to emphasize some pieces of evidence while deemphasizing others, refuting contradictory evidence or interpretations, and so on. On the other hand, all writing, not just argumentative writing, involves consideration of others' perspectives, a task which is very difficult for individuals using reasoning characteristic of the early reflective judgment stages.

The data in Table 12.1 are diagnostically useful for educators as they consider the nature of the challenges and supports that are needed to promote development. They suggest that students at different educational levels are prepared to tackle different kinds of writing tasks. With increasing sophistication of reasoning, there are changes in the kind of challenge and kind of support which are optimal. High school students are developing an awareness that uncertainty is an inherent quality of some intellectual issues. They seem to be learning that differences of opinion result from more than temporary errors of judgment or confusion on the part of those who should know the correct answer. Expecting high school students to use advanced reflective thinking is probably unrealistic and inappropriate. At the secondary level, the focus might appropriately be on developing the "preconditions" for reflective thought. It would be important to introduce different perspectives on the same event as an initial challenge to the assumption that there is a single, absolutely correct way to answer an ill-structured problem.

For instance, in an American history unit about the Revolutionary War, high school students might be asked to read essays by Patriot and Tory authors for and against colonial independence. Students could then respond in writing to a structured set of questions about the two views. For example, it may be useful to ask students to break each essay into its components: facts (ranging from formal data to anecdotal experience), appeals to authority, assumptions (both implicit and explicit), values, and conclusions or interpretations. Students need to understand the distinctions between these various elements of the essays, and they need to understand what role the former elements (i.e., facts, appeals to authority, assumptions, and values) play in the development of conclusions by an author. In a writing exercise, students could be encouraged to read essays by Patriot and Tory authors, describe the arguments on both sides in a relatively balanced way, and explain why reasonable adults of the time could not agree. One would not expect students to develop a coherent interpretation of their own, but simply to demonstrate an understanding of the alternative points of view by giving a clear explanation of those points of view and the arguments behind them.

As students develop an awareness of ill-structured problems, the next step is to develop their own interpretations within a context. The data in Table 12.1 suggest that such an awareness often does not develop until college. In analyzing the writings of others, students need to begin understanding how different assumptions and weighing of evidence can lead to different conclusions, and they need to begin asking why different authors start from different assumptions and why the authors might evaluate the same evidence differently.

In their own writing about ill-structured problems, students in the middle reflective judgment stages can begin developing a coherent interpretation of their own. For example, in that same American History unit, students might be asked to imagine that they are southern plantation owners whose cotton is sold to English manufacturers. They might be asked questions like the following: Would you be in favor of the colonies declaring their independence from England in 1776? What would be the reasons for your decision? In the middle developmental stages, it is sufficient for students to state certain assumptions or state a perspective and develop a position which is consistent with the evidence and the assumptions of their perspective. They need to present a coherent interpretation, but not defend it against alternative interpretations which begin from different assumptions or values.

When students are operating with Stage 5 or 6 assumptions, they should be encouraged to develop positions which transcend a particular perspective or point of view. Students might be asked to put themselves in the position of someone who has listened to the arguments of both the Tories and the Patriots and now must decide what is in the best interest of their country. Would they be in favor of independence from England in 1776 and for what reasons? Or the student might be asked to analyze two competing arguments, noting how the authors began from different assumptions, how they selected different evidence, how they weighed evidence differently, and how they relied on different authorities. Now, however, the student would be asked to evaluate which set of assumptions seemed the more plausible, which weighing of the evidence is more defensible, and which authorities are in the more knowledgeable position (or have the better argument).

If one begins to think about developing reflective judgment through writing, it seems wiser to think in terms of writing throughout the curriculum, rather than just one or two classes. The results in Table 12.1 suggest that the development of reflective judgment is slow. It requires more than one or two semester length courses. If the development of reflective judgment is incorporated into a curriculum spanning 3–4 years of high school or 4 years of college, students will have sufficient time to allow their thinking to mature.

Further, there is no particular reason to assign the development of reflective judgment to any one subject matter. This conclusion receives some indirect support from the studies which failed to find a relationship between college major and reflective judgment. Ill-structured problems occur in every field, from questions of literary to historical to scientific interpretation.

Educators may be somewhat discouraged by the small differences in Table 12.1 between high school, college, and graduate students. One must remember, however, that there is no reason to believe the students whose scores are presented in Table 12.1 were enrolled in curricula which systematically attempted to develop Reflective Judgment. Further, one must remember that even a change of one point can represent an important qualitative change in thinking. A shift from Stage 3 to 4 represents development of an awareness that ill-structured problems exist and that evidence plays a role, although the nature of the role is poorly understood. A shift from Stage 4 to Stage 5 represents a new understanding of how interpretations can be validated and compared. While neither of these represent advanced reflective thinking, they appear to serve as a foundation on which more complex and adequate assumptions can be built.

Several arguments can be given against the position that the schools (secondary and higher education) should attempt to develop reflective thinking. Some might argue that the schools have more than enough goals: to develop reading comprehension, written and oral expression, mathematical ability, social and emotional maturity, and so on. Adding the development of reflective thinking would be asking too much of our educational system. On the other hand, the "real-world" is full of ill-structured problems, from the choice of a senator to the safety of prescription drugs. If our educational system decides to ignore reflective thinking, it will have decided to neglect the preparation of students to deal with a type of problem which they will commonly encounter once they reach adulthood.

Further, and most important to the focus of this volume, since good writing involves taking the perspective of the reader, considering alternative points of view, and articulating arguments, it may be inexorably tied to the development of reflective judgment. For example, when grading argumentative essays, it is difficult to clearly distinguish the quality of the writing from the quality of the reasoning presented in the paper. Indeed, many educators may view the quality of the reasoning in such essays as being a critical component in evaluating the quality of the writing. According to Applebee et al. (1986) and Crowhurst (see Chapter 9, this volume), poor higher-order reasoning skills provide one possible explanation for the poor performance of students in argumentative writing. If so, then writing about ill-structured problems can help develop reflective thinking, and reflective thinking can simultaneously enhance the student's ability to write. For educators interested in enhancing both thinking and writing, this is clearly a no-lose undertaking, because the relationship between writing and reflective thinking is interactive.

REFERENCES

Applebee, A. N., Langer, J. A., & Mullis, V. S. (1986). *The writing report card: Writing achievement in American schools* (Research Rep. No. 15-W-02). Princeton, NJ: Educational Testing Service.

Anderson, R. D., DeVito, A., Odvard, E. D., Kellogg, M., Koch, L., & Weigand, J. (1970). *Developing children's thinking through science.* Englewood Cliffs, NJ: Prentice-Hall.

Banks, J. A. (1977). *Teaching strategies for the social studies: Inquiry, valuing and decision making.* Reading, MA.: Addison-Wesley.

Beach, R. (1987). Differences in autobiographical narratives of English teachers, college freshmen, and seventh graders. *College Composition and Communications, 38*(1), 56–69.

Beach, R., & Anson, C. M. (1988). The pragmatics of memo writing. *Written Communication, 5,* 157–183.

Brabeck, M. (1983). Critical thinking skills and reflective judgment development: Redefining the aims of higher education. *Journal of Applied Developmental Psychology, 4,* 23–34.

Broughton, J. M. (1978). The development of concepts of self, mind, reality and knowledge. In E. Damon (Ed.), *New directions for child development: Social cognition* (pp. 75–100). San Francisco: Jossey-Bass.

Churchman, C. W. (1971). *The design of inquiring systems: Basic concepts of systems and organizations.* New York: Basic Books.

Dunfer, M. (1978). *Social studies for the real world.* Columbus, OH: Charles E. Merrill.

Dewey, J. (1933). *How we think: A restatement of the relation of reflective thinking to the education process.* Boston: D. C. Heath.

Dewey, J. (1960). *The quest for certainty.* New York: G. P. Putnam.

Edwards, C. H., & Fisher, R. L. (1977). *Teaching elementary social studies: A competency based program.* New York: Praeger.

Esler, W. K. (1973). *Teaching elementary science.* Belmont, CA: Wadsworth.

Glatfelter, M. (1982). Identity development, intellectual development, and their relationship in reentry women students. (Doctoral dissertation, University of Minnesota). *Dissertation Abstracts International, 43,* 354A.

Griffith, J. (1984). *Reflective Judgment scores, Davidson College students.* Unpublished raw data.

Hays, J. N., Brandt, K. M., & Chantry, K. H. (1988). The impact of friendly and hostile audiences on the argumentative writing of high school and college students. *Research in the Teaching of English, 22,* 391–416.

Harvey, O. J., Hunt, D. E., & Schroder, H. M. (1961). *Conceptual systems and personality organization.* New York: Wiley.

Hayes, A. B. (1981). An investigation of the effect of dilemma content on level of reasoning in the reflective judgment interview. (Doctoral dissertation, University of Utah). *Dissertation Abstracts International, 40,* 2564B.

Jarolimek, J. (1977). *Social studies competencies and skills.* New York: MacMillan.

Kaltsounis, T. (1979). *Teaching social studies in the elementary school.* Englewood Cliffs, NJ: Prentice-Hall.

King, P. M. (1977). The development of reflective judgment and formal operational thinking in adolescents and young adults. (Doctoral dissertation, University of Minnesota). *Dissertation Abstracts International, 38,* 7233A.

King, P. M., Kitchener, K. S., Davison, M. L., Parker, C. A., & Wood, P. K. (1983).

The justification of beliefs in young adults: A longitudinal study. *Human Development, 26,* 106–118.

King, P. M., & Parker, C. A. (1978). *Assessing intellectual development in the college years.* A report of the Instructional Improvement Project, 1976–1977, Unpublished manuscript, University of Minnesota, Minneapolis, MN.

King, P. M., Wood, P. K., & Mines, R. (1990). Critical thinking among college and graduate students. *Review of Higher Education, 13,* 167–186.

Kitchener, K. S. (1977/1978). Intellectual development in late adolescents and young adults: Reflective judgment and verbal reasoning. (Doctoral dissertation, University of Minnesota, 1977). *Dissertation Abstracts International, 39,* 936B.

Kitchener, K. S. (1986). The reflective judgment model: Characteristics, evidence, and measurement. In R. A. Mines & K. S. Kitchener (Eds.), *Cognitive development in young adults* (pp. 76–91). New York: Praeger.

Kitchener, K. S., & King, P. M. (1981). Reflective judgment: Concepts of justification and their relationship to age and education. *Journal of Applied Developmental Psychology, 2,* 89–116.

Kitchener, K. S., & King, P. M. (1985). *Reflective Judgment scoring rules (Revised).* Unpublished manuscript, University of Denver.

Kitchener, K. S., & King, P. M. (in press). The reflective judgment model: Ten years of research. In M. L. Commons, C. Armon, L. Kohlberg, F. A. Richards, T. A. Grotzer, & J. D. Sinnott (Eds.), *Adult development, 2, Models and methods in the study of adolescent and adult thought.* New York: Praeger.

Kitchener, K. S., King, P. M., Wood, P. K., & Davison, M. L. (in press). Sequentiality and consistency in the development of reflective judgment: A six year longitudinal study. *Applied Developmental Psychology.*

Kitchener, K. S., & Wood, P. A. (1987). Development of concepts of justification in German university students. *International Journal of Behavioral Development, 10*(2), 171–185.

Kohlberg, L. (1969). Stage and sequence: The cognitive-developmental approach to socialization. In D. Goslin (Ed.), *Handbook of socialization theory and Research* (pp. 347–480). Chicago, IL: Rand McNally.

Lawson, J. M. (1980). The relationship between graduate education and the development of reflective judgment: A function of age or educational experience. (Doctoral dissertation, University of Minnesota). *Dissertation Abstracts International, 41,* 4655A.

MacDonald, S. P. (1987). Problem definition in academic writing. *College English, 49*(3), 315–331.

McKinney, M. (1985). *Intellectual development of younger adolescents.* Unpublished doctoral dissertation, University of Denver.

Mines, R. A. (1980/1981). An investigation of the development levels of reflective judgment and associated critical thinking skills. (Doctoral dissertation, University of Iowa). *Dissertation Abstracts International, 41,* 1495A.

Mines, R. A. (1982). Student development assessment techniques. In G. R. Hanson (Ed.), *New directions for student services: Measuring student development* (Vol. 20, pp. 65–92). San Francisco: Josey-Bass.

National Council for the Social Studies. (1971). *Social studies curriculum guidelines*. Washington, DC: National Council for the Social Studies.

Perry, W. G. (1968). *Forms of intellectual and ethical development in the college years*. New York: Holt, Rinehart, and Winston

Piaget, J. (1965). *The moral judgment of the child* (M. Gabain, trans.). New York: Free Press. (Originally published in 1932.)

Rest, J. R. (1979). *Development in judging moral issues*. Minneapolis, MN: University of Minnesota Press.

Rowe, M. B. (1978). *Teaching science as continuous inquiry*. New York: McGraw Hill.

Sakalys, J. A. (1982). *Effects of a research methods course on nursing students research attitudes and cognitive development*. Unpublished doctoral dissertation, University of Denver, Boulder, CO.

Sanford, N. (1966). *Self and society: Social change and individual development*. New York: Atherton Press.

Scarr, S., & Vander Zanden, J. (1984). *Understanding psychology* (4th ed.). New York: Random House.

Schmidt, J. A. (1983). *The intellectual development of traditionally and nontraditionally aged college students: A cross sectional study with longitudinal follow-up*. Unpublished doctoral dissertation, University of Minnesota, Minneapolis, MN.

Schmidt, J. A. (1985). Older and wiser? A longitudinal study of the impact of college on intellectual development. *Journal of College Student Personnel, 26*, 388–394.

Shoff, S. P. (1979). The significance of age, sex, and type of education on the development of reasoning in adults. (Doctoral dissertation, University of Utah). *Dissertation Abstracts International, 40*, 3910A.

Strange, C. C., & King, P. M. (1981). Intellectual development and its relationship to maturation during the college years. *Journal of Applied Developmental Psychology, 2*, 281–295.

Welfel, E. R. (1982). How students make judgments: Do educational level and academic major make a difference? *Journal of College Student Personnel, 23*, 490–497.

Wood, P. K. (1983). Inquiring systems and problem structure: Implications for cognitive development. *Human Development, 26*, 249–265.

13
Teaching English for Reflective Thinking

Barry M. Kroll

In the fall semester of 1986, I was assigned to teach, for the first time in my career, a large lecture course for freshmen. Although I had taught small classes of freshmen for more than 15 years at several universities, in this course, entitled "Literature and Composition," I was slated to lecture twice a week to a sea of faces—144 students, the number of seats in the lecture hall. (I also met 25 of them in a discussion section; my four graduate-student assistants met with the others). Instructors can choose their own readings for "Literature and Composition," and in most versions of the course these readings are organized around a theme, topic, genre, or author. I decided to focus on the literature of the Vietnam War, and I organized the course around a sequence of types of writing: memoir, history, journalism, and fiction.

I chose the Vietnam War as a topic because I believed undergraduates would be interested in it, but I also chose the topic because the war litera-ture raises the kinds of ethical and epistemological issues I wanted stu-dents to confront in the course. For while the syllabus indicated that the course was about the literature of America's most recent war—and more specifically about various modes of representing the nature and meaning of that war—lurking within the readings and the writing projects were complex and disturbing questions: How can a person know what really happened or what to believe about an event, especially when confronted with competing accounts and divergent points of view? How can one de-cide what actions are right or what it means to be good, particularly when there are several courses of action, none of them clearly right? Thus I saw the course as an experiment, of sorts, an attempt to find out how a group of freshmen would approach intellectual problems, to see how they would respond to projects that raised challenging questions, and to find out whether a one-semester course in literature and composition could stimu-late critical thinking and foster reflective analysis.

When I say that I conducted an experiment "of sorts," I mean, of course, that this project was a trial rather than a true experiment, an attempt to teach according to certain principles and observe the results. Thus my study fits the model of "action research" better than it does any paradigm of scientific investigation (Cohen & Manion, 1980). Because I was involved as both instructor and investigator, I was an engaged participant in the project, studying my own students—a group of freshmen I came to know and care about. If my involvement in this course sacrificed some measure of objectivity, it also provided a vantage point from which to observe—with some acuity and accuracy, I believe—the thoughts and responses of a group of freshmen who were embarking on their first course in college English.

I could not plan the course or my investigation without making some assumptions about college students' intellectual abilities and orientations. Those assumptions came mostly from reading I had done on the nature of critical thinking and intellectual development during the college years. My ideas about the nature of critical reflection owe a great deal to the work of John Dewey, particularly to his seminal book, *How We Think* (1933/1986). In Dewey's view, reflective thinking is called for in "perplexing, confused, or unsettled" circumstances (p. 248), or in what he also calls "forked-road" situations (p. 122) in which a person confronts problems for which there are discrepant solutions, conflicting explanations, or alternative courses of action. Although people often try to solve such problems as quickly as possible on the basis of whim, prejudice, stereotypes, or dogmatic beliefs, reflective individuals suspend judgment while they inquire more deeply into the alternatives: they "weigh, ponder, deliberate" (p. 175), "turning a subject over in the mind and giving it serious and consecutive consideration" (p. 113), seeking to "establish belief upon a firm basis of evidence and rationality" (p. 118).[1]

For my thinking about students' intellectual development, I found especially helpful William Perry's (1970, 1981) compelling account of undergraduate experience as an evolution from an initial state of dualistic and authority-centered thinking, through a middle period of multiplistic but largely uncritical thought, to a form of critical, contextual relativism.[2] And

---

[1] Other scholars in the Deweyan tradition have helped me refine my understanding of the nature of critical reflection. I have found Richard Paul's concept of "dialogic reasoning"—thinking "critically and reciprocally within opposing points of view"—particularly useful. See his article "Critical Thinking: Fundamental to Education for a Free Society," *Educational Leadership*, September 1984: 4–14. For a recent overview and critique of several important conceptions of critical thinking (including Paul's), as well as an exposition of his own "reasons conception" of rationality, see Harvey Siegel, *Educating Reason* (New York: Routledge, 1988).

[2] Others in the field of composition studies have found Perry's scheme useful for understanding their students as writers. The best informed work, in my view, is by Janice Hays. See "The Development of Discursive Maturity in College Writers" in Theresa Enos (Ed.), *A Sourcebook for Basic Writing Teachers* (New York: Random House, 1987), pp. 480–96—this reprinting includes an important postscript; and especially "Models of Intellectual Development and Writing: A Response to Myra Kogen," *Journal of Basic Writing*, 6 (Spring 1987): 11–27. For another thoughtful perspective see Patricia Bizzell, "William Perry and Liberal Education," *College English* 46 (1984): 447–454.

Reflective Judgment Theory provided another provocative source of insights into undergraduates' evolving conceptions of reality, knowledge, and the justification of belief (Kitchener, 1983, 1986; cf. Chapter 12, this volume). From such theories of critical thinking and intellectual development, I adopted several working assumptions.[3]

I assumed, first, that students tend to approach intellectual problems from a particular conceptual orientation, an interpretive framework from which they make sense of the ideas, questions, and projects that they encounter in their courses. I assumed, further, that these orientations could be adequately described by categories like those used in research on intellectual development, such as the major positions in Perry's scheme (dualism, multiplism, contextual relativism) or the primary stages of Reflective Judgment Theory (dogmatism, skepticism, rationality). But because I wanted to pursue different questions—using different methods—than either Perry or the Reflective Judgment group, I devised my own descriptive categories (which I will discuss later).[4]

I also assumed that students' orientations to knowledge tend to change during college, as students confront issues, questions, and points of view that challenge their ways of knowing. And I assumed that these changes follow approximately the kind of sequence outlined in the most widely accepted models of intellectual development: confidence that authorities

---

[3] I call these "working assumptions" because I accept them provisionally, as warranted by a good deal of evidence but certainly not established beyond dispute. In fact, there is currently a good deal of debate about the nature of rationality and intellectual development. One thoughtful perspective comes from recent studies of women's intellectual and ethical orientations, especially Mary Field Belenky, Blythe McVicker Clinchy, Nancy Rule Goldberger, and Jill Mattuck Tarule, *Women's Ways of Knowing* (New York: Basic Books, 1986). Within developmental psychology, there are ongoing debates about such complex topics as the stability of "stages" of development, the processes of stage transition, the relation of cognition and affect in human development, and the extent to which intellectual development is best conceived as social or individual in nature. In general, my thinking on many of these issues has been influenced by Robert Kegan, *The Evolving Self* (Cambridge: Harvard University Press, 1982).

[4] I've used elements from both the Perry scheme and reflective judgment theory to build a general framework for my thinking about students' intellectual development. In this paper, I have presented sketchy versions of the two theories, emphasizing similarities in their approaches. There are also important differences, both theoretical and methodological. For example, at the higher levels of development, Perry focuses on the ways students make commitments within a contextually relative world view, while reflective judgment focuses on the ways students make probabilistic judgments on the basis of rational reflection. The aim of my research was not, of course, to investigate students' levels of intellectual development, but rather to study a much more limited issue: the ways in which freshmen responded to the problem of conflicting accounts of an event. Therefore, although endebted to Perry's work and reflective judgment theory for many insights into the nature of students' thinking about problems of knowledge, my project is not an empirical test of a particular theory of intellectual growth.

know the truth; doubt in authorities and skepticism about being able to judge any views as truer than others; critical analysis of claims and evidence, within some frame of reference for rational judgment.

Finally, although I recognized that students' intellectual orientations change gradually throughout the college years, I assumed that instruction could foster critical reflection. The key, in my view, was to pose the right kind of problems—genuine problems that would engage students' emotional and intellectual resources, their hearts as well as their minds (to appropriate an infamous slogan from the Vietnam era). As Dewey points out, without such deep engagement, "problems and questions, which are the only true instigators of reflective activity, will be more or less externally imposed and only half-heartedly felt and dealt with" (p. 341). Thus my instructional model was based on a balance of "challenge" and "support" activities:[5] challenging reflection by posing a series of projects, problems, and questions for analysis; supporting reflection by encouraging group discussion, private expression (in journals), and personal engagement. Although I expected changes to be subtle, I believed that it made sense, even in a one-semester freshman course, to encourage students to become more thoughtful, reflective, and rational human beings.

In this chapter I am going to focus on one unit of the course and one part of my investigation, reporting what I have discovered about my students' orientations to historical writing, in particular the ways in which they made judgments about discrepant accounts of the same historical event. I had three broad aims in this investigation. First, I wanted to find out how the freshmen in my course would respond, at the beginning of the semester, to a situation in which they encountered two quite different accounts of the same battle. To do so, I gave them two accounts of the Battle of Ap Bac, an engagement between Viet Cong and South Vietnamese troops, and asked a series of questions about their reaction to the existence of two conflicting accounts of the same event. In analyzing the students' responses, I tried to describe both their overall orientations to the problem and the specific strategies they used to decide which account was better or more believable.

Second, I wanted to obtain students' responses to the same problem (the two accounts of Ap Bac) at the end of the 14-week course, so that I could compare the orientations and strategies in their initial and final

---

[5] I first heard about the concept of "challenge and support" variables in a provocative talk on "developmental instruction" given by L. Lee Knefelkamp several years ago. Knefelkamp adapted the concept from Nevitt Sanford, *Self and Society: Social Change and Individual Development* (New York: Atherton, 1966). For an overview of these and other principles of developmental instruction, see Carole Widick and Deborah Simpson, "Developmental Concepts in College Instruction," in C. A. Parker (Ed.), *Encouraging Development in College Students* (Minneapolis: University of Minnesota Press, 1978), pp. 27–59.

responses. I realized, of course, that dramatic changes were unlikely in the space of only a single semester. And I recognized that even if I were to find changes, it would be impossible, given the design of my study, to attribute them conclusively to anything in the course. Nevertheless, I was curious about what I would find if I took a careful look at students' responses to the same problem at the beginning and end of the semester.

Finally, I wanted to find out whether a unit that focused on the history of events in Hué during the Tet Offensive of 1968 would achieve its goals of provoking reflection about the problematic nature of historical accounts. In this unit, which occupied the sixth and seventh weeks of the course,[6] students were given the project of sorting out conflicting claims about the nature and meaning of the "Hué Massacre," an incident which occurred during the North Vietnamese occupation of the city of Hué in February 1968. This incident, in which perhaps 3,000 South Vietnamese died, was interpreted by U.S. officials as a carefully planned bloodbath, while critics of U.S. policy saw the bloodbath account as a "myth," an attempt both to conceal the destructiveness of American retaliatory strikes and to score a propaganda victory against the enemy. By examining the students' journal entries for this unit, I hoped to discover the nature of their responses to this complex and challenging project. I was also curious to see whether there would be any indication that the Hué unit exerted an influence on students' post-course responses to the Ap Bac problem. I recognized, of course, that my "action research" methods would yield only quite tentative conclusions. Nonetheless, as a teacher I was eager to find out whether there would be any evidence, however tentative, that the Hué unit had influenced students' thinking about the problem of judging conflicting accounts of an event. The first step in the investigation, however, was to examine students' responses to the Battle of Ap Bac.

---

[6] Other units in the course also promoted reflection, but not specifically about the problem of conflicting accounts of the same event. For the first five weeks of the course, students read some of the oral histories in Al Santoli's collection *Everything We Had* (New York: Ballantine, 1981) and they read sections of memoirs by a Marine officer and an Army nurse: Philip Caputo's *A Rumor of War* (New York: Ballantine, 1977) and Lynda Van Devanter's *Home Before Morning* (New York: Warner, 1983). My goal was both to orient students to the nature of soldiers' experiences in the war, and also to encourage them to think more critically about how those experiences are represented. Following the Hué unit, students examined reporting on the war, reading Michael Herr's *Dispatches* (New York: Avon, 1978) as the key text. Next they read a novel, Tim O'Brien's complex tale *Going After Cacciato* (New York: Dell, 1975). For the final unit, "legacies," students read Ron Kovic's memoir, *Born on the Fourth of July* (New York: Pocket Books, 1976). In addition, students read a number of articles, viewed several films, and listened to relevant music. Throughout the course, students were encouraged to be more critical and thoughtful in their reading and writing, but most of the units were focused on issues of representation or moral judgment, rather than problems of conflicting accounts.

THE BATTLE OF AP BAC

During the first week of the course, students were asked to respond in writing to two divergent accounts of the Battle of Ap Bac, a clash between American-advised units of the Army of the Republic of Vietnam (ARVN) and the communist Viet Cong (VC).[7] I wrote the two accounts myself, basing them on actual reports and interpretations of the battle (see Appendix). In general, Account #1 attempts to put the South Vietnamese attack against a small VC unit in the best possible light, while Account #2 tries to portray the attack as poorly executed and unsuccessful. But neither account is superior in every respect, and both are vulnerable to criticism.

After reading the two accounts, students were asked to respond to three questions, printed on a single sheet of paper with room for them to write their responses:

> When historical accounts of the same event are different, can you believe one of the accounts more than another? Why?
> Is either of these two accounts more likely to be true? Please explain your answer.
> What *really* happened at Ap Bac? Why do you think so?

I hoped that these questions would elicit responses that revealed not only the students' overall conceptual orientations but also the specific strategies they used to evaluate two accounts that presented different facts and rendered different interpretations of the same event.

A total of 110 students (50 men and 60 women) responded to the Ap Bac problem during the first and last weeks of the course. (Although the students worked on the problem during the initial and final weeks, for convenience I will use the terms "pre-course" and "post-course" re-

---

[7] In constructing this problem, I drew on a research tradition in which dilemmas or controversial statements are used to elicit individuals' reasoning processes—for example, Kohlberg's well-known studies of moral reasoning. In particular, I was influenced by a task that D. Kuhn, N. Pennington, and B. Leadbeater devised for their research on "cognitive relativism" [see "Adult Thinking in Developmental Perspective." In P. Baltes and O. Brim (Eds.), *Life-Span Development and Behavior: Vol. 5* (pp. 157–95). New York: Academic Press, 1983]. In that task, individuals were asked to evaluate two accounts of a war between the fictional countries of North Livia and South Livia, each account supposedly written by the official historian of one of the two rival states. An interviewer asked a series of questions about the two accounts, and the subjects' statements were categorized according to their epistemological stance (e.g., realist, perspectivist, relativist). My task was similar in that I gave students two accounts of a battle and asked several questions about them, but the accounts I used were about a real battle—a battle from the war the students would be reading about in the course (although they did not study Ap Bac during the course).

sponses.) To analyze the students' responses, I decided to use a coding system consisting of four types of "conceptual orientation" and four kinds of "evaluative strategies." The students' responses were rated twice, once by a coder who was unfamiliar with the project, and once by me. Because the coder and I agreed only moderately well on our initial judgments (e.g., for ratings of conceptual orientation we were in exact agreement on 65% of our codings), I decided that the most accurate scores would result if we compared and discussed ratings, reaching a consensus on the best assessment of each student's response. We followed this procedure both for our assessment of conceptual orientation and for our rating of evaluative strategies.

Conceptual Orientation

The first rating task involved assessing the predominant "conceptual orientation" in a student's response to the Ap Bac problem. I devised a set of descriptive categories that seemed to account for most of the orientations the students adopted when they evaluated the two accounts of the battle: dogmatic, perspectivist, intuitive, and analytical. (Although these categories may seem similiar to the ones used in research on intellectual development, the categories in my study reflect students' approaches to alternative accounts of an event—they do not index students' overall level of thinking or stage of intellectual development.) The rating procedure involved making a global or holistic judgment about the predominant orientation in a student's response to the Ap Bac problem. Although students' responses often reflected more than one orientation, we tried to determine the central tendency in a response. In most cases, this tendency was clear; in a few responses, however, students adopted adjacent orientations nearly equally, and in these cases we assigned the response to a "mixed" category (e.g., perspectivist/intuitive). The scheme is described in more detail below. (I've placed in brackets the percentage of pre- and post-course responses that were assigned to each category.)

- (1.0) *Dogmatic Orientation:* The student approaches the problem as a search for one true authority, or for a true account against which to compare these versions of the event, or for a true ideology to use to decide which account is correct. [1%, 0]
- (1.5) *Mixed Dogmatic/Perspectivist Orientation.* [1%, 0]
- (2.0) *Perspectivist Orientation:* The student approaches the problem as a matter of opinion and personal perspective, so that both accounts will be true to the persons who wrote them, or so that all facts will be

Table 13.1.   Students' Responses to the Ap Bac Problem Categorized by Conceptual Orientation

	Percentage of Students' Responses	
Conceptual Orientation	Before Course	After Course
Dogmatic/Perspectivist[a]	20	06
Intuitive	66	71
Analytical[b]	14	23

[a]includes mixed perspectivist/intuitive responses.
[b]includes mixed intuitive/analytical responses.

plausible from a particular point of view, or so that both accounts will be consistent with the "facts" as held by particular individuals. [12%, 4%]

- (2.5) *Mixed Perspectivist/Intuitive Orientation.* [6%, 2%]
- (3.0) *Intuitive Orientation:* The student attempts to judge one account (or parts of an account) as better, but relies on intuitive, impressionistic, or quasianalytical methods: One account seems to be telling the truth or to be distorting things; one account seems more realistic, or more specific, or more factual; one account is consistent with the student's general impressions of the war. [66%, 71%]
- (3.5) *Mixed Intuitive/Analytical Orientation.* [4%, 10%]
- (4.0) *Analytical Orientation:* The student bases judgment on reflective analysis: Assessing the credibility of the sources in the accounts; evaluating the quality of the claims and facts presented; analyzing the extent to which specific facts or claims are consistent with knowledge gained from other sources. [10%, 13%]

As is clear from the percentages reported above, two-thirds or more of the responses clustered in the intuitive category, while some categories contained few responses. Because of this clustering, I have, for ease of presentation and discussion, combined some of the categories to form three groups: A group comprised of responses that contained any elements of dogmatism or perspectivism (categories 1 to 2.5), a group containing only the intuitive responses (category 3), and a group consisting of those responses that contained any elements of analytical thought (categories 3.5 and 4). The results, expressed as percentages of total pre- or postcourse responses, are depicted in Table 13.1. Grouped in this way, the results indicate that, from the beginning to the end of the course, there was a decrease in the frequency of dogmatic/perspectivist orientations, as well as a slight increase in the occurrence of intuitive and analytical approaches.[8]

Nevertheless, a majority of the students—two-thirds at the beginning of the course, an even larger percentage at the end—took an intuitive approach to the Ap Bac problem: they made judgments about the accounts but typically based their decisions on impressions, feelings, unreflective generalizations, or quasicritical reactions. (And slightly more than half the students who were rated as intuitive on their precourse responses received the same rating on their postcourse responses.) But these ratings of overall conceptual orientation, while they give an indication of the ways students approached the Ap Bac problem, do not reveal what procedures the students used to make judgments about the two versions of the battle. To find out more about these specific procedures, I examined the students' use of four "evaluative strategies."

Evaluative Strategies

Three of the evaluative strategies were procedures that a student might use to assess the two versions of the battle: Examining the trustworthiness of sources of information for the accounts, assessing the plausibility and/ or quality of claims and facts in the accounts, and judging the consistency of the accounts with prior knowledge of, or beliefs about, the war. The challenge of the Ap Bac problem comes from the fact that neither account is clearly superior. In fact, both are slanted toward a particular point of view. For example, in Account #1 the VC are referred to as the "battle-tested 514th Viet Cong battalion, about 500 soldiers, including specialists in anti-aircraft and anti-tank tactics"—the writer's obvious attempt to make the enemy appear strong in order to account for the difficulty of the battle and the ARVN's heavy casualties. In Account #2, by contrast, the enemy is "two companies of Viet Cong (about 240 soldiers) reinforced with about 50 local guerrillas"—a clear effort to portray the VC as relatively weak, so that their ability to repell the attack will seem heroic.

---

[8] To further explore this trend, I assigned scores to the responses on the basis of the rating they had received for conceptual orientation (e.g., assigning a score of 1 for a dogmatic orientation, 2 for a perspectivist orientation, 3.5 for a mixed intuitive/analytical response, etc.). Scores could thus range from 1 to 4. The mean score for precourse responses was 2.94 (SD = .55); the mean for postcourse responses was 3.12 (SD = .43). I performed a paired-observations t-test in order to compare the means for the pre- and postcourse responses. The difference between the means was statistically significant ($t = 3.01$, df = $109, p < .01$). However, the strength of the effect, as measured by eta squared, was .08, reflecting a relatively weak relationship between conceptual orientation and time of response to the problem (pre- or postcourse).

One approach to evaluating these accounts involves examining the sources on which they are based. Although both accounts cite apparently authoritative books about the war, Account #2 includes comments from an American commander who was on the scene, as well as assessments by French and Australian journalists, who may reasonably be expected to be less biased than American or Vietnamese commentators, especially from the military.[9] By contrast, Account #1 cites the optimistic judgments of American and South Vietnamese generals who were not themselves at the battle, as well as the assessment of an American military analyst. To complicate matters, however, Account #1, has a slightly more "objective" tone in much of its recounting of the battle, even though it ends with the obviously biased comments of Generals Harkins and Cao. Account #2 sounds almost like a communist propaganda broadcast in its rendering of the battle. Nevertheless, it ends with the quite credible statement from Lt. Colonel Vann and the assessments of two foreign journalists. Thus, in terms of credibility of sources, Account #2 seems superior.

In terms of plausibility of claims, however, Account #1 has an edge. To begin with, the numbers cited in Account #2 seem suspicious: According to this account, the VC unit, outnumbered 10 to 1 and armed with only light weapons, stopped 6 tanks and inflicted heavy casualties on the ARVN troops, while losing only a few men (3 left on the battlefield). In Account #1, on the other hand, the numbers of dead are roughly equal for the two sides (although the statistic for the VC is an estimate), and this seems plausible because the ARVN's superior numbers and firepower are counterbalanced by the VC's choice of position and superior fortifications.

However, whether sources are taken as credible or claims accepted as plausible depends, in part, on an individual's knowledge of the politics and tactics of the war. For example, if a student believes that the Viet Cong typically defeated larger and better armed units, then he or she will have a reason to accept Account #2, despite its biases and apparently exaggerated claims. Thus a third strategy involves assessing the consistency of an account with one's knowledge of the facts of the war.

In sum, the Ap Bac problem gave students an opportunity to display

---

[9] Students tended to refer to these sources as "neutral," a reasonable assessment, considering the constraints of the problem and how little information they had to go on. Bernard Fall was indeed a highly regarded journalist and respected Vietnam scholar, the author of a series of important books on the French and American military involvement in Indochina. Burchett, the Australian, is a self-proclaimed Communist, and hardly a neutral observer. Vann is a complex and intriguing figure, a man who is currently receiving a good deal of attention: see Neil Sheehan's biography of Vann, *A Bright Shining Lie: John Paul Vann and America in Vietnam* (New York: Random House, 1988); and also two articles by Mark Perry in *Veteran*, "The Resurrection of John Paul Vann" (July 1988) and "The Messiah of Ap Bac" (August 1988).

their evaluative strategies: To assess the accounts on the basis of their sources, their claims, and their congruence with students' beliefs about the war. In addition, the problem elicited another kind of response—a fourth "strategy"—in which students stated reasons for their skepticism about the possibility of judging discrepant accounts.

To code the evaluative strategies in a student's response, the raters considered each of the four strategies separately, looking through a student's response for all of the comments that reflected use of that strategy (for example, all comments about trustworthiness of sources were considered together). The raters then made a holistic judgment about the predominant conceptual orientation reflected in those comments, considered as a group (for example, if a student claimed that certain sources "seem to be telling the truth" while others "sound like they're lying," those comments would be taken to reveal an intuitive or impressionistic approach, so that the student's use of the strategy "trustworthiness of sources" would be coded as "intuitive").

Table 13.2 shows, for each evaluative strategy, the percentage of students whose statements reflect each of the four orientations. What this table depicts is the way in which students' statements were distributed across the various categories of strategy and orientation. In discussing these results, I focus on shifts in orientation from the beginning to the end of the course. And since a majority of students tended to use intuitive or analytical approaches, I will illustrate those orientations with examples.

Trustworthiness of sources. Almost equal numbers of students made statements about trustworthiness of sources at the beginning (55) and end (53) of the course. Table 13.2 shows how these statements were distributed across the four orientations. Only two responses (or 4%)—both from the initial task—included elements of a dogmatic orientation to sources (a statement of faith in an authoritative or partisan source), and relatively few students adopted a perspectivist orientation (claiming that since people inevitably see things differently, discrepant views can be equally true and trustworthy)—with a decrease in the percentage of perspectivist responses at the end of the course.

The majority of students who referred to trustworthiness of sources did so from an intuitive orientation, typically claiming that a source "seems" to be telling the truth or "sounds" more objective or "appears" biased, but without analyzing the evidence for the source's credibility. As one student wrote:

> Account #2 is more likely to be true, because the story sounds more objective. I think Account #1 was saving the reputations of the American military advisors.... The article as a whole gave me the impression that the author was trying to cover up a military blunder.

Table 13.2. Students' Use of Evaluative Strategies

	Evaluative Strategies							
	Trustworthiness of Sources		Plausibility/Quality of Claims and Facts		Consistency with Prior Knowledge		Skepticism about Judgment	
	Before Course ($n=55$)	After Course ($n=53$)	Before Course ($n=71$)	After Course ($n=56$)	Before Course ($n=32$)	After Course ($n=32$)	Before Course ($n=57$)	After Course ($n=61$)
Orientation	Percentage of Responses Assigned to Each Orientation							
Dogmatic	4	0	0	0	13	0	2	0
Perspectivist	15	9	3	0	0	0	33	13
Intuitive	65	76	89	84	78	75	56	75
Analytical	16	15	8	16	9	25	9	12

As is apparent in Table 13.2, there was a slightly higher percentage of intuitive responses at the end of the course than at the beginning. On the other hand, analytical responses occurred with nearly equal frequency before and after the course, though in both cases the frequency was low. In an analytical response, a student assesses the credibility of the sources by examining specific evidence of bias or trustworthiness, as the following excerpt illustrates.

> I think it is quite probable that the ARVN performed badly. What led me to believe this was the last paragraph of each account. General Harkins said that the battle for Ap Bac was a victory. True it was a victory—the ARVN eventually achieved their objective. But how would Harkins know about their performance? He wasn't even there. General Cao also said that it was a victory, but he is their commander. What is he supposed to say, that they screwed up? He wasn't there either. On the other hand, an American who was there (the senior advisor) and who would have no motive for saying that Ap Bac was a miserable performance except to tell the truth, said the ARVN performed badly. Plus, a neutral observer, French journalist Bernard Fall, said that it was a disaster. Another neutral, Australian war correspondent, Wilfred Burchett, said that it was a turning point and gave the Viet Cong a psychological advantage.

In sum, the results suggest that there was a slight shift in the students' orientation to the sources: a shift away from dogmatic and perspectivist orientations and toward somewhat more frequent use of intuitive approaches. Nevertheless, in both sets of responses, intuitive statements predominate. With minor variations, this pattern holds true for the next two evaluative strategies as well.

Plausibility and quality of claims and facts. Although more students mentioned plausibility/quality criteria in the precourse responses (71) than in the postcourse ones (56), in both sets of responses the students' statements clustered in the intuitive orientation. None of the students' statements were judged to be dogmatic in orientation, and only two statements (both precourse) were coded as perspectivist: based on the idea that all claims and facts are plausible to the person giving a particular account.

The intuitive statements reflect the view that an account that sounds more "realistic," seems less exaggerated, or appears to be more factual is more likely to be correct.

> Yes, sometimes you can tell just by the way things are explained whether they are true or whether they are blown out of proportion and sarcastic. Sometimes a person can tell which one may be true just because of some subconscious information that they may have on the subject. Account #1 seems more likely to be true.

Students who took an analytical approach to the claims and facts in the accounts went beyond the kind of general, impressionistic judgments represented in intuitive assessments, using rational criteria to evaluate the plausibility of specific facts and claims.

> I believe the first account because it seems to me more probable. The VC having advanced warning of 500 soldiers is more likely than the VC armed with only 4 machine guns and rifles against 3000 crack soldiers. Even more improbable was the casualty count. The VC only lost 3? . . . I think the first account is more believable, if only because of the statistics involved.

Consistency with belief or prior knowledge. In both pre- and postcourse responses, less than a third of the students (29%) considered whether information in the accounts was consistent with their beliefs about or knowledge of the war. It is rather striking, however, that 13 percent of the responses to the initial exercise were judged to be dogmatic, whereas no responses from the end of the course were assigned to that orientation. The dogmatic responses tended to assert that an account was believable if it was consistent with the student's political ideology or supported what the student considered to be "our side" in the conflict. None of the students' responses reflected a perspectivist orientation to claims and facts. But once again the majority of the students' responses, both pre- and postcourse, were identified as intuitive: They asserted that an account was better if it conformed with their general impressions of the war.

> I think Account #2 is [true] because I know and have read about the ARVN and they were one of the worst armies ever. They refused to fight most often, and when they did they usually lost. I'm just using outside knowledge to help me decide.

Analytical responses, by contrast, drew on more specific knowledge to examine the validity of statements in the two accounts.

> Sometimes you can favor one more than the other . . . if one story runs true or contrary to things you already know. I favor account 2 but only slightly. . . . One big question is whether or not the VC were well armed. Things I have read have led me to believe that the VC weren't well armed especially in the beginning, that is one reason I favor #2.

As Table 13.2 illustrates, by the end of the course a larger percentage of the students who considered uses of prior knowledge were doing so from an analytical orientation. That certainly makes sense: The students learned a good deal about the war from their reading for the course, so that at the end of the semester they had more specific knowledge to bring to bear on the details in the two accounts.

The trend that emerges for these three strategies is a pattern of small but consistent decreases in dogmatic and perspectivist approaches, some increases in the percentage of analytical approaches (especially for consistency with knowledge), and relative stability in the most prevalent approach—the intuitive. These results suggest that, regardless of whether they were analyzing sources, claims, or prior knowledge, and regardless of whether they were responding at the beginning or end of the course, these students tended to rely on intuitive methods of evaluation.

Skepticism and judgment. While many students were willing to assess the validity of the two accounts of Ap Bac, more than half expressed reservations, sometimes quite strong ones, about the possibility of judging conflicting accounts of a past event (57 students made such statements in precourse responses, while 61 did so at the end of the course). Most of these students voiced their reservations in response to the first question about the accounts: "When historical accounts of the same event are different, can you believe one of the accounts more than another?" Students who answered "no" to this question were judged to be expressing skepticism about the possibility of rendering a rational assessment of the two accounts. (There were also a few cases in which a skeptical attitude emerged later in a student's response.)

The skeptical responses were particularly interesting, in part because they represented a more pessimistic attitude than was apparent from the students' positive judgments about the accounts. Although many of the students who initially expressed skepticism responded to subsequent questions by choosing an account that they thought was more likely to be true (and justifying that choice on the basis of better sources, more plausible claims, or greater consistency with prior knowledge), a note of skepticism often remained, sometimes accompanied by a hint that the student felt compelled to choose an account. As one student wrote, "if I was forced at gunpoint to pick, I would choose the second."

Another intriguing aspect of the skeptical responses is apparent from the data in Table 13.2: There is a fairly strong decrease in the percentage of perspectivist responses—along with increases in the intuitive and analytical responses—from the beginning to the end of the course. At the beginning of the course, a third of the students who took a skeptical approach did so from a perspectivist orientation, asserting that there is no basis for saying that one account is more believable or more truthful than the other, since different accounts are equally legitimate.

> When historical accounts of the same event are different, I do not think you can believe one of the accounts more than another. Two men witnessed the

same occurance but their positions on the field and point of view were different. Both are telling the truth as seen through their eyes.

By the end of the course, there were many fewer of these kinds of statements, while three-quarters of the skeptical comments expressed reservations about whether one could really tell which account is better. For example, a number of students felt that the pervasive bias in both accounts made it impossible to get a clear sense of which was more plausible. Others acknowledged that—lacking personal knowledge of the event—their intuitions or impressions gave them an insufficient basis for saying what happened at Ap Bac. But while they recognized the limits of intuitive approaches, these students saw no alternatives for evaluation or critical judgment. Hence they expressed uncertainty and skepticism about judging one account as better than the other.

> I think it is almost impossible to tell which is more likely to be true because you have no idea what is going on, so it is very hard to judge. Each side will have its own story and will not budge on the facts. So I believe it is almost impossible to believe totally one story. I honestly cannot say what happened at Ap Bac. There are two different stories, so who am I to judge what did or did not happen. I wasn't there. I don't know the background. This is not just a cop out because I don't want to write anything or think. I honestly don't know and I honestly cannot say.

The responses that were coded as analytical went a step further, either in the sophistication with which the limitations of judgment were explored or in the recognition that, while such limitations might preclude certainty in judgment, they do not necessarily prevent an assessment of probability. The following example illustrates the first type of response.

> No, I do not believe one or the other more. I could never infer what happened because one story sounds more possible than the other. (There are impossible sounding stories that really did happen.) ... To be honest, I don't know how to answer this. I could use facts from both or look it up in a history book, but who would know if that is more factual than what was written in the [course] packet.

What the data in Table 13.2 suggest, I believe, is that there was a tendency for the students to become more sophisticated skeptics by the end of the course. A larger percentage of the final responses reflect not just a reluctance to judge conflicting accounts because each represents a different person's view, but a more thoughtful skepticism about the efficacy of judgment, a skepticism based on distrust of sources, or on a sense of inadequacy about judging discrepant views and competing claims, or on a tentativeness about the validity and relevance of one's knowledge. Is it likely that the course contributed to this skeptical attitude?

Given the nature of this study, it is impossible to be sure. A growing sense of skepticism, relativism, and even cynicism is probably part of many students' first year of college. On the other hand, certain features of the course were designed to promote reflective, interrogative, and analytical attitudes. While every unit in the course called for some kind of reflective analysis, the two-week unit on the Hué Massacre was specifically designed to stimulate analytical thinking about historical accounts. Did it have any effect on the way students responded to multiple accounts? While I have no proof, I do have some quite suggestive evidence from the students' own analyses of their pre- and postcourse responses to the Ap Bac problem.

Self-Analysis of Ap Bac Responses

During the final week of the course, I gave the students both of their responses to the Ap Bac problem—the one they had completed at the beginning of the course, as well as the one from the end—along with a worksheet on which they were to analyze their responses, summing up the similarities and differences that they saw in their own answers. Then I asked them to respond to the following question:

> Did anything in the course have an influence on how you now look at accounts of historical events?

Five students did not answer the question. Two said that nothing in the course influenced their views. But the rest of the students all indicated that the course had, indeed, made an impact on their thinking about historical accounts. The majority of these responses fell into two categories. The first—which accounts for approximately 30 percent of the responses—consisted of general statements about how the students had become more analytical, more critical, or more skeptical about historical accounts.

> Yes, this course changed the way I looked at historical accounts a lot! I used to think that if it was from some fairly reputable source (especially in print) it was true. (The old saying "You can't always believe everything you read" was aimed directly at me.) I learned that there are almost always, at least, two sides to all stories and you have to look carefully at the sources.

But in a second group of responses, nearly half of the students (48%) attributed a shift in their views to a particular unit in the course: the unit in which they studied multiple accounts of the Hué Massacre. The following statements are quite representative:

> The unit on the Hué massacre.... Now I tend to look at accounts of historical events with a skeptical eye. I can't seem to believe half of what I read anymore.

> I think that when we studied about Hué ... I learned to be more curious and suspicious about historical accounts. I was forced to question the authenticity of a writer. Before I believed anything that was written. Now I'm more cautious.

To understand how the Hué material could have had such an impact on students' thinking, we need to examine that unit—and students' responses to it—more closely.

UNIT ON THE HUÉ MASSACRE

The first assignment for the unit was to read two quite different interpretations of what happened at Hué during the 1968 Tet Offensive, when the Vietnamese communists occupied the city for nearly a month. According to one view, communist forces systematically massacred many South Vietnamese civilians because they were politically suspect. But according to a second view, official reports of a massacre were actually an elaborate myth concocted to conceal the fact that many of the dead and missing civilians could be attributed to the ruthlessness of the U.S. counterattack against Hue.[10] The point of presenting these opposing views was, of course, to provoke the students into thinking about the nature of historical accounts. The students kept journals throughout the course, and their entries during this unit illustrate the ways in which the material had an impact on their thinking. Some students were confused:

> In reading the assignment for today I found myself very confused.... By the time I was done with those articles I don't have any idea what to believe.

Other students, however, began asking serious and vexing questions:

> The papers ... raise some important questions. First and foremost, why do they completely disagree about what happened at Hué? It almost seems as

---

[10] The first view was presented in Stephen T. Hosmer's book, *Viet Cong Repression and Its Implications for the Future* (Lexington, MA: Heath, 1970). For the second view, students read part of a monograph by Noam Chomsky and Edward S. Herman, *Counter-Revolutionary Violence: Bloodbaths in Fact and Propaganda* (Andover, MA: Warner Publications, 1973).

if they were about two different events! ... Both seem to be supported by "true" evidence, but which is right or more truthful?

After the two introductory readings, students read 13 more articles or book chapters, including short articles from the popular press, longer accounts by journalists or commentators, and additional critiques of the standard version of the massacre. Taken altogether, this material presented students with a more complex version of the Ap Bac problem: conflicting accounts of the nature and meaning of an historical event. Their assignment was to analyze this material and write a paper in which they presented the best case they could for what really happened in Hué during Tet 1968. Thus students confronted—many of them for the first time, apparently—a genuine problem of historical interpretation and judgment.

As teachers, my graduate-student assistants and I saw our role as one of provoking and encouraging critical reflection. Although we talked about evaluative strategies in an informal way, most of our energies throughout this unit were directed toward engaging students in the struggle to decide what to believe about the Hué Massacre. Because we wanted students to wrestle with discrepant interpretations of events in Hué, we were careful not to endorse one viewpoint. Instead, we supported our students' efforts—both individually (in their journals) and collectively (in group discussions)—to articulate alternative positions, to determine which claims supported which interpretations, and to subject all sources, claims, and facts to critical scrutiny.

Evidence From Journal Entries

The students' journal entries provide examples of how they struggled with the material on the Hué Massacre. For some students, the discrepant accounts provoked anxiety, alarm, and near panic.

> Well, I'm about to have a heart attack! You guys scare me to death sometimes! I just read the articles on Hué (at least the first few) and I can't believe how contradictory they are. ... I don't know really know how to approach these articles. I mean, I wasn't there, I really don't have any idea what truly happened, yet how will I EVER know? I won't! I may get a basic idea, but I'm never really going to know for sure. It's going to be really hard to convince someone that I know what's going on when I don't. How am I going to know what to believe??

Other students recorded efforts to base judgments on an examination of the accounts, often by considering the sources of information for various accounts of the massacre.

Can one really believe what he reads in his history book? This is an account from one person. Who is this person? What are his credentials? Was he there? If so, did he see what happened or did he talk to people? If not where did he get his facts from and are they able sources? I never thought about pondering questions like that when reading my history book but the readings from the Hué Massacre have opened my eyes a bit.

Although most students were willing to critique the sources for their biases, limitations, or lack of objectivity, in many cases their strategies for making a judgment on the basis of fallible and contested sources were "intuitive," based more on impressionistic judgment—or even emotional response—than on rational evaluation. As one student put it, "The tendency, from my point of view, is to sympathize more, and therefore believe more, the emotional and depressing accounts." Nevertheless, a number of students saw the possibility for reaching a rationally warranted conclusion, despite lingering doubts about sources and facts.

I would like to form an opinion of what I think happened at Hué. I believe that in the beginning the communists did have a few people executed such as members of the Hué secret police, soldiers, Americans, and foreigners having anything to do with the South Vietnamese military. As time went on, the VC committed individual acts of execution without orders. . . . It is quite possible that the South Vietnamese officials tripled or even quadrupled the number of bodies found in the communist dug mass graves. It is likely that the US gov't knew these numbers were false but used them anyhow for their own purposes. What about the rest of the bodies? I would surmise that most of those were civilians who were killed in the allied retaking of Hué.

The student's consistent use of qualifying phrases ("I believe," "it is quite possible," "it is likely," "I would surmise") suggests that he is writing his way toward a qualified judgment, a reflective, provisional conclusion.

While such journal entries illustrate the ways in which students responded to the Hué unit and suggest the impact it had on their thinking, the question remains whether the Hué material influenced students' post-course responses to the Ap Bac problem. Because my study was not designed to determine whether a certain intervention caused a particular result, I cannot answer that question definitively. However, I want to present some reasons to believe that, in a number of cases, the Hué unit did have an influence on students' subsequent thinking, and that the unit was implicated in—if not solely responsible for—some of the shifts in students' approaches to the Ap Bac problem.

As I pointed out in an earlier section, the most intriguing change from pre- to postcourse responses to the Ap Bac task involved students' skeptical comments: a notable decrease in comments about being unable to judge equally valid perspectives, and an increase in statements that revealed skepticism about the efficacy of intuitive or analytical judgments. While this skeptical attitude often prevented students from analyzing and evaluating the two accounts, it nonetheless led many of them to another kind of critical reflection: an assessment of judgment itself. Although several units probably contributed to increased skepticism, the Hué unit was the only one specifically designed to encourage a more sophisticated, critical attitude toward the process of assessing multiple accounts, an attitude involving distrust of sources, suspicion of claims, and uncertainty about whether one could know "the truth."

Moreover, at the end of the course many of the students claimed that the Hué unit had influenced their thinking about the Ap Bac accounts, and in particular that the unit had made them more analytical or skeptical about what they read. Although students might be unreliable judges of such influences, their claims have a certain amount of face validity. It certainly seems plausible that a unit in which students struggled with different interpretations of a historical event would have an impact on their subsequent thinking about Ap Bac, a problem that also posed the problem of rival accounts of the same battle. And while examples do not prove the point, I saw a number of cases in which the kind of reflective skepticism that emerged in a student's final Ap Bac response appeared to be related to discoveries the student had made during the Hué unit, as these discoveries were reported in the student's journal. I want to consider one example in some detail, the case of a student (Donna) whose journal entries offer at least a partial explanation of the change in her responses to the Ap Bac accounts, a shift from a perspectivist orientation at the beginning of the semester to an intuitive, quasianalytical approach by the end of the course.

A Case of Conceptual Reorientation

Donna's first Ap Bac response reflects the orientation that I have called "perspectivism"—the view that different people will inevitably perceive and portray an event differently, but that all accounts of that event are equally true.

When historical accounts of the same event are different, can you believe one of the accounts more than another?

> No, because writers have bias and see an event differently. It is up to the reader to investigate a topic and find many different opinions before he forms his own.

Is either of these two accounts more likely to be true?
No. Both accounts have some fact and some personal feeling in the articles. Which makes both of them true.

What really happened at Ap Bac?
The Ap Bac battle can be seen in three different ways, the ARVN's won, the VC's won, or a draw. Reading both accounts it seems to be a draw.... [Noncontroversial details of the battle]

Although Donna says that a reader must "investigate" in order to form "his own" opinion, she does not seem to have a clear sense that readers can exercise critical analysis. When asked to make her own judgment about what "really happened," Donna decides that the battle was "a draw," the conclusion that is most consistent with her claim that both accounts are "true."

In the Hué unit, Donna was put in a situation in which she had to make and defend a judgment about a complex and contested historical event. To do so, she had to confront the possibility that some views are better than others, and she had to consider whether there might be ways of deciding which claims are most likely to be true. Her journal entries during the Hué unit reveal her initial confusion and anxiety, followed by her effort to try out various analytical and critical strategies, and at last her struggle to reach a conclusion about what really happened at Hué. What we see in these excerpts, I believe, is a student's nonjudgmental perspectivism beginning to give way to a more analytical approach to historical accounts.

October 8: In the history unit, how can I tell who is right and who is making up a story, when in both sides they have sources to back them? Now that I've read two articles on Hué, I am very confused.... I still don't know what to believe or if I will be unbiased. Right now I tend to believe the second article just because it has more detail and less numbers.... I hope I form an opinion that I can back up with facts but I have a feeling I'll be in the middle and agree with a little of this and a little of that.

Donna feels a good deal of anxiety about the assignment for this unit, probably because it asks her to make a judgment about what really happened, and she fears that she will see truth in several views, steering a middle course between accounts (precisely as she did in her response to Ap Bac) and thus failing to complete the assignment. Apparently, her principal strategy for assessing the two accounts is intuitive, based on her impression that one account has "more detail and less numbers."

In the next entry, made two days later, we see Donna undertaking a more sustained evaluation of specific sources.

October 10: Jones ... had some strong evidence that the massacre did happen, but he doesn't always back it up. For example he states that blacklists were distributed into "target" areas but doesn't say where he found the information. In other articles I've read and in class we've talked about the blacklist, plus there have been sources to back up the information, so I guess that part of the [story] about Hué is true.... The stories seem to be similar so part of me wants to believe what Jones and Oberdorfer and other pro-massacre authors say.... But this story and others are from hear-say, but how true is hear-say? Everyone sees and hears things a little different. Plus people want their story to be the one told so they could alter the facts to make it more exciting.

Urged on by the assignment (and undoubtedly her discussion leader) to compare and assess various claims, Donna tackles the central question of whether there were blacklists of victims. She finds "strong evidence" in one article, as well as corroborating evidence in other sources. Therefore, she decides to accept the claim that the communists had blacklists ("I guess that ... is true"). While this decision is partly analytical (based on her examination of sources and evidence), it also seems to be partly intuitive (based on her sense that, because certain stories "seem to be similar," part of her "wants to believe" them).

By the end of the excerpt, Donna reveals her unhappiness with her decision. She is torn between affirming the conclusion that, in her view, is supported by most of the evidence and rejecting that conclusion because she is still skeptical about the reports on which it is based (they are "hear-say"). Moreover, Donna is still troubled by the notion that people see things differently and that their personal biases influence their accounts. Given these difficulties, how can she say that one version of events is "true"? In the next entry, we see this skepticism deepen, as she discovers that official reports might have been systematically distorted for political purposes.

October 13: I was shocked to read that the U.S. multiplied the number of bodies found in the graves seven times in order to make the U.S. people feel for Vietnam and it gave Nixon a reason to leave the troops in the country.... Thus, if these facts are true, our government who is to tell its people the whole truth is lying to us.... Were the documents the US claimed to be real changed? How can you prove it one way or another? The communists aren't going to help the US [figure out the truth]. Who can you trust and what is right?

The questions at the end of this journal entry reveal that Donna has gone beyond the simple perspectivism of her early Ap Bac response. At this point she is confronting difficult issues of knowledge and belief, and while she has tried to find a basis on which to analyze claims and arrive at a conclusion about the Hué incident, she is still confused and uncertain. Her final entry—after she had written her paper on Hué—reflects her distress over this uncertainly.

> October 17: I'M STILL UNSURE! I don't know what to believe about Hué, everyone seems to be right and everyone seems to be wrong. I wrote my paper on Hué believing there was a massacre but I just don't know.... I know in every situation there are two sides and it is up to the person to choose a side, so based on what I've read and how I feel, I think (but still a little unsure) there was a massacre.

Donna has succeeded in examining certain claims (concerning the blacklists), and she has worked her way to a conclusion that she can present in her paper. And yet, while she has practiced some of the tactics of analytical thinking, Donna has not discovered an easy path to rational inquiry. On the contrary, the Hué material has upset her comfortable perspectivism, replacing it with a more distressing kind of uncertainly and skepticism: a distrust of sources and an awareness of the difficulty of evaluating discrepant claims.

At the end of the course, Donna again responded to the Ap Bac problem. Her answers to the standard questions are quite different from her precourse responses. Most importantly, she no longer thinks that both accounts are "true" or that it is impossible to assess the accounts for their credibility.

When historical accounts of the same events are different, can you believe one of the accounts more than another?
> Yes, because it is easier to believe an account if there are a lot of details and well known people are documented. Also, if you know more about a topic, more than from just one author, it is easier to form an opinion.

Is either of these accounts more likely to be true?
> Both accounts have some very believable facts. In the first case it said that the U.S. won. This can be believed because in our readings it said that when the U.S. fought a battle, knowing where the enemy is, they win. In the second story there is more detail, which makes the reader lean toward this version. The first story uses some vague language such as "light" or "some," which implied that the U.S. was doing well, and like from our reading we have seen how the officials use vague language. Account 2 is more straightforward. Anyway, both accounts are lacking all of the information and are biased.

What really happened at Ap Bac?

> I believe that there was a battle and that the ARVN did take Ap Bac. I think when the second account claims there were many losses for the ARVN, that this is true because the first account said that there were "light" losses. The word "light" when used by the Army can mean a few or a lot wounded, it just depends on how the government wants the war to look to the American people. Both articles state that the V.C. were well prepared, so I guess that is believable if two sources state it. From doing other reading about the ARVN, I believe that they fought poorly. In other readings the ARVN would run off and leave the U.S. soldiers to fight.

Donna's response reflects the kind of partly intuitive, partly analytical thinking that had begun to emerge in her journal entries on the Hué Massacre. For example, she shows that she has developed a feel for some of the tactics of interrogating and assessing historical accounts (how much detail is provided, how reputable the sources are, and how consistent a particular account is with other accounts or with one's general knowledge of the event)—although she needs to refine these evaluative strategies. As in her Hué paper, Donna has difficulty coming to a confident conclusion about what really happened at Ap Bac, but this reluctance seems to reflect her awareness of the difficulty of making judgments on the basis of limited information. As she says in the self-assessment of her Ap Bac responses, "you can believe one account of a historical event if there are a lot of details and if you know a lot about a topic. But on this subject I can't believe one or the other because I don't know enough about this battle."

Moreover, Donna shows that she is aware of the limitations of sources, both because they "lack all of the information and are biased" and because of political manipulation ("it depends on how the government wants the war to look")—the same kinds of skepticism about sources that she expressed in her journal during the Hué unit. I'm sure that there were multiple and complex influences on Donna's thinking about judging discrepant accounts. But the Hué unit seems to have been the most salient influence. I examined all of Donna's journal entries quite carefully (41 pages, 29 entries, from September 3 to December 9), and in none of them—apart from the entries during the Hué unit—does she grapple with the issue of how to decide what to believe. In addition, Donna herself suggests that the Hué unit was a significant influence on her thinking. When asked to reflect on the lessons she had learned in the course, Donna wrote:

> Prior to this course, I believed everything the history books said, but now I feel publishers and the historians can be biased by telling only one side of an event. Reading about Hué forced me to ask a lot of questions.

I do not want to imply that Donna's shift from a perspectivist orientation was "typical": On the contrary, my analyses indicate that most of the students began the course using intuitive strategies, and that about half of them approached the Ap Bac problem from that same orientation at the end of the course. But even when the analyses indicate that a student's conceptual orientation was not transformed, quite often there are other indications—more difficult to quantify—that growth has occurred:[11] perhaps the student's journal entries suggest a deepening of reflection; or the student exclaims, in her self-analysis, that she has discovered what it really means to be a critical reader; or a student's post-course response to Ap Bac reveals a more thoughtful skepticism about his ability to say what really happened at a long-ago battle in a faraway place.

SUMMARY AND CONCLUSION

My aims in this project were straightforward: I wanted to know how a group of college freshmen would handle the problem of conflicting accounts of the same event, and I wanted to find out whether the orientations and strategies they used to respond to that problem would change over a semester—and if they did, what role a particular unit in the course played in that change.

When I examined their orientations at the beginning of the course, I discovered that the freshmen in my class were neither rigid dogmatists

---

[11] In several cases, students expressed surprise that their postcourse responses were so similar to their precourse answers, as in the following journal entry.

> I just compared my responses to the problems you gave us at the beginning of the year. Wow! I cannot believe how similar my solutions were. I mean, they were almost identical. "Well," I thought to my astonished, confused self, "I just went full circle!" I wondered why I didn't resolve the problems differently, how come my original ideas hadn't changed . . .? Well, as I tried to justify and justify, I realized that the fact that I had gone in a full circle wasn't bad at all, in fact it was so cool. I started this course with your basic academic inspiration "Ugh, let me just make it through." Quickly, however, I got interested (despite my resistance). I wanted to learn all about Vietnam and the people involved. . . . So, I learned and read and absorbed all the different facts about the war and came up with the same conclusions, Except, this time I had all that information to back me up. I am not, anymore, just some overly-ambitious, want-to-be-liberal that really has no basis for her position. I am an eighteen-year-old college kid that knows a hell of a lot about the Vietnam War and I am so proud and confident of my opinions about it. This sounds cocky as hell, but I think this course inspired me in a lot of ways. I want to feel that way about other parts of my life. I want to know EVERYTHING!!!

Such comments force me to question how well comparisons of pre- and post-course responses reflect changes in students' thinking.

nor naive perspectivists, at least not according to their responses to the Ap Bac problem. That will surprise those who have assumed that freshmen are so fundamentally mired in dogmatism or simple relativism that they cannot—or will not—think analytically.[12] While it is true that few of them were able to assess the accounts from a fully analytical stance, many of the students nevertheless made judgments about which sources seemed most reliable, which account appeared to be most realistic, or which version seemed most consistent with their impressions of what the war was like.

When I compared students' postcourse responses to the Ap Bac problem with their precourse responses, I found decreases in the percentage of dogmatic and perspectivist orientations and increases in intuitive and analytical approaches—although modifications of orientation and evaluative strategy tended to be small and subtle, rather than large and dramatic. I also found a somewhat stronger decrease in perspectivistic skepticism (a reluctance to assess views because they are all equally legitimate) and an increase in the percentage of intuitive skepticism (a reluctance to assess views because they are all too incomplete or biased to provide a sufficient basis even for impressionistic judgment).

Moreover, I found additional evidence, in other materials, that students had altered their thinking about historical accounts. In their self-analyses, more than three-quarters of the students claimed that the course in general, or the Hué unit in particular, had made them more reflective and skeptical about the things they read. Further evidence came from journal entries, where a number of students revealed an increasing propensity for analytical, interrogative, and critical thinking. Thus, while I would not want to claim that the course transformed students' intellectual abilities or reshaped their habits of mind, I believe there is ample evidence that the course accomplished its goal of promoting critical reflection about conflicting accounts of a historical event.

Finally, I have some ideas about what projects and teaching practices were successful in promoting reflective thinking. As I have said before, the unit on the Hué Massacre stimulated a good deal of reflection and analysis, judging from students' journal entries. Faced with discrepant accounts and conflicting opinions, the students had to pursue a line of inquiry into the claims and facts of the massacre, assessing the cogency and credibility of quite different explanations of events in Hué.

---

[12] For example, in "The Perry Scheme and the Teaching of Writing," *Rhetoric Review* 4 (January 1986), Christopher Burnham claims that "The Perry Scheme, by describing the characteristics of freshmen and sophomores ... gives us insights into why our students behave, think, and write the way they do. The majority are functioning in the dualistic stage and most of the rest are in the multiplistic stage" (p. 156).

During the two-week unit on the massacre, students had several kinds of opportunities to scrutinize and assess the numerous claims about—and interpretations of—the incident. For example, they had opportunities to talk about the massacre with other students, both informally and in meetings of their discussion sections, where they were encouraged to voice their opinions and raise questions about the Hué materials. Students also responded to the massacre by writing in their journals. This exploratory writing helped them articulate and examine their reactions and emerging insights, and because the instructors commented on the journal entries, students received a response to their ideas while they were still being formulated.

In sum, the key factors in the Hué unit seem to have been a significant and engaging problem, a forum for discussion with peers, an opportunity to react to the readings by writing in a journal, and an assignment that asked students to make and defend a reasonable judgment. Exactly how these factors worked—individually and together—is, quite clearly, a matter beyond the scope of my study. My observations suggest that all of them were important, though in different ways for different students.

From one point of view, it would be accurate to say that I did not really attempt to teach my students to be reflective thinkers, if by "teach" one means systematic training in the structures and strategies of critical thinking.[13] Instead, I tried to elicit reflection by giving students a project that challenged them to use their best evaluative strategies. And I worked hard at supporting their efforts to question sources, scrutinize claims, and evaluate evidence, while also accepting their doubts, their tentativeness, their humility in the face of complexity. If I succeeded in teaching English for reflective thinking, the reason, I suspect, is rather simple: I gave students opportunities to think reflectively, and I took their reflections seriously.

---

[13] There are a number of programs for teaching the skills of critical thinking, many of them involving instruction in elements of formal or informal logic (i.e., studying fallacies). For a review and critique of such programs see John McPeck, *Critical Thinking and Education* (New York: St. Martin's, 1981). For a review of research on the efficacy of teaching critical thinking skills see James H. McMillan, "Enhancing College Students' Critical Thinking: A Review of Studies," *Research in Higher Education* 26 (1987): 3–29. In general, I am most sympathetic to proposals that take a developmental approach to instruction in thinking, for example Janet Schmidt and Mark Davison, "Helping Students Think," *Personnel and Guidance Journal* 61 (1977): 563–69. However, my approach in this course followed Dewey's principles for how to teach reflective thinking. In Dewey's view, the teacher's major task is to arrange conditions that call for active thinking, creating contexts that allow students to exercise and thereby extend their reflective powers. As Deanna Kuhn succinctly summarizes this view, "the only effective way to teach people to think is to engage them in thinking" (p. 502). Although Kuhn acknowledges that this view has been powerful and pervasive, she finds "virtually no empirical research literature that pertains to it" (p. 503). See "Education for Thinking," *Teachers College Record* 87 (1986): 495–512.

REFERENCES

Cohen, L., & Manion, L. (1980). *Research methods in education.* London: Croom Helm.

Dewey, J. (1986). *How we think. The later works of John Dewey, 1925–53* (Vol. 8). Carbondale, IL: Southern Illinois University Press. (Original work published 1933.)

Kitchener, K. S. (1983). Educational goals and reflective thinking. *The Educational Forum, 48,* 75–95.

Kitchener, K. S. (1986). The reflective judgment model: Characteristics, evidence and measurement. In R. A. Mines & K. S. Kitchener (Eds.), *Adult cognitive development: Methods and models* (pp. 76–91). New York: Praeger.

Perry, W. G. (1970). *Forms of intellectual and ethical development in the college years.* New York: Holt, Rinehart and Winston.

Perry, W. G. (1981). Cognitive and ethical growth: The making of meaning. In A. Chickering (Ed.), *The modern American college* (pp. 76–116). San Francisco: Jossey-Bass.

APPENDIX: THE BATTLE OF AP BAC

In the early years of the Vietnam War most of the fighting in South Vietnam consisted of skirmishes between two factions. One faction was the Army of the Republic of Vietnam (the ARVN). The ARVN forces were loyal to the South Vietnamese government. The other faction was the Viet Cong (or VC), a guerrilla army opposed to the established government.

One of the first major battles between ARVN and VC forces occurred on January 2, 1963, when South Vietnamese intelligence reported a VC radio station operating near the village of Ap Bac. A larger number of ARVN troops, with American military advisors, converged on the village in an effort to engage the smaller VC force that was supposed to be guarding the station.

However, accounts of what happened at Ap Bac—and what these events meant—differ. On the following pages you will find two historical accounts of the ARVN operation at AP Bac, both based on documented reports from participants, observers, and military analysts.

ACCOUNT #1

At the battle of Ap Bac, the ARVN 7th Infantry Division went after the battle-tested 514th Viet Cong battalion, about 500 soldiers, including specialists in anti-aircraft and anti-tank tactics.[1] Although the ARVN had a well-conceived plan of attack, they had received poor intelligence information and therefore misjudged the size and location of the VC force. The VC, on the other hand, had learned the details of the coming attack from their spies.[2] With this advanced warning, the VC were able to pick the ground they wanted to fight on: They were dug into positions along a canal and tree line, giving them excellent protection and concealment, as well as a murderous line of fire on anything that tried to cross the open rice fields in front of them.

The ARVN engaged the VC unit, but the attack against the well-fortified VC quickly bogged down. The ARVN lost some helicopters and light tanks, and were unable to advance to the VC fortifications before nightfall. But that night, under the cover of darkness, the VC fled from their positions. The next morning the ARVN forces took control of Ap Bac.

The VC lost perhaps 50 or more killed and an unknown number of wounded; ARVN casualities were about 60 killed and 100 wounded.[3] Thus, in terms of casualities, some military analysts (such as Colonel D. R. Palmer) felt the battle had been "a draw."[4] Nevertheless, the ARVN achieved their objective at Ap Bac: they forced the VC to retreat from the village. Thus the American high command viewed the battle as an ARVN triumph, and a sign that the South Vietnamese army could accomplish its missions. General Paul Harkins, head of the U.S. military command in South Vietnam, called Ap Bac a "victory" for the ARVN.[5] And the ARVN Corps Commander, General Cao, announced that the battle was "a victory that laid the foundation for our success. . . . Ap Bac is a symbol of the South Vietnamese people's will to resist."[6]

---

[1] Dave Richard Palmer, *Summons of the Trumpet: A History of the Vietnam War from a Military Man's Viewpoint* (New York: Ballantine Books, 1978), p. 44.

[2] Kuno Knoebl, *Victor Charlie* (New York: Praeger, 1967), p. 84.

[3] Palmer, p. 50.

[4] Palmer, p. 50.

[5] David Halberstam, *The Making of a Quagmire* (New York: Random House, 1965), p. 156; Knoebl, p. 91.

[6] Quoted in Knoebl, p. 81.

ACCOUNT #2

At the battle of Ap Bac, a vastly superior ARVN force of over 3000 soldiers, most of them from the crack 7th Infantry Division, went after two companies of Viet Cong (about 240 soldiers) reinforced with about 50 local guerrillas.[1] Even with this 10 to 1 advantage, with American advisors, and with vastly superior firepower (including bombers, artillery, helicopters, and armored vehicles), the ARVN were unable to over-run the VC unit, which was armed with only 4 machine guns, some automatic rifles, and carbines.

The ARVN attacked at dawn, but the assault went badly. As soon as they took casualties, the ARVN troops panicked and refused to advance. When 10 helicopters tried to land more soldiers, 5 of the aircraft were destroyed and 4 others damaged by VC machine-gun fire. And when the ARVN armored vehicles attempted to advance, a VC squad of 15 men destroyed 4 of the tanks and damaged 2 others, stopping the assault.[2] After a full day of fighting, the VC were still secure in their positions, having taken very few casualties. Under the cover of darkness, the VC unit escaped from the ARVN "trap."

ARVN losses were heavy (61 killed and about 100 wounded) compared to VC losses (3 bodies left on the battlefield and losses estimated at no more than 12).[3] It seems clear that the ARVN had performed badly in the fight. Even the senior U.S. Army advisor to the ARVN division, Lt. Colonel John P. Vann, called the ARVN attack on Ap Bac "a miserable damn performance."[4] French journalist Bernard Fall called the battle "disastrous," a "humiliating defeat" for the ARVN.[5] For the VC, on the other hand, this first major battle provided a new confidence that their small guerrilla units could repulse much larger forces armed with superior weapons. Thus Australian war correspondent Wilfred Burchett proclaimed the battle a "turning point" in the war,[6] since it gave the VC a psychological advantage and won new recruits to its cause.

---

[1] Wilfred G. Burchett, *Vietnam: Inside Story of the Guerilla War* (New York: International Publishers, 1965), p. 88; Kuno Knoebl, *Victor Charlie* (New York: Praeger, 1967), p. 84.

[2] Knoebl, p. 86.

[3] Stanley Karnow, *Vietnam: A History* (New York: Viking Press, 1983); Terrence Maitland and Stephen Weiss, *The Vietnam Experience: Raising the Stakes* (Boston: Boston Publishing, 1982), p. 51.

[4] Maitland and Weiss, p. 51.

[5] Bernard B. Fall, introduction to Knoebl, p. xii.

[6] Burchett, p. 88.

14
Reading, Writing, and the Prose of the School

Cy Knoblauch
Peter Johnston

> *Daddy says there was a king who rained for forty years.*
> *Daddy says there are forks in the road.*
> *Mommy says lambs gamble on the lawn.*
> *Sometimes mommy says she has a frog in her throat.*
> *Daddy says there's a head on his beer.*
> *I've heard daddy talk about the foot prince in the snow.*
> *Daddy says some boars are coming to dinner.*
> *Did you ever hear such a bunch of fairy tails?*
>
> F. Gwynne (1970)

The phrase "becoming readers and writers" that heads this collection of essays means different things as it is viewed in different ways. It might mean, for some, a particular form of cognitive development, for others an acquiring of some range of technical and/or functional skills, and for still others an entry into cultural life. Contributions to this volume will probably articulate, explicitly or implicitly, these meanings and more besides. We do not propose to critique the various interpretations presented in this volume, although each could usefully be scrutinized for the assumptions it maintains and the limitations it conceals. Instead, we will describe our own preferred interpretation and make explicit its limitations and consequences. Indeed, our view of what it means to become readers and writers demands rigorous critique of all language including one's own articulated position.

From our perspective "becoming readers and writers" is part of developing literateness, which denotes the emergence of what Paulo Freire calls "critical consciousness"—a developed capacity and sustained willingness to turn language practices upon themselves. Becoming "literate" means, in this context, not some rudimentary or unreflective mastery of of reading and writing for some narrowly functional purpose (usually defined by others who possess a competence or at least an authority beyond that of the intended learner), but an alertness to the sociopolitical nature of language. It involves an awareness that language practices are learned in the context of institutional arrangements, which have been given factual status by the language itself, and in the context of particular distributions of power. Literacy means to us, then, an awareness beyond competence of the motives and agendas that inform texts, the authorizations that make some texts more powerful than others, and the tactics that enable texts to weave their illusions of coherence, necessity, and certitude. We do not regard initial consciousness as a dessert to be allowed once more basic skills have been learned—a "higher level thinking"—but, rather as basic, as the first priority in the context of which other skills and knowledge might be acquired.

For us, the notion of "development"—a linear, or at least progressive, acquisition of increasingly elaborate competences—is misrepresented to the extent that it is perceived as a neutral concept, a merely cognitive or otherwise "organic" reality to be empirically, and acontextually, specified as the basis for deriving responsive school curricula. On the contrary, descriptions of "development" are always embedded in ideological conditions, emerging from specific social and educational realities. Jerome Bruner (1986) makes the point plainly in *Actual Minds, Possible Worlds*, when he characterizes the different ways in which Freud, Vygotsky, and Piaget "may be constituting the realities of growth in our culture rather than merely describing them" (pp. 134–45). It is hardly surprising that the socialist Vygotsky should find the child at first a socially constituted being who then "develops" an independent subjectivity, while the structuralist and logician Piaget would celebrate the inherent reasoning capacity of the individual child who then grows "outward" toward the world by discovering rational means of controlling it. What society believes about itself and wants in its members is readily transmuted to a myth about human growth that ratifies educational practices designed to replicate those beliefs and instill those traits or capacities. The myths define a "natural" progression from a state of innocence or incapacity to a state of maturity. That progression is readily broken into "stages" or "levels" (what the 10-year-old can do, or the 20-year-old), representing the learning priorities necessary for the reproduction of desired social forms.

In the United States, for instance, a technological society that values practical know-how and the management of information, literacy is typically conceived in functionalist terms, where language is a code, where the code transmits "messages," and where the primary function of language is communication. Not surprisingly, therefore, the agenda of schooling is to teach, first, the mastery of the code, then the proper means of encoding (writing) and decoding (reading), and eventually the practical contexts of exchanging information. There is nothing "natural" about the growth of the American code user, although, to be sure, a person on the way to becoming a code user will be more or less competent to encode or decode at different ages: more or less serviceable to the American economy. Our point is that what the child is "ready for," according to some developmental argument, is usually less a question arising out of biological considerations than one arising from social priorities: development is fundamentally political. We are proposing a theory of language (no less politically situated than any other) which has the effect of questioning functionalist theories along with the social realities and educational practices that those theories serve to rationalize. To the extent that reading and writing activities take place in schools with the tacit support of a developmental model founded upon functionalist notions of language, we urge a radical instructional praxis that can call conventional school realities into question to the extent that they perpetuate ideas of literacy that serve the interests of privileged groups and traditions at the expense of the freedom and opportunity of other people. Furthermore, we urge the fundamental theoretical importance of the play of language, and of language play, as the means by which a plenitude of worlds is spoken into reality, and by which individual worlds are kept from domination.

Our starting point is the premise that language is fundamentally figurative rather than denotative or referential. Since this assertion about language is not age-dependent, we will not make a separate argument for adolescents and adults. The insight about figuration is hardly novel: It has served as a cornerstone of semiotics since Kant and has been appropriated in recent times for various philosophies of language, including deconstruction theory. Much of the argument that follows will, in fact, depend on deconstruction in particular for its conceptual underpinnings. Inevitably, our argument derives from values that we hold—assumptions about the ends of schooling, the importance of language, the nature of society, the purposes of life. Inevitably, those values exist in a context of other, different, even opposite values, which, in turn, lead to the articulation of positions we would oppose, or at least not support. We are at no pains here to insist that our view is the only correct one, or to convert others to the same position. Rather, we wish to assert, explore, and critique our view with the realization that any educational practice is motivated somehow, and that its adoption has human and institutional consequences. Jerome Bruner has commented on the:

> impossibility of ever settling institutional questions of education without first making a decision—yes, a political decision—on the nature of learning and learners. . . . At the heart of the decision making process there must be

a value judgement about how the mind should be cultivated and to what end. (1986, p. 5)

A position dependent to any significant extent on deconstructive principles cannot, as a matter of definition, claim a privileged vantage point on language or education—cannot insist on its own superiority. It can only claim to have consequences that serve to realize the values from which it derives, including, as we see it, the construction and enhancement of an egalitarian, democratic society. At the same time, a deconstructive perspective is obliged to remain conscious of its own limits, its own self-serving rhetoric, requiring that these be made fully as plain as the benefits of its application.

Given the premises of a deconstructive perspective, meanings are always slippery, always changing, always multivalenced. The process of deconstruction is the critical process of revealing all of the gaps, all of the slipperiness, all of the multiple possible meanings in language, and to show that the writer or reader cannot insist on a univocal significance because it is not in the nature of language to yield it. The process of deconstruction reveals the kind of games that are played in order to make a statement look the way it looks: The statement that pontificates, the statement that insists on its own authority. So it assumes a playful attitude toward language in a very profound sense. It doesn't deny meaning, it luxuriates in it. Essential to playfulness, for instance, is a freedom of choice among alternative meanings, a freedom which implicitly challenges the current insistence on teaching students to extract *the* main idea from text. It makes any attempt at a univocal reading a self-evidently political activity and reveals its political character. It is at once playful and seriously political. The story that is valued in school for its "moral lesson" (singular) about "obeying your parents" (and by extension other structures of authority) is revealed to be more complicated than that, to offer meanings that qualify or even subvert such tidy advice. The practice of insisting on that moral is perceived to be a political act, a way of reinforcing power relationships that extend beyond family into all the venues of social life.

Plainly, then, a deconstructive pedagogy involves more than superficial changes in classroom practice. It assumes a political consciousness of the act of teaching. Jacques Derrida has insisted on more than one occasion, but notably in a 1980 address at Columbia University, that there is a necessarily close connection between deconstructive thinking and pedagogy, that it properly influences not just teaching practice but also the educator's critique and reconstituting of that practice along with the institutional reality in which it is situated. This argument comes, in part, with the recognition that teaching and learning are inevitably discursive in nature, comprised of talk, reading, and writing. In effect, they involve the production of "texts" which are just as open to critique as any other texts. These texts include, for example, statements of "knowledge," student reproductions of those statements, dialogic encounters among teachers or students or both, "explanations" of what constitutes knowledge and what shape or importance it is supposed to have, arguments about how learners are to be introduced to knowledge, and judgments about when or how well they have learned what they are "supposed" to learn. These texts are in continuous process of composition amidst the phenomenal circumstances of school life. They are also, as texts, accessible to deconstructive critique, which offers a powerful instrument for revealing the features and meanings of school discourse, along with possibilities for their revision.

At the same time, as with any aspect of social life, schools entail complexly textured configurations of power and authority, networks of intellectual and historical rationalization (verbal and otherwise), political and economic ties to other sociocultural realities, and a play of internal and external crosscurrents and tensions (conflicting significations) reflecting the ceaseless opposition of alternative possibilities for the (re)conceiving of the school world. These layerings of institutional arrangements, codifications, and contending arguments are, by the terms of deconstruction, also discursive in nature, and comprise texts which are equally appropriate subjects of deconstructive critique. Together, the institutional orders, administrative and curricular patterns, evaluative policies, and teaching and learning practices of educational life constitute "the prose of the school," which a deconstructive reading may open to critical inspection. In other words, while deconstruction insists that it is important to critique texts like *King Lear*, it also insists on the importance of critiquing the text of the curriculum which requires *King Lear* to be read. Furthermore, deconstructive criticism highlights the political nature of the production and interpretation of these texts.

Vincent Leitch (1985) has made an argument of this sort with admirable energy in an article titled, "Deconstruction and Pedagogy," in which he points, as demonstration of the political engagement of deconstructive thinking, to Derrida's affiliation with the Group for Research on Philosophic Teaching (GREPH), established in Paris in 1974 to challenge state intrusions into the teaching of philosophy. Leitch points out that for Derrida, where teaching is concerned, "neutrality is unacceptable and activism is essential" (p. 17). Teachers act in the world, and acting always entails the making of choices, the expression of commitments. Teachers, among others, compose the world of educational life through the choices that they make, whether these are local judgments about what happens in their classrooms or broader judgments about school curricula, the nature and character of instruction, the means of assessment, or the value of the educational enterprise. Since teachers' actions have consequences for people's lives and for the always emerging circumstances of school reality, noninvolvement is a mythic condition and the claiming of noninvolvement an irresponsible posture (this is, of course, no less true of administrators and parents). Critical reflection on one's own praxis and a critical reading of the prose of the school, each of which can be assisted by the deconstructive habit of mind, are thus obligations of principle.

Deconstruction can be seen as at once a means and also an end of educational critique. It is advanced as a means insofar as it seeks to destabilize canonical or otherwise "transcendent" discourses such as curricula and power structures, as well as readings of texts, by pointing out the inherently mischievous nature of language, which always allows greater meaningfulness than any particular ideological stance will allow. The diversity of interpretations of the title of this book reflected in its chapters stands as evidence to this characteristic of language. It is also advanced as an end, an altered praxis, insofar as the attitudes toward language and discourse that it rationalizes encourage distinctive teaching activities and the production of liberating educational conditions in which all voices and statements, including those marginalized or silenced by hitherto canonical discourses, are allowed to flourish. Briefly, deconstructive inquiry subjects texts to a pressured interrogation that reveals the conditions and tactics that enable them to constitute themselves, the claims by which they entitle themselves to speak, and the discursive continuities and disruptions in terms of which they assert their identity. This exploration is always subversive, for it reveals the ideological nature of language use: the strategies by which texts deny the contingencies of their production or the plurality of their readings, the unselfconscious delimitations and preservative rhetorics that enable "positions," "institutions," "movements," "traditions," and "histories" to forget their ephemeral and problematic articulation. It aims in short, to reveal the nature of discursive practices, and one consequence is to destabilize not only the texts they produce but also the institutional realities both supporting and supported by those texts.

Evidently, deconstruction offers a disquieting portrayal of language— language the joker, as it were, forever composing and subverting the world. It is also a use of language, albeit bedeviled by reflexivity, toward an understanding of discourse which escapes the distorting limitations of isolated perspective. Its intent is to witness the play, the fullness, of signification by reading texts beyond the boundaries they imagine they have set for themselves in the pursuit of their own interests. It proceeds obliquely, at the margins of those texts, at points of beginning or closure, at places of disturbance or resistance where unreconciled or barely suppressed meanings strain the effect of coherence. It reveals the secret jests lurking within even our most earnest or reverent assertions, implicitly celebrating the exuberance of language, its irreducibly—and incorrigibly—figurative disposition.

Mischievousness and mirth are integral to a deconstructive frame of mind, where puns, double entendres, ironic twists, aporia, contradictions, runaway metaphors, and bizarre angles of vision are often the vehicles to a subversive understanding. Foucault writes at the beginning of *The Order of Things* that his book arose out of laughter, a comic insight that shattered all the familiar landmarks of his thought—and ours as well. Reading a passage from Borges he comes upon a reference to a Chinese encyclopedia which states that animals may be divided into (a) belonging to the Emperor, (b) embalmed, (c) tame, (d) sucking pigs, (e) sirens, (f) fabulous, (g) stray dogs, (h) included in the present classification, (i) frenzied, (j) innumerable, (k) drawn with a very fine camelhair brush, (l) etcetera, (m) having just broken the water pitcher, and (n) that from a long way off look like flies. "In the wonderment of this taxonomy," Foucault writes, "the thing we apprehend in one great leap, the thing that, by means of the fable, is demonstrated as the exotic charm of another system of thought, is the limitation of our own, the stark impossibility of thinking *that*" (1970, p. xv). Nor is it, he goes on, merely the oddity of unusual juxtapositions that makes this taxonomy inaccessible to us; it is also the unimaginability of a space in which such connections might be possible: The discursive site of the taxonomy is itself unthinkable. Yet, there, somewhere, it lies, a palpable fact of language, a testimony to the excesses of meaning, a denunciation of the earnest priority we assign to our own assertions. This comic and unsettling glimpse of the radically different, the absurdly unfamiliar, discourse leads Foucault to the puzzles that preoccupy his thought: the foundations of discursive practices, the manner of their emergence, the modes of their action, the possibilities and impossibilities of utterance that they define, the character and dispersion of their objects and relationships, the nature of the documents that they produce, but above all the play of language that both constitutes and deconstructs those documents and ultimately the practices themselves.

This last, or better first, concern—the inherent instability of language as an endless play of signifiers—is the most persistent theme of deconstruction. Discourse, for the deconstructive critic, is a *practice*, not a structure; an activity, not a container or enclosure: it *has* form but it is not *a* form; it is momentarily regular but not a system of precise or timeless rules; it exists within, not beyond, history; it is a site, shaped by phenomenal, shifting conditions, not a model or a code; it makes meanings but the meanings are contingent rather than determinate, dispersed more than unified, absent more than present, and, in the end, uncontrollably prolific. As Terry Eagleton (1983) has put it, there is something in discourse itself, not just some forms of discursive practice, "which finally evades all systems and logics . . . a continual flickering, spilling, and diffusing of meaning [which poses] a challenge to the very idea of structure: for a structure always presumes a centre, a fixed principle, a hierarchy of meanings, and a solid foundation" (p. 134).

Foucault's "discursive formation"—that network of "enunciative modalities" which articulates the conditions of meaningfulness for some particular discourse—is characterized, as he says in *The Archaeology of Knowledge*, "not by principles of construction but by a dispersion of fact"; it is, in other words, a phenomenal reality of language practices: "it does not form a rhetorical or formal unity, endlessly repeatable, whose appearance or use in history might be indicated"; it is "not an ideal, timeless form that also possesses a history"; it is rather, "from beginning to end, historical ... a unity and discontinuity in history itself." Similarly, the "statement," which for Foucault is a "modality" of the existence and operations of signs, is also "not a structure (that is, a group of relations between variable elements ...); it is a function of existence that properly belongs to signs and on the basis of which one may then decide ... whether or not they 'make sense', ... of what they are the sign, and what sort of act is carried out by their formulation." Discursive practice, he insists, is "a place in which a tangled plurality of objects is formed and deformed, appears and disappears," so that the task of analyzing it is not a matter of "treating discourses as groups of signs (signifying elements referring to contents or representations) but as practices that systematically form the objects of which they speak." Finally, the texts which emerge from the conditions of a discursive formation are themselves neither structures nor fixed unities, their superficial appearances notwithstanding. "The book is not simply the object that one holds in one's hands: its unity is variable and relative. As soon as one questions that unity, it loses its self-evidence; it indicates itself, constructs itself, only on the basis of a complex field of discourse" (1972, pp. 115–117). Plainly, there are no constants, no fixities, no absolutes or timeless artifacts at any point of this description: There is only language, endlessly producing the possibilities of utterance, endlessly exploiting the gaps, discontinuities, and disruptions within texts in order to reconstruct and, of course, to be reconstructed by, those generative possibilities.

The evident implication of this type of inquiry, Eagleton explains, is "that language is a much less stable affair than the classical structuralists had considered. Instead of being a well-defined, clearly demarcated structure containing symmetrical units of signifiers and signifieds, it now begins to look much more like a sprawling limitless web where there is a constant interchange and circulation of elements, where none of the elements is absolutely definable and where everything is caught up and traced through by everything else" (1983, p. 129). This view is a familiar, though hardly dominant, conceptual starting point for much contemporary literary criticism, which strives, from this perspective, to open the plurality of the literary text instead of delimiting its possibilities by reference to a privileged Reading, as New Criticism had done and as current classroom practice enforces through textbooks and tests. A deconstructive reading aims to retrieve the concreteness, the palpableness, and therefore the fecundity of the text from formalist reductions. As an interpretive style, deconstruction revels in the play of language, luxuriating in the unbounded richness of meaning while also attacking its repression in the service of narrow, dominating, or manipulative interests. Ultimately, of course, the very concept of literature is rendered suspect in such reading, for "Literature" seeks to appropriate to certain favored texts capacities of language which serve, in fact, to produce all texts and all discourses. The deconstruction of a text entails deconstruction of its discourse as well, a breaking out of the circle of certainty and self-referentiality that they form for their mutual support.

At the same time, and unfortunately we should say, the view of language and discourse that deconstruction proposes has made little headway in reading or in composition theory, despite its intellectual interest and its provocative rendering of the processes of writing and reading. Where it has appeared, particularly in the United States, its advocates have been selective about the texts to which they apply it. Its application to literary works has seen considerable virtuosity, if not virtue. Indeed, despite Derrida's commitment to activism, the texts which have been avoided are the sociopolitical conditions and responsibilities of literacy instruction. The reasons for this apparent oversight are located in the strongly conservative commitment in American education to the objectivism of empirical science, the formalism of linguistics and cognitive psychology, and the static historicism of traditional rhetoric and poetics. Even the currently popular social-construction arguments about language within the field tend to emphasize an ontological, ahistorical view of so-called "interpretive" or "knowledge" communities, along with traditional notions of individualized writers and readers whose activities are more or less precisely bounded by the "generic rules" to which those communities presumably subscribe. More speculatively, the emphasis on language *play* at the heart of a deconstructive style—Vincent Leitch speaks of the "licentiousness" of language, its inherent tendency to subvert its own assertions—may simply be incompatible with the overpowering earnestness of the American educational enterprise in general and the minimalist, vocational preoccupations of so much literacy instruction in particular. For the most part, reading and writing specialists present their teaching arguments in terms of straightlaced school survival, socialization, and professional preparation, remaining faithful adherents to the Calvinist and Franklinian traditions of American life. Reading and writing are sober business in school and are to be soberly attended to.

We would like to believe that literacy instruction could proceed from a revealing and encouraging of language play in all the specific ways that advocates of deconstruction have proposed—where students have opportunities to compose playfully (highlighting narrative and metaphor, formal experiment, parody, and digression, rather than expository logic and the design of the business letter), to read playfully (by challenging traditional interpretations or subverting privileged meanings), and to question the presumed boundaries of texts and genres (by rewriting a "literary" work or probing the secret rhetoric of a journal article). Students learn less about discourse practices, not more, when they are presented with monolithic, institutional constraints on reading and writing that are both fictitious and institutionally self-serving. They learn timidity; they learn to accept rather than truly to *read* the illusions of coherence and certainty that texts designedly impose upon them. They learn to compose the same illusions themselves and to forget the importance of disbelief. A greater educational service might be to destabilize students' typically ontological views of such notions as "author," "text," "reading," and "knowledge," by encouraging them to examine and write about the structural disharmonies, the ambiguous intentions and claims, the conflicting assertions, the secret rhetorical tactics of the professional discourses to which they are introduced, beginning with their own textbooks. The exuberance of language, the joker at its core, makes all texts and all readings suspect, elusive, self-aggrandizing, and self-deflating. Revealing the play of language effectively renders language use a more problematic, a more conscious, and interesting activity to students while also situating it within all the complex social realities that it both engenders and serves—realities that students must come to understand if they are to read and write productively. The goal is freedom—not freedom from language, which is impossible, but freedom from our own as well as other people's dominating uses of language. The essentially comic insight into vanities and pieties of prose that deconstruction engenders can humanize practices which otherwise, in their ritual authority, have more power to seduce than inform, and more power to stifle than to create.

Whatever the theoretical merits of a deconstructive pedagogy, however, one discursive reality that it cannot afford to overlook is the prose of the school, which composes the roles of teachers and students, along with the possibilities of instruction, in vastly different, more "serious," and less jovially accommodating terms than those assumed within the comic world of poststructuralism. The heroes of contemporary literacy theory are not Derrida and Foucault, but Allan Bloom and E. D. Hirsch, latter-day reincarnations of John Calvin and Benjamin Franklin, respectively, the first offering the American imagination a sober, postlapsarian lament about the decay of culture, the second offering a soberly practical guide to its quick and easy reconstitution. For Hirsch, knowledge is concrete, atomic, and specifiable, while discourse is a vessel, a container, enabling its preservation as cultural heritage and its communication to the uninitiated. Specially designated texts, the Great Books, offer the essential content of Western civilization much as a vault offers the dollars and cents that constitute "wealth." Literacy education is a process of learning the practical steps to unlocking the vault. For Bloom the container metaphors remain but the kinds of container are different. The Great Books are the same but are conceived as sacred texts, chalices containing transubstantiated wine, but alas in a cultural setting where people prefer to drink beer from paper cups. While Hirsch provides the mechanistic praxis for literacy instruction, Bloom provides the escatalogical vision that lends earnestness and intensity to the enterprises.

The U.S. Department of Education, and (judging by the best-seller lists) the American public, listen to Hirsch and Bloom, not to Derrida and Foucault. And what they hear is a serious story about objectified knowledge (called "information") and the codes, structures, and algorithms by which the information is transferred from person to person and place to place. Henry Giroux (1981) has characterized the situation succinctly:

> The notion of "objectified" knowledge as it operates in the classroom obscures the interplay of meaning and intentionality as the foundation for all forms of knowledge. Absent from this perspective is a critical awareness of the varying theoretical perspectives, assumptions, and methodologies which underlie the construction and distribution of knowledge. Unfortunately, the notion of "objectified knowledge" represents more than a conceptual problem; it also plays a decisive role in shaping classroom experience. . . . One is apt to find classroom situations in which "objective" information is "impartially" relayed to "able" students willing to "learn" it. (pp. 54–55)

Students who lack the correct information can have it deposited in their heads through "direct instruction" or authoritarian lecture formats in schools and can then be tested, "objectively," to see whether it was retained there or not. A massive and lucrative textbook industry supports the authoritarian transfer of information while a massive and lucrative assessment industry supports the measurement of teaching and learning "effectiveness." The authoritarian relationship encouraged between teachers and students is maintained, although in different terms, between administrators and teachers: In the first case, the knowledgeable are separated from the ignorant, the masters from the apprentices; in the second case, managers are separated from workers, those who have power and those who don't. The social reality of the American school is, therefore, not only objectivist but also hierarchical and meritocratic, replicating the larger social reality in which the school is situated. And its "mission" is a peculiarly American vocationalism, where the learning of job skills is rationalized in terms of perpetuating a certain cultural superiority—manifested by beating the Soviet Union to the moon and (if math "skills" can be brought from their current depths) the Japanese to a better television set.

To be sure, our quick, parodic reading of the prose of the school fails to include the internal stresses and discontinuities, the conflicting assertions and agendas, the sheer complexities that make educational reality a vital, changing, and changeable life-world rather than a fictional monolith serving our own polemical interests. But the point here is to juxtapose as forcefully as possible the world of language play and playfulness which we would happily propose with Giroux's (1981) "culture of positivism" that is concretely realized and powerfully situated in American schools. There can be no serious advancing of a deconstructive pedagogy if the prose of the school is not scrutinized as carefully, as critically, as unnaively, as the prose of Rousseau and Hawthorne has been in more purely "literary" deconstructive praxis. It is easy for those of us in universities, for the most part in literature departments, whose confidence in American critical pluralism can be absolute as long as we keep our work within the boundaries of discretely local literary readings, to cheerfully proffer pedagogical recommendations to other (preferably tenured) university colleagues provided that they do not go so far as to challenge established curricular interests and the other institutional realities that constitute the university. Deconstruction in a university setting is certainly the play it announces itself to be, but it is also for the most part "play" in a less nobly philosophical sense—a harmless amusement that has everything to do with academic preening and nothing to do with educational change. Yet, even that play has attracted the attention of the Department of Education and the other bureaucracies that compose the prose of the school, where howls of protest in newspapers and government reports about the loss of the West's literary and philosophical canons combine with ominous hints about the redirection of public spending if the scholarly community continues its irresponsible pursuit of intellectual exotica. But imagine the howls if a more fundamental and more overt proposal for educational revision were to offer itself beneath the banner of deconstruction.

An authentic deconstructive praxis must truly and self-consciously grant the implications of its own premises—and they are extraordinarily uncomfortable even at a theoretical, let alone at a practical, level. If teachers are to play the games that their better-protected university colleagues play, they will have to deconstruct the prose of the school—from *A Nation at Risk* to the curriculum guide to the principal's memo about committee assignments—more subtly, more substantially, and more courageously than their university colleagues have so far done or been compelled to do by the goals they have set themselves. It is unacceptably naive to imply that one can radicalize teaching, change schools, change school boards and public officials, change parents and children, by talking about *Hamlet* in a different way. It is just as naive to suppose that it is a simple matter to get teachers to talk about *Hamlet* "differently." They know perfectly well what is at stake, what they risk of themselves, by so seemingly innocuous a variation: not just their jobs, though that would be a lot, but their sense of intellectual and pedagogical security, their beliefs about language, meaning, and culture, their educational as well as other social commitments. And so far we have spoken only of rereading *Hamlet*, the relatively cozy business of the English curriculum, where what is at stake is only the status and meaning of "fiction." Suppose the deconstructive critique were to originate, as it theoretically well could, in the science curriculum, where the culture of positivism receives its most cogent rationalization, or even in the history department, where the Latin root "historia"—theme, account, or *story*—is forgotten in the interest of an "objective" depiction of the self-portrait and hegemonic values in which Americans wish to believe. Suppose it were to originate, not in the schools at all, but in the judicial system or in a rereading of the American Constitution, where— beyond even the values of positivism—our most cherished myths reside. The deconstructive project offers the tools for so radical a critique, to be sure. It does not shrink, in principle, from the rereading of science and history, the prose of the school, or even the myths of the culture, in its ceaseless subversion of texts.

Meanwhile, if life for teachers is radically altered in the context of a deconstructive pedagogy, what becomes of the life of students, in this instance adolescents on the way to adulthood? Students, after all, are not encouraged to "develop" the imaginative flexibility, the playful attitude toward language, that deconstruction commends. On the contrary, they are socialized with systematic effectiveness into the culture of positivism, from those early moments when they are assured that texts have single and determinate meanings, that writing is a transfer of value-neutral information, and that science produces incontrovertible facts that serve as the necessary standard for evaluating all other modes of discourse. What would be the consequence of challenging so comfortable, so economically convenient, a view of the world and of their relationships to it? How will changing students' views of themselves (and others) as knowers, as free subjects who constitute knowledge no less than others do, affect the normal hierarchical relationships, in schools as adolescents and in the workplace as adults, that constitute social life? The issue at stake here is not really the biological aspect of development: Young children are fully sensitive to the play of words and of discourse (witness the "story" that begins our essay); even before they come to school, children are able to appreciate irony, a central trope of deconstructive theory. The issue, rather, is a confrontation between alternative modes of socialization: The effect of denying the deepest assumptions of traditional educational practice in the interest of making students more self-conscious about the nature of language and therefore more capable and willing to claim authority to speak.

Finally, the deconstructive frame of mind, cultivated in deconstructive praxis, contains within itself an epistemological worm. The painstaking reflectiveness at the heart of its problem posing creates a vexed self-consciousness and some awkward paradoxes for anyone who seeks to carry out its projects. The intellectual energy that a critical perspective devotes to scrutinizing the secret assumptions and agendas of other ideologies, including that of the culture of positivism, must sooner or later turn reflexive, even at the risk of consuming its own source. Deconstructive analysis is relentless and undiscriminating—ultimately turning on itself to raise paralyzing questions about the legitimacy of political action in the service of any directed educational or other social change. In other words, it appears to undermine the very political will necessary to vigorously dissent, to ardently persuade, and to stand so visibly in a certain place. Where in fact does it allow itself to stand? To undertake a critique, to commence a project, to oppose one reality and offer an alternative, to act in any fashion in the world is to accept, however contingently, the validity of a premise. Yet no premise, no authorization to act, is free from deconstruction, nor is any commitment to prefer one reality over another and struggle for its realization. How can the deconstructive stance remain politically viable when it is also required, by its own rationale, to remain problematic? How are political will and direction to be sustained when their conceptual sources are permanently bracketed as unstable and indeed mischievously figurative? Why should anyone prefer that stance to a positivistic ideology? To what lengths may one go in persuading others to prefer it? We have our evidences about the oppressive conditions sustained by the culture of positivism, but the problem is hermeneutic, not empirical. Deconstructively speaking, such contentions are plausible readings of the prose of the school, but they have no compelling interpretive authority that offers a mandate for social change. They are in fact endlessly modified in the ceaseless self-scrutiny that language necessitates.

Given the fact that struggle for social change, in education as elsewhere, involves an enormous expenditure of energy over long periods of time, how shall activists sustain their righteousness while the light that guides them flickers so uncertainly? We can offer some tentative answers but with no illusion that they erase questions that are merely superficial. We have argued that deconstruction is itself no less ideological in character than is the culture of positivism. To the extent that it seeks to privilege itself over some contrary that it opposes, it is implicated in the same grubby struggle for power that it reveals with such mischievous relish in the midst of other discourse practices. As a desired "end" of educational critique, therefore, it raises plentiful problems of its own, not least the fact that, if it were to achieve such privileging, it would only have replaced one form of domination with another, even if its own brand of tyranny were the imposition of a continuous state of discursive and institutional disorder (or at least unrest). Administrative hierarchies and curricular structures would destabilize beyond any practical ability to carry out their organizing responsibilities. Teachers could be obliged to bracket their statements about knowledge to a point where the only substance communicated to students would be their own compelling philosophical insecurity. Students would be obliged to tolerate a degree of creative dissonance, of intellectual ambiguity, aspiring to neurotic proportions. The nurturing function of schools could largely collapse through an inability to discover, let alone believe in, stable values to impart to the future. Obviously, this state of affairs could come to pass only hypothetically as the final reduction of deconstructive premises. But at the particular point where commonsense and an instinct for cultural survival modify the deconstructive agenda, as they surely would do, a decision will have been made to accept premises that lie outside its portrayal of itself: Deconstruction will have given way to something else.

And so, it appears that a critical praxis can flourish only in circumstances where other, dominating interests exist for it to critique—that its function, therefore, is to work from the margins as its proper place. It cannot aspire to the center, except at cost to its own critical aspirations: Its marginality is what makes it ethical. The point of educational critique should not be to replace one set of dominating conditions with another set, but to retrieve the consciousness of alternative choices that enables the maintenance of human freedom, a consciousness that oppression invariably seeks to extinguish for its own survival. Since dominating conditions are a fact of human life, the deconstructive project—as a means to the relief of oppression—remains permanently vital and productive, directing its comic and chaotic energies toward all the earnest, supercilious, and self-important rationalizations of hegemonic realities that privileged interests strive to keep in place. We have put a name on one of those realities in the context of educational life—or rather we have borrowed Giroux's name for it: the culture of positivism. More specifically, we speak of contemporary arguments about the nature of literacy that highlight either a narrow vocationalism, as in "functional literacy," which teaches meek subordination to the hierarchical and socioeconomic status quo, or an intellectualized ethnocentrism, as in "cultural literacy," which teaches a fear of "outsiders" and a "civilized" way to keep them outside.

To the extent that deconstructive critique may serve to reveal the assumptions, values, and discursive tactics of these sadly limited and ominously limiting "stories" about what it is to become readers and writers, offering in their place a story about the play of language and the happiness of language play, it will be telling, as we see it, a joyful tale indeed.

REFERENCES

Bruner, J. (1986). *Actual minds, possible worlds.* Cambridge, MA: Harvard University Press.

Eagleton, T. (1983). *Literary theory: An introduction.* Minneapolis, MN: Minnesota University Press.

Foucault, M. (1972). *The archaeology of knowledge.* New York: Harper and Row.

Foucault, M. (1970). *The order of things: An archaelogy of the human sciences.* New York: Vintage Books.

Giroux, H. (1981). *Ideology, culture, and the process of schooling.* Philadelphia: Temple University Press.

Gwynne, F. (1970). *The king who rained.* New York: Simon & Schuster Prentice-Hall.

Leitch, V. (1985). Deconstruction and pedagogy. In G. D. Atkins & M. L. Johnson (Eds.), *Writing and reading differently: Deconstruction and the teaching of composition and literature* (pp. 16–26). Lawrence, KS: Kansas University Press.

V
The Field Stance

15
Telling Secrets: Student Readers and Disciplinary Authorities

Carolyn C. Ball
Laura Dice
David Bartholomae

Socrates: What do you think, Meno? Has he answered with any opinions that were not his own?

Meno: No, they were all his.

Socrates: Yet he did not know, as agreed, a few minutes ago.

Meno: True.

Socrates: But these opinions were somewhere in him, were they not? So a man who does not know has in himself true opinions on a subject without having knowledge.... if the same questions are put to him on many occasions and in different ways, you can see that in the end he will have a knowledge on the subject as accurate as anybody's.... This knowledge will not come from teaching but from questioning. He will recover it for himself.

—Plato, The Meno

'Fellowships of discourse' ... function to preserve or to reproduce discourse, but in order that it should circulate within a closed community, according to strict regulations, without those in possession being dispossessed by this very distribution. An archaic model of this would be those groups of Rhapsodists, possessing knowledge of poems to recite or, even, upon which to work variations and transformations. But though the ultimate object of this knowledge was ritual recitation, it was protected and preserved within a determinate group, by the, [sic] often extremely complex, exercises of memory implied by such a process. Apprenticeship gained access both to a group and to a secret which recitation made manifest, but did not divulge. The roles of speaking and listening were not interchangeable.

—Michael Foucault, The Discourse on Language

INTERROGATING A PEDAGOGY OF RECOLLECTION

Meno, the straight man to Socrates' wit, asks one of the fundamental questions of education: "Can you tell me Socrates—is virtue something that can be taught? Or does it come by practice? Or is it neither teaching nor practice that gives it to a man but natural aptitude or something else?"

Despite the clichèd nature of the question (and it is a clichè the moment Meno voices it), the answer one imagines radically determines the activities of the classroom—not only what the characters do (teachers and students) but how they stand in relation to each other and to knowledge of their subject. If we assume that language produces truth—that both the person knowing and what the person knows are constructions, and that language, culture, history, ideology, institutions, and not only the individual alone are doing the constructing—then the class hour will be organized differently than if we assume that language originates in and expresses a transcendent Truth. If teachers needed only to tell the truth, and students to listen, then the important problems of education would be limited to problems of delivery, getting the goods to the consumer. If, with Foucault (1972), the classroom is where certain ways of speaking (each expressions of the "will to truth") are organized and controlled, produced and protected, distributed and appropriated, then the problems of education have a more complex economics, one that involves the necessarily unequal distribution of power, authority, and value.

Socrates has played a powerful role for modern teachers, if only through the general evocation of a "Socratic method," where teachers question rather than lecture, and knowledge is represented by a method as well as by a set of received (and paradoxically also "discovered") truths. Teachers have used Socrates to name their desire for a scene of instruction where the positions of speaker and listener (if not their roles) could become interchangeable, erasing any inequalities that could be attributed to class, culture, gender, or history. In the course of his dialogue with Meno, Socrates argues that knowledge is not "taught" but recollected by making one of Meno's slaves, who is completely uneducated, reason out geometrical truths "by himself." Socrates uses the slave boy's experience to argue that the soul "remembers" truths from before birth and that these truths can be recollected with the help of questioning, his version of dialectic. Thus, a pedagogy of recollection is one in which the teacher questions the student, who may be as uneducated as the slave boy or as naive as Meno, in order to elicit truths which would otherwise remain hidden, unremembered in the depths of the soul.

Such talk of souls and the transmigration of knowledge is enough to set most educators today laughing, bearing more resemblance to the psychobabble of crystals and Shirley MacLaine than educational theory. Nevertheless, much of what we do as teachers bears startling resemblance to a pedagogy of recollection, and to some degree it must, for it is in the nature of teaching that we must always begin, in some sense, with what our students know. It was the revolution of process-centered pedagogies to acknowledge this fact. Since Mina Shaughnessy (1977), Basic Writing teachers have seen the grammatical errors in a student's paper as evidence of knowledge, as attempts, however mistaken, to approximate the conventions of correctly written prose. Such a pedagogy begins with the student's text, with the "knowledge" she has, and works from there. A similar pedagogy is in operation when students are asked to use their personal experience as the subject of their essays and comments in class. More subtly, but nevertheless a product of the pedagogy of recollection, is the advice to "Remember your audience," followed by a series of questions designed to elicit information about that particular group, whether it be the readership of *Seventeen Magazine* or the editor of a local newspaper or the president of the university. In each of these scenarios, students are asked to draw on what they know in order to do the work of writing, whether it be constructing a sentence or composing an autobiography or imagining an audience.

In this essay we wish to honor the motive to credit the knowledge students already possess, a motive underlying most of the progressive pedagogies deservedly receiving attention in efforts to reform the teaching of reading and writing, including reading and writing in the subject areas. Our primary concern, however, is to raise questions about the knowledge that is said to reside "in" students, the knowledge that could be said to reside "in" the academic disciplines (the knowledge that stands as currency in the academy), and the possible relationships between the two, at least as these relationships are acted out in the classroom and in the students' work.

Students' "common" understanding of things places them outside the specialized ways of knowing in the academic disciplines; education is the process of bringing students into the circle of disciplinary understanding by a combination of practice, recitation, and ritualized initiation.[1] While this opposition between "inside" and "outside" ultimately breaks down, it nevertheless grounds cultural attitudes and academic theorizing. The very rootedness of the distinction we make between communities of discourse marks it as both a necessary and fruitful place to begin

---

[1] For other discussions of the ways in which students' acts of reading and writing are constituted by disciplinary conventions and institutional power relations, especially for students who enter the university speaking a language different from the language expected in the classroom, see Bartholomae (1985, 1986, 1987).

thinking about how knowledge is imagined to relate to the self and the institution.[2]

When we started work on this chapter, we began by collecting a set of student essays written for various courses at our school, the University of Pittsburgh, and by reviewing both what the students wrote and what their professors said about what they wrote (usually in marginal comments). In particular, we asked the faculty to give us examples of students who, in their minds, could and couldn't do what the discipline expected them to do with texts, who could and couldn't do the reading and writing necessary for work in their course and, by extension, in their discipline. We have used these documents as the material for our study of how students are positioned, and how they position themselves, in relation to disciplinary authority—to their professors and to the texts that they are asked to read, to understand, and to use as material in their own writing.

It is our contention that the positions which students take in relation to authority—the ways in which they insert themselves into the discourse of the discipline—determine in crucial ways their academic success or failure. Yet, knowledge of the status relations surrounding discourse production is kept out of the classroom and away from students, who are left to "remember" it for themselves. Such a pedagogy pretends that this crucial knowledge is located "inside," in a student's native intelligence or powers of logic or intuition. In actuality, however, this knowledge is socially constructed; it is itself cultural coinage, simultaneously minted and won through elaborate and ongoing culture wars in which various groups struggle for the power to define knowledge and set standards of language and behavior.[3] Michael Apple (1986) identifies the connection between cultural warfare and education in his introduction to Ira Shor's (1986) *Culture Wars:*

> We should always ask a series of questions about the knowledge that schools teach and the ways they go about teaching it. 'Whose culture?' 'What social group's knowledge?' 'In whose interest is certain knowledge being taught in our educational institutions?'

In this perspective, our educational system provides an arena in which differ-

---

[2] The opposition of "inside" and "outside" ultimately breaks down insofar as subjectivity—what we commonsensically think of as "inside"—is structured by linguistic, psychoanalytic, and institutional factors. How this structuring occurs is the subject of current theoretical debate. A useful introduction to this debate can be found in Wolff (1984). For a specific treatment of how education structures subjectivity, see Althusser (1971).

[3] Carr (1988) examines the set of student positions constructed and made available through the McGuffey Readers. She discusses how the Readers represent and constitute literacy as cultural coinage, and how students from multiple cultures are positioned by such a practice.

ent groups with different conceptions of what is important to know, and often different power, fight it out, so to speak. The culture that ultimately finds its way into the school is the result of these battles, compromises, and what has been called 'accords.' (p. ix)

The wealth of legitimated knowledge must be acquired; it can never, we would argue, be produced by acts of remembrance: monetary standards are always cultural constructs, arbitrary assessments of worth rather than measurements of innate or essential value. When we fail to recognize in our teaching that some knowledge can never come from inside, from the self, we implicate ourselves in an educational practice which locates "error" in the student rather than as an effect of discursive systems which marginalize some students and reward others.[4]

In this chapter we argue for a pedagogy which makes apparent the status relations surrounding discourse as well as the systems of discourse production which operate in the academic disciplines and the university at large. We want to examine how knowledge becomes legitimated as school knowledge and how such knowledge, riddled with gaps and silences, helps to position students in relation to texts, institutions, and their own lives.

SYSTEMS OF DISCOURSE AND DISCURSIVE CONVENTIONS

Meno's slave boy was able to bring forward knowledge about geometry which consisted of facts about squares and triangles. Being a mathematician, however, consists of more than possessing factual truths about numbers; it involves knowing what kinds of questions to ask, what objects are appropriate for study, what methods are acceptable to a mathematician— not a person good with numbers but a member of the profession of academic mathematicians. These questions and methods are routine, habitual. They seem natural. Sociology claims a field different from, but related to,

---

[4] We have to some degree oversimplified the process of educational reproduction since some students, those with access to traditional elite education, seem able to produce knowledge by acts of remembrance. For these students, however, there was still a time when this knowledge was not already known, although it does seem to become "natural" for them earlier and more easily than for most students without access to this form of education.

The process by which this knowledge becomes naturalized for some students (and not others) needs further research, at both the institutional and individual levels. Such research is underway in studies of education and the reproduction of class structure. See Apple (1982), Aronowitz and Giroux (1985), Bowles and Gintis (1976). These authors examine how educational institutions, through specific practices such as labeling and tracking, reproduce existing hierarchies of social class. A useful introduction to this perspective on education can be found in Ferguson (1988).

anthropology, and these institutional divisions, too, seem obvious and natural, an inevitable part of the landscape of reasonable inquiry. Foucault's
(1972) definition of an academic discipline is a useful one, for it highlights
the artificial nature of divisions which seem commonsensical to us:

> Disciplines are defined by groups of objects, methods, their corpus of propo-
> sitions considered to be true, the interplay of rules and definitions, of tech-
> niques and tools: all constitute a sort of anonymous system, freely available
> to whoever wishes, or whoever is able to make use of them. (p. 222)

The student who is asked to write like a sociologist must find a way to
insert himself into a discourse defined by this complex and diffuse conjunction of objects, methods, rules, definitions, techniques, and tools. He
must master, to be successful, the conventions of written discourse, rules
of grammar and syntax, rules of style and diction, rules of structure and
organization, all varying with purpose and audience. In addition, he must
be in control of specific field conventions, a set of rules and methods
which marks the discourse as belonging to a certain discipline. These vary
even within disciplines; a reader response critic will emphasize one set of
textual elements, a literary historian another, and the essays produced will
contain these differences. To perform successfully as a practitioner, one
must be more than reasonable: One must have more than information
about a subject.

A third set of conventions to be accounted for are institutional, rules
which mark the discourse as belonging to a specific institutional setting.
An essay on literacy written within the English department will differ from
one written under the auspices of United Nations development work. And
even within the academic setting, the rules vary; an anthropologist writing
about literacy produces an essay markedly different from a composition
researcher's. *College English* and *Research in the Teaching of English*,
both journals located within an academic setting, provide forums for related yet discontinuous disciplinary activity. The texts appearing in these
journals differ markedly as to style, diction, format, rules for citation, acceptable subject material, and methods. Moreover, the journals themselves constitute institutions, complete with ruling boards and financial
resources. This example only begins to suggest the ways in which these
sets of conventions, complex in themselves, interact in elaborate and intricate ways to form discourses which, to complicate matters further, are
continuously changing. Thus, the student who is set the task of writing a
history paper must be aware not only of written discourse conventions,
field conventions, and institutional conventions, but she must possess at
least an inchoate sense of how these sets of conventions interact in multi-
directional relationships. Students must be able to produce the appro-

priate intersection of conventions at the appropriate time (although they need not be able to say what this intersection is).

It is no wonder that Foucault corrects himself when he writes that the anonymous system of discourse is "freely available to whoever wishes," adding the crucial qualification: "or whoever is able to make use of them." This qualification of "whoever wishes" to "whoever is able to make use of them," precisely defines the position of the sociology student who may very much wish to make use of that anonymous system but either doesn't know it exists or is only conversant with a portion of it.

But familiarity is not the only issue here. It is not as though a student could freely choose or freely reject (or freely manipulate) those ways of speaking that are quickly at hand, that constitute her cultural heritage and enable her to speak. It is not as though, in reaction to the difficulties of academic writing (writing sociology, for example), the student could turn freely to personal experience (an exercise that is often offered as a starting point or an alternative for the student having trouble with "academic" discourse). This discourse of personal experience carries little value in the academy. Students may write in journals in the sociology class, but these are private, ungraded. And at the moment at which experience is cast into language, it becomes language. Correctly written prose is produced by an elaborate and arbitrary set of rules which dictate not only the order of words in the sentence, but the movement from the beginning of writing to the end, a movement we fondly call the movement of mind but which is more appropriately the disciplining of language, a determined program to insure that students will produce predictable and recognizable discourse. School is the place where this discipline is ritualized by department and degree; schools are institutional sites organized to produce reading and writing, readers and writers. The students' knowledge—or experience, of sociology, of language—is never freely transcribed but instead is shaped and mediated by an "anonymous system" which produces knowledge and text. When asked to write about a moment in her own life, a student becomes instantly enmeshed in the activities of choice and selection, where she cannot ever freely choose or know the experience as it happened. To this degree, writing for school, in whatever form, will always be writing for school, even though school sanctions a multitude of types of writing—the sociology paper, the journal, the lab report, literary criticism, the essay exam.

In each of these situations, a student is asked "naturally" and "freely" to produce a text which is in actuality highly mediated and artificial. In the movie *Educating Rita*, the English professor gives Rita, a minimally educated working-class woman, an essay exam which asks how she would work with the staging problems of a well-known play. She writes the single sentence response, "Do it on the radio." Despite the fact that a radio production would adequately solve the production problems, that the response is in its own way quite brilliant, the professor points out that it is nevertheless in error, for it lacks the elaborate set of field conventions which surrounds the activity of writing literary criticism. Few students are as blissfully unaware (or as consciously resistant?) as Rita, and the story of her education is of her journey away from this naive but happy ignorance. Most students are painfully aware that these anonymous systems of knowledge production exist, but they are equally aware that the workings of these systems are just that, anonymous, a ubiquitous disciplinary secret attributable to and recoverable from no person or source. It is no wonder students fall silent when asked to account in some way for a text they've read; they are being asked to act as if they possess what they very well know they lack, and to take on a role they have not mastered in front of the powerful figures who help to determine how their lives might proceed.

THE SITUATION OF THE NOVICE AND THE AUTHORITY OF THE INSTITUTION

Perhaps the quickest index to both the possibilities and problems students face when they situate themselves in relationship to the disciplines can be seen in the way students make use of the words and ideas of experts in their own writing. In quotation and paraphrase students are literally as well as figuratively creating a relationship with the past, with tradition, and with the authority of that discourse privileged by their teachers and the institution.

Here, for example, is a selection from a student paper in an entry-level composition course. The student has read a chapter from Paulo Freire's *The Pedagogy of the Oppressed* (1970), a chapter in which he develops the metaphor of education as "banking" (that is, where teachers make deposits in students), and the student has been asked to use Freire as a way of reading a moment in his own education.[5]

> As a high school senior, I took a sociology class that was a perfect example of the "banking" concept of education, as described by Freire. There were approximately thirty students enrolled in the class. Unless each of our brains was computerized for long memorization, I don't understand how we were expected to get anything out of the class.
>
> Each class began with the copying of four to five pages of notes, which were already written on the blackboards when we entered the classroom.

---

[5] This assignment appears in "The Aims of Education" sequence in Bartholomae and Petrosky (1987).

Fifteen to twenty minutes later, the teacher proceeded to pass out a work-sheet, which was to be filled out using only the notes we previously copied as our reference. If a question was raised, her reply was, "It's in the notes." . . . . In order to pass the class, each piece of information printed on her handouts needed to be memorized. On one occasion, a fellow classmate summed up her technique of teaching perfectly by stating, "This is nothing but education by memorization!"

Anyone who cared at all about his grade in the class did quite well, according to his report card. Not much intelligence is required to memorize vocabulary terms. Needless to say, not too many of us learned much from this class, except that "education by memorization" and the "banking" concept of education, as Freire puts it, are definately not an interesting nor effective system of education.

The figure of the reader here, we would argue, is typical of students whose strategies in the face of texts are limited to that form of agreement that is functionally equivalent to submission, to silence. In the face of what Freire says, the student says "me too," his words are mine. It is a grand, if empty gesture, appropriating Freire's authority wholesale. It is, in a sense, a student's somewhat desperate attempt to make the roles of speaker and listener interchangeable. The story he tells is designed to show his professor that he has read Freire, understood him "perfectly," and can now reunderstand his experience "perfectly" in Freire's terms: "Needless to say, not too many of us learned much from the class, except that 'education by memorization' and the 'banking' concept of education, as Freire puts it, are definately not an interesting nor effective system of education." He agrees with Freire's evaluation of traditional education "totally," we can almost hear him say, because it coincides with his own experience. He demonstrates his agreement with, and intellectual debt to, Freire by telling a story which is "covered" by Freire's terminology of banking education. What he fails to acknowledge, probably fails to realize, is the degree to which the story is a representation made to fit, and fit perfectly, Freire's framework. This perfect fit, what we see as caricature, constitutes his bid for authority. He establishes his right to speak by deferring to Freire and speaking through him, a move designed to both establish his textual expertise and free him from the responsibility of entering the discourse in his own name as a speaker, as someone who can have a converstation with Freire.

From this position, everything does become "Needless to say," for the essay is predicted from the start; the writer will restate Freire's main points and provide a story which "fits" his argument. Anyone who has read Freire and attended school can spin out this essay or one very like it, making the whole exercise "Needless to say," except for the student's felt need to establish simultaneously his authority and apprenticeship, a seemingly contradictory position which the student believes cannot be achieved by asking questions.[6]

This oddly aggressive and deferential stance, arising in part from contradictory needs, locates the student in a passive relation to the text he is reading and writing about. This passivity is inscribed in the final sentence of the text in which the student attempts to critique his high school experience as an example of banking education. The (mis)construction of this sentence suggests instead that he learned about Freire and banking education in the very class he was critiquing for its reliance on a pedagogy of memorization. This (mis)construction is particularly apt because it represents the writer's position in relation to Freire's text as the same as that required by the high school teacher he critiques: In both cases the student has taken a passive, banking approach to learning. This passivity is so pervasive among today's students that educators have diagnosed a crisis in literacy and begun designing curricula to teach critical thinking skills.

In a provocative essay "Writing and Criticizing Texts," Olson and Torrance (1983) argue that students' "uncritical attitude . . . results not simply from a logical incapacity but rather from a lack of social authority. The reader does not believe that he or she is in a position to criticize authoritative persons or texts (except perhaps with groans and marginalia)" (p. 39). Olson steps out of the framework of cognitive science to posit in institutional terms what is often described as a reading problem when he acknowledges that all acts of reading occur within a social context and therefore are fraught with the "managing of status relations." Such a view begins to recognize the anonymous system of methods, truths, and rules which constitutes the discipline.

Olson suggests by way of solution that both readers and writers need to recover "a sense of authority, not necessarily of superiority to an audience, but of an equality to the readers who make up the writer's peer group. . . . As a reader, one must come to see the writer of a text as basically equal to oneself, and as a writer, one must come to see the audience, including the teacher as reader, as basically equal to oneself" (p. 40). Such a vision is an attractive view of the academy and of the discipline, positing teachers and students as dedicated equals in the ongoing search for truth where the roles of speaker and listener are interchangeable, where there is an exchange of value and yet nothing is lost. It is, in its own way, as lovely a vision as the classroom which empowers students by acknowledg-

---

[6] The extent to which it is acceptable practice for students to question and critique an authoritative essay varies from program to program. The teacher for whom this essay was written expected more than a summary of Freire's text; most high schools, however, discourage the kind of questioning which would lead to a more sophisticated reading of Freire and of the student's own experience. This is another example of how discourse practices vary with institutional setting.

ing their knowledge and experience as solely or primarily valid in the learning process. Both visions fail to adequately recognize the status relations within the classroom, the discipline, and the university. The sociology student's problem, when writing a sociology paper, will not be solved because she manages to talk herself into believing she is the equal of her professor as well as of Emil Durkheim and Karl Marx. Nor will it be solved by relying on her own experience to stand in as or magically become sociological knowledge, a kind of educational pulling one's self up by one's own bootstraps. Either stance would more than likely lead her astray, one leading to the bluster and arrogant caricature of the previous essay, the other to credulity and provincial blundering. The status relations the sociology student must manage are exceedingly tenuous and tricky: She is asked to speak as a professional sociologist would speak, aware at every moment that she lacks the knowledge she needs to do so, but simultaneously she must speak as a student speaks, acknowledging that she lacks the knowledge she is supposed to pretend she has. Our refusal to recognize these parameters, to uncover the anonymous systems of our disciplines, only further invites students to produce discourses which remain on the edges of knowledge, unrecognized and unrewarded.

SELF-EFFACEMENT AND ERROR

We can begin to uncover disciplinary systems (and secrets) by examining the ways in which the institution, through its representatives, rewards or censures the positions students assume in relation to disciplinary authorities. The excerpt which follows is taken from a research prospectus written for an upper-level course in Anthropology.

Prospectus

The Mulligan Company has been contracted by John Forni Construction, Inc., to perform market research on the feasibility of a miniature golf course facility within the Oakland area. The proposed project has many commercial and structural aspects. That the Mulligan Company will not attempt to ana- A lyze. Rather, examine a single feasibility consideration, i.e., the consumer perception of the proposed miniature golf complex. The Mulligan Company performed a detailed study of the public's attitude and its acceptance-denial ratio. John Forni Construction has placed an additional emphasis for this report to reflect any probability that the black minority of the population using the miniature golf facility would have an adverse effect on the white majority's usage of the facility. This is a sensitive racial issue but one that must be explored for a comprehensive analysis of the proposed plan and for an informed decision to be reached

With the consultation of John Forni Construction, the Mulligan Company has developed a list of variables which ~~shall~~ provide pertinent and necessary data for this study. These variables are placed in questionnaire form and cover particular aspects concerning such items as age, sex, and academic status, and personal views concerning the proposed miniature golf course complex (Appendix B). ~~Observed~~ data ~~from these variables was~~ *were* analyzed through statistical means. Statistical analysis provided basic concepts, including mean, midrange, and graphic representation of these variables.

Use double spacing. It is difficult to edit a typescript otherwise.
p. 1A This research has only a single feasibility consideration, which is the attractiveness of such a facility as determined by consumer perception.
p. 1B Variables do not provide data, they give guidance for seeking data. Variables are not placed in questionnaire form. Questionnaires are designed to elicit data addressing specified variables.
p. 1C You should say that data obtained using these variables were subjected to statistical analyses of mean and midrange. (You should also justify using particular statistical analyses.)
You have problems of clear communication. The writing is far from lucid.

This paper received a D. Let us be quick to say that we are not concerned with this grade as a teacher's judgment. For our purposes, we want to take this moment as evidence of the discipline, acting through a representative, encouraging the production of certain forms of knowledge and discouraging others. To that end, it is useful to recall the discourse the student is attempting to reproduce. In "Fieldwork in Common Places," Mary Louise Pratt (1986) discusses the practice of ethnographic writing within the discipline of anthropology. She describes the difference between ethnographic fieldwork which "produces a kind of authority that is anchored to a large extent in subjective, sensuous experience" and "the text which the ethnographer must produce to describe the experience" (p. 32):

> But the professional text to result from such an encounter is supposed to conform to the norms of a scientific discourse whose authority resides in the absolute effacement of the speaking and experiencing subject.

The student who hopes to perform as an anthropologist must understand this difference in forms of authority and produce a text which represses all references to an experiencing self and which pretends the objectivity of science. Yet, as the commentary on this student's performance demonstrates, an understanding of this difference is not enough to insure success. Here we have a student who is obviously aware that he must produce a self-effaced, "scientific," discourse. At no point in this excerpt does he refer to himself either as student or as writer; the facade of "The Mulligan Company" is never directly broken. And even within the fiction of the

Mulligan Company, the student never directly reveals the presence of a human researcher at work behind the scenes (except perhaps with the sentence about sensitive racial issues). Moreover, he knows that in order to achieve this pretense he must use certain syntactic forms, like the passive voice, and the specialized language of his discipline. It is in his attempts to deploy the specialized language and syntax of his discipline, however, that he fails: His grammatical error and misappropriation of terms betray his subjectivity, his position as a student. He attempts to take on the master's role, but in the end his position as apprentice betrays him.

Much of the institutional commentary on this paper is aimed at what are often characterized as the "fundamentals" of writing and seen as rooted in an abstract English free from the specific historical or cultural context of its user. The marks on and through the text of the essay are designed to point out and in some cases correct grammar and punctuation errors, violations of written discourse conventions. These grammatical lapses are analogous to the student's inability to master the discourse of statistical analysis which is so valued by the discipline. By the third comment [1c] on this (the first) page, the professor has moved from explaining the proper use of terms like "feasibility" and "variables" to offering a general comment about the student's project: "You have problems of clear communication. The writing is far from lucid."

Versions of this comment appear throughout the paper and become the dominant and overriding explanation of the student's failure. For example, in marginal comment 12A the professor again points out the student's misuse of statistical terminology: "Analysis does not commence (begin) a study. The writing style strains to be formal but slips easily into being pretentious. Greater clarity comes with simplicity and directness."

These comments, which imply that anthropological discourse is simple and direct, locate the origin of the student's problem in the domain of writing (*qua* writing). They suggest that the methods of anthropology, the forms of argumentation and proof, the conclusions such methods produce, are inevitable and obvious. Thus, in this representation of disciplinary work, the student's difficulty lies not in construing anthropological knowledge but in the later stages of the project, the stages of writing, when predetermined knowledge is cast into language.

This separation of disciplinary knowledge and language allows for scientific discourse to derive its authority from claims to transubjectivity (experienced by all observers rather than a single observer) and therefore objectivity. When the writer removes herself from the process of writing (not just the product), the whole enterprise proceeds properly and smoothly as the right words attach to their objects without the indiosyncratic interference of the writer, or so these comments imply. This student fails because he overcomplicates and obfuscates what would otherwise, naturally, be "clear" and "lucid"'—if he didn't get in the way. There is no room for the writer in the almost mathematical formulation, "Greater clarity comes with simplicity and directness," nor is there space in anthropological discourse for any language which calls attention to itself, either by error or misappropriation (or irony or metaphor or any of the other textual elements off limits in anthropological discourse).[7] It may seem odd to include what we see as obvious errors in the same category with the most valued of literary devices. This juxtaposition allows us to understand, however, why misuse of terminology is so severely censured: Such textual excesses, identified here as "pretension," call attention to the text as a constructed rather than a natural object and thereby undermine the discursive claim to objective rather than constructed (and self-interested) truth. A failure to be clear is in practice a failure to cloak the many acts of construction and representation which constitute the process of writing, and which, when apparent, direct the reader's gaze to the asserted rather than effaced subject. Ironically, then, it is an act of cloaking which is required to produce the illusion of transparency and complete self-effacement which authorizes scientific discourse. And it is in these terms that the professor summarizes the problem of the paper as a whole:

> It is cloaked in a writing style that pretends to be objective, factual, and analytical, but which fails to mask the absence of organized data supporting conclusions that meet the objectives of the research problem.

The professor's comment, with its negations and inversions of presence and absence, is no more clear, meaning easy to read, than the student's "misspoken" sentences. It begins to suggest, however, the complexity of disciplinary activity which requires a student to negotiate between clarity and cloaking, between simplicity and pretense, between directness and masking (comment 10A: "The pretense of being a professional marketing survey is carried too far"). This student will move no closer to a correct approximation of anthropological discourse by working on his writing, by trying, for example, to be "simpler" or "more direct," because a discourse only appears simple and direct to those who already know the lay of the land— the terms, rules, conventions, objects, and methods which define a disciplinary field. It is this subtle complex of injunctions and limitations which the student must begin to master. In practice, a discourse is "clear" when all members sharing disciplinary space can understand each other, when they

---

[7] Chamberlain (1989) examines how composition textbooks and handbooks on writing discourage students from the use of irony (as they might use it to excess) and thereby deny them access to one language of power. Such advice reproduces a structure of relations in which the practitioners of a discipline have and are able to deploy knowledge which is kept from those who are supposed to be learning what the practitioners know.

all draw the same lines marking textual excess, when they all understand, for example, how far to carry the pretense and what is carrying it too far. A student cannot enter this circle of understanding by willing himself into it, by willing himself equal to those in the know, for he simply cannot will the knowledge he needs to establish his equality. Against Olson's assertion that students need to see themselves as equal to their teachers and the writers of the texts they read, we place Foucault's reminder that the roles of speaker and listener, in an apprenticeship, are not interchangeable.

Within this context, we can re-understand the often short comments which mark student success. "Very nice introduction." "This is excellent." "These are brilliant insights." Comments like these mark the students' conformity to disciplinary lines. The Professor is saying, "You are doing what we do, and you know what that is because you're doing it." What is masked, however, are the terms within which the authority of niceness or excellence or brilliance has been granted. "This is clear" in practice means, "You have shown me a self which pretends not to be a self but which we both know is really and truly a self; let us be happy in sharing this secret." Both Professor and student continue, however, to talk about "clarity" as a characteristic of writing rather than as disciplinary performance. This deflection serves a purpose. The comments pretend that the successful student's authority resides *in* his text, in the style or structure or ideas, a deception which reinforces the belief that this textual brilliance originates in the student. In actuality, the student succeeds because he matches the lines drawn by his discipline; the crucial element lies not so much in the lines themselves, in the specific styles or structures or ideas, but in the act of conforming, of controlling excess. Because the comments themselves cloak the ways in which the discourse operates, the ubiquitous secrets of disciplinary activity and discursive success have been passed on without ever having been revealed. The professor is not dispossesed of his knowledge, and the closed space of the discipline (and the power of its practitioners) has not been threatened by the revelation and circulation of knowledge about how the discipline protects, defends and preserves itself.

The deflection of a student's gaze away from the discipline and onto writing serves yet another function. Positioned thus, they cannot question, or revise, the discipline: only their papers. When disciplinary operations are uncovered, we can posit that the critical reading problem is produced in part by an anonymous system of discourse which to some degree expects and rewards a passive relation to disciplinary authority.

SELF-ASSERTION AND ERROR

The contradictory and deceptive messages given to students about the practice of self-effacement also surround the practice of self-assertion.

One of the most common and powerful pieces of advice offered to student writers is that they develop their "own" ideas and write in their "own" words. The complexity of assuming a position of self-assertion, of "owning" the words one writes, is exemplified by the institutional response to an essay written for a survey course in Sociological Theories. The professor describes the problem of the paper as he explains the grade of D−:

> This paper suffers from a major problem that makes it very unsatisfactory: it draws too much of its sentences directly from the text with minor changes. When you do not do this, you directly quote very often, filling up the space with lines from the textbook. There is no way such a paper can convince me you understand the theories. When you do write your own sentences from your own ideas, you are caught in another basic problem: your choice of Coser and Simmel is a poor one. Coser was working very closely with Simmel's ideas. As a result, you have to strain to find some difference which is barely there. If you revise this paper, I would suggest starting over fresh. Use the Coser theory in some application context or compare Coser with a different theorist. Use some examples of your own and discuss them in order to develop the ideas in your own words.

This writer has engaged in many of the activities of academic writing: paraphrase, quotation, comparison. She has, nevertheless, failed because she hasn't achieved the proper balance. How many words must one change in order to paraphrase rather than plagiarize and at the same time stay close enough to the text that one isn't charged with idiosyncratic interpretation? How many lines must one quote in order to provide textual support without quoting *too* many? How different must two theorists be before differences can be located "without strain"? These questions point to the complexity and artificiality of textual activities which teachers often assume are simple and straightforward. The primary advice offered to this student directs her back to herself, however, rather than outward into the discipline: "Use some examples of your own and discuss them in order to develop the ideas in your own words." This final directive suggests that the student's problem will begin to be solved if she relies on her own experience and her own language instead of that of the text, that is, if she asserts rather than effaces her "self." A sociology text, however, is not primarily a medium for authentic self-expression, as such advice would indicate, but is instead, like anthropology, a form of scientific discourse requiring some degree of self-effacement. An examination of a successful sociology paper will reveal the hidden principles behind the directive to write "in your own words."

An A paper from the same sociology class begins with a two-page story, unintroduced, about a group of five students who worked together on a class project. At the top of page three, the writer explains the intention of her paper: "In this paper I am going to analyze this group based on three theorists and their ideas." The next two pages are given over to explanations of the theories. For example, the writer defines Parsons' AGIL Model: "AGIL stands for how a system adapts to its environment, how it defines and attains goals, how it integrates its parts, and how it goes about latent pattern maintenance. The AGIL Model is a structural-functional model of society analysis." The remaining four pages are devoted to a discussion of the class group in terms of the three theories.

This paper is successful in part because it offers as a subject for analysis an extended example drawn from the writer's personal experience. This narrative no doubt contributes to the impression that the writer has indeed managed to write "in her own words." However, the story itself offers no surprises. The group was formed on the basis of "common interests" and "people who could work well together," and it did work well together because each of the members could contribute to the group in a unique but necessary way: "The psychology and sociology majors could do most of the research, the writing major could write the paper, the communications major could type the paper, and the computer science major could do most of the work on a video...." In the formation of the narrative, we can already see the sociological perspective providing a representational framework; the group is already being represented in terms of function, a sociological concept which has so saturated our cultural consciousness that the story itself is highly conventional and stereotypical, hardly an original idea of the writer's.

Nor does the writer explain the theories "in her own words," as the section quoted earlier on the AGIL Model demonstrates. These lines are not taken word for word from the textbook, as infelicities such as "society analysis" suggest, but the language is very close. This particular writer, however, is not chided for drawing the sentences from the text with only minor changes. She realizes, and is rewarded for knowing, that in order to claim authority as a sociologist she must produce the self-effaced discourse of science. She knows when it is appropriate, and indeed necessary, to sound like the textbook, to efface herself, and when it is better that she assert herself.

The "original" sections of the paper are those where she offers her view of the theories and her application of them to the extended example from personal experience. These are moments in the text when she locates herself in relation to the textual authorities she has read. She offers this translation of the theories she has described:

> Durkheim, Goffman, and Parsons all share a common view. Each of these theorists see people as being motivated, but the source of motivation differs. For Durkheim the motivation is the sacred object. Goffman sees the individ-

ual as being the motivation, and to Parsons there is a specific goal that is doing the motivating. The actions performed in regards to these motivations are what promote group stability and solidarity.

This is the moment in a paper when we expect the writer to produce an insightful and interesting translation of the theories. What we get in this case is a statement of the obvious: These theorists see people as being motivated, but the source of motivation differs. One need hardly have read these theorists to produce such a bald generalization. While the D − writer failed to convince the teacher that she had read the text because she quoted extensively from it, this particular writer succeeds, even though she could easily have written these lines without ever having read Durkheim, Goffman, or Parsons.

While the institution does censure this paragraph, it remains clear that the lapse falls within the realm of acceptable error, while the D − writer has erred in ways that the discipline simply will not excuse. The marginal comment alongside this paragraph reads: "This is neither clear nor convincing." As was the case with the anthropology paper discussed earlier, the problem of this paragraph is represented as a writing problem, a matter of "clarity." We would argue, however, that the problem is not that the writing lacks clarity, but that what it presents is so obvious. Rather than addressing the complex issue of what constitutes an acceptable translation or reading of sociological theories, an issue which threatens to raise disciplinary questions, the institutional voice has displaced the problem as a writing problem. As a result, the anonymous machine of the discipline is kept anonymous and what is in actuality a very complex and difficult problem is made to seem clear-cut and trivial, a problem of "clarity," which could be solved by choosing more accurate words, or of persuasion (being "convincing"), which could be solved by offering more explanation or support. None of these strategies, however, can rescue this paragraph from its shallow "sociological" commentary.

The other moments of textual translation occur when she applies the theories to her own experience. At these points she often relies on such clichés as "it was the good aspects of deference and demeanor and the realization that people don't have to like each other to work well together that kept this group together," or "Each of the members tried hard to work with all of the other members, and they tried not to let personal feelings get in the way of what had to be done." Again, the writer fails to provide powerful translations in the moments we expect them, offering instead cultural commonplaces we all recognize.

Nevertheless, this writer succeeds, despite the commonness of her observations (and perhaps because of them; it may be an aspect of the role of student to speak in clichés, as Plato understood when gave Meno his voice). She succeeds because she knows how to sound like a student of sociology: She knows how to use the languages of sociology and of the commonplace in such a way that she sounds "like herself," a sociologist and a student. This particular example foregrounds the ways in which the "self" is composed of multiple languages drawn from different settings and different cultures: advertising, textbooks, cultural commonplaces, church, the neighborhood, and on and on.[8] In institutional settings, some languages are designated appropriate in some situations (and these situations can vary, as we have seen, from paragraph to paragraph); some languages are almost never appropriate. Thus, speaking "in your own words" means speaking the words that are acceptable in a particular context, not words which are familiar from personal settings, as any student from a background of nonstandard dialect well knows.

This institutional wisdom, "be yourself," "use your own words," is obviously curious advice, since what is being asked for is often some repetition of knowledge and language which originates elsewhere, in the discipline and the culture at large. Such directives function in much the same way as the comments discussed in the previous section: to occlude the discovery that knowledge is constituted rather than natural. Students are therefore placed in a position of relative powerlessness in relation to the discipline and disciplinary knowledge; prevented from working on the discipline, they are left to work on themselves as learners—to memorize faster, study longer hours, read more books—but these activities cannot guarantee the learning of disciplinary knowledge necessary for success in school.

POSITIONING STUDENTS AS WORKERS IN A DISCIPLINE

When a student positions herself in relation to disciplinary authorities, she must in every case grapple with determining what "self" to present. In some cases, she must "efface herself" and show forth the anonymous face of scientific discourse (an elaborate deception which involves cloaking the interpretive self-interest of all acts of writing). In these rhetorical and classroom settings, to err is to let one's self appear. In other cases, she must "assert herself" and produce an organization and language "of her own" (an elaborate deception which involves pretending one creates language and organization which have already received authorization in other institutional contexts). In these settings, to err is to choose the wrong

---

[8] The concept of the author as a unified and originary source of meaning, and as a figure of "genius," is critiqued in Barthes (1977) and Foucault (1977). The implications of this critique for the composition classroom are explored by Berlin (1988).

language or balance of languages, to let the "non-self" appear, to copy or to be inauthentic. Whether self-effacement or self-assertion, the position the student assumes is in actuality a textual construct composed of complex and elaborate sets of conventions. An authentic self is as much a textual construct as an effaced self; neither is a direct transcription of the individual who is doing the writing. Thus, knowledge of which "self" to show forth in a particular rhetorical context can never be gotten simply by looking inside as if searching one's closet for the appropriate outfit: Outfits must be made. One must know what materials and designs are appropriate to the social event in question; one must know how to make or acquire the materials and how to design the designs; one must know what's been worn before, which variations would be fresh and which outrageous. It is this kind of knowledge, however, the constitutive knowledge of the discipline, which is naturalized and kept hidden by institutional representations of disciplinary work.

We can pull at two of many threads in this complex problem of educational success and failure. On the one hand, we must reassert that knowledge must be taught and learned in order to balance pedagogies of recollection which may, with all good intentions, overemphasize the role of the student's own language and experience in learning. In doing so, we must remember the spirit of those good intentions: a desire to see students—all students—as whole and powerful figures in their own learning and living.

The other thread of the problem pulls less easily. We must recall the culture wars which surround the educational enterprise and determine which knowledge gets taught and which languages and behaviors become standard. It is not enough to reassert the necessity of teaching certain kinds of knowledge to disadvantaged students. We must also contend with disadvantage; that is, we must examine the ways in which cultural warfare legitimates the knowledge, language, and behavior of one group and marginalizes or exiles that of others. Many "back to basics" programs reassert that knowledge, "the basics" or "fundamentals," must be taught and learned. They fail, however, to address the issues of cultural contention, legitimation, and domination which run through any pedagogical practice. We question whether it is enough to provide suitable wardrobes, "cultural literacy," for the disadvantaged without asking in a persistant and hard-minded way who sets the standards of "suitability," who benefits, and who loses.[9]

---

[9] E. D. Hirsch's (1988) educational program (argued for in *Cultural Literacy*) is an example of a "back to basics" curriculum which fails to address in a serious way the ideological question. His list of items with which every "culturally literate" person must be familiar imposes a set of legitimated knowledge on all who would be educated. The construction of the list, however, is not a neutral activity, and it remains to be asked who sets the list and whose interests are represented? The list itself becomes a powerful weapon of cultural warfare.

We have only begun in this essay to show how the positions available to students for entering disciplinary discourse require and reinforce a passive relation to discursive and institutional authority. Certainly the process of disciplinary and cultural reproduction is more complicated than what we have outlined in these brief sketches of disciplinary activity. The simple and bold strokes of these scenes can only suggest in a crude way patterns which must be more fully, more minutely investigated. Even such incomplete sketches as these, however, argue against an idealized scene of instruction in which teacher and student are equal, their roles interchangeable. Students will not be empowered as disciplinary practitioners by relying on their own experience and language to stand in as disciplinary knowledge; nor will their passive positions be made active by teaching them one segment of disciplinary knowledge, the "basics" or "content," while keeping secret knowledge of how the discipline operates. If students are to see themselves as something other than "inspired" or "shooting the bull" or "guessing"—representations of disciplinary activity which posit them as essentially passive in relation to the work at hand—we must begin to make visible and available the machinery which produces the university's disciplines and its multiple discourses.

REFERENCES

Althusser, L. (1971). Ideology and the ideological state apparatuses (notes toward an investigation). In B. Brewster (Trans.), *Lenin and philosophy and other essays* (pp. 127–186). London: Monthly Review Press.

Apple, M. W. (Ed.). (1982). *Cultural and economic reproduction in education: Essays on class, ideology and the state.* London: Routledge & Kegan Paul.

Apple, M. W. (1986). Series editor's introduction. In I. Shor (Ed.), *Culture wars: School and society in the conservative restoration 1969–1984* (pp. ix–xiii). New York: Routledge & Kegan Paul.

Aronowitz, S., & Giroux, H. (1985). *Education under siege: The conservative, liberal and radical debate over schooling.* South Hadley, MA: Bergin & Garvey.

Barthes, R. (1977). The death of the author. In S. Heath (Ed. and Trans.), *Image-music-Text* (pp. 142–148). Glasgow: Fontana/Collins.

Bartholomae, D. (1985). Inventing the university. In M. Rose (Ed.), *When a writer can't write: Studies in writer's block and other composing-process problems* (pp. 134–165). New York: Guilford.

Bartholomae, D. (1986). Wanderings: Misreadings, miswritings, misunderstandings. In T. Newkirk (Ed.), *Only connect: Uniting reading and writing* (pp. 89–118). Upper Montclair, NJ: Boynton/Cook Publishers, Inc.

Bartholomae, D. (1987). Writing on the margins: The concept of literacy in higher education. In T. Enos (Ed.), *A sourcebook for basic writing teachers* (pp. 66–83). New York: Random House.

Bartholomae, D., & Petrosky, T. (1987). *Ways of reading: An anthology for writers.* New York: St. Martin's Press.

Berlin, J. (1988). Rhetoric and ideology in the writing class. *College English, 50,* 477–494.

Bowles, S., & Gintis, H. (1976). *Schooling in capitalist America.* New York: Basic Books.

Carr, J. F. (1988). *McGuffey Readers and the construction of American literacy.* Unpublished essay. University of Pittsburgh, PA.

Chamberlain, L. (1989). Bombs and other exciting devices, or the problem of irony. *College English, 51,* 29–40.

Ferguson, M. (1988). Teaching and/as reproduction. *The Yale Journal of Criticism, 1,* 213–222.

Foucault, M. (1972). The discourse on language. In A. M. S. Smith (Trans.), *The archaeology of knowledge & the discourse on language* (pp. 215–238). New York: Harper & Row.

Foucault, M. (1977). What is an author? In D. F. Bouchard (Ed.), *Language, counter-memory, practice: Selected essays and interviews* (pp. 113–138). Ithaca, NY: Cornell University Press.

Freire, P. (1970). *Pedagogy of the oppressed.* New York: The Seabury Press.

Hirsch, E. D., Jr. (1988). *Cultural literacy: What every American needs to know.* New York: Vintage Books.

Olson, D. R., & Torrance, N. (1983). Writing and criticizing texts. In B. Kroll & G. Wells (Eds.), *Explorations in the development of writing* (pp. 31–42). New York: John Wiley.

Plato. (1961). Meno. In E. Hamilton & H. Cairns (Eds.), *The collected dialogues of Plato* (pp. 353–384). Princeton, NJ: Princeton University Press.

Pratt, M. L. (1986). Fieldwork in common places. In J. Clifford & G. E. Marcus (Eds.), *Writing culture: The poetics and politics of ethnography* (pp. 27–50). Berkeley: University of California Press.

Shaughnessy, M. (1977). *Errors and expectations: A guide for the teacher of basic writing.* New York: Oxford University Press.

Shor, I. (1986). *Culture wars: School and society in the conservative restoration 1969–1984.* New York: Routledge & Kegan Paul.

Wolff, J. (1984). *The social production of art.* New York: New York University Press.

16
Assessing Literacy Learning With Adults: An Ideological Approach*

Susan L. Lytle
Katherine Schultz

Adults who enter literacy programs in the United States rarely enroll for instruction for the first time. Almost all have been to school previously and many have completed several years of high school. Yet when they come to programs as adults—bringing with them diverse and often quite extensive experiences using print in their daily lives—they feel they are starting over, hoping to learn to read and, less often, to learn to write. Schooled, but not educated, they recount poignant histories of failure in traditional classroom learning. Indeed, unlike many adults seeking literacy instruction in the Third World, adult literacy students in the United States have been "schooled into illiteracy" (Holzman, 1989). Programs in this country designed for adult learners—whether for beginning literacy, adult basic education, or high school equivalency—differ dramatically from each other. In some cases, they closely replicate the routines of prior schooling. In others, program planners acknowledge and build curriculum around what adults bring to learning based on the reasons why, at this later point in their lives, they have come again to learn.

Diversity in learners and programs would seem to suggest the need for a similar diversity in approaches to assessment. Yet most programs depend primarily on commercially available standardized tests adapted from instruments developed for primary and secondary schools. Under increasing scrutiny for their effectiveness in measuring literacy growth in chil-

* The authors would like to acknowledge the contributions of our colleagues at the Center for Literacy in Philadelphia and the Literacy Research Center at the University of Pennsylvania; Tom Marmor and Faith Penner for their work on an earlier paper related to this chapter; and the Philadelphia National Bank for its continuing support for this project.

359

dren, these tests are even more problematic when administered to adults who come late to the acquisition and development of literacy. When used to derive "reading levels" for adults, these tests lead to a view of adults as 'deficient' learners while yielding little useful information about their progress. Furthermore, labeling adults in this way contributes to a public perception of adults who lack literacy skills as part of an "epidemic" and to the view of illiteracy as disease or pathology. As Carman St. John Hunter (1987) has pointed out, literacy becomes defined as a remedial program, designed by "missionaries" for those "in need." Literacy levels will increase, she argues further:

> where there is serious commitment to goals of equity and justice and where the educationally disadvantaged are able to be involved in shaping their own learning within the context of reshaping the social, political, economic and cultural environment within which they live. If we are able to begin with programs that promote participation and direction by learners, that degree of openness can become a first step . . . Literacy is either a tool of oppression or liberation. Management and methodology contribute either to the increased dependence or to the empowerment of participants. Our decisions make a difference. (p. 7)

If adults are to shape their own learning, as Hunter argues, assessment would seem a critical feature of this vision of participatory literacy education.

From the perspective of research on literacy, the issue of assessment is similarly problematic. If we assume that adults' literacy abilities cannot be ranked along a continuum from the unskilled to the highly proficient, illiterate to highly literate, and if we do not just replace the single scale of reading levels with multiple scales that measure fixed competencies, we set ourselves the complex task of understanding literacy development from the multiple perspectives of learners, texts, tasks, and contexts (Lytle, Marmor, & Penner, 1986). Fundamental questions about what constitutes growth or change in reading and writing during adulthood—and about the factors which foster growth—argue the need for a different approach, one which accomodates the diverse social, cultural, and rhetorical contexts informing adult learning.

In this chapter we describe a conceptual framework for assessing literacy learning which has evolved from our work with adult learners in an ongoing longitudinal study called the Adult Literacy Evaluation Project (ALEP). ALEP is a collaborative action research project being conducted by university-based researchers in collaboration with administrators, staff, and adult learners at a large, urban literacy program providing instruction to adults who present themselves as needing "basic" reading and writing skills. The staff and adult learners' dissatisfaction with the current assessment procedures available to them and their commitment to practitioner research make this program an ideal site for designing alternate ways to conceptualize and assess the literacy learning of adults.

The chapter begins by reviewing research from a sociocultural perspective providing insight into differences in the literacy practices of adults within and across contexts. In particular, Street's (1984) "autonomous" and "ideological" models of literacy establish a useful structure for unpacking prevailing assumptions about adults as learners. We show how autonomous models inform, and often constrain, current programs for literacy instruction. Working from this ideological perspective, we describe our framework for learner-centered literacy assessment, contrasting it with traditional assessment and describing its use in our longitudinal study of adults as learners. Using excerpts from interviews, we show how adults' concepts of literacy and learning as well as their literacy practices in everyday life constitute important dimensions of literacy growth in adulthood.

SOCIOCULTURAL PERSPECTIVES ON ADULT LITERACY

In comparing theoretical perspectives on literacy, two divergent models proposed by Street (1984) provide useful starting points. The "autonomous" model assumes literacy is a neutral and objective skill or set of skills, independent of any specific social context or ideology. In presupposing acceptance of the cultural norms or values of the dominant group in a society, the autonomous model, in Street's view, allies itself with a notion of universal cognitive consequences for the acquisition of literacy. The "ideological" model, on the other hand, focuses on the social, political, and economic nature of literacy practices, which may differ from group to group within a society as well as from society to society. This model questions, rather than accepts, the status quo, and argues that claims for the cognitive consequences of literacy rest on the valuing of particular literacy conventions and thus the privileging of the literacy practices of specific groups within a society.

In the ideological model, it is assumed that all approaches to literacy are informed by ideology, whether implicit or explicit. Rather than a polar alternative, Street's ideological model is a synthesis of the two tendencies. As Street (1985) explains this model:

> It approaches literacy quite explicitly from the point of view of its location in ideological and cultural contexts but it does not attempt to deny technical,

skill or cognitive aspects. Rather the mental set within which these aspects are handled encapsulates them within the cultural whole and within structures of power, resisting attempts to represent them as independent or "autonomous." (p. 1)

In Street's view, by abstracting the technological aspects from their cultural and ideological location, advocates of the autonomous view set up a polarity which assumes these aspects can actually be considered independently, with the "cultural bits" added on later. Rejecting the autonomous view entails recognition that literacy practices cannot be considered neutral or objective. In contrast, the ideological model takes an anthropological perspective, defining literacy as a "culturally organized system of skills and values learned in specific settings" (Heath, 1980) and focusing on the uses of reading and writing and on their social, economic, and political meanings. From the ideological perspective, being literate means using knowledge and experience to make sense of and to act on the world, not merely encoding or decoding a set of technical symbols.

Challenging the concept of a universal literacy, the ideological model suggests instead a "plurality of literacies" which reflect the different roles literacy plays in the lives of individuals and communities (Szwed, 1981; Cook-Gumperz, 1986). In the work of Heath (1983), in the Piedmont Carolinas, Scribner and Cole (1981) in West Africa, and others, there is ample evidence that individuals can be expected to vary greatly in their purposes for reading and writing, in the texts they choose to read and write, as well as in the contexts for the performance of reading and writing abilities. As compared to a "machine-made" standardized product, then, an individual's literacy profile might be conceptualized as a contemporary quilt in progress, a kind of patchwork whose configuration is closely linked to specific settings characterized by specific opportunities and constraints (Lytle, Marmor, & Penner, 1986). As Scribner (1987) explains it, literacy is not a feature or attribute of a person but should be considered literacy-as-practice, a range of activities that people engage in for a variety of purposes. Intra- and interindividual differences in literacy ability reflect context-of-use, so that any individual's patchwork will be both unique and dynamic.

The cross-cultural research clearly suggests that in order to understand the literacy practices of different adult learners, we need to explore the particular types of reading and writing which adults themselves see as meaningful under different circumstances and which reflect their own purposes and aspirations. Reder's (1987) studies of three ethnic American communities (Eskimo, Hmong, and Hispanic), for example, describe connections between the social organization of literacy in each setting and its social meanings. In all three communities literacy is organized as collaborative practice in which reading and writing are both used and transmitted. Within each of these collaborative group activities, however, individuals participate in the same literacy practices with different modes of engagement. Some actually handle the materials while others provide knowledge or expertise or are engaged in the activity solely from a social perspective. Adults acquire different types of knowledge about literacy from these practices, with each type being learned in practice-specific ways.

What is evident from these and other cross-cultural studies is the profoundly social nature of literacy, and the problems inherent in the concept of literacy as a technical skill, extracted from its context. If literacy is culturally learned and practiced, an ideological approach to assessment would involve the systematic study of what counts as literacy to different groups and individuals within the society. This would include the perceptions of literacy—of language and learning, reading and writing, and of themselves as learners—adults bring to literacy instruction and the conventions adults learn when they encounter different texts and tasks in various contexts. From this perspective we have the potential to learn considerably more about learners' intentions, about their knowledge of specific uses and functions of literacy, and about the varied literacy events or activities in which they participate. Looking at literacy as sociocultural practice thus subsumes the cognitive psychological processes (e.g., how adults use their prior knowledge to read and write strategically), and foregrounds adults' purposeful use of print to create and communicate meaning in their daily lives.

Historical analyses of what counts as literacy in the United States point to shifts from multiple literacies to a single, standardized schooled literacy and from informal to formal strategies for its acquisition (Cook-Gumperz, 1986). Beginning with the 18th century view of literacy as pluralistic, grounded in everyday practice, and including the use of reading and writing skills for many social purposes, Cook-Gumperz traces its evolution to the 20th-century notion of literacy as singular, stratified, and designed to be taught in schools as the acquisition of universal, cognitive, and technical skills. While originally literacy was acquired through informal interactions around such texts as personal letters, diaries, notes, books, and almanacs, with the advent of mass schooling, literacy instruction was formalized and functioned to define and control access. In this new schooled sense, literacy "drove a wedge through the working class" (Laqueur, 1976, as cited in Cook-Gumperz, 1986) and "changed forever the relation of the majority of the population to their own talents for learning and for literacy" (Cook-Gumperz, 1986, p. 27). Cook-Gumperz's analysis furthermore characterizes the time from the 18th to the 20th centuries by a shift from the perception of literacy as dangerous to illiteracy as dangerous. Associated with popular culture and radical politics, before mass

schooling literacy was understood by some to be empowering and therefore threatening to existing social structures. At the same time, it was
viewed as potentially useful for social control. The current public perception of the close link between literacy and economic opportunity exists
alongside a public conception of illiteracy as a societal but ultimately an
individual failure. When schools link self-improvement with successful acquisition of reading and writing skills, then the learner's sense of goodness
or worth is inextricably tied to literacy. This moral dimension places responsibility on individuals who learn to blame themselves when schooling
does not allow or provide them opportunities to learn (Tyak, 1977, as cited
in Cook-Gumperz, 1986).

ASSUMPTIONS ABOUT ADULTS AS LEARNERS

Given the historical relationship between literacy and schooling, it is not
surprising that one of the most overused metaphors in the field of adult
literacy is the portrayal of illiteracy as pathology, which by extension implies that illiterate adults are the diseased who require curing. Newspaper
articles and posters recruiting students and tutors often portray adults as
helpless and needy; an illiterate adult, like a sick child, must be helped by
others to surmount his or her predicament. Illiteracy, like a disease, is
assumed to be *in* a person and must be 'cured' by an outsider in order for
change to occur. The autonomous view of literacy, as Street (1984, 1987)
has pointed out, connects literacy with cognitive consequences—the
transformation of minds and the creation of special cognitive abilities
(Goody & Watt, 1968; Olson, 1977). The resulting negative view of illiterate
adults is often internalized by the adults themselves, thus limiting their
capacity for change (Eberle & Robinson, 1980, as cited in Fingeret, 1983).
Practitioners point out that adults in literacy programs frequently mention
the feeling of being stigmatized and the accompanying need to hide what
they do not know.

Yet the image of incompetent and dependent adults marginalized by
society because of their deficiencies does not match the people who come
forward for instruction. Adults who enter literacy programs in the United
States bring with them a diversity of literacy abilities and behaviors; they
are clearly neither a homogenous nor an incompetent group. In a recent
study of adults as learners, Fingeret (1983) concludes that illiterate adults
do not necessarily fit the stereotypes of dependency, weakness, and failure affixed to them by the mainstream literature culture. Rather, the adults
she studied operate within complex social networks in which they are
interdependent, offering skills of their own in exchange for the literacy
skills of others within their network. She concludes that "illiterate" adults

have as varied interests, abilities, and self-perceptions that are as diverse as "literate" adults. In a similar vein, Reder's studies (1987; Reder & Green, 1985) document in minority communities the spontaneous acquisition of literacy skills outside of formal programs. Although these informal community practices may not actually "teach skills," they provide adults with the opportunities to learn about specific uses of literacy and to acquire skills. As a consequence, these adults can hardly be called "illiterate".

Some argue that the high attrition rate (over 50%) in U.S. adult literacy programs (e.g., Harman, 1984) suggests that many programs may be incongruent with what we know about adults as learners and thus fail to meet adults' needs. As Harman points out, adults rarely remain in programs over a long period of time and are unlikely to be interested in texts that have little meaning or use in their lives. In contrast to children, they are free to leave if they do not perceive the teaching and learning to be relevant to or useful in advancing their goals. Thus literacy defined as learning skills may reinforce negative stereotypes and lead to dropping out of programs and diminished self-esteem among adult learners.

PROGRAMS AS SOCIAL CONSTRUCTIONS OF LITERACY

Adult literacy programs have been characterized by Fingeret (1984) as either "individually-oriented" or "community-oriented." In individually oriented programs, literacy (generally conceived as the teaching of reading skills) is the primary focus of instruction; the goal is essentially to "mainstream" the adults into the middle class. Although often located in the community they serve, these programs do not usually become involved in working with community members to solve local problems. They are, however, concerned about "meeting the complex, interrelated needs of the individuals they serve" (p. 20). Instruction may incorporate materials pertaining to housing, employment, or other concerns, but the primary focus is on teaching skills rather than on the content (Fingeret, 1984). Based on a fundamental belief in improving individuals' circumstances through education, most literacy programs in this country are individually oriented and reflect society's desire to give those who have failed in traditional schooling a "second chance." These programs usually offer one-to-one tutoring by a volunteer or classes which meet with a teacher in a convenient location, generally a public library, church, or community building. Instruction generally emphasizes improving reading and writing levels through a variety of activities, frequently adapting materials and techniques developed originally for teaching young children and utilizing commercial materials patterned after the formats of school workbooks prepared for adult learners by national literacy organizations.

As compared to individually-oriented programs, community-oriented literacy programs are based on a different set of values and assumptions (Fingeret, 1984). Literacy instruction in these programs uses as a starting point issues identified by members of the community. The intent is to focus on culture and empowerment, that is, on "increasing the ability of persons and groups to control their lives" (p. 21). Community-oriented programs often integrate literacy instruction with employment counseling, child care, drug counseling, and other supportive services. Although individually-oriented programs also seek to empower adults, they differ from community-oriented programs in that the latter programs frequently advocate collective action for the improvement of conditions in the entire community. Literacy instruction is just one of many services; literacy learning is participatory, embedded in a variety of activities intimately tied to central concerns in people's lives. These programs are often initiated by adult learners who see a need for particular skills in order to make personal or political changes in their lives.

Within the broad categories of individually-based and community-based, literacy programs differ from each other in their orientation to teaching and learning. Some programs reflect the teaching methods and content of traditional schooling, while others consciously reframe and reconstruct the notions of literacy, teaching, and learning. When a program resembles school, the adults and their teachers or tutors tend to play their expected roles. There may be assignments and homework, spelling tests and grades. Often these programs focus almost entirely on remediating skills so that adult learners can perform predetermined functional tasks or pass standardized tests. Other programs begin with participants' personal, social, and political concerns and build the entire curriculum around the evolving needs and interests of the adult learners.

Programs also differ in the extent to which they provide opportunities for individual and collaborative learning. Reder (1987), Heath (1983), and Fingeret (1983) among others have described the collaborative nature of many out-of-school literacy practices among groups of adults. As mentioned above, Reder (1987) found that in the three sites he studied, "literacy development [was] heralded by the emergence of collaborative literacy practices, in which reading and writing tasks [were] accomplished collectively" (p. 256). While Reder does not mean to imply that all literacy activities are done collectively in the communities he studied, he argues that emphasis on solitary activities misrepresents the group contexts in which much of the reading and writing takes place. Study of the nature of collaborative relationships around reading and writing tasks and the functions and uses of print within the community provides insights into ways to promote literacy acquisition and development (Reder, 1987). Whether individually- or community-based, programs may choose to incorporate these collaborative literacy practices into the design of the curriculum.

AN IDEOLOGICAL VIEW OF LITERACY ASSESSMENT

The cross-cultural literature on literacy provides a compelling picture of differences within and across communities and underlines the elusiveness and complexity of defining what should be assessed. Rejecting a normative model in favor of one reflecting multiple social uses and meanings entails recognition that there is no "true" definition and that each definition of literacy "must be designed for the purpose to which it is put" (Bormuth, 1975). Furthermore, as Fingeret (1984) explains, "to establish a national set of standards for a concept that is relative in relation to time and culture will, to some extent, undermine efforts to develop literacy programs that are appropriate to the varying needs of adults in their social contexts." (p. 7)

Currently available standardized tests for adults reflect an autonomous view of literacy (see, for example, the analysis of the TABE, the Test of Adult Basic Education, in Hill & Parry, 1988). Conceptualizing literacy as a set of technical skills and assessment as measurement have led to dependence on decontextualized tests of letter and word recognition and to paragraphs with questions keyed to reading subskills. Applying reading levels and subskills to adult learners involves the deceptively simple transfer of models and practices used to describe the acquisition of reading in children. In a comprehensive survey of assessment in reading, Johnston (1984) argues that the reading field has historically relied on quantitative methods in order to create the appearance of being scientific and objective. He contrasts two models of reading performance currently in use: the "ability" model and the "learning" model. According to Johnston, the ability model is grounded in Darwinian notions of intelligence and focuses on stable abilities or "traits" which are frequently described as deficits (e.g., processing limitations) and thus less amenable to change. The learning model, in contrast, is concerned with "states" in which the learner's strategies are presumed to vary with the context or situation and thus are more responsive to instruction. The diagnostic or trait model of assessment is typically seen as appropriate for assessing adult literacy learners because, from this perspective, adults have failed to respond to earlier "treatment." Viewing assessment from a medical/diagnostic/prescriptive orientation fits neatly with the identification of adults as reading at the grade levels of elementary school children. In the deficit mode, illiteracy is an in-the-

Table 16.1. Contrasting Frameworks for Assessment in Adult Literacy

	Current Traditional	Learner-centered
View of Literacy	• autonomous model • literacy as a set of technical skills (neutral, objective, decontextualized) • universal literacy	• ideological model • literacy as social practice, context-dependent • multiple literacies
View of Learner	• learner as object of assessment • emphasis on deficits	• learner as active participant and co-investigator • emphasis on practices, strengths and strategies
Why Assess	• measurement/testing • diagnosis/prescription • placement and program monitoring • select graded materials	• evaluation • self-assessment • placement and program monitoring • select materials • inform curriculum and instruction
What to Assess	• "traits" • reading levels	• "states" • variety of texts, tasks and contexts
How to Assess	• standardized tests which measure vocabulary and comprehension in addition to functional skills • primarily quantitative • predetermined procedures and roles for assessor and assessee	• one-to-one scripted and ethnographic interviews; inventories and profiles; reading and writing tasks in context; portfolio analysis • quantitative and qualitative • dynamic, recursive, and collaborative
Who Assesses	• instruments • teachers as testers	• adult learners (self-assessment-individually and collaboratively- with each other and with teachers/tutors/program coordinators)

reader phenomenon compatible with the view of literacy as disease or pathology and the literacy problem, nationally, as an epidemic. Under this system failure is a given, the first line of failure is the individual, and the current modes of assessment efficient ways to manage and explain that failure.

In Table 16.1 we present two contrasting frameworks for assessment in adult literacy based on Street's autonomous and ideological models. Current traditional assessment (defined as assessment that is congruent with the autonomous model) views literacy as a technical skill and the learner as the object of assessment. Procedures assess learners' traits or deficits and yield quantitative information about reading levels with sub-skill data for vocabulary and comprehension abilities. Thus, the current traditional model does not provide information that is critical to our understanding of adult literacy. We are left with many questions, primarily because much of what is apparently central to these processes goes undocumented. When we reconceptualize literacy as more than a set of technical skills, and the assessment of literacy as more than measurement, we move toward an ideological approach or framework for assessment which we are calling "learner-centered." This framework can be used not only to analyze but also to foster adult learning in more informed ways. It is built on several assumptions: (a) adults come to literacy programs with particular goals or objectives; (b) adults bring with them perceptions of literacy and illiteracy, reading and writing, teaching and learning—all of which affect what and how they learn; and (c) assessment procedures themselves communicate notions about literacy. These three assumptions lead to a fourth: Adults' expectations and learning may be strongly influenced by what the literacy program chooses to assess and by the particular methods used. Assessment is an informing process, a fundamental act of educating which can play a significant role in teaching and learning. Inappropriate tests teach beliefs and shape learners' notions about literacy and about themselves as learners. These tests also drive many curricular and teaching decisions.

Current cognitive and sociopsycholinguistic theory and research define reading and writing as constructive and dynamic processes and emphasize the role of metacognition or knowledge of one's own thinking for the strategic control of language. This aspect of reading and writing seems to have particular relevance to adults' literacy development. In a recent essay about adult disabled readers, Johnston (1985) presents case studies in which a myriad of difficulties arise for individuals from misconceptions or more precisely "missing conceptions" of various aspects of reading. When an adult learner thinks that writing is spelling or reading is primarily remembering (as did one of Johnston's cases), the person's operating theory tends to limit his or her progress. Another direction in the current research is the importance of a reader's or writer's prior knowledge in acquiring literacy. If the acts of reading and writing are characterized by the meaning and intentions people bring to them, and if all meaning is made in the context of prior meanings, then people can be expected to differ stylistically in the ways that they read and write. This does not mean merely that adults differ in their prior knowledge, but also in how they organize and use what they know. Acknowledging these individual differences within and between readers and writers suggests assessing adult learners in ways which go considerably beyond the limiting concepts of levels or discrete skills (see, for example, Lytle, 1982, 1985).

"Learner-centered" assessment, as we have argued above, assumes that literacy is a diverse set of cognitive, social, and cultural practices which are context-dependent. Adults are active participants, co-investigators in determining and describing their own literacy practices. To demonstrate their particular reading and writing interests, strengths and strategies, they select and interact with a wide range of texts and tasks in different contexts. Learner-centered assessment departs from the narrow focus on measurement and testing to a broader view of evaluation, one which integrates skills and content, foregrounds observation, documentation and self-assessment, links assessment with curriculum and instruction, and diversifies assessment procedures for different purposes and audiences (Lytle & Botel, 1988). Adult learner participation and ownership are considered central to the learning process so that learner-centered assessment is participatory, with adults necessarily taking an active role in designing their own assessment.

Table 16.1 summarizes and contrasts our conception of the key characteristics of the current traditional and learner-centered frameworks for assessment.

THE ADULT LITERACY EVALUATION PROJECT

One could imagine a wide range of assessment practices congruent with the learner-centered framework which we have proposed. Indeed, it is axiomatic that with an ideological approach to assessment, the rationale and methods for assessing growth over time vary considerably from learner to learner, setting to setting, and program to program. The assessment procedures, and thus the data available for analysis, reflect the overall goals and emphases of each program, whether individually- or community-oriented. If we wish to learn about adult literacy acquisition and development as it occurs within the contexts of literacy programs, then we need to regard this variation as both expected and interesting. What constitutes growth in literate behaviors in adulthood reflects what counts and is valued by groups and individuals in particular settings.

The site for the Adult Literacy Evaluation Project is an urban literacy agency which offers to adults who describe themselves as "illiterate" both one-to-one tutoring by volunteers and small staff-taught classes held in churches, libraries, and businesses throughout the city. Because the curriculum at this agency is designed in response to individual needs and interests, staff members have been particularly dissatisfied with the available standardized assessment tools and several years ago recognized the need to develop alternatives. At the same time an interest in alternative forms of assessment was being explored by faculty and graduate students at the university. This, in turn, led to a proposal for collaborative research which was funded by a local corporation.

Because they were designed for use in an action research project, the assessment procedures were intended to serve a dual purpose: to generate new knowledge about adults as learners and at the same time to perform programmatic functions such as matching adults with tutors and/or teachers and providing information for planning curriculum and instruction. In this program, assessment occurs primarily through a set of *planning conferences*, conducted by staff coordinators when adults enter the program and thereafter at six-month intervals. Intended to engage the adults in a variety of literacy-related activities in which they would explore practices as well as abilities, the planning conferences were initially developed as part of a six-month research seminar held by staff-and university-based researchers and informed by input from adult learners. As the project staff learns more from and with these adults, the conferences continue to be revised.

Our conceptual framework for the assessment procedures in this agency includes four dimensions of literacy development: practices, strategies and interests, perceptions, and goals. The first dimension focuses on *the role of literacy in everyday life.* Learners describe the variety of settings in which they engage in literacy practices, including what, when, where, and with whom they read and write as well as their mode of engagement in literacy activities. Home, community and work environments are explored in order to understand the social networks and contexts in which learners currently use or may want to use literacy skills. Over time, adults report changes in the frequency and variety of their literacy activities such as participating more actively or playing new roles in community meetings. To assess the adult learner's repertoire of *reading and writing strategies and interests*, a variety of texts and tasks are used, including an array of materials such as newspapers, novels, manuals, and adult learner-authored texts. Word recognition is evaluated by using photographs taken in urban Philadelphia of signs on buildings, streets, and public transportation. At both initial and periodic planning conferences, learners bring with them a portfolio of accomplishments and work-in-progress which they examine and critique in collaboration with the coordinator and tutor. Criteria for assessing growth include more efficient and effective use of a range of reading and writing strategies, a broader range of task-appropriate types of transactions with texts, and increased ability to use written language for multiple purposes.

The third dimension of the assessment focuses on adult learners' *metacognitive perceptions of reading and writing, teaching and learning.*

This involves exploration of adults' theories of reading and writing including their own histories and their current conceptions of reading and writing processes, tasks, texts, and strategies. Adults examine their own beliefs, attitudes, and expectations about who reads and writes and what it means to be a "good" reader and writer. These constructions of adults' past and present experiences with teaching and learning—in and out of school—in both literacy-related and other domains provide self-portraits which are refined and elaborated over time. Finally, adults identify, prioritize, and discuss their *goals and purposes* for literacy learning based on a list of goals compiled from adults who previously participated in this literacy program. Adults indicate in which areas—home and family, social and business, personal, and job-related—they already feel competent; these goals become the basis for constructing their curriculum. As the assessment processes are further refined, they are becoming increasingly integrated into the tutoring and teaching programs.

The four dimensions described above are used to structure assessment. An ongoing portfolio of reading and writing artifacts functions as the primary resource for selecting, analyzing, and synthesizing data to indicate growth. At any point in time, procedures can be used to construct a profile which captures not only the four dimensions but also their interrelationships—a rich and nuanced picture of the literacy beliefs, experiences, and abilities of the adult. Over time, each dimension represents a continuum of literacy development. For example, assessment of goals involves not only demonstration of competence at particular self-selected tasks (e.g., reading aloud to children) but also setting new goals, reassessing old ones, or changing priorities over time. Changes in goals, even to what appear to be somewhat "simpler" tasks or to tasks which adults previously indicated they could do, are not necessarily signs of going backwards. Instead a change in goals may indicate a more realistic appraisal of what is entailed in accomplishing that particular activity or in adapting it for a different context, purpose, or audience. For example, adults may redefine what it means to help their children with their homework from checking to see that it has been done to interacting about what is to be learned and how to go about it. In Table 16.2 we summarize each of these dimensions for assessing change or growth.

In the remainder of this chapter we analyze examples taken from assessment interviews to demonstrate how learner-centered assessment can be used to further our understanding of literacy learning in adults. These examples have been selected from a longitudinal study of the literacy practices and abilities of 85 adult learners who, seeing themselves as "illiterate," came to an urban literacy program for instruction (Lytle, Marmor, & Penner, 1986; Lytle, Belzer, Schultz, & Vannozzi, 1989). The examples illustrate some of what can be learned about literacy development from

Table 16.2.   Design for Assessment in ALEP: the Adult Literacy Evaluation Project

Dimension of Assessment Procedures	Purposes: Learner & Program	Processes	Criteria for Assessing Change
Literacy Practices: Role of Literacy/ Learning in Every-day Life	To describe con-texts and practices	Discuss uses in home, community, workplace, etc.	Frequency and vari-ety in types of par-ticipation in literacy-related events
Reading, Writing, and Learning Strate-gies and Interests	To provide opportu-nity to display and take risks in display-ing reading and writ-ing repertoire	Construct and ana-lyze portfolio of lit-eracy activities; range of reading and writing texts and tasks	More efficient and effective use of a wider range of strat-egies
Perceptions of Reading and Writ-ing, Teaching and Learning	To understand adults' histories of reading & writing, teaching and learn-ing; knowledge of processes, strate-gies, texts & tasks	Discuss percep-tions in general and in relation to spe-cific activities above	Changes in knowl-edge about reading and writing pro-cesses, strategies, texts and tasks
Goals	To identify current abilities and inter-ests and set priorit-ies for learning	Discuss and com-plete checklist of goals; (home and family; social and business; personal and job-related)	Demonstration of competence at self-selected tasks re-lated to goals; set-ting new goals; reassessing previ-ous goals; changing priorities

learner-centered assessment, in this case from the exploration of adults' literacy histories and their perceptions of reading and writing, teaching and learning. By unpacking the prior knowledge and experiences adults bring to literacy programs, we show how their understanding of language and learning evolves over time, enabling them to participate in literacy activities more successfully and with increased awareness of the functions of written discourse.

Planning conferences, as described above, are complex, multifaceted interactions from which adults and staff members construct a literacy pro-file at a given point in time. For our discussion of adults' literacy histories and perceptions, we have selected excerpts from the portions of the plan-ning conferences which resemble ethnographic interviews in that they are efforts to uncover the learners' own understandings or meanings about literacy in practice. As conducted in the ALEP project, these interviews are both scripted and open-ended, so that spontaneous adaptations for individual learners can be made. Questions are designed to engage the adult in a dialogue informing to both interviewer and learner. As a form of dynamic assessment, these interviews are directed toward learners' strengths; when appropriate, interviewers assist learners in coping with any difficulties. At various points in the interview, the adults are encouraged to reflect back on what has occurred so far, to reframe or revise what they have said or done, and to make connections among different aspects of their experiences. Conversational in tone, the assessment interviews attempt to engage learners in self-revelation and self-reflection, to provide a climate for risk taking, and to make it possible for adults to assume the roles of experts on their own learning.

LITERACY HISTORIES

Although adults may come to literacy programs with the self-image of a nonreader or writer, when encouraged to tell stories about their own past experiences, the ensuing narratives reveal distinctive concepts of themselves as readers and writers and of reading and writing in general. Furthermore, it is not unusual for adults to describe the extraordinary efforts they made to teach themselves how to read and write outside of formal schooling. In the first example, an adult explains her use of writing to decode the print in her environment prior to participation in the literacy program:

> Example 1. Trying to memorize was hard. So I used to write. When I was walking down the street, I used to take little notes on the signs and stuff and writing them down and go home and break them down into syllables. Even though I couldn't pronounce them, I used to break them down still. And I came home and I started looking into the newspapers more so or I picked up the horoscope, that was my main option for reading. Because I love . . . I didn't know too much about the horoscope but I liked to read them. I guess the good things and the adventures you may have and whatever. That was more of an inspiration to read too.

In this example we see how the adult has developed her own strategies for learning to read by taking notes on signs. Unlike many adult literacy students who initially may see little relationship between writing and reading, this adult knows how to use writing to help her read. Yet her focus is on reading as decoding: "breaking words down," and in literally carrying the words out of their meaningful context, she undoubtedly makes her reading task more difficult. From this description, however, we also learn that although she claimed she couldn't read when she first began working with her tutor, in fact she was already reading and developing preferences for particular types of material. One of the functions of the interview then is to bring into awareness uses of literacy in everyday life that the adult herself had discounted.

While adults use print in numerous ways, they may not consider themselves to be "readers" or "writers" because what they are doing does not match what they have come to believe about reading and writing based on years of formal schooling. This occurs even when their strategies are clearly acquired in school, as in Example 1 where the learner invoked a script for decoding by breaking words into syllables. In the examples below, the same adult reports how she spontaneously invented her own version of the Language Experience Approach (LEA) for composing letters, a method for learning reading and writing she had not encountered in school:

> Example 2. I had a friend and he was in Germany. And I never knew how to write letters. And my cousin used to always, I used to contradict [dictate] my letters to her. And she used to write them. And I used to say, "Well it seemed kind of bad. They are my words, but you actually written the letter." So she said, "Don't worry about it. You'll learn how to write your own letters." And I used to write it and she'd say "read it back." But it was funny, even though I couldn't write it, I was always able to read whatever I contradict [dictate] to someone. So I read my letters. And afterwards I rewritten them in my own handwriting . . .

In Example 2, when the adult uses her own prose as the text, to her surprise she is able to read. While claiming on the one hand to be a "nonreader," given the opportunity to talk about her own reading and writing she begins to describe a full range of literacy activities. This example also illustrates how adults work collaboratively to accomplish literacy-related tasks and ways they modify these relationships as they begin to acquire new skills. In Example 3, we see how this adult perseveres in reading and writing so that her understanding of the task deepens as her independence as a writer grows:

> Example 3. And then afterwards I say, "Okay I'm going to write my first letter." And I took all the letters that she ever written for me and spread them all over the bed. And I was able to read all of the letters, though. And I just kept on reading and reading them. And I said, "Okay, get plain paper, pencil." And I started writing my own letter. When I first write my first letter, it's like a three page letter. But it was out of a lot of the words that I was writing that was already written already. But they were still my own

thoughts. And most of the time when you write letters, it's almost, say about fifty percent of the same words. But adding different things and different timing. So, what I did, I written it in scrabble like what I really wanted to say, and whenever that might have happened at a newer time, or something that I wanted to ask about previous time that I didn't get a response to.

Distinguishing between copying and composing, she reuses words from old letters to create new meaning. Furthermore, through many repetitions of the same process, she comes to an insight about language use which allows her to gain control over the genre. In a continuation of this same narrative, she describes how she empowered herself as a reader and writer:

Example 4. And before I knew it I was able to write letters. And from there on, I told her, "See you don't have to write any more letters for me. I can write them now." She said, "How do you do it?" I say, "I write over. I take the letters that you write out and I analyze what was written." I must have read them over and over and over. And I still have the letters. I read them. And I write over and now I don't even have to go back over them, I can write now. Which I don't have to write to him because we don't talk any more. But being able to write them was a big expression.

We see from these examples that in learner-centered interviews, even when adults attest to their inability to read and write, they often go on to describe a wide variety of accomplishments in which literacy plays a role. Some of these experiences are imitative of school routines while others reveal original strategies and tenaciousness in accomplishing personal goals.

While out-of-school literacy learning is often successful, adults' school memories are consistently about failure and blame. The following examples show two recurrent themes:

Example 5. I don't want to go to school until the third grade. I didn't go to the first grade and the second. The third grade, the teacher [would ask me to read] . . . I didn't want him, you know, to get mad . . . The teacher would hit me because I didn't know how to read. Half the time they scared me, you know.

Example 6. When I started going to the high school, it was the same way, you know. And it was just like all my life it was like this little corner, you know. And [now that I'm learning to read and write] it's getting out of that corner and learning.

Typical of many adult literacy learners, in the first excerpt the adult remembers unexplained irregularities in school attendance and notes that when he was unable to learn to read, his teachers became angry and punishing. Often failure to perform in school has caused isolation, as Example 6 suggests; adults lacking literacy skills have been outsiders, excluded from learning. Many assessment interviews are punctuated with similar stories; adults allude to placement in special education and remedial classes as a result of missing school from serious illness, or being ridiculed and excluded from academic learning by assignment to classes, presumably vocational, in which one adult we interviewed remembered a curriculum composed of "making things."

Revealing both creative strategies for coping with print and painful memories of schooling, these literacy histories illustrate the complexity of the experiences adults who consider themselves to be "illiterate" bring to literacy programs, experiences which inform present learning and must be taken into account in the assessment of literacy development. By uncovering previously unarticulated strategies the adults use in their daily lives in the initial assessment conference, it is possible to begin the program by building on strengths rather than by identifying deficits. What is apparent from these interviews is that even though the adults initially present themselves as lacking reading and writing skills, they have been involved in literacy learning throughout their lives. Any assessment of adults as learners must begin with that assumption.

KNOWLEDGE OF LANGUAGE PROCESSES AND STRATEGIES

Reading

Many of our assessment interviews indicate that adults bring to literacy programs their own conceptions of reading, including knowledge of strategies and of the features of different texts. As they recount their own experiences and their observations of other readers, operating frameworks or theories of reading are often embedded in their talk. In the examples below, three adults present contrasting views of reading:

Example 7. In the mill up there, you've got some good readers up there ... They've got some guys up there that just glance at something and can just about tell you what the whole thing is ... all of them are highly educated, very highly educated.

Example 8. I read more so better then I ever read in a long time. And I enjoy it. I like to read now. I never knew reading had so much meaning to it because there are so many words, you know. We talk a lot, but to be able to read the words out of a book and analyze them, what they mean or what they saying, is something really important.

Example 9. So being able to open a book is just like a dream. Being able to keep following it. Not knowing what's going to happen in the book. Not knowing what's in the book. So I keep on traveling and reading. And each time I read a sentence or a paragraph and I get a smile—it makes me—boy, I wonder what the next sentence is going to be like ... and I just keep on going until I finish the story. When I finish the story, it's like, boy, I really enjoyed that.

In Example 7, the speaker is responding to a question about what it means to be a "good reader," and how one might identify skillfulness. The respondant's reply suggests that he believes good readers can simply glance at a page and read what is on it, that their process is rapid and effortless, and that good readers can retell whole texts by merely perusing them. In Example 8, the adult reflects on her experience in the literacy program, recalling a previous time when reading was not as easy or enjoyable. In saying "I never knew reading had so much meaning to it because there are so many words," she juxtaposes an earlier view of reading as knowing or recognizing words with her current meaning-centered orientation. In Example 9, another adult learner tries to capture the intense sensation of fluent reading by comparing it to a kind of dreamlike journey, one in which new experiences occur again and again as the reader accesses previously unknown worlds through print. When an adult becomes a reader relatively late in life, it is not surprising that such descriptions of the process often suggest a kind of wistfulness and wonder at being able to make sense of what has been for so long inpenetrable.

Adults also reveal the extent to which social networks support reading and writing in their daily lives. Often even beginning literacy learners help members of their own families with literacy tasks, an illustration of the shifting and mutually supportive roles played by adults who may work together to decipher newspapers or write letters collaboratively. In the example that follows, this experience of reading as a fundamentally social process is further explained:

Example 10. Well I written a story about the world. The title was "The World." In order to write about it I had to get different points of view from different people. And I may talk to my boss about things. Sometime I read the paper to find out different ideas about what's going on around the world. And my teacher. And sometimes my neighbors. And my nieces and nephews. They're younger than me but they have a lot of goals and dreams. And it's just like myself, even though I'm an adult and they're children. I find that a lot of my ideas and goals come from my nieces and nephews. Because they make me ... when I see them wanting to learn how to read and write, really wanting to see what's out there in this big world, it makes me want to just go out there and grab for it even more. And that's where a lot of my writing came—through the children.

In a later interview this same adult describes checking books out of the library for herself and for her nieces and nephews. Now that she can read, they read to each other:

> Example 11. So we just get together around the table. Sometimes we all get together and read now. And that was something I never been able to do because of my pride or not being able to read. A lot has opened up since the program and I wouldn't trade it back for nothing.

As adult learners become more skillful readers, their patterns of participation in literacy events do not reflect less dependence on others (Fingeret, 1983) but rather suggest the development of more complicated forms of interdependence and a broader range of modes of engagement with written language.

Writing

Adult learners' descriptions of themselves as writers are similarly informing. Because many associate writing with handwriting, however, their concepts of writing as composing or making meaning are often not apparent in their initial responses. In replying to the question "how would you describe yourself as a writer," one adult, for example, replies:

> Example 12. And I mean, I always did love to write. I mean, I loved to write so nicely and so neat, you know. I try to learn just all kind of writing, and I love a lot of fancy writing. I love that. And if I could get into the upper level, I love all kind of fancy ways and everything like that.

In an effort to learn to write neatly, he describes taking poetry books home from the library and staying awake until three in the morning writing, or more precisely, copying the poems. Yet when the interviewer encourages him to elaborate further, he begins to speak of topics he would like to write about—his family, literacy, his progress—moving from a conception of writing as encoding to a view of writing as a way to communicate ideas and construct meaning for himself.

Other adults describe strategies they have invented for coping with the demands of transcription while focusing on meaning. Many of these resemble what is currently taught in the primary grades as "invented" or "inventive" spelling and the use of placeholders for unknown words or letters. In Example 13 the speaker describes the way she overcame her inability to spell which prevented her, she believed, from keeping a diary. Example 14 displays the kind of internal dialogue some adult learners use to impel their composing processes forward:

> Example 13. Whatever comes to my mind I just put it down. I mean I can't spell all of the words, but I just put them down. If I have to draw a little picture in between there to camouflage the word itself. And I just keep on going. I just write.

> Example 14. And a lot of time when I am writing I always think out loud, like "what about if somebody read my story, they don't like it?" Or "what about if the words don't sound right?" Or maybe I write the story and somebody else might write the same thing. Or "should I make it short or make it long? Do I keep using 'I', 'I', 'I', like I always do? Or do I start it with large paragraphs or small paragraphs? Do I just talk about literacy or I talk about myself in general?

Using placeholders is apparently a self-invented strategy the adult in Example 13 uses for maintaining the flow of writing when she doesn't know how to spell a word. Later interviews revealed that this approach is actually an adaptation of an earlier strategy, using pictures to take notes in class, something she had taught herself to do while studying to become a painting contractor before she ever entered the literacy program. In the second excerpt we see the ways in which a beginning adult writer has internalized many of the same kinds of questions more experienced writers raise. Her self-interrogations reveal an appreciation for a diverse set of problems writers encounter, including decisions about invention, purpose, originality, audience, style, and the use of conventions.

Descriptions such as these argue for the value of self-reports of strategies in use, both when adults enter programs and as they progress over time. As we have pointed out above, the assessment interviews provide opportunities for adults to describe in some detail their own processes or methods for reading and writing, and thus have the potential to make what is being learned more accessible not only to tutors, teachers, and program planners but to the adults themselves. In addition to these descriptions, the assessment interviews include opportunities for adults to demonstrate and reflect on responses to various texts, on their strategies for reading and writing, and on ways they have developed for dealing with difficulties. These examples suggest that assessing adult literacy development entails careful tracking of how learners metacognitive perceptions of reading and writing change as they become more skillful readers and writers.

VIEWS OF TEACHING AND LEARNING

Scaffolding

Adults also come for instruction with expectations about what it means to be a teacher or a learner. One adult expressed the delicate balance a teacher needs to maintain between being helpful and nurturing independent learning:

> Example 15. And I might tell them a story about myself or a story about something. They might write it . . . And they helped me out . . . [and they also] let me go for myself and that's what it is about. You know, if they helped me out, I wasn't going to get nowhere. So they get me to go for myself.

Rather than requiring adults to continue to attempt more and more difficult tasks until they fail, as in conventional assessment, in learner-centered assessment a relationship is established from the beginning that is co-investigative and collaborative. The coordinator who is conducting the assessment notes, for example, independent as well as assisted or scaffolded reading and writing (Cazden, 1979; Palincsar & Brown, 1984; Applebee & Langer, 1984). A collaborative process, however, may interrupt the adult's notions about traditional roles of teachers and students, and may make the adult uneasy about not being able to demonstrate competence "all by herself." Yet we have also found in conducting a large number of initial interviews that under these scaffolded conditions adults generally exceed their own expectations, that is, read and write much better than they thought they could. As one adult put it, "I don't know why I can read this tonight. Usually I'm not able to."

Choice and Control

For adult learners (and for children and youth as well) choice and control appear critical to learning (Hunter & Harman, 1979; Knowles, 1970; Cross, 1981). In an ideological approach to assessment, the processes of selecting materials and methods for learning begins with the initial interview. As one adult expresses her concern with ownership:

> Example 16. The thing is being able to do something you want to do. Because when you get out in the world, as you get older and come out of high school. Yes it's true . . . if your boss say, "I want this here done", you're still going to have to do it. He's going to say, "I want it done good." But the same time, you learn your own techniques, how to do it to get it done. And it's the same thing with a book too.

From this woman's perspective learning involves constructing one's own methods for understanding and accomplishing reading and writing tasks. In later interviews, she speaks explicitly about sharing control with the tutor, and she attributes her failure to learn in school to the absence of opportunities to choose what and how to read or write:

> Example 17. Whenever I have a class, my teacher always ask me what do I want to do. Most of the time when I go [went] to the school, the teacher never ask you what do you want to do. It's what they want you to do. And I feel sometime when we, when they let us use our own discretion, our own intelligence—it kind of gives you some type of drive or goal to step out there. And if we never get the opportunity, we never are going to go anywhere. I mean I could sit up here and read all the books you want me to read, but it doesn't mean I'm going to remember them all. Because it wasn't nothing I really wanted to remember from the beginning; it was something you wanted me to remember. And I think that's the reason why I can't read today.

This person emphasizes that adults are accustomed to exercising options in other areas of their lives. Working with their tutors and teachers to select goals, set priorities, and choose materials and methods all contribute to the adult's control of the learning experience. Furthermore, programs which do not provide opportunities during assessment for choice (e.g., of texts and tasks) will yield data about adult literacy development that reflects the judgments and world views of program planners or tutors, not the learners themselves. There appears to be little to gain in assessing adult development as displayed in progress through prestructured materials and standardized tests. Whether learner-centered or more traditional, assessing literacy apart from the context of teaching and learning has little to contribute to our understanding of adults as learners and can be misleading. When programs are participatory and adults structure their own learning, we get a dramatically different picture of literacy development.

CONCLUSION

The focus of this chapter has been a conceptual framework for assessing literacy acquisition and development in adults who come to literacy programs lacking what they regard as the basic skills. In the first part we argue that a sociocultural or ideological view of literacy and literacy learning suggests an approach to assessment which values what literacy means to individual adult learners and within that framework aims to understand the meaning of growth and the factors that contribute to it. This learner-centered framework may be useful to both researchers and practitioners, as it provides a structure for designing procedures to document change over time along a number of dimensions, including adults' practices, strategies, perceptions, and goals. In this approach to literacy assessment, the adult learner is not the object of scrutiny but rather an active participant in the process.

In the second part of the chapter we present excerpts from interviews in which adult learners trace their literacy histories and tell stories of learning in and out of school. Assessing literacy development necessarily takes place within a set of parameters of expectations determined initially by the learners themselves. Learner-centered assessment is a problem-posing process rooted in the expertise of the adult learner and connected to daily life. Intended to inform and enable, this type of assessment attempts to create the conditions under which learners may empower themselves. In contrast to tests that often mask ability, in this form of assessment adults typically exceed their own expectations.

Moving between public and private worlds of spoken and written language, adults who come late to learning develop literacy abilities within an intricate web of memories and life experiences. Theories of literacy acquisition in children and adolescents may provide only the roughest blueprint for what happens when adults bring lifetimes of coping to the learning process. The adults with whom we are studying changes in literacy practices and the effects of literacy on their lives have much to teach us about their own experiences. By linking assessment in literacy programs to action research, we are making an effort to study what literacy means to different learners without imposing models or expectations based on what some assume should have been learned in school.

REFERENCES

Applebee, A. N., & Langer, J. A. (1984). Instructional scaffolding: Reading and writing as natural language activities. *Language Arts, 60*(2), 168–175.

Bormuth, J. R. (1975). Reading literacy: Its definition and assessment. In J. B. Carroll & J. Chall (Eds.), *Toward a literate society* (pp. 61–100). New York: McGraw Hill.

Cazden, C. B. (1979). Peekaboo as an instructional model: Discourse development at school and at home. *Papers and Reports on Child Language Development, 17*, 1–19.

Cook-Gumperz, J. (1986). Literacy and schooling: An unchanging equation? In J. Cook-Gumperz (Ed.), *The social construction of literacy* (pp. 16–45). Cambridge: Cambridge University Press.

Cross, K. P. (1981). *Adults as learners.* San Francisco: Jossey-Bass.

Fingeret, A. (1983). Social network: A new perspective on independence and illiterate adults. *Adult Education Quarterly, 3*(3), 133–146.

Fingeret, A. (1984). *Adult literacy education: Current and future directions.* Columbus, OH: ERIC Clearinghouse on Adult, Career, and Vocational Education, Ohio State University.

Goody, J., & Watt, I. (1968). The consequences of literacy. In J. Goody (Ed.), *Literacy in traditional societies* (pp. 27–68). Cambridge, MA: Cambridge University Press.

Harman, D. (1984). *Functional illiteracy in the United States: Issues, experiences and dilemmas.* Far West Laboratory and the Network, Inc. (Prepared for the National Adult Literacy Project).

Heath, S. B. (1980). The functions and uses of literacy. *Journal of Communication, 30*(1), 123–133.

Heath, S. B. (1983). *Ways with words: Language, life and work in communities and classrooms.* Cambridge: Cambridge University Press.

Hill, C., & Parry, K. (1988). *Reading assessment: Autonomous and pragmatic models of literacy* (LC Report 88-2). New York: Literacy Center, Teachers College, Columbia University.

Holzman, M. (1989). Evaluation in adult literacy programs. In M. Cooper & M. Holzman (Eds.), *Writing as social action.* Portsmouth, NH: Heinemann.

Hunter, C. (1987). Literacy/Illiteracy in an international perspective. *World Education Reports, 26,* 1–4.

Hunter, C., & Harman, D. (1979). *Adult illiteracy in the United States.* New York: McGraw-Hill.

Johnston, P. H. (1984). Assessment in reading. In R. Barr, M. L. Kamil, P. Mosenthal, & P. D. Pearson (Eds.), *Handbook of reading research* (pp. 147–182). New York: Longman.

Johnston, P. H. (1985). Understanding reading disability: A case study approach. *Harvard Educational Review, 55*(2), 153–177.

Knowles, M. S. (1970). *The modern practice of adult education: Androgogy versus pedagogy.* New York: Association Press.

Laqueur, T. (1976). The cultural origins of popular literacy in England: 1500–1850. *Oxford Review of Education, 2,* 255–275.

Lytle, S. L. (1982). *Exploring comprehension style: A study of twelfth-grade readers' transactions with text.* Unpublished doctoral dissertation, University of Pennsylvania, Philadelphia.

Lytle, S. L. (1985, April). *Comprehension styles of twelfth grade readers: What verbal protocols can (and can't) tell us.* Paper presented at the American Educational Research Association, Chicago, IL.

Lytle, S. L., Belzer, A., Schultz, K., & Vannozzi, M. (1989). Learner-centered literacy assessment: An evolving process. In A. Fingeret & P. Jurmo (Eds.), *Participatory literacy education.* San Francisco: Jossey-Bass.

Lytle, S. L., & Botel, M. (1988). *PCRP II: Reading, writing and talking across the curriculum.* Harrisburg, PA: The Pennsylvania Department of Education.

Lytle, S. L., Marmor, T. W., & Penner, F. H. (1986, April). *Literacy theory in practice: Assessing reading and writing of low-literate adults.* Paper presented at the American Educational Research Association, San Francisco, CA.

Olson, D. R. (1977) From utterance to text: The bias of language in speech and writing. *Harvard Educational Review, 47,* 257–281.

Palinscar, A. S., & Brown, A. L. (1984). Reciprocal teaching of comprehension-fostering and comprehension-monitoring activities. *Cognition and Instruction, 1,* 117–175.

Reder, S. M. (1987). Comparative aspects of functional literacy development: Three ethnic communities. In D. A. Wagner (Ed.), *The future of literacy in the changing world* (pp. 250–270). Oxford: Pergamon Press.

Reder, S. M., & Green, K. R. (1985). *Giving literacy away: Alternative strategies for increasing adult literacy development.* Portland, OR: Northwest Regional Educational Laboratory.

Scribner, S. (1987). Introduction to theoretical perspectives on comparative literacy. In D. A. Wagner (Ed.), *The future of literacy in a changing world* (pp. 19–24). Oxford: Pergamon Press.

Scribner, S., & Cole, M. (1981). Unpacking literacy. In M. F. Whitman (Ed.), *Writing: The nature, development, and teaching of written communication* (Vol. 1, pp. 71–87). Hillsdale, NJ: Lawrence Erlbaum Associates.

Street, B. V. (1984). *Literacy in theory and practice.* London: Cambridge University Press.

Street, B. V. (1985). *The "autonomous" and "ideological" models–A further note.* Unpublished manuscript.

Street, B. V. (1987) Literacy and social change: The significance of social context in the development of literacy programmes. In D. A. Wagner (Ed.), *The future of literacy in a changing world.* Oxford: Pergamon Press.

Szwed, J. F. (1981). The ethnography of literacy. In M. F. Whitman (Ed.), *Writing: The nature, development, and teaching of written communication* (Vol. 1, pp. 13–23). Hillsdale, NJ: Lawrence Erlbaum Associates.

Tyak, D. (1977). City Schools: Centralization of control at the turn of the century. In J. Karabel & A. H. Halsey (Eds.), *Power and ideology in education.* Oxford: Oxford University Press.

17
Developmental Challenges, Developmental Tensions: A Heuristic for Curricular Thinking*

Louise Wetherbee Phelps

SETTING THE PROBLEM

It is remarkable how long it took to notice the oddity of "freshman writing" as part of a university curriculum. No other subject at the university is conceived as a single, freshman course with no sequel. The institution of "freshman" English expresses powerfully, in symbolic and political terms, the academic community's folk wisdom that writing has no adult elaboration and growth beyond mastery of a trivial competence. Even more important, as a practical unit of curriculum the freshman writing course has made any developmental concept of literacy unimaginable. The classroom teacher worked, as she had to, in a developmental zone defined by the semester or year boundaries of the freshman course. She could not concretely know its antecedents or predict its consequences; she was cut off from the rest of the curriculum as a source of real writing and reading experiences. With formal instruction ending at the freshman level, teachers felt compelled to design curriculum as damage control and crisis management.

* I want to thank all my colleagues at Syracuse for their work in developing a writing program that engages all its members collectively and collaboratively in heuristic thinking about a developmental curriculum. The ideas here are proposed for their interpretation and critique. Members include the teachers who are becoming reflective practitioners; Faith Plvan and the coordinators who are leaders and mentors in that effort; and the research faculty whose generative ideas constantly renew the curriculum: Carol Lipson, Catherine Smith, Margaret Himley, James Zebroski, and visiting professor Brian Huot. In particular, I should acknowledge Margaret Himley and the profiling group, whose inquiries and reflections are contributing to a communal understanding of students' experiences and attitudes. Margaret, along with Carol Lipson, also bears major responsibility for creating a climate in which the program could come into being in 1986.

Writing across the curriculum changed this situation dramatically, spreading consciousness and practices of writing into the disciplines and into the upper division, sometimes in the form of broadly subscribed or required advanced writing courses (Kinneavy, 1987). Expanding writing instruction across time and contexts created for the first time, at the college level, the demand and the intellectual possibility for truly developmental curricular thinking (cf. Moffett, 1968; Moffett & Wagner, 1976/ 1983). This situation calls for a new paradigm in which program planners must take into account complicated interactions and multiplistic casual relations among different dimensions of person, curriculum, and broader cultural environment (see pluralist, ecological models of explanation: for human development, Dixon & Nesselroade, 1983; Cairns, 1979; Magnusson & Allen, 1983; for literacy, Kintgen, Kroll, & Rose, 1988; Goelman, Oberg, & Smith, 1984; Phelps, 1988b; see also Chapter 1, this volume). However, this transition to comprehensively developmental planning has not yet taken place in most programs despite the introduction of new courses and writing across the curriculum.

I approach this problem from a theory that situates personal growth in literacy within human development over the life span, which in turn represents a complex, reciprocal transaction between an active individual and a dynamic context (Phelps, 1984, 1988a, 1988b). Literacy is understood here to mean the forms and practices of spoken, written, and inner language related to writing as a symbol system and productive cultural activity (in the rich Soviet sense) (see Zebroski, 1983; Wertsch, 1985; Kozulin, 1986). Such a broad concept of writing requires study of literacy development and how the culture supports it over the lifespan and across contexts of use. The 1987 Coalition on the Future of the Teaching of English has reawakened such a vision of rhetoric in human life, affirming the commitment of educators at all levels to helping persons to develop the arts of language as the basis for creating, clarifying, communicating, relating, and applying knowledge in all fields of cultural experience. Once articulated, such a vision transforms the practical problems of teaching at any point or phase in the educational system.

My question in this chapter is, what strategies or principles might guide the process of curriculum design at a particular school—Syracuse University—at a particular historical moment, when the intention to develop a comprehensive program of writing instruction made the developmental question concrete, material, and urgent for curriculum planners and classroom teachers. My focus is not on the answers this program is developing, but on *the processes of inventive thinking and critical action* needed to plan and implement a curriculum of this sort.

From this perspective, working on a curriculum (like any kind of composing) calls for heuristics—strategies for systematically approaching a creative problem, one that can't be solved by simply applying a rule (Perkins, 1981). One common type of heuristic is a set of concepts representing topics of categories for inquiry. Such a terminological heuristic provides an analytical or analogical framework for mapping out distinctions, contrasts, questions, and relations between phenomena or domains of experience (Young, 1987).

A powerful heuristic for thinking about developmental aspects of curriculum can be derived from a distinction between two aspects of time, proposed by Saussure (1915/1959) in the context of linguistic analysis and extended by Jakobson (1960; Jakobson & Halle, 1956/1971) to represent two fundamental and intersecting dimensions of human experience. These two dimensions are *sequence* and *simultaneity*, originally presented by Saussure as orthogonal axes or coordinates on a graph (p. 80). Sequence represents experience as linear, chronological, logical, casual, and progressive (as in episodic memory or narrative). Simultaneity refers to that virtual dimension of experience in which actualities or possibilities coexist and connect (as in semantic networks or presentational art). These coordinates will be translated here for curricular planning into "developmental challenges" (for ordering or sequence) and "developmental tensions" (for simultaneous, opposed motives generating conflicts).

What this conceptual heuristic does is provide a way of mapping the developmental territory by distinguishing between two types of issues and problems, suggesting ways to think about relationships between them. However, in a practical situation a conceptual heuristic, providing a strategy or tool for thinking, must be specified in procedural (strategic) terms as a process enabling participants to act and to make decisions. Further, it is not enough for a heuristic to provide an organizing scheme, enabling teachers to make broad, abstract, initial choices for an instructional program. Curriculum is not a text of statements about what is or should be (though it begins as one): it is the dynamic by which teachers actually design syllabi and course plans, realize them experimentally (in daily choices), and constantly update and adjust instruction, thereby interpreting and revising "theory texts." Heuristic strategies must therefore help enable teachers, with their students, to make and remake the curriculum as reality and as text, individually and collectively.

THEORETICAL AND INSTITUTIONAL BACKGROUNDS

A Contextualist Philosophy of Development

In previous work I have argued for contextualism as the basis for a psychology of composition (Phelps, 1984) and a philosophy of composition in resonance with postmodern thought (Phelps, 1988a, 1988b).

Contextualist themes dominate contemporary discourse in many fields, in the form of metaphors modeling reality on the communicative relationship. Developmental psychology is one discipline where thinkers (e.g., Lerner, 1983a; Hoffman & Nead, 1983) have explicitly turned to contextualism as a philosophical basis for theory and research. Many have cited the seminal work of Stephen Pepper (1942) to contrast contemporary emphases on process (change, flux) and context (field, system, relation) with earlier reliance in psychology on organic and mechanistic metaphors.

Pepper described four root metaphors constituting relatively adequate bases for understanding the world philosophically. Contextualism frames the world as event, a concept that has developed in contemporary thought in the categories of *change* and *context*, often through textual or discursive metaphors. Organicism uses the living organism as a metaphor for understanding reality. Others are formism—the world as rules or logical forms, and mechanism—the world as machine. Given its focus on the individual, organicism is the obvious philosophical base for a discipline concerned with human growth in all dimensions including the psychological, and is highly developed in the work of Piaget, where it is combined with formism. However, in the 1970s developmental psychologists found problems with an unmodified organicism as a basis for research and practice. First, by starting with the individual organism, or person, as the primary unit of analysis, it perpetuates Cartesian dualities between individual and environment, subject and object, mind and matter. More important, this paradigm provides no motivation for change, since organicist theories conceive of change largely as transitions between tightly structured, relatively static and autonomous stages. This model assumes that development moves toward a known end state, adulthood or maturity, ignoring the possibility of continuing development as well regression from mature states.

I will be working from a view of human development strongly influenced by contextualist premises (see Lerner, 1983b, for a historical synthesis). Contextualist psychologies, while not abandoning the organic metaphor entirely, tend to see even human beings as events, that is, in terms of their ability to change and to enter into relationships.

Contextualist psychologies center on the "person-in-the-environment" (Magnusson & Allen, 1983), assuming that there is no meaningful notion of self apart from transaction and communication with the physical and social environment. The self is differentiated from this relationship rather than being taken as a primordial fact—paradoxically deriving its capacity for self-organization, autonomy, self-organization, novelty, and unpredictability from its interdependence, even interpenetration with the world. (See Prigogine & Stenger, 1984, on self-organizing systems). In the "developmental synthesis" (Cairns, 1979), an interdisciplinary treatment of social development, this relationship is called the "bidirectionality of structure and function." Bidirectionality is complete in that the environment continually shapes the person while individuals transform their environment, both physically—through tools—and culturally—through signs. As Cairns puts it, "the experiences of the individual—even self-produced ones—can change its biological properties. These changes, in turn, help to control and direct social behavior. Development is a two-way street; it is not just the unfolding of potentials, nor the shaping by experience" (p. 24).

A particularly important kind of bidirectionality for humans is interpersonal. Urie Bronfenbrenner, in setting up a classification of nested ecological contexts, begins with the dyad or pair and moves gradually outward to larger and larger social interactions, culminating in cultural institutions and societies as wholes. Bidirectionality in a dyad such as mother and child or teacher and student has the property of *synchrony* (Cairns, 1979; Bronfenbrenner, 1979), meaning that their actions are mutually supported and coordinated. Reciprocity, one form of synchrony, means that actions of partners in a dyad become more similar: thus, for example, students' learning may depend on the colearning of their teachers. The relationship between personal development and major institutional or cultural change may, as in the Syracuse Writing Program, display complex relationships of cause and effect or synchrony.

Contextualism deals with the problem of developmental change by positing a paradox. Self-organizing structures like human beings, while holistic in function and capable of improvement or progress, are always imperfect wholes that cannot achieve some final, mature state. It is hard for them to either stabilize or stagnate, since they are always subject to new external influences through interchanges with their environment. For the developing mind, this means that any cognitive structure contains imbalances, tensions, inconsistencies, and contradictions, which paradoxically enable and motivate continuing life-span growth.

I translate these philosophical premises into the following working definition of development:

> Development is bidirectional change over time leading to an increasingly complex patterning of activity, through which both autonomous individuals and their products and environments may become increasingly complex structures, separately and in relationship.

Given the biological basis for individual development, some capabilities unfold on a maturational schedule, but formation and transformation of mental structure is largely driven by the individual's own activity, or what is called in language arts education "active learning." "Activity" also refers more broadly to transactive social practices or to the social meaning of behavior (see Bissex, 1980 for an account, focused on invented spelling, of how a child's inventive activity relates to maturation of his linguistic and cognitive abilities and to social practices and language conventions).

The overall movement of this growth-through-activity in human beings is towards more power over the environment and towards self-regulation or control of one's own behavior. This means that development moves toward consciousness. Paradoxically, the person becomes increasingly individual and autonomous, on the one hand, and more connected into environmental networks on the other.

Piaget (1977, see index) calls this overall process of change by virtue of activity "equilibration," a continual balancing and unbalancing of the organismic patterns. This concept subsumes two processes: (a) assimilation of information or energy to a continuing, relatively stable structure—evolutionary or quantitative change; and (b) accommodation—revolutionary, qualitative transformations of large parts of the structure or the whole. Both figure in development, but it is revolution that gives development its characteristic wave pattern.

Complexity of patterning refers here to the way a mental or cultural structure becomes more finely differentiated into new parts and connections and more highly organized through multiple relationships. As experience feeds information into the system, it becomes denser and richer, creating the need to form new patterns and transform old ones. This model of the mind says that learning creates *dis*order as well as order, stimulating the creation of more powerful ways of containing and controlling the proliferating information. The notion is similar to models of the writing process or of problem solving that begin with a contradiction, ambiguity, or felt tension arising from new experiences or ideas that do not fit with old knowledge. Such cognitive dissonance leads a writer or problem solver to reorganize and reconceptualize networks of information. The idea of "productive error" captures the same insight: Experiences of disorder, failure, or dissonance are necessary conditions for developmental change in the face of complexity.

This definition of development is normative, expressing ideal tendencies of growth. It is important, therefore, to acknowledge certain negative possibilities working against development. First, development itself incorporates a negative principle in that its impulse to order must be constantly defeated if growth is to occur. The internal principle for change is disequilibrium. In order to be flexible and adaptive, our mental state must be always somewhat unfinished, disorderly, with potential for new arrangements and novelty generally.

Second, development is not inevitable, especially if we distinguish biological and physical growth, which seems to follow a predictable course toward maturity and decline, from mental and spiritual growth, which can in principle continue until death. At any point in the psychosocial life history, development may be countered, blocked, and weakened in various ways. In fact, the very control of development in adulthood means an enhanced power to choose *not* to develop. (Perry's [1968] description of intellectual and moral development in college men shows the ambivalence, paradox, and pain these choices entail, the possibility of stagnation as well as sudden leaps and advances.) So while change is inevitable, since one must cope with the onslaught of new experiences just by being immersed in the stream of life, development is not.

Multiple Perspectives on Literacy Development

The philosophy of development so far described leads me to conclude that literacy is not a unitary cognitive phenomenon that follows a single, predictable course of growth. Instead it is a psychosocial function of great complexity, in which many streams of development come together and many kinds of ability and knowledge are coordinated.

Because of this ad hoc, opportunistic nature of literacy as a psychological function, trying to construct a single, universal model of its development is fruitless and unproductive. Instead one must adopt a pluralistic approach that multiplies perspectives on literacy development without attempting to synthesize or combine them. I have suggested that productive perspectives might include literacy in relation to personal, life-span development; literacy as language or semiotic activity; literacy as a domain of skillful performance; literacy as critical consciousness; literacy as an esthetic sphere; and literacy as a practical-moral activity involving work, power, and conflict (Phelps, 1988b).

This view presented so far, of a contextualist philosophy and its implications for literacy, underlies both the concept of the heuristic and the process for implementing it proposed in this work. First, however, I want to present a set of concepts on *writing* development that have contributed to the decision-making processes of curriculum discussed here.

The following description of writing and development over the college years, drawn from a document prepared for program planners and teachers (Phelps, 1988d), is couched in more explicitly pedagogical and curricular terms. It makes selective use of some theoretical perspectives on literacy to help teachers reconceive writing as developing over the undergraduate years. Rhetorically, it also addresses an argument for viewing writing developmentally to university faculty and administration, in support of a proposal to transform existing courses into a new four-year sequence of writing instruction. These goals explain the selection of particular perspectives to frame a view of writing and development. Some lenses (writing as a cultural tool, writing as skilled and reflective practice, writing as language) were chosen for the Syracuse Writing Program because they harmonize with intellectual themes at the university emphasizing symbolic systems, processes, and advanced technologies. Other emphases fit with institutional facts at Syracuse like the strength of professional fields requiring artistry of performance.

Clearly, rhetorical and pragmatic considerations invade the pure domain of "theory" itself long before we begin talking about pedagogical application. In a contextualist curriculum, designers who understand literacy pluralistically select theoretical frameworks both to fit the institution as it is and to realize its potential for change.

Writing and Development in the College Years

Modern composition has redefined writing in a way that changes what we mean when we call it a "basic" skill. Before, "basic" meant elementary knowledge of a limited number of rules and conventions. Now we mean that the written word—verbal literacy—is fundamental to critical action and information exchange in an advanced technological culture. In this view, to teach writing is to help learners master a symbol system and use it as a multipurpose cultural tool.

Jerome Bruner (1973) describes cultural tools like language as amplifying devices for extending a human organ or capacity, as a hammer extends the hand or a telescope extends vision. Writing is a special form of language with new properties as a cultural tool; it has a close relationship to other technologies including drawing and electronic media.

In a high-literate culture, writing amplifies the capacity of individuals to think, learn, remember, and plan as well as to exchange information, influence beliefs, and get things done. Electronic design environments allowing thinkers to combine writing flexibly with reading and iconic communication promise to further amplify and diversify its power as a cultural tool. Judgments of writing "skill" along with teaching strategies need to address the whole range of writing functions and, especially in an academic context, support the cognitive development and applications of writing ability as much as communicative ones.

What, then, does it mean to "know how" to write? To use a symbolic system, writers must orchestrate and apply many kinds of knowledge besides the rules of the system itself. What they need to know is indeterminate, depending on the task. Writers draw on a rich, evolving knowledgebase including, for example, the following:

- cognitive skills
- knowledge about social conventions and interpersonal relationships

- "cultural literacy" and situational information
- field-specific knowledge about subject matter
- technological skills
- visual, auditory, and motor skills.

Only a small subset of this knowledge is identifiably "writing" or even linguistic knowledge. Composition teachers cannot conceivably provide students with all this knowledge. They must rely heavily on the growth of students' knowledge and skills through casual and formal language use. Writing "specialists" are really generalists who help writers acquire, access, coordinate, and control needed knowledge and skills by learning more about the nature of cultural codes and conventions, the processes of inquiry and composing, and the rhetorical (communicative) functions and contexts for writing. They do so primarily by providing learners with opportunities for writing practice, offering them feedback, selectively drawing lessons and general principles from practice, and encouraging students to accomplish and to reflect on their own learning.

Each literacy task at the college or university requires some context-specific knowledge of subject matter, of other experts' views, of the teaching-learning situation, and of operative local conventions for carrying out particular discourse purposes—asking questions, making criticisms, testing a hypothesis, arguing a point, and so on. What writing specialists try to do is prepare students to cope with these cognitive and rhetorical expectations by applying and adapting what they already know and by using learning strategies that depend on language. Teachers hypothesize that such reflective thinking about language use, along with specific attention to analyzing new rhetorical tasks, may help students to make the transfer of language skills from speech or from one writing situation to another, and to act critically in those situations. Later these same abilities to analyze, contrast, and analogize between discourse situations, and to ask useful questions of informants, should serve students as they move into post-college environments.

One important role for writing programs is to familiarize students and content teachers with developmental patterns of learning and help academics adjust teaching and learning to fit them. There are important differences between these patterns and modes of learning in those academic disciplines defined by rationalized content (see Schön, 1987, on reflective practice). Writing development more closely resembles learning in other fields of *skilled practice* like acting, musical performance, clinical medicine, or sports—for example, in their use of models, their tolerance or encouragement of trial and error, and their reliance on tacit, unspecifiable knowledge rather than explicit criteria for right and wrong practices. Many other professional practices at Syracuse have a dimension of artistry that follows similar developmental paths of learning and requires, like writing, a pedagogy that emphasizes coaching and learning by doing. Such fields—for example, architecture, engineering, industrial design, or nursing—tend toward studios, clinics, labs, workshops, and internships where students try out ways of behaving or making things and subject their actions or products to criticism and revision for effectiveness in a pragmatic context.

Writing is strongly developmental not only because it is a skill rather than a content but also because as a form of language it has a genetic base. For instruction to be effective in writing, students need to be developmentally ready, based on linguistic and cognitive maturation that depends significantly on appropriate social experience. Maturation cannot be speeded up much through effort or instruction; experience and the sheer passage of time are often prerequisites or corequisites of instruction. Often an individual's social, cognitive, and linguistic abilities do not develop in synchrony, and people differ greatly in maturation rate over a broad normal range. As with speech, knowledge of the writing system relies on unconscious acquisition of complex codes and strategies that cannot be learned directly, or can be learned consciously only when embedded in a problem-solving situation. Finally, developmental progress is not incremental and step-by-step. It is holistic and proceeds in leaps that require considerably risk taking and tolerance for productive error. Improvement may involve long latency periods of apparent stagnation or even regression. As writing skills mature, there remain so many indeterminacies in writing situations that one cannot automatically expect either an easy or a successful performance on a new task.

The college years are particularly crucial for writing development. The combination of maturing abilities (linguistic, cognitive, and social) and an environment that foregrounds literacy sets the stage for intensive writing growth. However, writing, unlike speech, does not develop inevitably or without conscious instruction. The university has the potential to provide a comprehensive environment for challenging writing skills in a developmentally sound sequence and for supporting writers as they respond to these challenges. The ultimate goal of teaching writing in a college environment is to help writers make the transition to producing and managing their own writing development. For this to happen writers must learn to diagnose their writing problems, replace dependence on formal teaching with peer collaboration or expert advice, analyze new writing situations, and assess their own written work and writing abilities.

The circumstances of college writing—the student's developmental ripeness, the rich role of literacy in an academic setting—can, if exploited, stimulate intensive growth in writing skill, broadly defined. Conversely, intensive and varied writing experience can stimulate intellectual development and disciplinary learning in the college environment because it amplifies the potential for reflection and critical thinking.

The Institutional Context

One consequence of the theoretical position taken here is that a writing curriculum should be adapted to fit an institutional context. I do not mean simply the range of academic and professional fields taught, but the institution in its most comprehensive sense, including everything from its size, geographical setting, classroom space, and financial resources to its fundamental values and leadership style. Some of these factors are enduring, while others mark a particular historical moment of conflict or opportunity. The institutional context as a whole acts as a set of design constraints for a writing program, which must be planned elastically not only to fit the current possibilities but to adapt to (and sometimes catalyze) institutional change. Although the Syracuse program design responds to this whole context, I will limit myself to its broadest features, emphasizing the academic character of the university.

There was an unusual opportunity to design writing instruction at Syracuse in terms of a comprehensive plan for the university, incorporating both courses offered on the traditional format (a sequence of writing studios from freshman year through graduate school) and collaboration with other faculty to develop nontraditional instructional formats and writing in the disciplines. The current working plan attempts to meet this demand in terms that suit the administrative and curricular structures of the university and maximize its institutional themes and strengths.

Syracuse University is a mid-sized university (about 13,000 undergraduates) set in urban upstate New York. Its most striking feature is an array of professional schools (13), mostly undergraduate, coexisting with a strong arts and sciences college from which come many of the top-level administrators. These academic units, and Syracuse in general, are further distinguished by curricular and research interests clustering around rhetorical themes: symbolic systems and practices of communication (verbal, iconic, numerical-logical, electronic, multimedia); information systems and exchange; design; theory-into-practice; and the technologies of communication. In recent years the university has been improving its position as a research institution, at some cost to the quality of its undergraduate education. Recently the administration has set the goal for Syracuse to right this imbalance and has taken steps to improve and reward teaching, especially at the undergraduate level.

In 1986, Syracuse University made a decision to establish a new writing program based on contemporary theory and research in composition. The decision was triggered by dissatisfaction with an outdated freshman English program in which traditional content was implemented through a modular curriculum based on concepts of incremental learning (mastery learning). Although initially proposed for the College of Arts and Sciences, the program quickly became an all-university project. In its first year, the new program was chartered as an independent academic unit with faculty appointed jointly in English or (potentially) other departments and colleges. The charter established a broad though vague mandate for the Writing Program to offer, coordinate, and integrate instruction in writing for the university at large. These structural decisions set the stage for the program to begin reconceptualizing and improving the quality and coherence of writing instruction for which it was then responsible, while developing and arguing for a long-term design of instruction integrated with the whole educational program. This design envisioned a sequence of writing courses (now being implemented) to be called "studios," as part of a comprehensive package including "horizontal" writing instruction tied to the content curriculum. The latter aspect of the plan will not be discussed here (see Phelps, 1988d), though its cross-curricular exchanges are vital to studios. Both sides of the program emphasize these features, among others: inquiry and its connections to writing; focused forms of literate talk; reflective writing by both teachers and students; collaborative learning and collaborative teaching; reflections in writing leading to "publication" by both teachers and students; expanding thinking and communication through sophisticated electronic environments; and the rhetoric of discourse communities and professional cultures in and out of the university.

The immediate impetus for institutional change was the challenge presented by the concept of a sequence of writing studios. The Writing Program was faced with the need to help part-time instructors and new teaching assistants suddenly begin teaching a radically different set of courses, for which the documentation was still abstract and sketchy. It could not be otherwise until these teachers themselves began through inventive, critical practice to reimagine and concretize the new curriculum. In this situation, developmental questions emerged with startling clarity and force, because studios posed them as a function of *curriculum* rather than a matter of individual teachers' decision making.

To this point, developmental theories have been discussed in the composition and reading literature largely as something an individual teacher can draw on to decide how to respond to student papers, or to plan and organize a single writing course. The teacher uses scholarly sources to account (abstractly, deductively) for the ways in which students do and don't perform as expected or desired, or to predict their behavior, and thus make teaching choices. Nothing in this model of application compels or helps the teacher to envision what is going on simultaneously in the student's literacy life that may change this account, or provides reality checks in the form of information about student's subsequent writing development.

This limitation was particularly the case at Syracuse, where a sequence already existed in fragments, taught by teachers who did not form an intellectual community with opportunity to correlate their experiences and curricular content at different levels. If anything, the later courses became substitutes for the writing course not taught earlier (because Freshman English was largely a literature course, except for an opening unit on a highly prescribed form of argumentation). Program planners saw immediately that it was necessary to differentiate the new course content from year to year on developmental premises, and to test these hypotheses and revise them in practice. Classroom teachers more slowly realized the need as they taught studios in sequence, or tried to rethink content for courses coming later in the sequence. They were brought up against the consequences of their decisions, either by students or by their colleagues, now engaging in constant conversation about what their students had and hadn't learned in previous courses, what they needed or wanted next, and so on.

In one of the early curriculum documents produced in the program, "Thinking 'Studio': A Speculative Instrument" (Phelps, 1987b), "studio" was treated as an emerging genre which teachers were invited to analyze. A distinction was made there between "text" and "subtext," as follows:

> TEXT: the continuing, stable content that distinguishes the Studio curriculum—its primary topics, activities, and goals.
> SUBTEXT: underlying, changing patterns of writing-related issues and problems that recur throughout the studios and help to organize the interpretation of the curricular text in particular studios ... themes that emerge from the complex situation in which the text is taught.

Two other terms were also introduced: "developmental challenges," defined as "specific problems of writing, thinking, learning, and communicating presented to learners by the symbolic and practical environment"; and "tensions" as a synonym for the many subtexts that took the form of polarities, conflicts, and oppositions. Developmental challenges served to differentiate the way TEXT (e.g., inquiry as a practice) changed over curricular time, from studio to studio, while SUBTEXTS were identified with developmental tensions (for example, being "critical" vs. "belonging"—becoming a member of a new discourse community).

I mention this source because it reveals that, contrary to most accounts, heuristics stand in the middle between two conceptual operations, rather than at the beginning. Many discussions in composition picture application of a heuristic as the first step in a thinking process (to generate ideas). What happened here (typically, in my experience) is that some terms, concepts, and connections articulated in relation to a problem stimulated a search for analogous terms or categories in another context that might make my own more powerful, useful, and simple. Recalling the coordinates introduced by Saussure and profoundly extended by Jakobson, I *reinvented* their categories as a heuristic for improving my own thinking. This is a form of analogous practical reason called "abductive" (White, 1983, adapting Charles Peirce, 1978) that does not happen just once, but is a constant feature of curricular thinking. The heuristic works because it simplifies, organizes, and transforms existing insights. As category, it enables one to make distinctions and connections; and as metaphor, it brings a new field of meanings to bear on the situation.

The Axes of Succession and Simultaneity: Saussure and Jakobson

In his *Course in General Linguistics*, Saussure (1915/1959), sketched a distinction between simultaneous and sequential linguistic phenomena in a simple diagram picturing an orthogonal relation between the "axis of simultaneities" and the "axis of successions," respectively (p. 80). In Saussure's definitions, AB stands for the time-independent relations among present elements of a structure (system), CD for things as they change over time, moment to moment. In linguistics, synonyms fall on the AB axis, since they are items within the lexical system related by their similarity; the grammatical relations of words in sentences fall on CD since they represent meaning through ordering in time. Figure 17.1 shows Saussure's coordinates as modified by Jakobson.

Jakobson (1960; Jakobson & Halle, 1956/71) extended this graph brilliantly in his work on aphasia, identifying the axis of simultaneity with metaphor (right-brained aphasia) and the axis of successions with metonymy (left-brained aphasia). He shows that the twofold character of language recognized by Saussure implies different cognitive operations: (a) relating phenomena through their conceptual associations (which coexist in the virtual world created by memory and imagination); and (b) relating phenomena by their contiguity and succession in real time. Jakobson generalizes these interpretations to the different types of cognition that aphasia links to the right and left hemispheres, called respectively the metaphoric way (RH) and the metonymic way (LH).

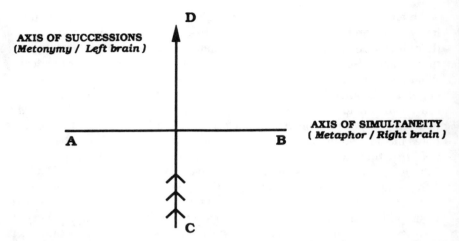

FIGURE 17.1. Bipolarity of Language and Mind: Saussure/Jakobson Coordinates

Ultimately Jakobson identifies a great variety of linguistic and symbolic phenomena with these axes. Here are some of his alignments:

	AXIS OF SIMULTANEITIES	AXIS OF SUCCESSIONS
	metaphor	metonymy
	analogy (analog)	analysis (digital)
	similarity/dissimilarity	sequence, causality
	selection, substitution (in the code)	combination (in sentence, discourse)
	virtual (knowledge system)	actual (history)
(Freud)	identification, symbolism	displacement, condensation
(literature)	romanticism	realism
	right hemisphere	left hemisphere

In Jakobson's hands Saussure's definitions, originally a technical distinction in linguistics, become essentially metaphors themselves, representing not just the structure of language, poetry, psychoanalysis, magic, and other semiotic systems, but the bipolarity of the human mind itself: "The dichotomy discussed here appears to be of primal significance and consequence for all verbal behavior and for human behavior in general" (1956/1971, p. 93). It is this generalization and expansion to a universal meaning that makes the Saussure-Jakobson scheme potentially heuristic or portable to other contexts.

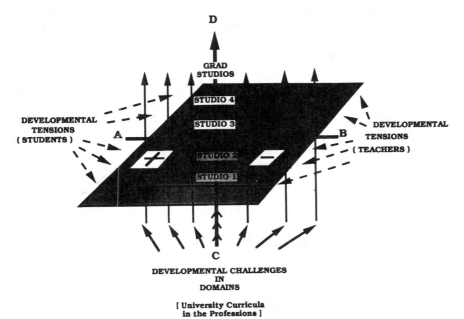

FIGURE 17.2.   Heuristic for Curricular Thinking

A HEURISTIC AND ITS INTERPRETATION IN REFLECTIVE PRACTICES

The Heuristic: A Translation

Figure 17.2 translates the coordinate system of Saussure and Jakobson from the realm of language and brain functions to the realm of curriculum. The new coordinates AB and CD distinguish two dimensions of development so that we may attend to them directly, differently, and relatedly in making curricular decisions for a writing program.

The coordinate CD (the "arrow of time") represents the student's experience of moving through a curriculum. The central arrow stands for the writing curriculum, specifically the core curriculum of writing studios at Syracuse, encompassing a course at each level of undergraduate experience, plus graduate studios. Other locations (upward arrows) in this space represent the advancing curriculum in content domains, which students follow concurrently with the writing studios they take in each year. The diagram oversimplifies in several respects. Respecting the studios themselves, there is not really a four-year sequence (students take *either* Studio 3 *or* Studio 4), and students' course choices in a particular academic year correspond only roughly to the designated developmental levels in any subject. The diagram also omits the communication and interdependence of studios and content curriculum that is integral to the program design.

The concept of "developmental challenges" links decisions about the writing curriculum to information about the actual literacy tasks that challenge students to advance in writing, reading, and critical judgment as they progress through the university year by year. It is assumed that the writing curriculum should respond directly to the context of literacy practices that students actually face at the university in the various disciplinary and professional domains. We necessarily begin with general hypotheses: that students need to take notes in class, lab, or field; read and interpret texts; take essay exams; write research papers, reports, proposals, talks, and so on. But the heuristic directs us to find out not only what these tasks are, concretely and as they vary from one context to another; but also at what point and where they appear in the curriculum of various fields, as *developmentally sequenced* challenges to the student's growing expertise in its subject matter and discourse expectations. For example, a simple progression found in many curricula is from shorter papers, less dependent on expert sources, to longer, highly intertextual ones.

The coordinate (AB) in the heuristic represents experiential themes and relationships in development that co-occur and recur, rather than falling into progressive sequences. On this plane we can analyze aspects and relations of development that are more holistic and less time-dependent; recurrent and repetitive; co-present, parallel, and interactive, rather than linear, successive, progressive, and discontinuous. (Compare the distinction between motif and transition as semantic and episodic types of cohesion, Phelps, 1988a.)

The concept of developmental *tensions* focuses the heuristic particularly on relations of conflict, ambivalence, and dissonance that emerge in the simultaneous influence of co-occurring motives and values at any given moment in the curriculum. As pictured, on this plane polarities complicate development when conflicting desires pull students simultaneously in different directions, represented here as plus (+) and minus (−) poles. These tensions—often echoed or complemented by ambivalencies within teachers themselves—create elements of risk and resistance at every point in the chronology of development. For example, students' mixed feelings about authority-dependence relationships with teachers are in synchrony with teachers' ambivalence about their own powerful roles in the classroom as experts, representatives of the culture, models, judges, and so on. Developmental theories like those of Perry (1968) and Gilligan

(1982) illuminate and help teachers to recognize and categorize the tensions of this axis of development. For example, many tensions seem to cluster around issues of identity and autonomy, and are closely related to the intertextuality of authorship and to the fears and resistance associated with joining new discourse communities. However, developmental tensions are so fluctuating and context-dependent that to take them into account in curricular planning teachers must study them continually as participant-observers.

Developmental Challenges

The boundaries between courses and semesters, creating the typical discontinuities of student life (different content, different teacher, examinations and grades, time lapses between academic terms), produce the effect of developmental stages in which students must make qualitative leaps in going from one course and one level to the next. Thus to design a curriculum of one-semester writing studios offered at each level of the curriculum requires a practical theory of stages. At the first decision point, when curriculum proposals are written, designers must differentiate studios from one another by criteria of increasing challenge, new tasks, and advancing skill. These abstract descriptions must then become concrete through interpretive course plans and teaching experiences. In our curriculum, this work is not done by designers creating a central program "syllabus," but by teachers designing and changing their own writing courses semester by semester.

What kind of information might guide planners in making such a dynamic curriculum developmentally sensitive? Available research sources seem to adopt different emphases in a scheme of discourse interactions (e.g., the pentad, Burke, 1945/1969; Jakobson, 1960; the communication triangle, Kinneavy, 1971). For example, those emphasizing the biological and psychological basis for development seek deductive explanations and predictions in *universals* of cognitive development unfolding within the individual. Others try to generalize categories, factors, and stages in growth by microanalysis of *cognitive processes* across chronological ages. Some approaches examine written *products* to evaluate what learners have done, therefore what they can do, and by extension to predict what others like them in age or background can be expected to do. More recently, research in development has foregrounded the *codes*, conventions, and practices of discourse communities students seek to join.

This kind of knowledge seems indispensable as a background for interpreting and organizing observations made in the practical situation, but it is rather suspect as a basis for predicting and hypothesizing, especially if program planners rely on only one approach. It is insufficiently sensitive to the immediate context, being either outdated, limited, or invalid for the situation. Above all, it is static when what is needed is a dynamic and highly contextualized type of information, of a type that teachers can gather, interpret, apply and update themselves. Where these research methods can be adopted by teachers themselves informally, they become practically useful (for example, teachers can use protocol techniques, examine bodies of texts together, observe social interactions in class observations of one another, and so on).

But the most obvious source of information for constructing stages in a developmental writing curriculum is the rest of the curriculum. It is the content sequences in other fields and disciplines, paralleling and following the writing studios, that pose challenges to students' literacy requiring developmental growth. In this notion, stages of writing development are what the contexts for student writing require them to be. Since curricula differ and students' programs may be idiosyncratic mixtures of fields, the stages of their writing development as determined by developmental challenges may vary widely.

To pursue this idea, I want to draw on the work of David Feldman (1980) on nonuniversal domains of development. These are areas of human capability ranging from species-specific ones (hand-eye coordination, language) to unique works of genius or extremely specialized areas of expertise, with academic and professional fields falling somewhere in the middle. Feldman argues that many realms of human activity are developmental, that is, sequential and hierarchically integrated over time, but not governed by universal timetables or achieved by all humans in all cultures without instruction. Activities can be ranged along a spectrum, whose regions include universal, cultural, discipline-based, idiosyncratic, and unique types of development. He presents a new theory of transitions (qualitative leaps from one stage to another) based on the idea that *both universal and nonuniversal stages are located in the domain,* not the child. In Feldman's view, "developmental *levels* exist in the psychological structure of domains. . . . A developmental level . . . is one idealized system for dealing with certain kinds of knowledge which, in conjunction with other such systems or parts of systems, can be used as templates against which to gauge the child's intellectual repertoire—his or her present developmental state" (pp. 58–59).

Any curriculum within a field or discipline at the university presents students with a sequence of tasks within a domain, most of which are associated with specific demands on literacy in the broadest sense (connecting the written word to speech, reading, thinking, nonverbal symbolic systems, and technologies of communication). The subject-matter work is designed by faculty to fit an increasingly sophisticated learner—older, more knowledgeable, more experienced, more skilled—over the college years. Developmental challenges in each domain define a sequence of increasing expertise, which can be directly connected with increasing demands on literacy skills. This connection implies that to construct a developmental curriculum in writing we should take *inventory* of the literacy tasks set for students progressively in various content domains at the university, analyze them, and consider their implications for what we teach at different levels. At Syracuse we plan to begin by asking faculty in each of the undergraduate colleges (e.g., social work, information sciences, public communications) to help us develop such an inventory, treating the college as the content domain, as defined by common college requirements. Later we will differentiate by discipline within colleges where there is wide variance. We already know that in some colleges with tightly prescribed curricula there is a well-known sequence of literacy tasks, both formal and informal. For example, faculty in architecture have pointed out in which required course their students first encounter an essay exam requiring historical comparisons and noted that in an upper division class where students design a building, they keep a planning notebook combining sketches and words.

So far I have assumed that literacy tasks throughout the curriculum are determined solely by the logic of the domain, which requires that certain content or skills be learned before others. However, the situation is more complicated and interesting than that. As illustrated in Figure 17.3, the writing and reading tasks presented to students in any curriculum (like the curriculum in general) represent a *negotiated* conception of developmental stages determined by the interaction of learners and domains in the past.

We all know that school writing in any domain is not exactly what professors write in a discipline or what professionals in the field write. In fact, school writing seems to have its own genres and subgenres (e.g., essay exams, lab reports, learning logs). School writing is generically distinctive not merely on account of its special functions (e.g., demonstrating learning) but because assignments reflect what professors have discovered, or believe, students can or will do. In that sense, developmental challenges (sequenced literacy tasks within a disciplinary domain) embody a tacit theory of development—of what is hard, when, and why—that responds to all the facts influencing development within individuals and populations.

The institutional history of a given curriculum, including its literacy tasks, demonstrate how this theory is constantly being renegotiated as a result of the ongoing collision between the developmental states and demands of students, on the one hand, and the requirements of a domain, on the other. *Both* are changing: students, their readiness, capabilities, ex-

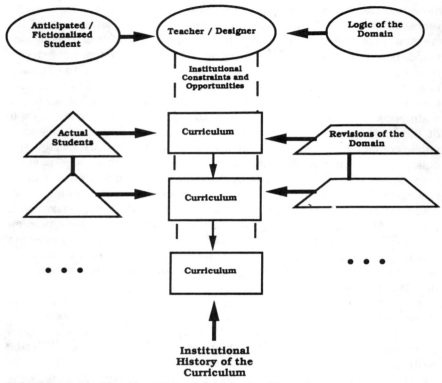

FIGURE 17.3. The Negotiated Curricular Domain

perience, and attitudes in flux generationally and culturally; the domain, in which knowledge is constantly growing and being revised, often radically. Indeed, an interesting question is to what degree the domain itself (e.g., history as a field of inquiry) is shaped by the nature of schooling and the academic institutionalization of it as a "subject" for education.

To use CD, the sequential dimension of the heuristic, for practical theorizing requires, then, at least two, complementary types of inquiry:

1. Constant efforts to inventory and to analyze contrastively the writing and writing-related activities required of students in the curricula of every field
2. Ongoing, in-depth study of students as they actually encounter these tasks in the curriculum and as they participate in writing studios.

In both instances teachers should engage students collaboratively in their studies.

In our program, both types of inquiries have originated in a grass-roots fashion from the interaction between practitioners' needs and questions and scholars' commitments to inquiry. (As part of ongoing program design, we are trying to coordinate these efforts and propose theoretical frameworks like this heuristic for expanding them in a productive partnership of teachers, students, researchers, and theorists.) With respect to developmental challenges and their relation to curricular sequence (the CD axis), contrastive analysis of literacy tasks in different disciplines is built especially into our second (sophomore) studio, although all studios collect assignments and information about writing and reading throughout the curriculum as part of students' inquiries into literacy at the university. Professor Brian Huot and others are currently designing an inventory project, working with the undergraduate colleges of the university to collect information on the informal and formal writing challenges their curricula set progressively for students. Both kinds of information will help to shape and revise not only content decisions for the writing studio sequence, but also initiatives in nontraditional teaching through stand-alone workshops, computer programs, and other resources to develop writing in the curriculum.

Professor Margaret Himley (work in progress) is working with more than 25 teachers on a "profiling" project, where instructors are studying students developmentally in a variety of informal modes, often through projects in which students are coresearchers. The profiling project began when she presented teachers with a hypothetical "George" (a portrait of an entering student as writer and reader) and asked them to test its validity by having students investigate literacy backgrounds and attitudes in their class (for example, through literacy autobiographies and composing process inventories.) Next year we will recommend that teachers incorporate profiling or profiling updates at the beginnings of all studios, in conjunction with self-assessing writing throughout. In both inventory and profiling, this teaching community is not carrying out a narrowly conceived or time-limited research project, but taking joint responsibility for ongoing investigations and reflective activity engaging the deepest issues of curriculum and development.

One consequence of conceiving practical theorizing in terms of continuing inquiry is that the relation between the writing studios and the curriculum is not a passive, service function. In the first place, that is impossible because the heterogeneity of developmental challenges demands active analysis and synthesis to make decisions for the studio curriculum. Second, it is obvious that curricular literacy tasks do not always fit well the capabilities, developmental levels, and learning needs of the students. Teachers in the Writing Program can play a constructive part in the constant student-teacher renegotiation of the literacy dimensions in content curricula, to harmonize better the requirements of the domain with students' developmental needs, including active learning. Finally, the fact that curricula and students not only vary greatly but also change historically means that writing teachers must continually update and reevaluate their own views of the curricular writing challenges.

Developmental Tensions

Whereas developmental *challenges* have a concrete reality in the content curriculum, developmental *tensions*, experienced as resistances and "hot spots," are a pervasive, often tacit feature of the everyday life of writing classrooms. These tensions surface most vividly when teachers and students are engaging difficult and important issues of development.

Over time, we have come to see development tensions (originally perceived as idiosyncratic "subtexts" in studios) as issues concerning relationships among individuals, culture, and education that carry significant developmental meaning. What is at issue in those relationships is historically, culturally, institutionally, and individually specific. They have multiple sources, and can originate (as a factor in the classroom) with either students, teachers, or both. The intense feelings of teachers often seem to mirror those of students: See Schön's (1987) concept of the "hall of mirrors" and the "bidirectionality" theorem (Cairns, 1979). This is particularly the case at Syracuse since teachers are themselves often going through important periods of intellectual and emotional growth, in graduate programs (teaching assistants) or in the transition to a new paradigm of teaching (professional instructors).

Recently, for example, a teacher sensitively reported on a case study of a student in her class. This student is shy and intensely private, disinclined to display her writing to classmates and to subject her deepest thoughts to criticism. She regards her drafts as "messes" and her relationship to the teacher as privileged communication. The teacher, a graduate student, commented on her sympathy and identification with her student. She went on to ask a series of intelligent, acute, and uncomfortable questions about the value of collaborative learning and the potential dangers of oppressing students (threatening their privacy or autonomy) that lie in a studio curriculum emphasizing social aspects of learning and the formation of intellectual community (cf. Stewart, 1988). This example falls in a broad category of tensions in American culture centering on individualism and commitment (see Bellah, Madsen, Sullivan, Swidler, & Tipton 1985). In this category cluster a number of polarities: for example, belonging, being initiated, joining a discourse community (Bartholomae, 1985; Bizzell, 1982) vs. individuation: resisting, rebelling, opposing (Himley, in preparation; see also Chapter 3); excelling, and being original (Phelps & Mano, 1983).

A second example comes from a teacher's correspondence to the class in a practicum course. The teacher described herself as initially proud when her class spontaneously concluded, following a discussion, that there is no objective truth, only subjective constructions reflecting terministic screens. On reflection, she became disturbed at the possibility that she had exposed her students to a dangerous idea, potentially leading them to a philosophy of despair. She asked how she could ethically introduce students to concepts and problems she herself was struggling with and could not resolve, in this case the dilemma of objectivism vs. relativism. Here are two culturally specific conflicts with profound developmental meaning for both student and (only slightly older) teacher. The first (philosophical) poses objectivism (absolutism) against relativism, a conflict that Perry (1968) finds central to development in the college years. The second is the struggle (interpretable both ideologically and psychodynamically) to deal with authority and power, a subject of pervasive concern to writing teachers and one that implicitly structures much student behavior.

The design of our curriculum permits teachers to thematize such tensions for studios as *developmental* ones by placing them in the context of students' intellectual growth and its relation to written language and the university context. In some cases this is done by making a general developmental issue a topic of inquiry as it relates to writing or to language (e.g., in studios organized around inquiries about authority, voice, and gender). Developmental tensions also become a structural feature of the curriculum when they are projected from the axis of simultaneities to the axis of successions (Jakobson's [1960] principle), muting or transforming conflicts by giving them more or less emphasis recursively at different points in the curriculum. One example is the opposition refigured in so many polarities of self and other: writing to learn vs. writing as rhetoric, "creative" vs. "structured" writing, process vs. product, and so on. Tentatively, we have set up studios to emphasize one or another motive and then to loop back to them in later courses in a "spiral," eventually examining the tension itself. However, we recognize the tension as constant, because each motive both represses and incorporates the other. Since developmental tensions are acknowledged, reflected on, exploited thematically, and built into the very structure of daily teaching, teachers in the program may be thought of as always "teaching along the tension."

In application, the heuristic described here serves to organize practical theorizing in a community that is planning and implementing a writing curriculum, in these ways:

- the concepts of the heuristic provide a basis for *speculative theorizing*
- the heuristic picks out sources of information accessible and important for *dynamic theorizing.*

Speculative Theorizing

In planning a curriculum, whether on the macrolevel (as a comprehensive curricular plan) or the microlevel (composing a course for next semester), there is a starting point that occurs without the student. At this point the teacher or planners must, like any composer, imagine the student audience for which they are "scripting" a learning experience (Rocklin, 1988). This teaching moment is speculative thinking.

The curriculum composer can consult appropriate research and theory (on composing processes, social cognition, discourse communities, academic or disciplinary conventions, human development, etc.), along with the wisdom of experience, as a base for practical projections. A heuristic selects particular elements and relations for attention, in this case the following:

ELEMENTS

Students entering the university, or a curriculum, or course within a sequence	←	studios	→ university *curricula*, specifically, their literacy require-
	←	mediate	→ ments (tasks in the domains)

RELATIONS

Conflict and opportunity, risk and resistance: the polarized, charged themes of identity, education, and culture derived from both psychological and environmental sources, including (for contemporary Syracuse students) creativity, gender, anti-Semitism, and professionalism, for example.

A crucial issue concerns the relationship between the logic of the curriculum and the psycho-logic of the way students and teachers experience it in terms of their own activities and responses. Through bidirectionality, the knowledge, values, sources, and conventions shaping an institution and its curriculum help to constitute students' selves long before they come to the university. Conversely, the curriculum is a negotiated one that reflects prior and present student responses to its demands, as negotiated by previous and contemporary students with their teachers.

To observe how the heuristic picks out certain elements and relations in speculative theorizing, look at how curriculum is *initiated*. At the macrolevel, studios rest on a set of theorems (Phelps, 1987a) that organize assumptions and hypotheses about developmental sequences and themes: For example, the idea that attention to particular issues and tensions in the curriculum recurs in a spiral form, with studios returning to re-engage them recursively over the years (cf.. Bruner, 1966). At the microlevel, classroom teachers hypothesize along each axis of the coordinate system in drawing up course plans and imagine possible relations, working sequence with and against tensions to make decisions about specific content, division and order, pacing.

Dynamic Theorizing

Curriculum dies if it becomes, as it did in the 15-year-old Syracuse Freshman English Program, fossilized, unresponsive to students' new needs, boring for teachers and insulated from their own critical and self-critical examination. Heuristics for curricular thinking support not only initial conceptualizations but also the dynamic process of critical action, by organizing informal inquiry to be carried out by teachers forming a community of "reflective practitioners" (Schön, 1987). For this purpose, the two coordinates of this heuristic distinguish these different foci as accessible topics of inquiry for practical theorizing:

- Students and teachers (people, as they actually engage the curriculum through activities and interactions)
- The texts they read and write
- The university curriculum and its tasks, as challenging students' to acquire or change literacy skills, habits, assumptions, and practices of thinking and communicating
- The content of studio courses themselves as they address—and themselves construct—developmental challenges, and as they express, respond to, and thematize developmental tensions.

Members of the writing/teaching community at Syracuse, in partnership with faculty scholars, have already begun addressing all these aspects of curriculum through observation, investigation, reflective writing, and experimentation.

The activities constitute ways for individuals and communities to create and revise knowledge that fall between teachers' lore and epistemic knowledge. There are two such ways (Phelps, 1988c): reflection-in-action (Schön, 1987), which creates personal artistry encodable for communication within a teaching community as an art of practice; and teacher inquiry, which creates context-bound propositional knowledge that is *local*, most often feeding directly back into practice. Both kinds of curricular knowledge making rely on "teacher talk," in an oral tradition, and on "publishing" informal writing in various program forums. By linking the artistry of practice to the systematic studies of a local and national research community, classroom teachers become simultaneously colearners with students (fostering their reciprocal development) and co-inquirers with their faculty colleagues. Not only do they dynamically construct and reconstruct a context-specific curriculum sensitive to real students and their development, but they model a form of curricular thinking that goes some small way toward reintegrating the roles and activities of research, teaching, and learning in higher education.

REFERENCES

Bartholomae, D. (1985). Inventing the university. In M. Rose (Ed.), *When a writer can't write: Studies in writer's block and other composing process problems* (pp. 134–165). New York: Guilford Press.

Bellah, R., Madsen, R., Sullivan, W., Swidler, A., & Tipton, S. (1985). *Habits of the heart: Individualism and commitment in American life.* Berkeley: University of California Press.

Bissex, G. (1980). *Gnys at wrk: A child learns to write and read.* Cambridge, MA: Harvard University Press.

Bizzell, P. (1982). College composition: Initiation into the academic discourse community. *Curriculum Inquiry, 12,* 191–207.

Bronfenbrenner, U. (1979). *The ecology of human development: Experiments of nature and design.* Cambridge, MA: Harvard University Press.

Bruner, J. (1966). *Toward a theory of instruction.* Cambridge, MA: Harvard University Press.

Bruner, J. (1973). *Beyond the information given: Studies in the psychology of knowing* (J. Anglin, Ed.). New York: Norton.

Burke, K. (1969). *A grammar of motives.* Berkeley: University of California Press. (Original work published 1945)

Cairns, R. (1979). *Social development: The origins and plasticity of exchanges.* San Francisco: Freeman.

Dixon, R., & Nesselroade, J. (1983). Pluralism and correlational analysis in developmental psychology: Historical and philosophical perspectives. In R. Lerner (Ed.), *Developmental psychology: Historical and philosophical perspectives* (pp. 113–45). Hillsdale, NJ: Erlbaum.

Feldman, D. H. (1980). *Beyond universals in cognitive development.* Norwood, NJ: Ablex.

Gilligan, C. (1982). *In a different voice: Psychology theory and women's development.* Cambridge, MA: Harvard University Press.

Goelman, H., Oberg, A., & Smith, F. (Eds.). (1984). *Awakening to literacy: The University of Victoria symposium on children's response to a literate environment: Literacy before schooling.* Exeter, NH: Heinemann.

Himley, M. (Ed.). (In preparation). *Risk and resistance: Teachers/students (Reflections in Writing, 9).* Syracuse, NY: Syracuse University, Writing Program.

Hoffman, R., & Nead, J. (1983). General contextualism, ecological science and cognitive research. *Journal of Mind and Behavior, 4,* 507–560.

Jakobson, R. (1960). Concluding statement: linguistics and poetics. In T. Sebeok (Ed.), *Style in language* (pp. 350–377). Cambridge, MA: MIT Press.

Jakobson, R., & Halle, M. (1971). *Fundamentals of language* (2nd rev. ed.). The Hague: Mouton. (Original work published 1956)

Kinneavy, J. (1971). *A theory of discourse.* Englewood Cliffs, NJ: Prentice-Hall.

Kinneavy, J. (1987). Writing across the curriculum. In G. Tate (Ed.), *Twelve bibliographical essays* (rev. and enlarg. ed., pp. 353–377). Fort Worth: Texas Christian University Press.

Kin, E., Kroll, B., & Rose, M. (Eds.). (1988). *Perspectives on literacy.* Carbondale: Southern Illinois University Press.

Kozulin, A. (1986). The concept of activity in Soviet psychology: Vygotsky, his disciples and critics. *American Psychologist, 41,* 264–274.

Lerner, R. (Ed.). (1983a). *Developmental psychology: Historical and philosophical perspectives.* Hillsdale, NJ: Erlbaum.

Lerner, R. (1983b). The history of philosophy and the philosophy of history in developmental psychology: A view of the issues. In R. Lerner (Ed.), *Developmental psychology: Historical and philosophical perspectives* (pp. 3–26). Hillsdale, NJ: Erlbaum.

Magnusson, D., & Allen, V. (1983). *Human development: An international perspective.* New York: Academic.

Moffett, J. (1968). *Teaching the universe of discourse.* Boston: Houghton Mifflin.

Moffett, J., & Wagner, B. J. (1983). *Student-centered language arts and reading, K-13: A handbook for teachers* (3rd ed.). Boston: Houghton Mifflin. (Original work published 1976)

Pepper, S. (1942). *World hypotheses: A study in evidence.* Berkeley: University of California Press.

Perkins, D. N. (1981). *The mind's best work.* Cambridge: Harvard University Press.

Perry, W. G., Jr. (1968). *Forms of intellectual and ethical development in the college years: A scheme.* New York: Holt.

Phelps, L. W. (1984). Cross-sections in an emerging psychology of composition. In M. Moran & R. Lunsford (Eds.), *Research in composition and rhetoric: A bibliographical sourcebook* (pp. 27–69). Westport, CT: Greenwood Press.

Phelps, L. W. (1987a). *The spiral curriculum* (Curriculum proposal). Syracuse, NY: Syracuse University, Writing Program.

Phelps, L. W. (1987b). *Thinking 'studio': A speculative instrument* (Working paper). Syracuse, NY: Syracuse University, Writing Program.

Phelps, L. W. (1988a). *Composition as a human science.* Oxford: Oxford University Press.

Phelps, L. W. (1988b). *Conceiving literacy developmentally.* Lecture presented at Purdue Seminar in Composition and Rhetoric, Purdue University, West Lafayette, IN.

Phelps, L. W. (1988c). *Praxis as wisdom in action.* Paper presented at Convention on College Composition and Communication, St. Louis, MO.

Phelps, L. W. (1988d). *The Writing Program: A design perspective. Stage 2, A strategic plan for program development* (Planning document). Syracuse, NY: Syracuse University, Writing Program.

Phelps, L. W., & Mano, S. (1983). Originality and imitation in the work and consciousness of an adolescent writer. In J. Niles (Ed.), *Solving problems in literacy: Learners, teachers, and researchers* (pp. 290–293). Rochester: NRC.

Piaget, J. (1977). *The essential Piaget: An interpretive reference and guide* (H. Gruber & J. J. Voneche, Eds.). New York: Basic.

Prigogine, I., & Stengers, I. (1984). *Order out of chaos: Man's new dialogue with nature.* Boulder: Shambhala.

Rocklin, E. (1988). *Being in action together: Converging transformations in teaching literature, composition, and drama.* Paper presented at National Conference of Teachers of English, St. Louis, MO.

Saussure, F. de. (1959). *Course in general linguistics* (W. Baskin, Trans.; C. Bally and A. Secheyaye in collaboration with A. Riedlinger). New York: McGraw-Hill. (Original work published 1915)

Schön, D. (1987). *Educating the reflective practitioner.* San Francisco: Jossey-Bass.

Stewart, D. (1988). Collaborative learning and composition: Boon or bane? *Rhetoric Review,* 7, 58–83.

Wertsch, J. (1985) *Vygotsky and the social formation of mind.* Cambridge, MA: Harvard University Press.

White, S. (1983). The idea of development in developmental psychology. In R. Lerner (Ed.), *Developmental psychology: Historical and philosophical perspectives* (pp. 57–77). Hillsdale, NJ: Erlbaum.

Young, R. (1987). Recent developments in rhetorical invention. In *Teaching composition: Twelve bibliographical essays* (rev. and enlarg. ed., pp 1–38). Fort Worth: Texas Christian University Press.

Zebroski, J. T. (1983). Writing as "activity": Composition development from the perspective of the Vygotskian School (Doctoral dissertation, Ohio State University, 1983). *Dissertation Abstracts International, 44/01,* 94A.

Author Index

Vander Zanden, J., 266, *286*
Vipond, D., 9, 13, *31*, *33*, 111, 112, 115, 116, 117, 123, 133, *135*
Vispoel, W.L., 249, 250, *260*
Vosniadou, S., 104, *109*
Voss, J.F., 104, *109*
Vye, N., 17, *30*
Vygotsky, L.S., 95, *109*, 113, *135*, 161, *180*

W

Waanders, J., 192, *197*
Wagner, B.J., 248, *261*, 387, *413*
Wall, S., 27, *30*
Walters, S.A., 161, *180*
Wang, Y., 104, *109*
Warren, R.P., 176, *178*
Watt, I., 94, *108*, 364, *384*
Weber, R.M., *261*
Weigand, J., 265, 266, *284*
Weinberger, J., 372, *384*
Weiss, R.H., 161, *180*
Weiss, S., 317, *317*
Welfel, E.R., 273, 278, *286*
Wells, G., 95, *109*
Wendler, L., 156, *158*, 230, *243*
Wendler, W., 11, 12, *29*
Wertsch, J., 387, *414*
White, J., 200, 201, 202, 203, 205, 206, 207, 209, 210, 211, 212, 213, 215, 216, 217, *221*, *223*

White, S., 399, *414*
Wignell, P., 217, *222*
Wilkinson, A.M., 203, 204, 208, 210, 214, 216, 220, *223*
Wilkinson, I.G., 250, *259*
Wilson, N., 176, *179*
Wimsatt, W.K., 113, *135*
Winnner, E., 139, 153, 156, *158*, *160*
Winograd, P., 8, 26, *31*
Winterowd, W.R., 163, *180*
Wittgenstein, L., 74, 76, 77, 78, 79, 89, *90*
Wittrock, M.C., 161, *178*
Wolcott, W., 257, *261*
Wolf, D., 228, *245*
Wolff, J., 340, *358*
Wollner, M.H.B., 140, *160*
Wood, L.A., 114, *135*
Wood, P.A., 278, *285*
Wood, P.K., 267, 269, 273, 274, 279, *284*, *285*, *286*
Woodward, V.A., 133, *133*
Woolgar, S., 93, *108*

Y

Yesner, S., 163, *179*
Young, R., 388, *414*

Z

Zebroski, J.T., 387, *414*
Zemelman, S., 163, *179*

Subject Index

Cooperative attitude in the reading of po-
etry, 145, 151, 154
Cooperative negotiation, 154
Critical consciousness, 318–319
Critical thinking, 287, 288–289, 313
Critical thinking, *see* Higher-order cognitive
skills
Cultivated disposition, 141, 145, 150, 153,
156
Cultural communication, 136–137
Cultural differences, 55–57
Cultural literacy, 25
Cultural loyalty, 136
Cultural socialization, 19, 26, 136–137
Cultural-developmental approach, 139
Culture of positivism, 329–330
Culture wars, 340, 356
Culture, 183, 190, 196, 197
academic disciplines as, 185, 186, 193,
195
cultural differences, 183, 184, 186
cultural groups, 183, 185
rhetorical communities as, 185, 187, 190,
196
Curricular models of writing, 163–166, 175–
178
Curricular thinking, 387–388, 399–411
as composing, 410
as dynamic theorizing, 411
heuristic for, 387–388, 399–411
as speculative theorizing, 410
Curriculum, 386–388, 396–399, 401–408; *see
also* Studios, writing
in content domains, 401, 404–408
in writing, 386–388, 396–399

D

Deconstruction, 321
educational critique and, 323
teaching and, 322–323, 327
reflexiveness and, 331–332
view of language, 323–326
Deconstructionism, 22
Decontextualized art, 93, 94–96, 101–103
Development of reading and writing
vs. acquisition, 66, 80, 90
social view, 66–67, 4–75
students as participants in, 80–81, 84–85,
85–86, 90
Development, 319–320, 386–414
bidirectionality in, 390, 408–409

complexity of patterning in, 390–391
definition of, 390
developmental synthesis, 389–390
domains of, 404–408
literacy, 387–388, 392–393
processes of change in, 390–392
accommodation, 391
assimilation, 391
disequilibrium, 391
equilibration, 391
synchrony in, 390
writing, 392–396, 403–411
Developmental challenges, 388, 398, 401–
408; *see also* Saussure-Jakobson coordinates
Developmental stages, 403–408
as negotiated concept in curriculum,
405–406
in relation to content domains, 403–408
Developmental tensions, 388, 398, 401–403,
408–409; *see also* Saussure-Jakobson
coordinates
Dialect, nonstandard, 355
Dialogic, 61
Dialogics, 18–19
Direct instruction, 252
Discipline, 341–342, 35–351
students' position in relation to, 344, 347,
355–356
Discourse community, 67–68
Discourse conventions, 68–69, 341–344
arbitrariness of, 69
and consensus, 73
defined, 68
vs. discourse practices, 68–80
field, 342
institutional, 342
meaning and, 70–71
teaching, 73–74
as verbal formulae, 73
written discourse, 342
Discourse practices, 68–69
defined, 68
vs. discourse conventions, 68–80
in First-Year English, 80–90
kinds of, 66, 70, 81–89
as motivated behavior, 69–73
as social action, 73–80
social contexts of, 68, 70, 72, 87, 88–
89
vs. mental states, 74–78

rules, 66, 68, 73, 76, 80
value and, 71–72, 74, 78–80
Language, nature of, 319–320
Literacy 3–28, 34–63, 93–107, 318–320, 364, 370–387, 392
  advanced, 93, 104–107
  assessment, 7, 20–22, 27–28, 41–42, 57–58
  autonomous model, 361–362, 368
  beliefs, 371–372
  critical, 318–319
  critical consciousness, 392
  definition of, 34–35, 387
  domain of skillful performance, 392
  esthetic sphere, 392
  functional, 319–320
  goals, 25, 372
  histories, 372, 373, 374–377
  ideological model, 361–363
  in relation to life-span development, 392
  instruction, 27, 59–63
  paradigms, 37–59
    "Basic skills," 37, 40–41, 51, 58–59
    "Belles lettres," 37, 40
    "Cultural tradition," 37–38
    "Personal growth," 37–39
  perspectives on, 3–7
    cognitivist, 3, 4–5, 7
    expressionist, 3, 5, 7
    social contextualist, 3, 5–7
  practices, 370–371
  social views of, 34, 59–61
  stereotypes of illiteracy, 364
  strategies, 371, 374, 377–380
Literacy programs, 365–367, 370
  community-oriented, 367, 370
  individual-oriented, 365–366
Literary awareness, 157
Literary response, 140
Literary symbols, 138–139
Literature, 44–45, 226–331, 339
  characters, 228
  definitions of, 44
  genres, 226, 330–331, 339
  text selection, 44–45
Literature instruction, 136–142

M
Main path/faulty path structure, 101–103
Mapping, 233–234, 236–237
  comprehension, measure of, 234
  degree of elaboration, 233, 236

Media, 236
Memory, 227
Meno, 337, 338, 355
Metacognition, 371
Metacognitive training studies, 253
Method, Socratic, see Socrates
Multiple perspectives, 271, 281–283

N
Narrative writing, 202, 203, 205, 212, 214, 216, 218
  performance in, 202, 203, 205, 218
Narrative, 95, 106, 227

O
Open symbolism, 139, 144
Organizing, 100

P
Participant, 249
Pedagogy, 65–90, 338–341
  of writing, 65–6, 73–74, 76, 79–80, 80–90
    peer discussion in, 85–86
    use of computers in, 81
Performatory activities, 141, 143
Personal voice, 353–355
Persuasive writing, 200–220
  definitions of, 200–201, 202
  difficulty, 214–215, 216, 218–219
    cognitively demanding, 214, 218–219
    schema lacking, 212, 213, 218
    varies with assignment, 214–215
  effect of context, 215, 217–219
  effect of reading persuasion, 219, 220
  influence of spoken language, 204, 208–209, 211–213
  performance in, 201–203, 206–212, 214–215, 217, 219–220
    age-related differences, 203–205
    assessments, large scale, 200–202, 206, 215, 219
    characteristic problems, 202, 206–212
    content, 202
    linguistic forms, 202–203, 211, 218
    structure, 202, 204–205, 210–211, 213, 218
    nonarguments, 26–210, 212–213
  compared with narrative writing, 202, 203, 218